D0820214

DISCARD

Geographic Perspectives in History

ESSAYS IN HONOR
OF EDWARD WHITING FOX

Geographic Perspectives in History

Edited by
EUGENE D. GENOVESE
and
LEONARD HOCHBERG

BASIL BLACKWELL

British Library Cataloguing in Publication Data

Geographic perspectives in history.
  1. Historiology
  I. Genovese, Eugene D. (Eugene Dominick),
    1930–   II. Hochberg, Leonard
  907'.2

ISBN 0-631-14521-4

Library of Congress Cataloging in Publication Data

Geographic perspectives in history/edited by Eugene D. Genovese and
  Leonard Hochberg.
     p.   cm.
  Includes index.
  1. Economic history.   2. Social history.   3. Geography, Economic.
  4. France — Economic conditions.   5. France — Social conditions.
  6. Europe — Economic conditions.   7. Europe — Social conditions.
  I. Genovese, Eugene D., 1930–   II. Hochberg, Leonard.
  HC21.G45 1989
  330.944 — dc19
    ISBN 0-631-14521-4

Typeset in 11 on 12½ pt Baskerville
by Dobbie Typesetting Limited, Plymouth, Devon
Printed in Great Britain by
Bookcraft Ltd., Bath, Avon

Contents

Editor's Preface

During the last decade or so the long and debilitating separation of geography from history and, more broadly, the social sciences has begun to be overcome. Not even the most optimistic among those who regard the separation as appalling, not to say stupid, would claim that the battle has been won or even that victory has been assured in what promises to be a long struggle for reintegration. But the publication fifteen years ago of Edward Whiting Fox's *History in Geographic Perspective* reopened the discussion at an impressively high level, stimulated creative thought among the practitioners of the relevant disciplines, and offered exciting theses and hypotheses on which to build.

Eschewing geographic determinism and reductionism, Edward Fox sketched a heuristically powerful and historically specific argument for the limits imposed – and opportunities offered – by geography on human action. We might reasonably claim for Edward Fox in relation to Arnold Toynbee, who clearly influenced him, what Marx claimed for himself in relation to Hegel: he stood Toynbee on his head–respectfully, lovingly, transformed a dialectical idealism into a materialist interpretation of social development. Fox's materialism, however, departs radically from that of Marx both as historical interpretation and as world view and attendant politics. At a time when 'liberalism' may fairly be said to be at bay, he has firmly reclaimed much of its historical and philosophical ground and has proudly reasserted its finest values, while impatiently, if politely, dispensing with its pretensions and cant.

Edward Fox's book represented the culmination of a life of the study and teaching of history and provided a hint, although probably no more than that, of the grounds on which his reputation as a great teacher have been based. In particular, as demonstrated by his editorship of Cornell's superb series of books on western civilization, he has compelled his peers, his students, and all who have been privileged to know him to value and cherish a great tradition that has – we hope temporarily – fallen on evil days. Certainly, as this volume demonstrates, his thought has had a profound impact on a wide variety of scholars from many disciplines and from most points on the ideological and political spectrum from, as it were, left to right.

This is not a festschrift, although it may have some of the attributes of one. Rather, it represents a many-sided attempt to come to terms with Edward Fox's thought and to demonstrate some of the possible lines of advance from it. The editors invited historians, geographers, anthropologists, political scientists, and sociologists to present their thoughts and the fruits of their research in relation to the problems posed by his challenging book. Each has proceeded independently but, we believe, in a manner that has produced a coherent if open-ended whole. The contributors agree with each other primarily in believing that Edward Fox has successfully challenged us to reconsider the geographic influence on history, not merely in general but with pregnant specificity, and has advanced ideas with which all serious historians, geographers, and social scientists must engage. But we also agree that the highest compliment that one scholar can pay to another is to *engage* with his thought, whether in agreement or no, and to build on it.

In that spirit this book will, we trust, speak for itself both as a series of contributions toward the reintegration of geography and the social sciences and as a modest tribute to the man who inspired it.

The editors wish to thank the Department of Cartography of Miami University for generous assistance with maps.

EUGENE D. GENOVESE
LEONARD HOCHBERG

PART I

France and Europe

1

First by Land, Then by Sea:
Thoughts about the Social Formation
of the Mediterranean and Greece

MARTIN BERNAL

It is surprising that the history of Ancient Greece should make so little sense. It is, after all, a country that is seen as central to European or 'western civilization', and it is the only one to have the larger part of an established academic discipline devoted to it. Conventional wisdom provides no coherent description, let alone any explanation, of Greek origins, of the rise and fall of Mycenaean society in the Late Bronze Age, or of the development of Archaic and Classical Greece in the first millennium BC. Before attempting a remedy, let us look at the historiography of the origins of Ancient Greece. Fully aware that models inevitably betray the complex texture of reality and that one should always be wary of reification, I want to distinguish between two models of Greek history, which I call the Ancient and the Aryan.

The Aryan, in which most of us have been educated, holds that Greek civilization originated in the conquest of the country from the north by Indo-European speakers. The native 'Pre-Hellenes' are seen as civilized but soft and, though not Indo-European, white and Caucasian – definitely not African or Semitic. Thus there was no 'racial' mixture. Greek culture, like the cultures of Medieval Europe and India, is seen as the offspring of this mating of Beauty and the Beast: a vigorous 'male' northern domination over a gentle 'female' culture.[1] Unlike the collapse of the

---

[1] For a discussion of the rise of the Aryan Model see my 'Black Athena Denied: The Tyranny of Germany over Greece and the Rejection of the Afroasiatic Roots of Europe, 1780–1980', *Comparative Criticism*, 8 (Spring 1986), pp. 3–69; and *Black Athena: The Afroasiatic Roots of European Civilization* (3 vols, Free Association Press, London, 1987), vol. 1: *The Fabrication of Ancient Greece, 1785–1985*.

Roman Empire or the Vedic conquests of northern India, however, no record or folk memory of such a conquest existed in Greece. As J. B. Bury, one of the leading practitioners of the Aryan Model, put it: 'The true home of the Greeks before they won dominion in Greece had passed clean out of their remembrance, and they looked to the east not to the north, as the quarter from which some of their ancestors had migrated.'[2]

What Bury saw as faulty memory, I describe as the 'Ancient Model'. This historical scheme was used by most Greek writers concerned with understanding their distant past, omitted by one or two, but denied by none. According to it, Greece had originally been inhabited by primitive tribes, Pelasgians and others, and had been settled by Egyptians and Phoenicians, who had built cities and introduced irrigation. The Phoenicians had brought many things, notably the alphabet, and the Egyptians had taught the natives the names of the gods and how to worship them.[3] Greece had continued to borrow culturally from Egypt and Phoenicia and most leading Greek statesmen, philosophers, mathematicians, and scientists were supposed to have acquired their pre-eminence after having studied in Egypt.[4]

This Ancient Model went unchallenged in Antiquity, the Middle Ages, and the Renaissance. During the Christian era the only debate was on the priority of Hermetic, that is, Egyptian, philosophy and religion over those of the Bible. Not surprisingly, the Church Fathers came down in favor of the latter. Neither side disputed that 'gentile' wisdom had come to Greece and Rome from Egypt. Despite the centrality of Hermetic learning to Renaissance humanism and the 'scientific revolution', most

---

[2] John Bagnell Bury, *A History of Greece to the Death of Alexander the Great* (Macmillan, London, 1900), p. 25.

[3] Herodotus, *The Histories*, Bk 2, 5.58 and 6.55; Aeschylus, *The Suppliants*; Euripides, *The Phoenician Women*; Isocrates, *Helen*, 10.68; Pausanias, *Guide to Greece*, especially 2.16 & 38; Diodorus Siculus, *The Library of History*, 1; and many others.

[4] Giorgio de Santillana, 'On Forgotten Sources in the History of greek Science', in *Scientific Change: Historical Studies in the Intellectual, Social and Technical Conditions for Scientific Discovery and Technical Invention, from Antiquity to the Present: Symposium on the History of Science, University of Oxford 9–15 July 1961*, ed. A. C. Crombie (Heinemann, London, 1963), pp. 813–28. See also George G. M. James, *Stolen Legacy: The Greeks Were Not the Authors of Greek Philosophy, but the People of North Africa, Commonly Called the Egyptians*, reprinted with intro. by Asa Hilliard (Julian Richardson Associates, San Francisco, 1976). For Phoenician sources see William Foxwell Albright, 'Neglected Factors in the Greek Intellectual Revolution', *Proceedings of the American Philosophical Society*, 116 (1972), pp. 225–42.

enthusiasts for Egypt and its religion were able to maintain at least the appearance of Christian orthodoxy. The convention was broken by Giordano Bruno, who, as well as proclaiming Copernican heliocentricity, openly called for a return to the religion of ancient Egypt, the *prisca theologia* – the religion behind all others. In this way he hoped to transcend the divisions within Christianity and those between it and other faiths.[5] Bruno's ideas seem to have been fundamental to the mysterious Rosicrucians of the seventeenth century.[6] They were certainly the basis of 'speculative' Freemasonry as it emerged at the beginning of the eighteenth.[7] This created a reaction against Egypt among defenders of Christianity and, because of new forces to be discussed below, by the middle of the century these attacks, for the first time, included attempts to raise the cultural status of the Greeks above that of the Egyptians.[8] They failed in the face of the authority of the Ancient Model and the Enlightenment's enthusiasm for Egypt. Thus, for the most part, the Ancient Greeks continued to be seen as poets but poor philosophers whose greatest achievement was in having preserved some part of the wisdom of Egypt and the Orient.[9]

This image was overthrown at the turn of the nineteenth century, by the revival of Christianity after the French Revolution and the triumphs of the concept of progress and of Romanticism. With a passion for peculiarity and small societies bound by kinship and rooted in a particular soil, the Romantics attacked the universality of the Enlightenment, with its preference for large 'rational' empires– Roman, Egyptian, or Chinese. Romantics asserted that demanding environments, particularly the cold of mountains or the north, produced the most virtuous people–those capable of maintaining free institutions. These assertions, coupled with a belief in the permanence of racial essences through all their changes

[5] Frances A. Yates, *Giordano Bruno and the Hermetic Tradition* (Routledge & Kegan Paul, London, 1964).

[6] Frances A. Yates, *The Rosicrucian Enlightenment* (Routledge & Kegan Paul, London 1972).

[7] Margaret C. Jacob, *The Newtonians and the English Revolution 1689–1720* (Cornell University Press, Ithaca, New York, 1976); Margaret C. Jacob, *The Radical Enlightenment: Pantheists, Freemasons and Republicans* (Allen & Unwin, London, 1981).

[8] William Warburton, *The Divine Legation of Moses: Demonstrated, on the Principles of a Religious Deist from the Omission of the Doctrine of a Future State of Reward and Punishment in the Jewish Dispensation* (6 vols, F. Gyles, London, 1738–41), vol. III, 1, pp. 395–8, and vol. IV, 5, pp. 229–61.

[9] See Bernal, 'Black Athena Denied', pp. 8–10.

of form, made it 'impossible' for the virtuous Greeks, with their free cities, to have derived their culture from the south and east.

Closely associated with Romanticism was the rise of systematic racism that projected an integral connection between virtue, manliness, intelligence, and skin color. Many pillars of the Enlightenment, including Locke, Hume and Voltaire, were racists. As others saw, however, racism contradicted enlightened universalism and the deep and widespread respect for China and Egypt, which was held especially by men like Bruce, Dupuis, Volney, and Champollion, who believed that Egypt was essentially African.[10] Thus connections between racism and the Enlightenment were contingent, while those between racism and Romanticism were necessary since the two systems, with their emphases on northern virtue, crude geographical determinism, and the importance of kinship and blood-ties, are neatly congruent.[11] Socially and politically, the rise of racism in the eighteenth century was clearly influenced by the northern Europeans' need to denigrate the peoples they were exploiting, enslaving, and exterminating in other continents.[12] European expansion also strengthened the new paradigm of progress. While in previous centuries paradigms of decline or historical cycles meant that the greater antiquity of the Egyptians and Phoenicians was to their credit, the idea that 'later is better' clearly benefited the Greeks, as did the growing and related cult of youthful dynamism. Ancient Greece was now seen as ancient Europe's childhood – itself a new concept that combined sentimentality and Romanticism with progress. Until the eighteenth century the antiquity and stability of Egypt had been foci of admiration; they now began to be seen as marks of failure.

These interwoven beliefs made the Ancient Model intolerable. Greece, the epitome of youthful and dynamic Europe, could not have gained

[10] James Bruce, *Travels to Discover the Source of the Nile, in the Years 1768, 1769, 1770, 1771, 1772, and 1773* (5 vols, Robinson, Edinburgh 1790); Charles François Dupuis, *Origine de Tous les Cultes, ou Religion Universelle* (2nd edn, 7 vols, Babeuf, Paris, 1822); Constantin François Chasseboeuf, Comte de Volney, *Les Ruines, ou Méditations sur les Révolutions des Empires* (Levrault, Paris, an. 3, 1795); Hermine Hartleben, *Lettres de Champollion le Jeune* (2 vols, Leroux, Paris, 1909), vol. 2, pp. 427–8.

[11] Herder's attempt to give equal worth to all nations including those outside Europe was not followed by his intellectual descendents.

[12] See Philip D. Curtin, *The Image of Africa: British Ideas and Action 1780–1850* (University of Wisconsin Press, Madison, 1964); Sander L. Gilman, *On Blackness without Blacks: Essays on the Image of the Black in Germany* (G. K. Hall & Co., Boston, Mass., 1982); Edward W. Said, *Orientalism* (Pantheon Books, New York, 1978).

its civilization from the static and senile, if not dead, culture of the southern and racially dubious Egyptians. The academic attack on the Ancient Model started at the University of Göttingen, which in retrospect can be seen as the embryo of all later German and American universities. Founded by George II, as Elector of Hanover, in 1737, it was free from medieval and religious shackles. It was also a center of German resistance to French cultural domination and an important conduit into Germany of British thought, which included not only the empiricism of Locke and Hume but also their racism and growing Scottish Romanticism.[13] Göttingen had many distinguished professors who were academics of a new type. They established exclusive disciplines defended by professional journals and began to write in jargons that, though originally German, were comprehensible to even smaller circles than had been the Latin of the educated, generalist *Gelehrtenstand*, which the new academics were replacing.[14] The new professors included the founders of romantic 'biographical' national historiography and Blumenbach, the first academic taxonomist of 'race' by skin color and the inventor of the term 'Caucasian'.[15]

The center of Göttingen was *Philologie*, a discipline dominated by C. G. Heyne, a professor there from 1763 to 1812.[16] Heyne developed the seminar from the Socratic method and promoted the new technique of 'source criticism' by which the modern scholar was required to discriminate between worthless texts and ones that represented their times or the *Zeitgeist* – a term invented by his colleague Meiners. Using 'source criticism', the scholar could dismiss the quantity or wide spread of ancient attestation and focus on the one 'good' source that suited his purpose. Whether or not this method was developed to counter the Ancient Model –

[13] Herbert Butterfield, *Man on his Past: The Study of The History of Historical Scholarship* (Cambridge University Press, Cambridge, 1955), pp. 125–36; Luigi Marino, *I Maestri della Germania: Göttingen 1770–1820* (Einaudi, Turin, 1975).

[14] R. Steven Turner, 'Historicism, *Kritik*, and the Prussian Professoriate, 1790 to 1840', in *Philologie und Hermeneutik im 19 Jahrhundert II*, eds. Mayotte Bollack and Heinz Wismann (Vandenhoeck & Ruprecht, Göttingen, 1983), pp. 450–77.

[15] Leon Poliakov, *The Aryan Myth: A History of Racist and Nationalist Ideas in Europe*, tr. Edmund Howard (Chatto & Windus, Heinemann, London, 1974), pp. 188–9; Bernal, 'Black Athena Denied', pp. 16–17.

[16] Ulrich von Wilamowitz-Moellendorf, *History of Classical Scholarship*, tr. Alan Harris, ed. with intro. by Hugh Lloyd-Jones (Duckworth, London, 1982), pp. 171–4; Rudolf Pfeiffer, *A History of Classical Scholarship from 1300 to 1850* (Clarendon Press, Oxford, 1976), pp. 171–2.

and it may have been – it proved effective against it.[17] The one drawback was the lack of a single early classical source that explicitly repudiated the Ancient Model. Scholars were forced, therefore, to rely on the 'tacit dissent' they saw in the few ancient historians who failed to mention the legendary invasions.[18]

The Ancient Model did not fall immediately. It fell only after the defeat of the French Revolution and the reaction of the upper classes against the Enlightenment that was believed to have caused it. The triumphs of racism and Romanticism and the revival of Christianity combined to discredit Ancient Egypt, and after the outbreak of the Greek War of Independence, worked to elevate Classical Greece. It was in the passionate Philhellenism of the 1820s that the Göttingen professor Carl Otfried Müller demolished the idea of there ever having been any Egyptian colonies in Greece, by bringing out internal contradictions in the legends. He also neatly maneuvered himself into a position of 'scientific' scepticism by demanding 'proof' of the invasions.[19] The requirement of proof, inappropriate for many subjects, is absurd for early Greek history. The best one can hope for is competitive plausibility. Even, if like Müller, one accepts the requirement, it is odd to demand it of those who follow a broadly based ancient tradition rather than from those who challenge it. The great and long-lasting success of the theories based on Müller's dubious methods simply shows how well his conclusions fitted the *Zeitgeist* of his and later times.[20]

The Aryan Model was not completed until after Müller's premature and romantic death in Athens in 1840. His ideas of indigenous development had to be integrated with the new theories on language that were coming from another wing of the romantic movement. Though dimly perceived for a considerable period, a clear picture of the Indo-European language family only emerged in the 1830s. From this time, it became accepted that the urlanguage *Proto-Indo-European* had been

---

[17] For an analogy, see the description by Stephen Jay Gould of the origins of factor analysis which 'was invented in a social context and for definite reasons', in his *The Mismeasure of Man* (W. W. Norton, New York, 1981), p. 238. Factor analysis has of course a far stronger mathematical and scientific base than *Quellenkritik*.

[18] Connop Thirlwall, *A History of Greece* (8 vols, Longman, Rees, Brown, Green & Longman, London, 1835–44), vol. 1, pp. 67–8. Thirlwall did not cite Plutarch's *De malign. Herod.* apparently because of Plutarch's 'lateness' (second century AD) and unreliability. Plutarch took it for granted that Greek religion derived from Egypt.

[19] Bernal, 'Black Athena Denied', pp. 35–6.   [20] Ibid.

formed in some central Asian mountains.[21] The theory received powerful support from Indian traditions of a northern Aryan invasion, which also encouraged the postulation of a similar Aryan invasion of the Balkans and Greece despite the absence of a supporting tradition. The tribal movement within Greece known as the Return of the Heraclids was renamed the Dorian Invasion, and attempts were made to push the Dorian homeland northwards. Unfortunately, since the Return took place after the Trojan War its identification with the Aryan Invasion requires the transfer of such Homeric heroes as Agamemnon and Achilles to the category of 'Pre-Hellenes', a price few scholars have been willing to pay. In the 1950s, the reading of the Bronze Age Script Linear B as Greek rendered the identification of the Aryan with the Dorian Invasion untenable. Some scholars still cling to the theory that the Dorian was the last in a series of invasions, but even this cumbersome theory does not provide any information about the arrival of Indo-European speech in Greece.

It is sometimes maintained that an important reason for the discrediting of the ideas that make up the Ancient Model was the disillusion with eastern cultures after Champollion's decipherment of hieroglyphics and the reading of Babylonian cuneiform. But these new sources of information only began to be accepted by the majority of classicists after the Aryan Model was firmly in place. Nor did the Aryan Model arise from archaeological discoveries, for the earliest work on Bronze Age Greece– Schliemann's – came in the 1870s. The new sources of information were simply fitted into the Aryan Model.

To proceed, we must distinguish between two branches of the Aryan Model, the 'Broad' and the 'Extreme'. The Broad, established by the 1840s, denied the tradition of Egyptian influence on Greece but for the most part accepted that of the Phoenicians. The Extreme denied even Phoenician influence. Since the end of the eighteenth century, there had been little doubt that the 'best race' was the Caucasian. The Caucases were the mountains in which Prometheus had been imprisoned. Prometheus, whose bold and self-sacrificing character was soon seen as typically 'Aryan', was the son of Lapetos who was identified with the biblical Japhet. Despite these non-Semitic connotations, many nineteenth century writers included the 'Semites' – a new linguistic term, soon used

[21] Holger Pedersen, *The Discovery of Language: Linguistic Science in the Nineteenth Century*, tr. John Webster Spargo (Indiana University Press, Bloomington, 1959), pp. 240–77.

racially – among the Caucasians.[22] With the demotion of the Egyptians, the Chinese, and all other peoples, and the establishment of the Indo-European and Semitic language families, two master races emerged: the Aryans and the Semites. These were seen in perpetual dialectic, the Semites having given the world religion and poetry, and the Aryans manliness, democracy, philosophy, and science.

In classical scholarship this view allowed the legendary Phoenician role in Greece to be tolerated. Indeed, the reputation of the Phoenicians actually rose to compensate for the disappearance of the Egyptians. The picture of stern seamen who spread civilization while making a tidy profit from selling cloth and from a little bit of slave-trading was especially appealing in England. In Germany, however, this positive image was never so widely accepted, and German scholarship was central to the new discipline of *Altertumswissenschaft*, or Classics, and to the formation of the Extreme Aryan Model.

As the nineteenth century wore on, Europeans increasingly resented the amount of credit given to the Semites. They mounted efforts, which coincided with the rise of racial, in contradistinction to religious, anti-Semitism, to deny a Jewish role in the creation of poetry and Christianity. At least since the Renaissance, scholars had rightly seen a relation between Phoenicians and Jews, for both spoke dialects of the same Canaanite language. Thus, with the Dreyfus case of the 1890s a number of influential articles denied any extra-European or Semitic influences on Greece.[23] Competition between the Broad and Extreme versions of the Aryan Model persisted until the 1920s, when the Semites, both Jews and Phoenicians, were firmly put in their place – outside European civilization.

Their expulsion was related to the prominence of Jews in the Russian Revolution and world Communism. It was also the result of supreme self-confidence. Europeans, with the world at their mercy, could afford to turn on an 'internal enemy'. The situation changed radically after 1945. The moral revulsion at the consequences of anti-Semitism and the simultaneous rise of the Third World, and of Israel as an 'outpost of western civilization', has led to the readmission of Jews as Europeans.

---

[22] For Schlötzer, see Poliakov, *The Aryan Myth*, p. 188.

[23] Outstanding among these were: M. Salomon Reinach, 'Le mirage oriental', *L'anthropologie*, 4 (1893), pp. 539–78 and 699–732; Julius Beloch, 'Die Phoeniker am Aegaeischen Meer', *Rheinisches Museum für Philologie*, NF. 49 (1894), pp. 111–32. For more on the whole process see Bernal, 'Black Athena Denied', pp. 49–53.

Increased Jewish self-confidence, though largely reflected in Zionism and religious revival, has had as an intellectual byproduct an attempt to restore the historical role of the Phoenicians. Thus, since the 1960s there has been a struggle to bring back the Broad Aryan Model. Resistance by the 'Extremists' seems to be motivated partly by academic inertia and a respect for authority, which is naturally high in such disciplines, and partly by the political conservatism of many classicists, which makes their scholarship respond far more readily to extra-academic pressures from the right than to those from the left.[24] Despite the resistance, the Broad Aryanists, led largely by Jewish scholars, are gaining ground and should succeed by the end of the century.[25] The restoration of the Ancient Model, with some necessary revisions, may take some time longer.

Now let us reconsider the change from the Ancient to the Aryan Model. Thomas Kuhn identifies no objective causes for a change of paradigms, which appear as more or less arbitrary shifts within a scientific community.[26] Lakatos tried to relate such changes to those in society as a whole and, unwilling to give up the concept of progress, insisted that the successful paradigm must have 'surplus explanatory value'. It must explain everything, or nearly everything, explained by the discarded one and some more.[27] This would seem reasonable with the proviso that the 'surplus explanatory value' need not be inside the paradigm or model concerned, but might be in its effectiveness in relating it to other or external paradigms. The Aryan Model may have been superior to the Ancient externally in its relations to the *Weltenschauung* of the historians concerned. It need not have provided any better internal explanation of the development of Ancient Greece. Since most scholars today do not share the romantic ethnicity and racial hierarchy that provided a large part of the basis for the dismissal of the Ancient Model and the creation

[24] Luciano Canfora, *Ideologie del Classicismo* (Einaudi, Turin, 1980), especially pp. 133–59; Mariella Cagnetta, *Antichisti e Impero Fascista* (Dedalo, Bari, 1979).

[25] See, for example, the new tone on this issue in M. I. Finley, *The Legacy of Greece: A New Appraisal* (Clarendon Press, Oxford, 1981), p. 23; Anthony Snodgrass, *Archaic Greece: The Age of Experiment* (Dent & Sons, London, 1980), pp. 32–4.

[26] Thomas Kuhn, *The Structure of Scientific Revolutions* (2nd revised edn, Chicago University Press, Chicago, 1970).

[27] Imre Lakatos, 'Falsification and the Methodology of Scientific Research Programmes' in *Criticism and the Growth of Knowledge*, eds. Imre Lakatos and Alan Musgrave (Cambridge University Press, Cambridge, 1970), pp. 106–111.

of the Aryan, it would seem appropriate to reopen competition between them.

The extraordinarily inefficient prevailing model cannot explain the 50 per cent of the Greek vocabulary and the 90 per cent of toponyms, divine and mythological names, that are non-Indo-European. Neither can it explain why so many ancient writers suffered from 'barbarophilia' and 'Egyptomania' – the delusions that 'barbarians', especially Egyptians, were central to the formation of Greek culture. With some revisions the Ancient Model can provide a relatively coherent view of Greek history, resolving many of the first set of problems and making the second disappear completely.

THE REVISED ANCIENT MODEL IN ITS MEDITERRANEAN CONTEXT

Edward Fox and Fernand Braudel have emphasized the critical importance of water transport. Fox has brought out the contrast between states' use of land for communication and military control, and the use of water to convey heavy goods and to link maritime and riverine trading or manufacturing communities. Braudel, in his work on the Mediterranean, one of the regions in which these communities have been strongest and territorial states proportionately weak, has stressed its unifying and centripetal forces.[28] Yet despite these Mediterranean unities there are important social and cultural distinctions between its northern and southern litorals. Some are the results of states' being initially land-based, such as the Arab and Turkish empires. Most, however, are not, and can only be explained by using a far greater time depth than is usually attempted.

During much of the Paleolithic, the populations of Africa, south west Asia and Europe shared similar or identical material cultures.[29] This

[28] Edward Whiting Fox, *History in Geographic Perspective: The Other France* (W. W. Norton, New York, 1971); Fernand Braudel, *The Mediterranean and the Mediterranean World in the Age of Philip II*, tr. Siân Reynolds (2 vols, Harper & Row, New York, 1972–3); Braudel, *La Méditerranée: les Hommes et l'Héritage* (Arts et Métiers Graphiques, Paris, 1978).

[29] J. Desmond Clark, 'The Legacy of Prehistory: An Essay on the Background to the Individuality of African Cultures', in *The Cambridge History of Africa*, eds. J. D. Fage and Roland Oliver (Cambridge University Press, London, 1978–), vol. 2: *From c. 500 BC to AD 1050* pp. 11–86; D. W. Phillipson, *The Later Prehistory of Eastern and Southern Africa* (Heinemann, London, 1977); D. H. Trump, *The Prehistory of the Mediterranean* (Yale University Press, New Haven & London, 1980), pp. 7–27.

would seem to have been the result of developments and innovations over hundreds of thousands of years among relatively small mobile populations. How far these resemblances extended into other aspects of life it is impossible to say. Linguistic evidence from Basque and dead non-Indo-European languages of Europe indicate that, in this respect at least, the cultures of Africa and Europe were very different from each other by the late Mesolithic – around 10,000 BC. Today the linguistic distinction between the two sides of the Mediterranean is that between the Afroasiatic and Indo-European language families. The two are, I believe, ultimately related, but the very latest a common proto-language could have been spoken is in the Mousterian period – 50,000–35,000 BP.[30]

We, however, are principally concerned with developments after the end of the last ice age c.10,000 BC. The rise in temperature around this time caused a reduction of the Polar ice caps and an increase of rainfall. During the following three or four millennia of climatic optimum, when much of the Sahara had become savannah, agriculture spread across north Africa, probably from the Rift Valley in the east.[31] On the basis of archaeological remains and later linguistic distribution, I maintain that it was this movement that established the Afroasiatic language families – Berber, (Ancient) Egyptian, and Semitic – along the southern Mediterranean coasts and their hinterlands.[32]

Professors Georgiev, Mellaart, and Renfrew have argued plausibly that Indo-European, or rather the broader linguistic family of Indo-Hittite, was the language of south Anatolian farmers during the eight and seventh millennia BC, and that the language traveled with agriculture

---

[30] See Allan R. Bomhard, *Toward Proto-Nostratic: A New Approach to the Comparison of Proto-Indo-European and Proto-Afroasiatic* (J. Benjamins, Amsterdam & Philadelphia, 1984); Aron Borisovich Dolgopolskii, *Sravitel'no-istoricheskaya fonetika kushchitskhikh yazygov* (Akademya Nauk, Moscow, SSR 1973); Carleton T. Hodge, 'Lislakh', *The Fourth LACUS Forum*, ed. Michel Paradis (Hornbeam Press, Columbia, South Carolina, 1978), pp. 414–22; Saul Levin, *The Indo-European and Semitic Languages* (State University of New York Press, Albany, 1971).

[31] See the many papers in *The Sahara and the Nile: Quaternary Environments and Prehistoric Occupation in Northern Africa*, eds. Martin A. J. Williams and Hugues Faure (A. A. Balkema, Rotterdam, 1980).

[32] See Martin Bernal 'Paleoclimate, Archeology and the Origins of Afroasiatic', paper presented to the *First International Conference of Somali Studies* (Mogadishu, 1980).

to Greece and the Balkans in the seventh.[33] I follow Professor Goodenough's claim that these rich Neolithic culture gave rise to the mixed agricultural and nomadic Kurgan Culture in what is now the Ukraine.[34] These claims are controversial, but we rejoin conventional wisdom in saying that the language of the Kurgan culture was Indo-European, though I would exclude Hittite and the other Anatolian languages. Derivatives of the Kurgan culture seem to have spread with its language: southeast to Iran and India, west to central Europe, and southwest to the Balkans and Greece. The development of agriculture in western Europe in the fourth millennium was clearly linked to that further east and seems to have spread by sea, or rather along the coasts. There is no evidence here of a radical change of population. Local Mesolithic cultures seem to have taken up – or to have been reduced to – farming.[35] This region nevertheless also became largely Indo-European speaking, possibly as early as the fourth millennium itself. In the eastern Mediterranean, however, the association of language with the much greater agricultural population meant the cultural and linguistic disappearance of the earlier hunter-gatherers.

It is difficult to say how much non-linguistic cultural baggage went with the languages, since it would have been obscured by later overlays. Thus, for instance, while it is likely that the common Indo-European word for 'king' – *rex* in Latin, *rix* in Gaulish, *ri* in Irish, and *rajah* in India – originally contained a common sense of 'kingship', as Dumézil claims,

---

[33] Vladimir Ivanov Georgiev, *Introduzione alla storia delle Lingue Indeuropee* (2nd edn., Ateneo, Rome, 1966); Vladimir Ivanov Georgiev, 'The Arrival of the Greeks in Greece: The Linguistic Evidence', in *Bronze Age Migrations in the Aegean: Archaeological and Linguistic Problems in Greek Prehistory*, eds. R. A. Crossland and Ann Birchall (Noyes, Park Ridge, New Jersey, 1974), pp. 243–54; James Mellaart, *The Neolithic of the Near East* (Thames & Hudson, London, 1975); Colin Renfrew, 'Problems in the General Correlation of Archaeological and Linguistic Strata in Prehistoric Greece: The Model of Autochthonous Origin', in Crossland and Birchall, *Bronze Age Migrations*, pp. 263–276; Trump, *Prehistory of the Mediterranean*, pp. 28–57.

[34] Ward Hunt Goodenough, 'The Evolution of Pastoralism and Indo-European Origins', in *Indo-European and Indo-Europeans: Papers Presented at the Third Indo-European Conference at the University of Pennsylvania* (University of Pennsylvania Press, Philadelphia, 1970), pp. 253–66 – *pace* Marta Gimbutas, 'Proto Indo-European Culture: The Kurgan Culture during the Fifth, Fourth and Third Millenia BC', *Indo-European and Indo-Europeans* pp. 155–98.

[35] Jean Guilaine, 'Problèmes Actuels de la Néolithisation et du Néolithique Ancien en Méditerranée Occidentale', *Interaction and Acculturation in the Mediterranean*, ed. Jan G. P. Best and Nanny M. W. deVries (B. R. Grüner, Amsterdam, 1980), pp. 3–22; Jean Guilaine, 'Les Origines de l'homme en Europe', in *L'Europe*, ed. Fernand Braudel (Arts et Métiers Graphiques, Paris, 1982), pp. 38–64, especially 46–7.

they are somewhat different when first attested historically.[36] The one clear-cut example of an association between language and another cultural trait is that of Afroasiatic with circumcision, and it is possible, though no more than that, that this denoted a distinctive attitude to communities and divinities. Nevertheless, I find it plausible that there were other cultural characteristics associated with the language families.

The origins of the differences between the Indo-European north and the Afroasiatic south coasts of the Mediterranean are also obscured by climatic distinctions between their hinterlands, which intensified with the increasing dessication of the south after the fifth millennium.[37] On the whole, however, the strongly Afroasiatic characteristics of such areas as the Atlas, the Ethiopian highlands, and the Lebanese mountains, which retained their rainfall, would suggest that the linguistic-cultural differences are more significant.

This view of the sea as a cultural barrier at this early stage differs from one held by a number of linguists, according to which originally there was a Mediterranean unity that was disturbed by later conquests. They have found the notion of a Mediterranean 'substratum' essential to explain fundamental features common to Indo-European and Afroasiatic, which for ideological as well as intrinsic reasons they believe to be genetically distinct.[38] This hypothesis is unnecessary, if one believes the two language families – of the Rift Valley and Anatolian agricultural centers – to have been related, and that substantial loaning went on in later times.

The appearance of human remains on islands from the ninth millennium shows that some kind of navigation was possible by then. But it seems plausible that ease of maritime transport of stock and goods only surpassed that of transport by land in the fifth or fourth millennia. If so, the centripetal forces in the Mediterranean would only have begun to operate after the two linguistic-cultural blocks were in place. During the period 40,00BC–AD1850, in which water transport dominated, an

[36] Georges Dumézil, *Mythe et Epopée: L'Idéologie des Trois Fonctions dans les Peuples Indo-Européens* (3 vols, Gallimard, Paris, 1968–73), 'Préface'.

[37] Michel Servant and Simone Servant-Vildary, 'L'Environnement Quaternaire du Bassin du Tchad', and Lionel Balout and Colette Roubert, 'Apports de la Préhistoire à la Stratigraphie et la Chronologie au Sahara et au Maghreb', *The Sahara and the Nile*, pp. 133–62 and 163–72.

[38] See bibliography in Eduard Schwyzer, *Griechische Grammatik* (3 vols, Beck, Munich, 1949–53), vol. 1, pp. 63–5.

extraordinarily fruitful pulling together of the two occurred, especially in areas in which the coast was cut off from the hinterland and state power was proportionately weak. The most significant regions in this respect are southern Spain, western Italy, and the Aegean. All of these received massive eastern influence during the Late Bronze Age and were urbanized and introduced to 'slave society' by Phoenicians between 1000 and 700 BC. In the Levant itself, I believe there was a much earlier example of the same pattern; that is to say, Semitic speech was established there by overland movement from Mesopotamia in the sixth and fifth millennia BC, but from the late fourth the coast was heavily influenced by Egyptian culture that came by sea.[39] From then on it took part in the general Mediterranean exchanges. Here, however, we are concerned with the Aegean.

According to the Revised Ancient Model, the Neolithic population of Greece and the Aegean as a whole was Indo-Hittite speaking. In some period or periods during the fourth and third millennia BC, Greece, though not Anatolia, was overrun by invasion or infiltration from the north by Indo-European speakers. Since Greek went through major later changes and Indo-European is a branch of Indo-Hittite – and therefore the two would have been related – it is difficult to detect traces of the substratum in Greek language, toponyms, or mythological names. Afroasiatic influences are much easier to see. There were almost certainly Egyptian and Semitic influences on the Aegean in the fourth and third millennia BC, but the major impact occurred in the first half of the second millennium, when Egyptian and Semitic speakers settled and colonized much of Greece, the islands, and possibly parts of coastal Anatolia. During this period the massive non-Indo-European component in Greek culture was introduced as an Afroasiatic superstrate on an Indo-European base. In language this would explain the similarity of the semantic range of the Indo-European elements in Greek to that of the Anglo-Saxon in English: basic verbs and adjectives; pronouns and prepositions; the names of family members, domestic animals, and agricultural terms. By contrast the non-Indo-European terms in Greek correspond to the French component in English. The military, political, religious and philosophical vocabulary is overwhelmingly non-Indo-European and, I maintain, Egyptian and west Semitic.

---

[39] Bernal, 'Origins of Afroasiatic', pp. 57–9. I am now convinced that most differences between Canaanite and other Semitic languages can best be explained in terms of Egyptian influence on the former. See Bernal, *Black Athena* vol. 2: *Greece European or Levantine? The Egyptian and West Semitic Components of Greek Civilization*.

COMPETITION BETWEEN THE TWO MODELS AND THE ORIGINS OF 'SLAVE SOCIETY'

The Aryan Model is not merely concerned with Greece in the second millennium. It consistently plays down later contributions attributed by the Ancients to the Egyptians and the Phoenicians. I hope to write elsewhere on the Afroasiatic roots of Greek science and philosophy.[40] Here, I should like to restrict myself to the origin of Marx's 'Slave Society' and its derivation from the 'Asiatic Mode of Production'.

Since the Greeks maintained that most of their cities had been founded during the Bronze Age, one should not expect any tradition of Near Eastern colonization between the ninth and seventh centuries BC, when the *polis* was established. Greek historians plausibly asserted that the new civic constitutions introduced during this period were created by Greeks. Most of the constitution makers, however, were supposed to have gone to Egypt and/or Phoenicia to study legal and constitutional forms. Lacking a clear-cut definition of their own economic system, the Greeks and Romans had no explicit traditions about the origins of what we would call 'slave society', but there are indications that they believed that it came from Phoenicia. As Cicero put it, 'The Phoenicians with their traffic in merchandise were the first to introduce into Greece greed, luxurious living and insatiable desires of all sorts.'[41] This of course fits the pattern of the Homeric epics in which all trade and slaving is carried out by Phoenicians. Thus the idea that slave society originated in Greece conflicts with ancient views.

Marx and Engels were products of the peak of Hellenomania in German educated circles between 1820 and 1840. Marx had a lifelong love for Greece and completely accepted the prevailing view that in every aspect of her civilization Greece was categorically different from and superior to all that had gone before. According to him, it was only in Greece that the individual had cut the umbilical cord from his community and had changed from a *Gattungswesen*, 'species being', to become a *zôon politikon*, 'political animal/city dweller'.[42] In Marx's concept of 'Asiatic

---

[40] For other writings on this subject, see n. 4 above.

[41] Cicero, *De Re Publica*, Fr. 3.3.

[42] *Grundrisse der Kritik der politischen Ökonomie* (Marx, Engels, Lenin Institute, Moscow, 1939, and Dietz Verlag, Berlin, 1953), pp. 375–413, tr. Martin Nicolaus (Vintage Books, New York, 1973), pp. 471–513.

society' or the 'Asiatic mode of production' as a historical stage, society, though technically advanced, had not broken free from the primitive tribal community and was characterized by self-sufficient village communities whose surplus production was taken directly by the state. Thus, there was no distinction between rent and tax. This mode of production was typically Asiatic and essentially static.[43] By contrast, Marx's slave society had private property in land, which mediated between the state and the lower classes, and its cities were typically ruled by landowners. Marx denied that trade and specialized manufacture were dominant, but he and Engels seem to have seen them as leading to the growth of commodities and private ownership of land and people – that is, the commercial or chattel slaves upon whose labor the economy depended.[44]

[43] See Anne M. Bailey and Josep R. Llobera, eds., *The Asiatic Mode of Production: Science and Politics* (Routledge & Kegan Paul, London, 1981); Stephen Porter Dunn, *The Fall and Rise of the Asiatic Mode of Production* (Routledge & Kegan Paul, London, 1982); Jonathan Friedman, *Systems, Structure, and Contradiction in the Evolution of 'Asiatic' Social Formations* (National Museum of Denmark, Copenhagen, 1979); Lawrence Krader, *The Asiatic Mode of Production: Sources, Development and Critique in the Writings of Karl Marx* (Van Gorcum, Assen, 1975); Jean Suret-Canale, *Sur le 'Mode de Production Asiatique'* (Centre des Études et de Récherches Marxistes, Paris, 1974); Ferenc Tökei, *Essays on the Asatic Mode of Production'* tr. W. Goth (Akademia Kiadó Budapest, 1979); Wu Dakun and others, 'Yaxiya Shengchan Fangshi Xueshu Taolunhui Jiyao,' (A Compendium of the Forum on the 'Asiatic Mode of Production'), *Zhongguoshi Yanjiu*, 3 (1981) no. 3, pp. 1–168. For the best bibliography on the Asiatic mode of production in the Near East, see Carlo Zaccagnini, 'Modo di Produzione Asiatico e Vicino Oriente Antico, Appunti per una Discussione', in *Dialoghi di Archeologia*, 3 (1981), pp. 3–65.

[44] M. I. Finley, ed., *Slavery in Classical Antiquity* (Heffer, Cambridge, 1968); M. I. Finley, *The Ancient Economy* (Chatto & Windus, London, 1973); M. I. Finley, *Ancient Slavery and Modern Ideology* (Viking Press, New York, 1980) – see pp. 187–8 for a bibliography of his other writings on the subject. See also Perry Anderson, *Passages from Antiquity to Feudalism* (New Left Books, London, 1974), pp. 18–28. Marx, Engels and their contemporaries were dazzled by the culture of Athens into taking it as the typical case. In my opinion it would be more useful to consider the Euboean cities, Aegina or Corinth. The last, which in the eighth and seventh centuries BC was economically far ahead of Athens, was famous for its manufacture and export of bronze and pottery as well as for its early establishment of colonies. These developments were clearly linked to its limited land area and lack of agricultural self-sufficiency. Corinth was also famous for the large number of its slaves and its 'Phoenician' characteristics. For details of the former and an attempt to deny the oriental impact, see J. B. Salmon, *Wealthy Corinth: A History of the City to 338 BC* (Clarendon Press, Oxford, 1984), especially pp. 101–58.

We now know that all recorded ancient societies in Asia had family land, as distinct from community, palace, or temple land. They also had considerable trade in both luxuries and essentials. Thus, only in some peripheral regions does there appear to have been any village autarchy.[45] Some slavery, especially of women, existed from the earliest times, and at least in later Mesopotamian society there was a pattern of servitude that Muhammad Dandamaev has shown to have been in every way as complex as those in Greece and Rome.[46] As Finley, Tökei, Zaccagnini, and Anderson hasten to assure us, these anomalies do not invalidate Marx's scheme, which does not refer to the whole society but only to its dominant mode of production, and, as Dandamaev demonstrates, most land was not cultivated by people whom it is helpful to call slaves.[47] Within these limits we may usefully distinguish Egypt, Mesopotamia, and the other territorial or riverine societies from those of the classical world of the Mediterranean.[48]

But is the division best drawn, as it was soon after the Greek War of Independence in the 1820s, between old and static Turkey/Asia and young and dynamic Greece/Europe? Against this we now have the paradox that Mycenaean Greece had a palatial economy and society of

[45] See I. M. Diakonoff, 'The Rise of the Despotic State in Ancient Mesopotamia,' tr. G. M. Sergeyev, in *Ancient Mesopotamia, Socio-Economic History: A Collection of Studies by Soviet Scholars*, ed. I. M. Diakonoff (Nauka, Moscow, 1969), pp. 173–202; Zaccagnini, 'Modo di Produzione Asiatico' pp. 22–36. See also the essays in *Oikumene* 2 (1978), based on the conference held in Budapest in 1974.

[46] Muhammad A. Dandamaev, *Slavery in Babylonia: From Nabopolassar to Alexander the Great (626–331 BC)*, tr. Victoria A. Powell (revised edn, Northern Illinois University Press, De Kalb, Illinois, 1984), pp. 67–101. The wide extent of the slave market in the Ancient Near East can be seen in the remarkably constant price of slaves, in terms of silver, during the Late Bronze Age, from Egypt to Mesopotamia. See Michael Heltzer, *Goods, Prices and the Organization of Trade in Ugarit* (Reichert, Wiesbaden, 1978), pp. 92–3 and 113.

[47] Marx, *Gründrisse*, pp. 377–94; Finley, *Ancient Economy*, pp. 28–9; Tökei, *Essays on the Asiatic Mode of Production*, pp. 21–24; Zaccagnini, 'Modo di Produzione Asiatico', p. 16; Anderson, *Passages from Antiquity to Feudalism*, p. 21; and Dandamaev, *Slavery in Babylonia*, pp. 646–54.

[48] *Pace* I. M. Diakonoff, 'Slaves, Helots, and Serfs in Early Antiquity', *Acta Antiqua*, 22 (1974), pp. 45–78; and G. Komoroczy, 'Landed Property in Ancient Mesopotamia and the Theory of the So-called Asiatic Mode of Production', *Oikumene*, 2 (1978), pp. 9–26.

the bureaucratic 'Asiatic' type.[49] Even more striking, we find Levantine slave societies. It would seem better to take up Weber's argument that slave society was overwhelmingly coastal and distinguish not between Asia and Europe but between the types proposed by Fox for land and waterborne societies.[50]

The connection between slave society and the sea was not accidental. Without the ease of bulk shipping of staples, food-deficient, specialized manufacturing economies could not develop. Diocletian's edict on maximum prices demonstrates that it cost less to ship grain from one end of the Mediterranean to another than to cart it 75 miles.[51] Moses Finley rightly draws a categorical distinction between helots, with their attachment to land and intact families, and deracinated chattel slaves, who were basically not self-reproducing, but he does not make an explicit link to maritime society.[52] Since in both slave society and capitalism, the rich and powerful monopolize sea passage, the slave could not run home. His or her choice was restricted to accepting slavery, suicidal revolt, or trying to join suspicious barbarians beyond the pale.[53] Nearly all chose the first and thus made it possible for slave-owners to use slaves in relatively unguarded, extensive and long term agriculture and extraction. The slave-owners were further secured by what seems to have been a conscious policy of mixing slaves from the very different cultures reachable by sea. These possibilities were not open to territorial empires. The nearest parallel is that of the Neo-Assyrian and Neo-Babylonian mass

[49] See Luigia Achillea Stella, *La Civiltà Micinea nei Documenti Contemporanei* (Ateneo, Rome, 1965). This, like the critically important work of Cyrus Gordon on Linear A, is omitted from John Chadwick's extensive bibliography in his *Documents in Mycenaean Greek* (2nd edn, Cambridge University Press, Cambridge, 1973). For the 'oriental' aspects of the society see also Suret-Canale, *Sur le 'Mode de Production Asiatique'*, pp. 178–82. Finely points out these anomalies in *Ancient Economy*, p. 182, n. 39.

[50] Max Weber, *The Agrarian Sociology of Ancient Civilizations*, tr. R. I. Frank (New Left Books, London, 1976), pp. 40–1 and 155–63, cited in Anderson, *Passages from Antiquity to Feudalism*, p. 20.

[51] Arnold Hugh Martin Jones, *The Later Roman Empire* (3 vols, Basil Blackwell, Oxford, 1964), pp. 841–2, cited in Finley, *Ancient Economy*, p. 126. An equally striking example of this under capitalism comes from a story my father used to tell of his grandfather's complaints that it had cost more to have a grand piano moved from San Francisco to their house in San José than to have it shipped around Cape Horn from Genoa.

[52] Finley, *Ancient Slavery and Modern Ideology*, pp. 70–1.

[53] This may have been a reason that Romans found north European slaves less tractable than Greeks, Asiatics and Africans.

movement of populations across their empires. Interestingly, however, these only took place after the development of the Phoenician 'slave economy'. In any event, even these mixtures left small communities more or less intact.

Marx had considerable difficulty in explaining the rise of slave society in noncommercial Greece.[54] Twentieth-century scholars' have been unable to do much better. Professor Michel Lejeune has tried to show that the system existed in embryo in the presence of slaves in the Mycenaean *damoi*, 'townships.'[55] Yet slaves existed in virtually all 'Asiatic Societies.' As Jean Suret-Canale points out, Mycenaean slaves did not form 'l'essentiel de la production,' and the survival of the system after the destruction of the palaces and 400 years of 'Dark Ages' is almost impossible.[56] Thus, while the geography of the Aegean lends itself to trade, it is hard to trace the steps by which Greek tribal society, even with a memory of the Mycenaean bureaucracy, became commercial in the eighth and seventh centuries BC.

In my opinion these difficulties come from having asked the wrong question. The place to investigate the origins of slave society is in Phoenicia, although there are great difficulties with the sources. Phoenicians made great use of writing and papyrus. It is no coincidence that Byblos, the Greek name for the great city of Gu/ebal, was used as the word for 'papyrus' or 'writing'. Phoenicians were renowned for their records and archives, but since they were defeated by the Greeks and lived in a rainfall climate, virtually nothing of their literature survives except that preserved in the Bible.[57] Paradoxically, we know much less about the Phoenician society than we do about that of Bronze Age Mesopotamia and Syria, when records were kept on clay. The patterns

[54] Gabriele Bockische is unable to do much better. See her 'Zur Entstehung der Produktionssklaverei im alter Griechenland', in *Produktivkräfte und Gesellschaftsformationen in Vorkapitalistischer Zeit*, ed. Joachim Herrmann (Akademie Verlag, Berlin, 1982), pp. 314–25. Finley promises to explain it but fails to, in his *Ancient Economy*, p. 71. In *Ancient Slavery and Modern Ideology*, p. 87, he is disarmingly modest: 'Little as we may understand the processes by which they [the necessary conditions for slavery] arose that is the critical, and most difficult, question. I do not pretend that I can answer it satisfactorily.' For Starr's linking the rise of Greek commercial society to the Assyrian conquests, see below, n. 103.

[55] 'Le Damos dans la Société Mycénienne,' *Revue des Etudes Greques*, 78 (1965), pp. 1–22.

[56] Jean Suret-Canale, *Sur le 'Mode de Production Asiatique'*, p. 179, n. 2.

[57] Josephus, *Against Apion*, 1.17, and Pliny, *Natural History*, 18.22

of Phoenician economy and politics have to be gleaned from
fragmentary and disparate scraps of evidence, usually in the writings of
their enemies.

Trade and manufacture had been important on the Levantine
coast since at least the fourth millennium BC. Family ownership
of land was well established there, as in the rest of the Middle
East by the middle of the second millennium BC, and from this
period there was a gradual 'laicization' of landed property until
'land became a commodity like any other.'[58] While many important
coastal cities of this time had sufficient arable land, others seem
to have been agriculturally deficient and dependent on exchanging
finished goods for grain. During the fourteenth century BC, we
have the first reference to the people as sovereign in a Levantine city.[59]
As Michael Astour points out, this situation was not unique:
'the ease of the transition from personal to collective rule demonstrates
that the city states of Canaan possessed the necessary institutions
even under the royal regime.'[60] In the Late Bronze Age, republics
were nonetheless unusual. The normal pattern on the Levantine
coast was that of a constitutional monarchy backed by a major land power –
the Egyptians or Hittites.

In the thirteenth and twelfth centuries BC the East Mediterranean
was devastated by a series of migrations and invasions carried out by
raiders whom the Egyptians called 'peoples of the sea' and who appear
to have come from the Aegean and Anatolia. Egypt managed to survive
but qualitative changes occurred elsewhere. In Greece the breakdown
was followed by 300 to 400 years of depopulation and very little town
life. Phoenicia, by contrast, recovered quickly, but with new economic
and political structures. Until the continuous Assyrian pressure of the
late eighth century BC there were no sustained threats to the coast from
land-based states. Thus from c.1050–750 BC, Phoenician cities, notably
Tyre, maintained political independence and generated enormous wealth.
The 'Tyrian Lament' cited in Ezekiel, which seems to refer to the early
ninth century BC, contains an astounding description of the city's trading

[58] Zaccagnini, 'Modo di Produzione Asiatico', p. 28.

[59] This was how Amenhotep IV/Akhenaton addressed the ruler of Arwad. *Tel el
Amarna Letters*, 149: 57–63.

[60] 'The Amarna Age Forerunners of Biblical Anti-Royalism', in *For Max Weinreich
on his Seventieth Birthday* (Mouton, Paris–The Hague, 1964), pp. 6–17, especially p. 14.
Astour cites the change from royal to republican regime at Aduna. *Amarna Letters*, 100.

network, which stretched from Spain to Persia and the southern Red Sea to Greece.[61]

By 850 BC Tyre was a major entrepôt for staples and luxuries transported by both land and sea. Much was re-exported, but as the historian of Tyre, H. Jacob Katzenstein, plausibly argues, much had to have been consumed in the city itself.[62] As early as the tenth century BC, king Hiram of Tyre, in return for help in building the temple at Jerusalem, asked Solomon for corn 'which we stand in need of because we inhabit an island.'[63] Solomon sent 20,000 *kor* of wheat annually, which appears to have been more than 60 per cent of the amount consumed by his own court.[64]

None of the goods mentioned on the list from Ezekiel appears to have come from a Tyrian colony, with the possible exception of Tarshish in Spain, but there is little doubt that colonization too was initiated by Phoenicians. Groups of merchants from one city, living corporately in another, had existed in the Near East at least since the early Bronze Age, and the establishment by cities of villages around their periphery is also ancient. The biblical metaphor is of a city as the 'mother'–metropolis– and the villages as 'daughters' over which she has authority. By the ninth century at the very latest, Phoenicians were establishing 'daughter cities' overseas.[65] Great efforts have been made to distinguish these from Greek colonies, but the Phoenician ones seem to have been founded and maintained for much the same reasons as the Greek: as markets for specialized manufacture, to increase supplies of staples and metals, for the export of population to ease social problems, and to provide protection

---

[61] Ezekiel 27. 12–24. For convincing arguments in favor of dating this Phoenician *Vorlage* to the early ninth century BC, long before the time of Ezekiel, see H. Jacob Katzenstein, *The History of Tyre: From the Beginning of the Second Millennium BCE until the Fall of the Neo-Babylonian Empire in 538 BCE* (Schocken Institute, Jerusalem, 1973), p. 154.

[62] Katzenstein, *History of Tyre*, p. 158.

[63] Quoted in Josephus, *Antiquities of the Jews*, 8. 54, tr. Henry St John Thackeray and Ralph Marcus, (4 vols, Harvard University Press, Cambridge, Massachusetts, 1930–43), vol. 2, p. 599.

[64] For this amount and those of barley and olive oil see 1 Kings 5. 11, and Katzenstein, *History of Tyre*, p. 99.

[65] It is possible that the ninth century BC Nora Stone refers to Tyre as the 'mother' of Tarshish in Sardinia. There is no doubt about the term's use in later inscriptions. See Naoum Slousch, *Otzar Hakkitabôt Happiniqiyôt* (Dvir, Tel Aviv, 1942), pp. 32, 34, and 46. See also 2 Samuel 8.1 and 20.19, and Ezekiel 16. 46–9, and the bibliography in Guy Bunnens, *L'expansion Phénicienne en Méditerranée: Essai d'Interpretation Fondé sur une Analyse des Traditions Littéraires* (Institut Belge de Rome, Brussels, Rome, 1979), pp. 281–2.

and refuge in time of trouble. In both cultures, colonies that had achieved political and economic autonomy, retained religious ties with the mother city.[66]

This shift to a predominantly commercial and manufacturing society with a food deficit seems to have been reflected in a change of emphasis in the pattern of labor. The Bible offers some guidance to the different kinds of labor in Israel, which presumably resembled those of similar Canaanite-speaking tribal federations or kingdoms – Moab, Ammon, and Edom. In these, the most important form was the *mas*, permanent helotry for subjugated peoples or temporary levies for the Israelites themselves.[67] Men in service were usually called *<abâdîm*, the general word for servants and slaves. For, despite the preponderance of helotry, commercial slavery played an important role in Israelite society in particular and Canaanite society in general, as can be seen from the references to Jahve as a slave dealer who 'sells' and 'redeems' his people.[68] Typically, slaves were foreigners captured or bought from

[66] *Pace* Bunnens, *L'Expansion Phénicienne*, pp. 280–284. For an analysis of the story of the foundation of Carthage in the late ninth century BC to avoid social conflict, see François Decret, *Carthage ou l'Empire de la Mer* (Seuil, Paris 1977), pp. 46–53; and Katzenstein, *History of Tyre*, pp. 186–91. Five hundred years later, Aristotle described a system by which social discontent was avoided at Carthage by sending some of the poor to outlying districts to turn them into men of property – see *The Politics*, 6, 5. See also Sallust, *Jugurtha*, 19. 1–2. Arguments among scholars as to which was the *essential* motive for colonization seem futile. See Alexander John Graham, *Colony and Mother City in Ancient Greece* (Manchester University Press, Manchester, 1964); 'Patterns in Early Greek Colonization', *Journal of Hellenic Studies*, 91 (1971), pp. 35–47; John Nicolas Coldstream, *Geometric Greece* (E. Benn, London, 1977), pp. 231–3; Robert Manuel Cook, 'Reasons for the Foundation of Ischia and Cumae', *Historia*, 9 (1962), pp. 113–14. It is clear that economic, political and social motives were all involved in varying proportions. For the political autonomy granted to the cities dependent on Carthage, see Maurice Sznycer 'L'"Assemblée du Peuple" dans les Cités Puniques d'après des Témoignages Épigraphiques', *Semitica*, 25 (1975), pp. 47–68, especially p. 51.

[67] For the Israelite *mas* see Judges 1. 28–35; 1 Kings 5.13, and elsewhere. *Mas* would seem to be borrowed from the Egyptian *m<*, Coptic *meeše*, 'troop, workgang', another probable example of Egyptian influence on Canaanite. For a short survey of Israelite slavery, see Hans Walter Wolff, *Anthropology of The Old Testament*, tr. Margaret Kohl (SCM Press, London, 1974), pp. 192–205. Finley has quite rightly pointed out that to squeeze the many and varied forms of labor in the ancient world into the three categories of slavery, helotry, and wage labor does violence to the complexities of the actual society – *Ancient Economy*, p. 65. See also Dandamaev, *Slavery in Babylonia*, p. 77. While accepting this, I still maintain that this categorization, however crude, has heuristic value.

[68] See Judges 2.14, 3.8, 6.2, 6.9, and 10.7 and 1 Samuel 12.9.

abroad. There were also temporary or bond slaves from the nation itself, who sold themselves or were sold as children because of debts or poverty. Distinctions between these and foreign slaves were often blurred, as can be seen from repeated attempts to have Israelite slaves released at regular intervals.[69] In addition to helots and slaves, there were wage-laborers and independent craftsmen.

The same types of labor existed in Phoenicia. Hiram, king of Tyre, sent <abâdîm to cut timber and build the temple at Jerusalem. Solomon paid Hiram for the work.[70] Some of these men came from a corveé, others seem to have been state or personal slaves. In contrast, Solomon appears to have dealt directly with Hiram the craftsman, who was clearly free.[71] Scattered evidence strengthens the plausible hypothesis that in Phoenicia, with its urban manufacture and commerce, chattel slavery was even more important than it was inland. The 'Tyrian Lament' reference to buying slaves from Greece, and the two major references to Phoenicians in the *Odyssey* are concerned with slaving. Odysseus' story of having been kidnapped by a Phoenician is particularly significant since untrue.[72] In the eighth century BC, Amos condemned Tyre for 'forgetting the ties of kinship' and selling Israelite refugees to Edom.[73] Two centuries later, Joel denounced Tyrians and Sidonians for selling Judeans to the Greeks.[74] Herodotus opened his work with a reference to Phoenician slaving.[75] In all cases except one the slaves were taken overseas.

Slaves appeared as a natural part of the city life described in Proverbs. In the fifth century BC, the author of Ecclesiastes described the life of a rich man: 'I built myself houses and planted vineyards: I made myself gardens and parks and planted all kinds of fruit trees in them; I made myself gardens and parks and planted all kinds of fruit trees in them; I made myself pools of water to irrigate a grove of growing trees; I bought slaves,

[69] Leviticus 25.41–6; and Deuteronomy 15.12–9. King Mesha of Moab used Israelite prisoners for construction. See W. F. Albright, 'The Moabite Stone', in *Ancient Near Eastern Texts: Relating to the Old Testament*, ed. James B. Pritchard (3rd edn., Princeton University Press, Princeton, 1969), pp. 320–1.

[70] 1 Kings 5.9.   [71] 1 Kings 7.13–14.

[72] Ezekiel 27.13; *Odyssey*, 14.290–300 and 15.403. Lexicographers of Greek are generally happy to accept that *doulos*, the most common word for 'slave', is non-Indo-European. The most plausible etymology is, despite some complication over the vocalization, from the Canaanite *dal* or *dâl*, 'poor, dependent'. The presence of *doero* in Mycenaean Greek, however, makes it impossible to associate the derivation with the introduction of slave society many centuries later.

[73] Amos 1.9.   [74] Joel 3.6.   [75] Herodotus, 1.1, and 2.55–6.

male and female, and I had my home-born slaves as well.'[76] This portrait of the environment of the archetypal slaveowner corresponds to Diororus' description of agriculture near Carthage, which also appears to have been based on slave labor.[77] With the advantages of sea transportation of slaves, Phoenicians in the West Mediterranean seem to have been able to base their agriculture upon slave labor, and Moses Finley is almost certainly right when he suggests that it was from the Carthaginians and other west Phoenicians that the Roman *latifundia* system developed.[78] Thus the evidence, though scanty, indicates that commercial slavery dominated relations of production in Phoenicia from the tenth if not the eleventh century BC, well before it dominated in Greece.

It seems to have been the Phoenicians who developed that symbol of slave-owning indolence, the couch for eating, taken up in Greece and another area of Phoenician influence, Etruria.[79] If Phoenicia had chattel slavery, it also had its opposite, free citizens, but this was not, as is sometimes suggested, the creation of slave society. The contrast between servility and freedom – *amargi* in Sumerian – existed in Mesopotamia since at least the third millennium.[80] In Canaanite the terms *ba<al* and *hôr*, mean both 'noble' and 'free', and *d'ror*, 'free', combines images of 'free flowing water' and 'swallows' that never touch the ground. Thus, it is European cultural arrogance to claim that the Greeks invented the concept of freedom.[81]

---

[76] Ecclesiastes 2.6–8. This book is generally considered to have been written in Hellenistic times. For a convincing argument for the earlier dating, see William Foxwell Albright, *Yahweh and the Gods of Canaan* (Doubleday, Garden City, New York, 1969), p. 224.

[77] See also Diodorus Siculus, 20.8.3–4; and S. Gsell, 'Esclaves Ruraux dans l'Afrique Romaine', in *Mélanges Gustave Glotz*, eds. Frank Ezra Adcock et al. (2 vols, Presses Universitaires de France, Pairs, 1932), pp. 397–415. Quoted by Finley, *Ancient Economy*, p. 191.

[78] Finley, *Ancient Economy*, pp. 71 and 191. See also Ferruccio Barreca, *La Sardegna Fenicia e Punica* (Chiarella, Sassari, 1974), pp. 30–5. Slavery was also important in western mines. Polybius (quoted by Strabo, *Geography*, 3.2, 10) described what must originally have been west Phoenician mines as having 40,000 men working in them. Finley plausibly describes them as slaves.

[79] See Amos 6.4. The Egyptians and Mesopotamians feasted sitting on chairs. See also Jean-Marie Dentzer, 'Aux Origines de l'Iconographie du Banquet Couché', *Revue Archéologique*, (1971), pp. 215–58. The idea that eating from couches symbolizes freedom is preserved in the Jewish tradition – see the *Haggadah sel Pesah*.

[80] See H. W. F. Saggs, *The Greatness that was Babylon* (Mentor, New York, 1962), pp. 169–71; Samuel Noah Kramer, *The Sumerians: Their History, Culture and Character* (University of Chicago Press, Chicago, 1963), pp. 78–80.

[81] *Pace* Finley, 'Between Slavery and Freedom', *Comparative Studies in Society and History*, 6 (1963–4), pp. 236–9; Anderson, *Passages from Antiquity to Feudalism*, pp. 21–3.

The nineteenth-century notion that private ownership of land began in Greece has been shattered by later discoveries. While temples and states owned immense territory, a considerable proportion of Mesopotamian and Egyptian documents are concerned with privately held land and its transfer: first within the family, then with fictitious kinship, and finally as a commodity.[82] The last seems to have been the predominant form of land ownership in Phoenicia.[83]

Most Phoenician cities had walls to protect the whole people and were dominated by the *hekal*. This word, deriving from the Sumerian *e–gal*, 'big house', changed its meaning, approximately with the crisis of the twelfth century BC, from 'palace' to 'temple', usually of the city or tribal divinity that represented the people as a whole. Many Jews and Tyrians chose to die rather than have this symbol of their corporate identity profaned. And note the biblical insistence that Solomon built the temple before and on a grander scale than his own palace.[84]

Free citizens participated widely in the running of Phoenician cities. Ancient Mesopotamia and Syria had long traditions of democratic and aristocratic rule.[85] Thus the Phoenician pattern was an option already available through general historical precedent and the specific institutions of Bronze Age Canaan. In Phoenicia, however, these local councils and assemblies were not subject to territorial monarchs.

As among the Greek states, the Phoenician cities and the inland Canaanite-speaking kingdoms of Israel, Moab, and Ammon shared a common language, literary culture, and religious practices, though they had their own gods. Politically they were often bitterly divided. In this respect, Phoenicia in the ninth and eighth centuries BC strikingly

[82] See V. A. Jacobson, 'Some Problems Connected with the Rise of Landed Property (Old Babylonian Period)', in *Beiträge zur Sozialen Struktur des alten Vorderasien*, ed. Horst Klengel (Akademie Verlag, Berlin, 1971), pp. 33–7; Zaccagnini, 'Modo di Produzione Asiatico', pp. 27–8.

[83] In upcountry Israel, the sale of land was clearly subordinated to the legality of 'ancestral land' – see Leviticus 27.20; and Ruth 4.1–6. See, however, the urban 'capable wife' in Proverbs 31.16. The story of Naboth's vineyard can be seen as a conflict between the traditional Naboth who refused to sell his ancestral land and the phoenicianized King Ahab who offered a good price for it – 1 Kings 21.1–8.

[84] 1 Kings 6.38–7.2; and 2 Chronicles 2–3.

[85] See n. 60 above; Dandamaev, *Slavery in Babylonia*, pp. 42–5; Thorkild Jacobsen, 'Primitive Democracy in Ancient Mesopotamia', *Journal of Near Eastern Studies*, 2 (1943), pp. 159–72; Kramer, *The Sumerians*, pp. 73–5; and Saggs, *The Greatness that was Babylon*, pp. 160–3.

resembled Greece of later times. As Bustanay Oded has described
Phoenicia, there was an 'absence of any attempt to unite, even
temporarily, in order to confront the enemy from without. The history
of the coastal cities is replete with internal strife arising from commercial
competition and territorial disputes'.[86] And like the later Greeks, the
Phoenicians had varied and changing political forms: monarchies,
plutocracies, aristocracies, democracies, and mixed constitutions. They
seem to have preferred constitutional monarchies, though Canaanite
republics existed at most periods between the Late Bronze Age and the
fall of Carthage.[87] As with their common rituals for different gods,
Canaanite-speakers had a common political vocabulary and probably
a common repertoire of political forms. Although one should not
exaggerate the extent of illiteracy in societies with nonalphabetic scripts,
the Mesopotamian practice of inscribing laws on publicly visible stone
stelae or tablets became something very different in Canaan, with its
alphabet and widespread literacy.[88] Some scholars have suggested
that the early Greek law code inscriptions derived from Phoenician
ones.[89]

When looking at the constitutions of the Canaanite states, the key
term is <am; this word has the basic sense of 'troop', either of sheep
or men. It appears in many Semitic languages with the meanings of
'patrilineal kinship group, troop of soldiers' or 'the people of a particular

[86] 'The Phoenician Cities and the Assyrian Empire in the Time of Tiglath pileser
III', *Zeitschrift des deutschen Palästina-Vereins*, 90 (1974), pp. 38–49, especially p. 40.

[87] See Astour, 'Biblical Anti-Royalism'. There are many striking cases of this in the
Bible. See, for instance, the idyllic description of 'free' Laish in Judges 18.7. For
constitutions in Phoenicia see Sabatino Moscati, *The World of the Phoenicians*, tr. Alastair
Hamilton (Weidenfield and Nicholson, London, 1968), pp. 51, and 169–75. For the
Carthaginian constitution in the fourth century BC see Aristotle, *The Politics*, 2.11. For
its later developments in a democratic direction see Polybius, 6.51–2. The most complete
study of the literary sources on the Carthaginian constitution is still that of Stephane
Gsell in his *Histoire Ancienne de l'Afrique du Nord* (8 vols, Hachette, Paris, 1914–28),
vol. 2: *L'État Carthaginois* (1918), pp. 183–244.

[88] Widespread literacy is suggested by the poverty of the material remains associated
with the abecedary found at Izbet Sartah. See Moshe Kochavi, 'An Ostracon of the
Period of the Judges from Izbet Sartah', *Tel Aviv*, 4 (1977), pp. 1–13, especially 1–2.
See also Judges 8.14, where a young man captured at random in a remote village was
able to write down the names of village elders.

[89] See Snodgrass, *Archaic Greece*, p. 120.

city or territory.'⁹⁰ There is little doubt that in Hellenistic and Roman time, the Phoenician ⁵m was used as an equivalent of the Latin *populus*, 'the people' or 'free citizens' and 'their assembly,' and there are indications from the Bible that the word was used in this sense much earlier. There is now little doubt that in the appropriate contexts, ⁵m found on a number of Phoenician inscriptions is the Canaanite word which Greek writers translated as *demos* when describing 'the people' of Carthage.⁹¹ Furthermore, it is also clear that in many biblical contexts, and especially in the compound ⁵am hå⁼ åres, 'people of the land,' ⁵m refers not merely to the free citizens but to land owners and to their assemblies.⁹²

In Carthage there were also two 'kings' – called *sufetes* in Latin, from the Canaanite šop̄'tîm, 'judges' – and 'a council of elders.' According to Aristotle's description of the city's constitution in *The Politics*, issues to be discussed by the *demos* were selected by the two kings and the elders, but, in theory at least, ultimate power rested with the people. Aristotle saw the Carthaginian kings and elders as the counterparts of the Spartan kings and *gerousia*. Another striking parallel between the two constitutions was that in Carthage there were mess-halls of companions – *sussitia tōn hetairōn* – very like the Spartan *phitidia*. Their exact constitutional position is unsure, but a Canaanite equivalent has been found in the root *hbr*, 'associate,' found in a Carthaginian inscription and frequently in the Bible.⁹³ Institutionally, traces of it have been seen in the *curiae*

---

⁹⁰ For a detailed analysis of this term see Robert McClive Good, *The Sheep of His Pasture: A Study of the Hebrew Noun <Am(m) and its Semitic Cognates* (Harvard Semitic Monographs 29; Scholars Press, Chico, California, 1983).

⁹¹ Diodorus, 14.1; Polybius, 15.1.2; Nahum Slousch, 'Representative Government among the Hebrews and Phoenicians', *The Jewish Quarterly Review*, 4 (1913), pp. 303–10, especially p. 308.

⁹² For a survey of discussions of this see Good, *The Sheep*, pp. 111–22. Earlier in this century Mayer Sulzberger referred to this as a 'Hebrew Parliament' – see his *Am-ha-aretz: the Ancient Hebrew Parliament* (Greenstone, Philadelphia, 1909). See also Gsell, *L'État Carthaginois*, pp. 226–30.

⁹³ *The Politics*, 2.11. It should be pointed out that Aristotle was not always consistent in his description of the Carthaginian constitution and that he was probably drawing on information from different periods. See Sznycer, 'L'"Assemblée du Peuple" dans les Cités Puniques' p. 48. In Psalms 107.32, a clear distinction is drawn between the 'assembly of the people' and the 'council of the elders', showing that the bicameral constitutions known in Mesopotamia were also present in Canaan. See also Gsell, *L'État Carthaginois*, pp. 193–226.

or 'voting colleges' within the assemblies found in the North African cities of the Roman period, which seem to have been part of the 'Carthaginian heritage.'[94]

Most Canaanite states seem – like Carthage – to have had councils or senates of elders or notables. Special rank was given to the conveners of the council or assembly of the people. In general, both elders and people met at the town gate, but in larger cities they may have met in a special building.[95] Decisions were often by acclamation. The question of whether there were votes or elections is basically semantic, for a fine line separates these from casting lots to discover God's wishes, which in Israel at least was by casting pebbles. This process usually took place at great assemblies and often involved large numbers of people, as is evident from the phrase 'both the small and the great' sometimes used with it.[96] In Greece 'casting lots' had what would now be seen as the two meanings of casting lots and voting, frequently done with *psephoi*, 'pebbles', often placed in a *ketharion* or *kêthis*, which like *kêd* ('funerary urn') and *kados* ('urn') comes from the Canaanite *kad* ('jar') and ultimately from the Egyptian *kd*.[97] Despite the six centuries that separate Davidic from late Carthaginian institutions, it would seem reasonable to see parallels between them. Aristotle insisted on the antiquity of the Carthaginian constitution, comparing it with the oldest – and best – in Greece, those of Crete and Sparta. At no point did he suggest that Carthage borrowed from Greek patterns.[98] Even if appointment by lot

[94] See Slousch, 'Representative Government among the Hebrews and Phoenicians', pp. 309–10; Sznycer, "L'"Assemblée du Peuple" dans les Cités Puniques' p. 50. I hope to be able to discuss elsewhere the striking institutional similarities between Carthaginian and Roman institutions and the possible Semitic origins of the latter.

[95] See, for instance, Job 29.7–10, and Proverbs 31.23. I hope to set out elsewhere my belief that the *bêt mîllô* at Shechem in Judges 9.6 and the *mîllô* in Jerusalem were 'senate houses'.

[96] Lots for allocating land or choosing leaders were usually made at assemblies. See for instance 1 Samuel 10.20–5, and Micah 2.5. The phrase 'the small with the great' appears in 1 Chronicles 24.31, 25.8, and 26.15, in reference to the appointment of officials under David. The passages are obscure. The King James Version treats the process as one of 'ward against ward'. However, the New English Bible rejects this, as does Jacob N. Meyers in the Anchor Bible *Chronicles* (2 vols, Doubleday, Garden City, New York, 1965), vol. 1, pp. 162–78.

[97] For Greek voting see Victor Ehrenberg, *The Greek State* (revised edn, Methuen, London, 1961), p. 56.

[98] See Robert Drews, 'Phoenicians, Carthage, and the Spartan Eunomia', *American Journal of Philology*, 100 (1979), pp. 45–58. James Henry Oliver clearly understood this in his *Demokratia, the Gods and the Free World* (Johns Hopkins University Press, Baltimore, 1960).

in Archaic Greece did not derive from Canaan, it is clear that conventional wisdom has been misled by European arrogance and anti-Semitism into the belief that Greek cities differed categorically from the Phoenician in being 'free' while the latter were authoritarian.[99] Assyrian 'oriental despotism' only became dominant on the Levantine coast in the late eighth century BC, and Tyre and the other Phoenician cities maintained considerable autonomy long after that. Thus, from 800 to 600 BC when the *polis* emerged, the Phoenicians, the Middle Easterners with whom the Greeks had most contact, were living in very similar city states. The presence of Phoenicians in the Aegean before the late eighth century BC is attested both in Homer and archeology.[100] Such statements as that of Professor Ehrenberg – 'There is no direct road leading from the territorial state under its kings to the Greek community of free citizens' – are therefore absurd.[101]

In short, whereas in Greece it is necessary to postulate the emergence of slave society *ex nihilo*, in Phoenicia it can plausibly be seen to have arisen from early Levantine patterns of trade and manufacture, the economic, social and political developments of the Late Bronze Age, the shock of the invasions of the peoples of the sea, and 300 years of

[99] See, for instance, Mason Hammond, *The City in the Ancient World* (Harvard University Press, Cambridge, Mass., 1972) pp. 172–3. Interestingly, he contradicts this when he refers to the antiquity of Canaanite civic councils on p. 87.

[100] The only scholar to articulate opposition to the claims of Gordon and Astour of an early Phoenician presence in the Aegean was James David Muhly. See his 'Homer and the Phoenicians: the Relations between Greece and the Near East in the Late Bronze and Early Iron Ages', *Berytus*, 19 (1970), pp. 19–64; and 'On the Shaft Graves at Mycenae', in *Studies in Honor of Tom B. Jones*, eds. Marvin A. Powell and Ronald H. Sack (Butzont Bercker, Kevelaer, 1979), pp. 311–23. Since then, however, Muhly has made a *volte face* and now sees massive west Semitic influence on Mycenaean Greece. See Muhly, 'The Role of the Sea Peoples in Cyprus During the L. C. 111 Period', in *Cyprus at the Close of the Late Bronze Age*, eds. J. D. Muhly and Vassos Karegeorghis (A. G. Leventis Foundation, Nicosia, 1984), pp. 39–56. Muhly is obdurate, however, on the question of Phoenician influence on Early Iron Age Greece. See his 'Phoenicia and the Phoenicians' in *Biblical Archaeology Today: Proceedings of the International Congress on Biblical Archaeology Jerusalem, April 1984*, eds. Avraham Biran et al. (Israel Exploration Society and American Schools of Oriental Research, Jerusalem, 1985), pp. 177–91. For archaeological evidence pointing to the presence of Phoenicians in the Aegean during this period, see the thesis by Muhly's pupil, Peyton Randolph Helm, *'Greeks' in the Neo-Assyrian Levant and 'Assyria' in the Early Greek Writers* (University of Pennsylvania, 1980), pp. 75, 95–6, and 126.

[101] Ehrenberg, *The Greek State*, intro., p. 9.

freedom from interference from land empires. This plausible origin, together with its appearance three to four hundred years earlier in Phoenicia than in Greece, and the literary and archaeological evidence for the presence of Phoenicians in the Aegean in the intervening period, make it virtually certain that slave society started in Phoenicia and spread to Greece. Weber saw the new society's development as having taken place in Greece and, true to the Extreme Aryanism of his time, had no chapter on Phoenicia in his *The Agrarian Sociology of Ancient Civilizations*. He admitted, however, that: 'The first great change in social relationships in Greece was due to the establishment of city-states (*poleis*). This seems to have been due to the arrival of Near Eastern cultural elements by way of the sea, and to the participation of coastal areas in overseas commerce.'[102]

It would seem useful to consider the Phoenician as the 'pure type' of commercial city state. If we accept Marx's view that most Greek cities – with the important exceptions of 'phoenicianized' Corinth and Aegina and the Euboean cities – were still self-sufficient in staples and were controlled by landowners, we must see them as a compromise between the Phoenician commercial city and the earlier tribal society. Culturally, the mixture can be seen in the twin processes of disarming citizens while maintaining their martial spirit by confining violence spatially in the gymnasium and temporarily in games. In literature there was a parallel elevation of Homer's heroic poems into national epics.

Why should the Greek 'compromise' have been more successful in the long run? It is generally safer to rely on your own citizens for fighting, as the Greeks did, rather than on mercenaries, as the Phoenicians did. This military advantage should not be overstated, since the social cohesion and good fortification of the Canaanites in general and the Phoenicians in particular made their cities much more more able to withstand long sieges than the Greek ones. There are no Hellenic parallels to the repeated heroic defences of Tyre, Carthage, and Jerusalem. Nevertheless, Greek, or at least semi-Greek Macedonian, armies did conquer the Phoenician cities of the East Mediterranean, and it cannot be overemphasized that Alexander owed his victories to the phalanx, not to any alleged superiority of Greek science, philosophy, or civilization in general.

---

[102] Weber suggested that the Greeks won out because they, unlike the Phoenicians, used coins. However, he admitted that: 'Greeks had commercial life as active as that of the Phoenicians hundreds of years before the first state coinage.' Weber, *Sociology of Ancient Civilisations*, p. 163. The Greek advantage had certainly been gained well before the sixth century BC, when coins became common.

Long before the fourth century BC, however, Greece had gained a critical advantage. Chester Starr sees an association between the rise of the Greek *polis* and the Assyrian conquests of the late eighth century.[103] This would seem less important than the consequence of the conquests brought out by William Robertson Smith who wrote, in nineteenth century-terms:

> The northern Semites . . . whose progress up to the eighth century before Christ certainly did not lag behind that of the Greeks, were deprived of political independence, and so cut short in their natural development, by the advance from the Tigris to the Mediterranean of the great Assyrian monarchs, who drawing from the rich and broad alluvium of the Two Rivers resources that none of their neighbors could rival went on from conquest to conquest till all the small states of Syria and Palestine had gone down before them. The Assyrians were conquerors of the most brutal and destructive kind, and wherever they came the whole structure of ancient society was dissolved. From this time on the difference was not one of race alone; it was the difference between a free citizen and a slave of an Oriental despotism.[104]

The Greek cities gained a critical advantage from their geography. Beyond the reach of the land empires, they rose to fill the voids left by the Phoenicians, who had been weakened by the Assyrians and Neo-Babylonians. But the Phoenicians were not destroyed. The Levantine cities retained considerable autonomy until the end of the Persian period. The Carthaginians and other west Phoenicians kept their independence until they were destroyed by land-based Rome. In the Greek archipelago, however, the eclectic Mediterranean culture and polities that had grown up there survived and flourished for four hundred years after the Assyrians had devastated the Levant. Thus, geography, not inherent cultural superiority, determined the triumph of Hellenic civilization over the Canaanite until the rise of Christianity.

[103] Chester G. Starr, *The Economic and Social Growth of Early Greece, 800–500 BC* (Oxford University Press, New York, 1977), p. 26.

[104] *The Religion of the Semites: The Fundamental Institutions* (Schocken reprint, New York, 1972: 1st edn 1894), pp. 34–5.

2

Towns, Regimes and Religious Movements in the Reformation

ROBERT WUTHNOW

Efforts to relate the religious movements of the Reformation to their social environment have increasingly focused on the role of towns. This emphasis has developed in the wake of dissatisfaction with earlier social histories that stressed the importance of corruption within the established church, of economic change, and of variations in political structure. Evidence on religious corruption has been difficult, at best, to glean without bias and has mostly produced inconclusive results: the undoubted widespread abuses at the time of the Reformation seem not to have been noticeably worse in areas that went Protestant than in areas that remained Catholic.[1] The role of economic change, while of obvious importance on the surface, has generally been specified in narrowly Marxist terms that have failed to gain fine-tuned support in detailed studies of religious innovation. That Protestantism was adopted mainly by the new commercial bourgeoisie as an ideology to legitimate its rising social position still finds currency in some literature,[2] but much evidence from

[1] Richard Crofts, 'Books, Reform and the Reformation', *Archiv fur Reformationsgeschichte*, 71 (1980), 21–36; Hermann Heimpel, 'Characteristics of the Late Middle Ages in Germany', in *Pre-Reformation Germany*, ed. Gerald Strauss (Macmillan, New York, 1972), p. 68; Bernd Moeller, 'Religious Life in Germany on the Eve of the Reformation', in *Pre-Reformation Germany*, p. 15; Gerhard Ritter, 'Why the Reformation Occurred in Germany', *Church History*, 27 (1958), pp. 99–106.

[2] See, for example, P. C. Gordon-Walker, 'Capitalism and the Reformation', *Economic History Review*, 8 (1937), pp. 1–19; Immanuel Wallerstein, *The Modern World-System: Capitalist Agriculture and the Origins of the European World-Economy* (Academic Press, New York, 1974), pp. 153–4.

in-depth research has cast doubt on the idea that Protestantism was exclusively or even primarily concentrated among the commercial elite as such.[3] The role of political variations has been addressed in an effort to account for broader regional variations in the adoption of the Reformation.[4] But this explanation has not proven widely acceptable to either historians or sociologists because of certain conceptual and methodological problems.[5] In contrast, the research initiated by Moeller, Davis, Ozment, and others, which locates Protestantism within the social context of the late medieval and early modern town, has generally been received as a welcome and challenging addition to Reformation historiography.[6]

Yet there remain two fundamental problems with which the growing literature on towns and the Reformation has not yet dealt effectively. The first is that of specifying the towns or kinds of towns most likely to adopt the Reformation and those inclined to confront it with indifference or opposition. The second is that of identifying more precisely what it was about towns – and their environs – which led some to become bastions of Protestant support: their communal nature of organization, type of industry, location, class structure, size, or some other feature. These questions are related. To specify more clearly what about 'town-ness' was conducive to Protestantism requires an understanding of the differences between pro- and anti-Reformation towns. Here, we shall examine these questions in the light of the rapid accumulation of historical studies that have appeared during the past few decades, with special reference to some theoretical considerations derived from Edward Fox's

[3] G. R. Elton, *Reformation Europe, 1517–1559* (Harper & Row, New York, 1963), pp. 305–8; Lucien Febvre, *Life in Renaissance France* (Harvard University Press, Cambridge, Mass. 1977), pp. 70–90.

[4] Guy E. Swanson, *Religion and Regime: A Sociological Account of the Reformation* (University of Michigan Press, Ann Arbor, 1967).

[5] Cf. William J. Bouwsma, 'Swanson's Reformation', *Comparative Studies in Society and History*, 10 (1968), pp. 486–91; Natalie Zemon Davis, 'Missed Connections: Religion and Regime', *Journal of Interdisciplinary History*, 1 (1971), pp. 381–94; Martha Ellis Francois, 'Reformation and Society: An Analysis of Guy Swanson's *Religion and Regime*', *Comparative Studies in Society and History*, 14 (1972), pp. 287–305.

[6] Bernd Moeller, *Imperial Cities and the Reformation* (Fortress Press, Philadelphia, 1972); Natalie Zemon Davis, *Society and Culture in Early Modern France* (Stanford University Press, Stanford, 1975); Steven E. Ozment, *The Reformation in the Cities: The Appeal of Protestantism to Sixteenth-Century Germany and Switzerland* (Yale University Press, New Haven, 1975).

work on early modern commerce.[7] The discussion is purposefully
limited to the 'early' Reformation (that is, up to about 1559) since
religious developments during the second half of the sixteenth century
were increasingly shaped by religious conflict, armed insurrection, and
civil wars that tended to overshadow the role of towns.

TOWNS AND THE REFORMATION

Although a relation has long been perceived between the growth of towns
in Europe at the end of the Middle Ages and the rise of Protestantism,
Reformation historiography that emphasizes the role of towns in recent
years has derived largely from Moeller's work on imperial cities in the
German territories. Moeller's principal observation is that 'the
Reformation penetrated the imperial cities far more deeply than the other
estates of the empire.' For more than fifty of the sixty-five imperial cities
in some way recognized the Reformation and over half of them remained
Protestant.[8] Studies of specific German, Swiss, and Dutch towns
published both prior to and since Moeller's book have tended to confirm
the impression that towns played a leading role in the Reformation in
central Europe. These include most notably studies of Nuremberg,
Augsburg, Strasbourg, Antwerp, Hamburg, Constance, Zurich, Geneva,
and Rostock.[9] Some of these studies indicate that town councils were

---

[7] Edward Whiting Fox, *History in Geographic Perspective: The Other France* (W. W.
Norton, New York, 1971).

[8] Moeller, *Imperial Cities*, p. 41.

[9] Franz Lau, 'Der Bauernkrieg und das Angebliche Ende der Lutherischen
Reformation als Spontaner Volksbewegung', *Luther Jahrbuch*, 26 (1959), pp. 109–34;
Miriam Usher Chrisman, *Strasbourg and the Reform: A Study in the Process of Change* (Yale
University Press, New Haven, 1967); Gottfried Seebass, 'The Reformation in
Nurnberg', in *The Social History of the Reformation*, ed. Lawrence P. Buck and Jonathan
W. Zophy (Ohio State University Press, Columbus, 1972), pp. 17–40; Harold J. Grimm,
'Social Forces in the German Reformation', *Church History*, 31 (1962), pp. 3–13; Harold
J. Grimm, 'Luther's Contributions to Sixteenth-Century Organization of Poor Relief',
Archiv fur Reformationsgeschichte, 61 (1970), pp. 222–33; Alastair Duke, 'The Face of
Popular Religious Dissent in the Low Countries, 1520–1530', *Journal of Ecclesiastical
History*, 26 (1975), pp. 41–67; H. Soly, 'The "Betrayal" of the Sixteenth-Century
Bourgeoisie: A Myth? Some Considerations of the Behaviour Pattern of the Merchants
of Antwerp in the Sixteenth Century', *Acta Historiae Neerlandicae: Studies on the History
of the Netherlands*, 8 (1975), pp. 31–49; Gerald Strauss, *Nuremberg in the Sixteenth Century*;

sometimes late in giving their support to the reformers and that they did so reluctantly.[10] But by the middle of the sixteenth century enough councils had thrown their weight behind the Reformation to give it a strong base of operations. Additional evidence has demonstrated the effect of towns on Protestant clergy, showing that most were sons of town magistrates, merchants, and artisans, while only one in nine were of rural origin.[11]

The Anabaptist movement, with its considerable importance to the theological development of the Reformation and its association with the peasantry, by and large also showed the towns to have been the principal carriers of the Reformation, for it initially had fairly strong appeal among urban residents and only gradually came to be concentrated in rural areas as a result of persecutions in the towns.[12] Claus-Peter Clasen's research, based on comprehensive membership lists, also reveals that the Anabaptist movement attracted a tiny proportion of the total rural population – perhaps as little as one per cent – compared to much higher rates of attraction to Lutheranism and Calvinism in the towns.[13]

Nor was the appeal of Protestantism to the towns limited to central Europe. In Scandinavia the Reformation became particularly strong in Copenhagen, Malmö, Stockholm, and Lübeck.[14] In Poland

---

E. William Monter, *Calvin's Geneva* (John Wiley and Sons, New York, 1967); Robert W. Scribner, 'The Reformation as a Social Movement', in *Stadtbürgertum und Adel in der Reformation: Studien zur Sozialgeschichte der Reformation in England und Deutschland*, ed. W. J. Mommsen (Klett-Cotta, Stuttgart, 1979), pp. 49–79.

[10] Ozment, *Reformation in the Cities*, pp. 127–31.

[11] Robert W. Scribner, 'Practice and Principle in the German Towns: Preachers and People', in *Reformation Principle and Practice: Essays in Honour of Arthur Geoffrey Dickens*, ed. P. N. Brooks (Scholar Press, London, 1980), pp. 95–118.

[12] Cf. George Hunston Williams, *The Radical Reformation* (Westminster Press, Philadelphia, 1962).

[13] Clasen, *Anabaptism: A Social History* (Cornell University Press, Ithaca, NY, 1972); Clasen, *The Anabaptists in South and Central Germany, Switzerland, and Austria* (University Microfilms International, Ann Arbor, 1978).

[14] I. Andersson, 'Sweden and the Baltic', in *The New Cambridge Modern History* (14 vols, Cambridge University Press, Cambridge, 1957–79), vol. III: *The Counter-Reformation and Price Revolution, 1559–1610*, ed. R. B. Wernham (1968), pp. 404–26; N. K. Andersen, 'The Reformation in Scandinavia and the Baltic', in *New Cambridge Modern History*, vol. II: *The Reformation, 1520–1559*, ed. G. R. Elton (1958), pp. 134–60; E. H. Dunkley, *The Reformation in Denmark* (SPCK, London, 1948); Conrad Bergendoff, *Olavus Petri and the Ecclesiastical Transformation in Sweden, 1521–1552: A Study in the Swedish Reformation* (Fortress Press, Philadelphia, 1965).

Lutheranism gained an early following in Danzig, Elblag, and Torun.[15] By 1526 popular uprisings with clear Protestant elements had broken out in at least twenty-seven Polish and east Prussian towns.[16] In England, in addition to the prominence of London as a center of reformed teaching, many of the smaller towns in the south east had been centers of Lollardy before the sixteenth century and served as Protestant havens during the main development of the Reformation.[17] In France the pattern was much the same: in the north Protestants were concentrated in the Seine valley, especially in the city of Rouen; in Ile-de-France Protestants were most likely to be found in Paris, Meaux, Beauvais, Senlis, and Soissons, while the rural population remained solidly Catholic; in Champagne the Reformation was centered at Troyes and in Brittany at Nantes; and in the south Lyons, Montpellier, and Nimes became focal points of the reformed movement.[18] Even in Spain

[15] R. R. Betts, 'Constitutional Development and Political Thought in Eastern Europe', in *New Cambridge Modern History*, vol. II: *Reformation*, pp. 464–80.

[16] Maria Bogucka, 'Towns in Poland and the Reformation: Analogies and Differences with Other Countries', *Acta Poloniae Historica*, 40 (1979), 55–74.

[17] A. G. Dickens, *The English Reformation* (Schocken, New York, 1964), p. 64; D. M. Palliser, *Tudor York* (Oxford University Press, Oxford, 1979), p. 223; Peter Clark, *English Provincial Society from the Reformation to the Revolution: Religion, Politics and Society in Kent, 1500–1640* (Harvester Press, Sussex, 1977), p. 40; Claire Cross, 'Priests into Ministers: The Establishment of Protestant Practice in the City of York, 1530–1630', in *Reformation Principle and Practice: Essays in Honour of Arthur Geoffrey Dickens*, ed. P. N. Brooks (Scholar Press, London, 1980), p. 210; Roger B. Manning, *Religion and Society in Elizabethan Sussex: A Study of the Enforcement of the Religious Settlement, 1558–1603* (Leicester University Press, Leicester, 1969), p. 243; T. M. Parker, *The English Reformation to 1558*, (2nd edn, Oxford University Press, Oxford, 1966), p. 19.

[18] Gabriel Loirette, 'Catholiques et Protestants en Languedoc à la Veille des Guerres Civiles (1560)' *Revue d'Histoire de l'Église de France*, 23 (1937), 503–25; David Nicholls, 'Social Change and Early Protestantism in France: Normandy, 1520–62', *European Studies Review*, 10 (1980), 279–308; David J. Nicholls, 'The Nature of Popular Heresy in France, 1520–1542', *Historical Journal*, 26 (1983), 261–75; Philip Benedict, *Rouen During the Wars of Religion* (Cambridge University Press, Cambridge, 1981), p. 53; Denis Richet, 'Aspects Socio-culturels des Conflits Réligieux à Paris dans la Seconde Moitié du XVI siècle', *Annales: Economies, Sociétés, Civilisations* 32 (1977), 764–89; Yves-Marie Berce, *Révoltes et Révolutions dans l'Europe Moderne* (Presses Universitaires de France, Paris, 1980); A. N. Galpern, *The Religions of the People in Sixteenth-Century Champagne* (Harvard University Press, Cambridge, Mass., 1976); Natalie Zemon Davis, 'The Sacred and the Body Social in Sixteenth-Century Lyon', *Past and Present*, 90 (1981), 40–70; Emmanuel Leroy Ladurie, *The Peasants of Languedoc* (University of Illinois Press, Urbana, Ill., 1974), pp. 158–64.

Protestant enclaves developed at Seville, Valladolid, and in several other port cities.[19]

The new doctrines held a variety of potential attractions for the various strata in the towns. The reformers' teachings in effect reincorporated religion into the collective life of the towns and thereby ended legal and political disputes that had resulted from the church's dual position as a town institution with outside loyalties and responsibilities. The Reformation embodied the principle of *corpus Christianum* that had been an explicit conception of the city in medieval political theory. Towns that adopted the reforms quickly vested control of clerical appointments in municipal councils, subjected the clergy to taxation, seized ecclesiastical holdings, and transferred legal jurisdiction from ecclesiastical to municipal courts.[20] For artisans and craftsmen the Reformation offered vernacular worship, access to the sacraments and scripture, and a greater sense of participation in religious services. It also held potential appeal to the magistracy and to the poorest strata, for the reforms often provided an excuse to seize control of relief chests and redirect church funds for relief purposes.[21]

In contrast, Catholicism remained much more deeply integrated in the social life of rural villages and manors. Its public rituals and symbols – from marriages, to baptisms, to the worship of saints, community festivals, and even seating arrangements – dramatized the social relations of agrarian society, reminding peasants of their dependence upon landlords; landlords of their social standing in relation to peasants; and both of their moral obligations, one to the other.[22] The church served

[19] Fernand Braudel, *The Mediterranean and the Mediterranean World in the Age of Phillip II* (2 vols, Harper and Row, New York, 1973), vol II p. 767; Bartolome Bennassar, *The Spanish Character: Attitudes and Mentalities from the Sixteenth to the Nineteenth Century* (University of California Press, Berkeley, Calif., 1979), p. 75.

[20] Cf. Robert W. Scribner, 'Civic Unity and the Reformation in Erfurt,' *Past and Present*, 66 (1975), 29–60; Strauss, *Nuremberg*, pp. 176–7.

[21] Grimm, 'Luther's Contribution', Robert M. Kingdon, 'Social Welfare in Calvin's Geneva', *American Historical Review*, 76 (1971), 50–69; Natalie Zemon Davis, 'Poor Relief, Humanism, and Heresy: The Case of Lyon', *Studies in Medieval and Renaissance History*, 5 (1968), 217–75; Robert Jutte, 'Poor Relief and Social Discipline in Sixteenth Century Europe', *European Studies Review*, 11 (1981), 25–52.

[22] André Burguière, 'Le Rituel du Mariage en France: Pratiques Ecclésiastiques et Pratiques Populaires (XVIe–XVIIIe Siècle)', *Annales: Economies, Sociétés, Civilisations*, 33 (1978), 637–49; John Bossy, 'The Counter-Reformation and the People of Catholic Europe', *Past and Present*, 47 (1970), 57; John Bossy, "Blood and Baptism: Kinship,

as a storehouse of public goods from which peasants and landlords could draw in emergencies or as protection against subsistence crises.[23] Communal ties were nurtured through religious interaction, vows and oaths sworn before the priest took on quasi-legal dimensions, and tithes figured importantly in the overall distribution of tax burdens.[24]

The appeal of Protestantism, although greatest in the towns, by no means reached evenly to all towns. Some towns succeeded in officially institutionalizing the Reformation; others remained largely unaffected by it; still others, despite a wave of popular enthusiasm, turned their backs on its demands or vigorously sponsored efforts to root it out. Major towns in central Europe, such as Cologne and Deventer, as well as many of the smaller towns in Flanders, failed to institute the reforms that were rapidly being adopted in neighboring towns. In Poland the initial enthusiasm for Protestantism in the towns quickly subsided. Thereafter,

---

Community and Christianity in Western Europe from the Fourteenth to the Seventeenth Centuries," in *Sanctity and Secularity: The Church and the World*, ed. Derek Baker (Basil Blackwell, Oxford, 1973), p. 131; John Bossy, "Essai de Sociographie de la Messe, 1200–1700," *Annales: Economies, Sociétés, Civilisations* 36 (1981), 44–70; A. C. F. Koch, 'The Reformation at Deventer in 1579–1580: Size and Social Structure of the Catholic Section of the Population During the Religious Peace', *Acta Historiae Neerlandicae: Studies on the History of the Netherlands*, 6 (1973), 51; R. W. Southern, *Western Society and the Church in the Middle Ages* (Penguin Books, London, 1970), p. 18; William A. Christian, JR, *Local Religion in Sixteenth-Century Spain* (Princeton University Press, Princeton, 1981); Janusz Tazbir, 'The Cult of St Isidore the Farmer in Europe', in *Poland at the 14th International Congress of Historical Sciences in San Francisco* (Polish Academy of Sciences, Institute of History, Warsaw, 1975), p. 107; Febvre, *Renaissance France*, p. 74.

[23] H. Van Werveke, 'The Rise of Towns,' in *The Cambridge Economic History of Europe* (7 vols, Cambridge University Press, Cambridge, 1941–78), vol. III: *Economic Organization and Policies in the Middle Ages*, eds. M. M. Postan, E. E. Rich and E. Miller, Cambridge, (1963), pp. 30–1; Tom Scott, 'Reformation and Peasants' War in Waldshut and Environs: A Structural Analysis, Part I', *Archiv fur Reformationsgeschichte*, 69 (1978), 82–102; Tom Scott, 'Reformation and Peasants' War in Waldshut and Environs: A Structural Analysis, Part II', *Archiv fur Reformationsgeschichte*, 69 (1979), 140–68.

[24] Marceli Kosman, 'Programme of the Reformation in the Grand Duchy of Lithuania and How It Was Carried Through', *Acta Poloniae Historica*, 35 (1977), 21–50; Ralph Houlbrooke, *Church Courts and the People During the English Reformation, 1520–1570* (Oxford University Press, Oxford, 1979), p. 7; Sidney Oldall Addy, *Church and Manor: A Study in English Economic History* (Augustus M. Kelley, New York, 1970); Pierre Goubert, *The Ancien Regime: French Society, 1600–1750* (Harper and Row, New York, 1973); Carlo M. Cipolla, *Before the Industrial Revolution: European Society and Economy, 1000–1700* (W. W. Norton, New York, 1976), pp. 54–8.

disaffected nobles in outlying regions carried the main thrust of the Polish Reformation, and by the end of the sixteenth century even this support had largely dissipated.[25] In France major towns such as Bordeaux and Toulouse remained virtually untouched by the Reformation. Paris, unlike London, increasingly sought to drive out the reformers, and even in Lyons and Rouen Protestantism never succeeded in gaining official sanction. Similarly in Spain, despite early successes in humanist innovations, despite the urban upheaval of the *comuneros* and despite the great rise of the Andalusian cities, Protestantism made scarcely any visible inroads. How can these differences be explained?

TRADING TOWNS AND COMMERCIAL TOWNS

Edward Fox's contrast between trade and commerce provides a useful starting point for attempting to sort out the characteristics that may have favored the adoption of Protestantism in some towns and deterred it in others.[26] The essential contrast is between local or regional markets and long-distance markets: *trade* is defined as 'the exchange of local products within the usual radius of the market town'; *commerce* as transactions over large distances, usually involving the importation and exportation of luxury goods. Because of the costs associated with long-distance trade throughout most of history, commerce has, at least until recently, been conducted mostly by water transportation, whereas trade is more likely to have been carried out on land. From this distinction it is therefore possible to identify two main types of towns: *trading towns*, which are likely to be located in landlocked, hinterland areas; and *commercial towns*, which are likely to be located along coasts and rivers.[27]

This distinction has a certain instinctive appeal since the rise of Protestantism coincided roughly with a dramatic increase in long-distance

[25] Kosman, 'Programme of the Reformation'; Aleksander Bruckner, 'The Polish Reformation in the Sixteenth Century', in *Polish Civilization: Essays and Studies*, ed. Mieczyslaw Giergielewicz (New York University Press, New York, 1979), pp. 68–87; Janusz Tazbir, 'The Fate of Polish Protestantism in the Seventeenth Century', in *A Republic of Nobles: Studies in Polish History to 1864*, ed. J. K. Fedorowicz, Maria Bogucka and H. Samsonowicz (Cambridge University Press, Cambridge, 1982), pp. 198–217.

[26] Fox, *History*, pp. 33–71.

[27] Cf. Edward W. Fox, '"History in Geographic Perspective" Revisited' (paper presented at the Social Science History Conference, 1983).

economic exchange and appears to have been more closely associated with commercial towns than with trading towns. After more than a century and a half of demographic and economic decline, Europe, toward the end of the fifteenth century, experienced a revival of commerce that flourished dramatically during the Reformation period and in many areas lasted until the beginning of the seventeenth century.[28] The main arteries along which commerce expanded were the Rhine, Danube, and Rhone valleys; the water routes that linked the Baltic, Low Countries, and England; and the Atlantic coastal zone, which extended from Spain and Portugal to France and England.[29]

The towns that became centers of Protestant activity tended to include a great number of those which were becoming engaged in long-distance commerce as opposed to towns that served only as local trading hubs. Zurich, Danzig, Antwerp, and London underwent huge population increases (between 200 and 400 per cent) during the sixteenth century as a result of their favorable location with respect to commerce.[30] Antwerp, Amsterdam, Strasbourg, Nuremberg, Augsburg, and Magdeberg all had populations of at least 25,000 by the start of the century and were linked with cities as far away as London and Seville. In northern Europe,

[28] Wallerstein, *Modern World-System*; Fernand Braudel, *Civilization and Capitalism, 15th–18th Century* (3 vols, Harper and Row, New York, 1983), vol. III: *The Perspective of the World*.

[29] Michael Postan, 'The Trade of Medieval Europe: The North', in *Cambridge Economic History of Europe*, vol. II: *Trade and Industry in the Middle Ages*, eds. M. Postan and E. E. Rich (1952), pp. 119–256; M. M. Postan, *Medieval Trade and Finance* (Cambridge University Press, Cambridge, 1973); Philipe Dollinger, *The German Hansa* (Stanford University Press, Stanford, 1970); S. T. Bindoff, 'The Greatness of Antwerp,' in *New Cambridge Modern History*, vol. II: *Reformation* pp. 50–69; Kristof Glamman, 'European Trade, 1500–1700', in *The Fontana Economic History of Europe*, ed. Carlo M. Cipolla (6 vols, William Collins Sons, Glasgow, 1972–6), vol. II: *Sixteenth and Seventeenth Centuries* (1974), pp. 427–526; Kristof Glamman, 'The Changing Patterns of Trade', in *Cambridge Economic History of Europe*, vol. V: *The Economic Organization of Early Modern Europe*, eds. E. E. Rich and C. H. Wilson, (1977), pp. 185–289; J. H. Parry, 'Transport and Trade Routes', in *Cambridge Economic History of Europe*, vol. IV: *The Economy of Expanding Europe in the Sixteenth and Seventeenth Centuries*, eds. E. E. Rich and C. H. Wilson (1967), pp. 155–219.

[30] Jerzy Topolski, 'Continuity and Discontinuity in the Development of the Feudal System in Eastern Europe (Xth to XVIIth Centuries)', *Journal of European Economic History*, 10 (1981), 373–400; Karl F. Helleiner, 'The Population of Europe from the Black Death to the Eve of the Vital Revolution', in *Cambridge Economic History of Europe*, vol. IV: Expanding Europe, pp. 1–95; Roger Mols, 'Population in Europe, 1500–1700', in *Fontana Economic History*, vol. II: *Sixteenth and Seventeenth Centuries*, pp. 15–82.

Copenhagen, Malmö, Stockholm, Reval, Riga, and Lübeck were all becoming increasingly involved in shipping and exports. Danzig was rapidly becoming the chief conduit for exports of Polish grain and cattle to western Europe.[31] Cracow, Poznan, Warsaw, and Lwow were also situated favorably to provide outlets for Polish grain.[32] In France Lyons served as the principal broker for the Rhone trade, while Rouen played a similar role on the Seine.[33] And of course London dominated England's rapidly expanding commerce in cloth and other commodities.[34] In short, it could be observed for the Reformation, as Fox has observed more generally, that 'the critical distinction . . . lies not between town and country, but between commerce and trade.'[35]

It is, however, not so much the distinction between commerce and trade itself that proves most helpful in understanding the Reformation, but the discussion Fox offers about the internal social and economic characteristics of towns rooted in commerce versus those rooted in trade. Trading towns are by definition economically dependent upon nearby agricultural production, whereas commercial towns are to a greater extent dependent upon one another since the flow of goods requires supplies and markets outside their immediate vicinity.[36] Trading towns were thus more likely to be influenced by the interests of local landowners, whereas commercial towns were to a greater extent free of these influences and in important respects concerned with maintaining good relations with merchants in other towns. In short, towns need to be considered not as strictly autonomous units but in the context of other relevant economic elites.

[31] Marian Malowist, 'The Economic and Social Development of the Baltic Countries from the Fifteenth to the Seventeenth Centuries', *Economic History Review*, 12 (1959), 177–89.

[32] Jan Ptasnik, 'Towns in Medieval Poland', in *Polish Civilization*, pp. 25–50; Antoni Maczak, 'The Structure of Power in the Commonwealth of the Sixteenth and Seventeenth Centuries', in *Republic of Nobles*, pp. 109–34.

[33] Josiah C. Russell, *Medieval Regions and Their Cities* (Indiana University Press, Bloomington, 1972), p. 117, 142.

[34] F. V. Emery, 'England *circa* 1600', in *A New Historical Geography of England*, ed. H. C. Darby (Cambridge University Press, Cambridge, 1973), pp. 293–301; Peter Ramsey, *Tudor Economic Problems* (Gollancz, London, 1965), p. 53.

[35] *History*, p. 31.

[36] James E. Vance, Jr, *This Scene of Man: The Role and Structure of the City in the Geography of Western Civilization* (Harper's College Press, New York, 1977), pp. 213–16.

Towns' policies toward the Reformation were often shaped by the degree of dependence or autonomy they experienced in relation to the nobility and other local landowners. Given the high degree of articulation between the established church and the moral economy of rural life, landowners not surprisingly supported the church wherever possible. Only those towns which enjoyed a relatively high amount of autonomy from the rural elite were in a strong position to sanction religious reforms that threatened to undo this mainstay of the rural economy.[37]

The towns in central Europe that adopted the Reformation tended to be ones that had gained a high degree of autonomy from the rural aristocracy: the imperial cities that had gradually developed a strong tradition of self-government; larger commercial towns with economies principally linked to long-distance trade; towns that had purchased the surrounding areas on which their food supplies depended and had created an indigenous artisan economy; and towns located in provinces in which smallholding had eroded seigneurial power.[38] Detailed studies of the process by which the Reformation was adopted in cities such as Nuremberg, Strasbourg, and Geneva uniformly demonstrate that the nobility's voice in municipal government was weak and that councils acted above all to preserve their autonomy.[39] Much the same was true

[37] Robert Wuthnow, 'Class Structure and State Autonomy: The Social Origins of Early Modern Reform' (paper presented at the annual meeting of the American Sociological Association, San Antonio, 1984).

[38] Manfred Hanneman, *The Diffusion of the Reformation in Southwestern Germany, 1518–1534* (University of Chicago Press, Chicago, 1975); Aldo de Maddalena, 'Rural Europe, 1500–1700', in *Fontana Economic History*, vol. II: *Sixteenth and Seventeenth Centuries*, pp. 273–353; L. G. Rogier, 'De Protestantisering van het Noorden', in *Algemeene Geschiedenis der nederlanden*, eds J. A. Van Houtte, J. F. Niermeyer, J. Presser, J. Romein, and H. Van Werveke (12 vols, W. de Haan, Antwerp, 1949–58), vol. V: *De Tachtigjarige Oorlog, 1567–1609* (1952), pp. 326–43; C. A. J. Armstrong, 'Had the Burgundian Government a Policy for the Nobility?', in *Britain and the Netherlands, Vol. II: Papers Delivered to the Anglo-Dutch Historical Conference, Utrecht and Amsterdam, 1962*, eds J. S. Bromley and E. H. Kossmann (J. B. Wolters, Gröningen, 1964), pp. 9–32; Norman Birnbaum, 'The Zwinglian Reformation in Zurich', *Past and Present*, 15 (1959), 27–47; Benjamin R. Barber, *The Death of Communal Liberty: A History of Freedom in a Swiss Mountain Canton* (Princeton University Press, Princeton, 1974).

[39] Strauss, *Nuremberg*; Gerald Strauss, 'Protestant Dogma and City Government: The Case of Nuremberg', *Past and Present*, 36 (1967), 38–58; Jackson Spielvogel, 'Patricians in Dissension: A Case Study from Sixteenth-Century Nurnberg', in *The Social History of the Reformation*, ed. L. P. Buck and J. W. Zophy (Ohio State University Press, Columbus, 1972), pp. 73–92; Chrisman, *Strasbourg*; Thomas A. Brady, Jr, *Ruling*

of cities in other areas, such as Copenhagen, Stockholm, Lübeck, London. In each of these cities the nobility had largely been excluded from municipal offices, while the growth of commerce had given the town a greater degree of financial independence from surrounding rural areas.[40]

Conversely, towns in which the nobility continued to exercise a strong voice were considerably less likely to adopt the Reformation officially. In the German and Dutch territories the two prominent cases of the failure of the Reformation were Cologne and Deventer, in both of which the lack of municipal autonomy appears to have been an important reason.[41] More broadly, the towns in Utrecht and Flanders, as well as those in the 'forest cantons' appear to have been inhibited in sponsoring religious reforms because of the relatively strong position in local affairs maintained by the nobility.[42] Similarly, in Poland the nobility acted to suppress the growth of Protestantism in the major towns. Most of the towns had only a weak indigenous merchant class because of the rising economic power of the nobility and their conscious efforts to 'sell direct.' The larger cities depended almost entirely upon trade initiated by the landlords, and the majority of smaller towns were under the private jurisdiction of local landlords. Urban patricians who sought to support the Reformation risked harming their own freedoms in relation to the nobility; and in several instances, noble armies forcibly suppressed religious uprisings.[43]

Class, Regime, and Reformation at Strasbourg, 1520–1555 (E. J. Brill, Leiden, 1978); Monter, *Geneva*; Thomas F. Sea, 'Imperial Cities and the Peasants' War in Germany', *Central European History*, 12 (1979), 3–37.

[40] A. G. Dickens, *The German Nation and Martin Luther* (Edward Arnold, London, 1974), pp. 163–5; Wilson King, *Chronicles of Free Cities: Hamburg, Bremen, Lubeck* (E. P. Dutton, New York, 1914), pp. 372–402; Stanford E. Lehmberg, *The Reformation Parliament, 1529–1536* (Cambridge University Press, Cambridge, 1970), pp. 81–2; Perez Zagorin, *Rebels and Rulers, 1500–1600* (2 vols, Cambridge University Press, Cambridge, 1982), vol. I: *Society, States, and Early Modern Revolution. Agrarian and Urban Rebellions*, p. 72.

[41] Robert W. Scribner, 'Why Was There No Reformation in Cologne?', *Bulletin of the Institute of Historical Research*, 49 (1976), 217–41; Koch, 'The Reformation at Deventer', p. 50.

[42] Jan DeVries, *The Dutch Rural Economy in the Golden Age, 1500–1700* (Yale University Press, New Haven, 1974), pp. 25–41; Armstrong, 'Burgundian Government', pp. 9–10; William Martin, *Switzerland from Roman Times to the Present* (Praeger, New York, 1971), pp. 81–4.

[43] Bruckner, 'The Polish Reformation', pp. 73–4; Bogucka, 'Towns in Poland'.

In France the role of the nobility is also evident, even in cities such as Lyons and Rouen. Although Protestantism proved attractive to merchants and artisans whose interests were linked to long-distance commerce, it gained few adherents among local nobility, which occupied strong positions in the provincial *parlements* and municipal councils. In Rouen, for example, the *parlementaires* were largely of rural landowning stock, even though they maintained residences in the city, and most had extensive landholdings from which the greatest share of their incomes derived. Since their estates tended to be scattered and were at some distance from the town itself, most of their time was actually spent away from Rouen. The absences weakened their ties with the commercial bourgeoisie and strengthened loyalties to the contryside. These elites loaned money to, and on occasion borrowed from, the crown. They thus exercised some degree of financial influence over the state, but had weak financial ties to the local bourgeoisie.[44] In short, the *parlementaires'* economic well-being depended primarily upon the land. When religious violence broke out in Rouen, they immediately opposed and then, with the assistance of neighboring landlords, suppressed it. At about the same time a similar uprising in Lyons was also forcibly suppressed, and soon thereafter Protestantism in the town was virtually extinct. In Reims and Troyes the town councils were controlled by local landowners, and only a few of these notables became Protestants.[45]

These examples point even more strongly to the importance of the balance of power between commercial and agrarian interests than to that of the distinction between commerce and trade. For the nobles played a strong role in preventing Protestantism from becoming officially adopted wherever they retained influence in municipal affairs – in commercial as well as in trading towns. Danzig, Cologne, Lyons, Rouen, Bordeaux, Seville were all port cities that served as brokers for long-distance commerce, but the local nobles were sufficiently powerful to present Protestantism with insurmountable obstacles. In contrast, many of the towns in which Protestantism flourished – Aachen, Colmar, Geneva, Heidelberg, York, Coventry, Worcester – were by Fox's definition regional trading hubs rather than commercial towns, but the surrounding nobility was too weak or divided to uproot Protestantism.

[44] Jonathan Dewald, *The Formation of a Provincial Nobility: the Magistrates of the Parlement of Rouen, 1499–1610* (Princeton University Press, Princeton, 1980); Benedict, *Rouen*; Nicholls, 'Social Change'.
[45] Galpern, *Religions of the People*, pp. 123–40.

These patterns, then, give pause to accepting Fox's dichotomy between commerce and trade as an absolute distinction that rests strictly on geographic location and on types of economic flows. While the distinction remains useful, it is, so far as understanding the Reformation is concerned, better conceived of as a distinction between degrees of autonomy or degrees of dependence between the governing bodies of towns and local landowners. The rise of long-distance commerce clearly augmented this autonomy in many commercial towns, but autonomy also depended upon regional social and political conditions which sometimes favored Protestant reforms and sometimes hindered them.

REGIMES AND REFORMATION POLICIES

To suggest that towns were influenced by regional social and political patterns necessarily raises the question of how broader territorial regimes affected policies toward the Reformation. Fox again provides a useful starting point. Commerce, he suggests, leads to a type of regime which, while more oligarchic than democratic, tends to recognize special interest groups and thus favor policies based on negotiation. Societies based on local trade in agricultural commodities, in contrast, are more likely to have regimes that rule by effectively administering their own and others' landholdings and are thus characterized by strong civil and military bureaucratic hierarchies. This time-bound distinction is not intended to apply to the modern welfare state, in which, despite advanced commercial relations, expansive bureaucracies administer social programs. Rather, it suggests a loose federation of commercial towns – such as the seventeenth-century Dutch Republic – in contrast to a heavily centralized authoritarian monarchy.

For the Reformation the critical distinction seems to be between regimes that remained financially and administratively dependent upon the landowning class and regimes that managed to extricate themselves from this dependence by engaging in or supporting commerce. At the municipal level, broader territorial regimes that supported the Reformation had the necessary autonomy to do so without having to face strong negative repercussions from the nobility, but regimes that remained heavily indebted to the nobility scarcely had the option of adopting even those religious reforms that might have proved beneficial to the regime in the long run. Thus it was not simply that some regimes were oligarchic while others were authoritarian, or that some favored negotiation while others favored administration; rather, it was that some regimes could more easily afford to ignore the nobility or violate its short-term interests, while others were bound to follow courses that the nobility either dictated or favored.

The relations between the nobility and monarchs or territorial rulers in the sixteenth century were, as they had been in preceding centuries, essentially conflictive, or as Fox suggests, 'largely limited to a simple struggle for power'.[46] The struggle varied in intensity from place to place but usually included conflicts over taxation and appointments to titles and offices as well as questions of dynastic succession. Thus religious policy was likely to be affected by the balance of power between rulers and this segment of the ruling class. In the sixteenth century commerce was the new variable in this relation, often providing the leverage rulers needed to shift the balance of power favorably in their direction. Fox writes: 'Not only did the territorial rulers and their courts provide an important ultimate market for the commercial cities; but the wealth produced by commerce was a continuing temptation to chronically impecunious monarchs.'[47]

The political situation along the Rhineland corridor differed from that in most other parts of Europe. Here the more than 200 free cities, cantons, and provinces had effectively resisted the imposition of any central regime and continued largely to defend themselves through their own resources by forming leagues and by cultivating temporary alliances with the more powerful territorial princes.[48] Accordingly, they enjoyed considerable freedom from interference by the nobility. In addition, two other political dynamics came increasingly to influence this region near the beginning of the sixteenth century.

First, the Hapsburg dynasty posed a growing threat to central Europe. When Charles V became Holy Roman Emperor in 1519 the lands from Holland to the Swiss cantons and from France's eastern border to Austria-Hungary fell under his ultimate jurisdiction, and the rich mining and commercial areas so encompassed were a prize that Charles wished to exploit, especially in the costly wars in which he was engaged against the Turks. The exigencies of his regime posed considerable danger for the traditional autonomy of the towns and territorial principalities, the

---

[46] *History*, p. 54.
[47] Ibid.
[48] Ibid., pp. 56–7.

rulers of which acquired an added incentive to champion local religious freedoms against the Catholic universalism to which the Spanish dynasty looked for legitimation.

Second, several territorial princes, particularly the Duke of Saxony and to a lesser extent the Landgrave of Hesse, enjoyed rising economic power. These princes gained in wealth and, accordingly, in autonomy from the lesser nobility and peasantry as a result of rapidly expanding incomes from mineral rights, levies on commerce, and loans from the urban patriciate.[49] The lower nobility, generally in decline (partly as a result of the princes' legislation), was being pressed into the ranks of the yeomanry, while the wealthier nobility shifted assets into the towns. Thus the princes' interests came to be increasingly articulated with those of the towns, and religious policies tended to follow suit. With Saxony and Hesse at the lead and eventually others following – Württenburg, Pomerania, Nassau, Brandenburg – the princes lent strong support to the defense of the Reformation.[50]

The Reformation in Scandinavia also received strong support from the prevailing regimes, without which its popularity in the towns would have doubtlessly been seriously thwarted by the nobility. In Denmark Charles II, Frederick I, and Christian III successively took an active hand in promoting Lutheranism by permitting increased freedom of preaching after 1527, and by sponsoring the wholesale secularization of church lands between 1533 and 1539.[51] In Sweden, Gustavas Vasa accomplished similar reforms, greatly adding to his own holdings as a result of the seizure of monastic lands.[52] Both crowns were enabled in pursuing these policies by the virtually unparalleled fiscal autonomy they had achieved in relation to the nobility. For the Danish crown the largest

[49] F. L. Carsten, *Princes and Parliaments in Germany* (Clarendon Press, Oxford, 1959); H. J. Cohn, *The Government of the Rhine Palatinate in the Fifteenth Century* (Oxford University Press, Oxford, 1965); Barber, *The Death of Communal Liberty*; Karl E. Demandt, *Geschichte des Landes Hessen*, (2nd edn, Barenreiter-Verlag, Kassel, 1972); Robert Brenner, 'Agrarian Class Structure and Economic Development in Pre-Industrial Europe', *Past and Present*, 70 (1976), 69.

[50] Hans J. Hillerbrand, *Landgrave Philipp of Hesse, 1504–1567: Religion and Politics in the Reformation* (Foundation for Reformation Research, Saint Louis, 1967); John C. Stalnaker, '*Residenzstadt* und Reformation: Religion, Politics and Social Policy in Hesse, 1509–1546', *Archiv fur Reformationsgeschichte*, 64 (1973), 113–46.

[51] Swanson, *Religion and Regime*, pp. 122–9; Andersen, 'Reformation in Scandinavia', p. 140.

[52] Michael Roberts, *The Early Vasas: A History of Sweden, 1523–1611* (Cambridge University Press, Cambridge, 1968), pp. 171–3.

source of independent revenue came from tolls on the rapidly expanding traffic through the Sound. The revenues were used to expand crown lands, extend central administrative powers over the nobility, and cultivate mercantile interests.[53] By the end of the century the Danish crown was taking in four times as much revenue as Poland, with only a tenth of Poland's population, and its revenue structure was virtually independent of the landowning sector: 50 per cent came from royal domains, 35 per cent from tolls, and only 15 per cent from taxes.[54] In Sweden the crown also succeeded in reducing the nobility's influence, largely by cultivating closer financial ties with Lübeck and deriving rapidly expanding revenue from exports of copper and iron.[55]

England was the other leading case in which the Reformation received strong support from the central regime, which had also succeeded in gaining a high degree of autonomy from the landed aristocracy. Although the motives behind Henry VIII's break with Rome may have been mixed, the success of his policy depended to a large extent upon the kind of autonomy that the crown had achieved during his father's reign and that it enjoyed until the middle of the sixteenth century. Parliament provided the strongest assistance to the crowns's efforts to institutionalize the Reformation. Unlike its counterparts elsewhere, the English Parliament had largely ceased to function as an agency of the nobility, and had instead become dominated for the time-being by a coalition of cloth merchants, burgesses, and royal officials allied with the crown. Overall, landed interests were outnumbered by a margin of two to one.[56] The merchants and burgesses in the Reformation Parliament strongly supported Henry's religious policies, both from broader loyalties based on his highly successful policies aimed at promoting trade and from specific religious grievances against the church for inhibiting commerce.[57] In addition to the support it received from Parliament the

[53] Thomas Riis, 'Town and Central Government in Northern Europe from the Fifteenth Century to the Industrial Revolution', *Scandinavian Economic History Review*, 29 (1981), 33–52.

[54] Maczak, 'The Structure of Power', p. 131.

[55] Roberts, *The Early Vasas*, pp. 5–31.

[56] J. W. McKenna, 'The Myth of Parliamentary Sovereignty in Late-Medieval England', *English Historical Review*, 94 (1979), 481–506; Lehmberg, *Reformation Parliament*.

[57] Susan Brigden, 'The Tithe Controversy in Reformation London', *Journal of Ecclesiastical History*, 32 (1981), 285–301; H. Miller, 'London and Parliament in the Reign of Henry VIII', in *Historical Studies of the English Parliament*, (2 vols, Cambridge University Press, Cambridge, 1970), eds E. B. Fryde and Edward Miller, vol. II: *1399–1603*, pp. 125–146.

crown had an unusually strong financial position in relation to the nobility – a position that proved temporary but that freed Henry from some of the negative pressures the nobility might have been able to mount. Largely as a result of its successful promotion of commerce, the crown's revenues by the beginning of Henry's reign were essentially independent of the nobility: 35 per cent came from customs, 35 per cent from crown lands, and 20 per cent from the royal mint and other special concessions. Thus only 10 per cent had to be raised from loans or taxes on land.[58]

In administrative affairs the crown also succeeded in extricating itself from the nobility's influence. Unlike other monarchic regimes, the Tudors followed a deliberate policy of excluding the nobility from high appointive office and refused to sell offices to the nobility to raise supplemental income. Instead, they selected officials from merchant and professional families, from the lower strata, and from the royal family itself.[59] The Tudors also administered justice and collected taxes largely without involving the nobility. Justices of the peace were subjected to the authority of royal lords-lieutenant; special commissions were used to execute crown policy rather than letting local bureaucracies develop; and coercive measures against insubordinate nobles and officials were applied with exceptional severity.[60]

As the Reformation proceeded, resistance came, as it did elsewhere, from the nobility, most notably in the Lincolnshire and York rebellions in 1536 and the Cornish rebellion in 1549.[61] But neither these rebellions nor the nobility's close ties with the church prevailed against the crown's reforms. They did succeed in containing the reforms so that popular religious practice remained little affected.[62] Yet the major ecclesiastical

[58] Penry Williams, *The Tudor Regime* (Clarendon Press, Oxford, 1979), p. 58.

[59] G. R. Elton, *The Tudor Revolution in Government: Administrative Changes in the Reign of Henry VIII* (Cambridge University Press, Cambridge, 1953), pp. 33–4.

[60] Clark, *English Provincial Society*, pp. 16–23; G. R. Elton, *Policy and Police: The Enforcement of the Reformation in the Age of Thomas Cromwell* (Cambridge University Press, Cambridge, 1972).

[61] Claire Cross, *Church and People, 1450–1660: The Triumph of the Laity in the English Church* (Humanities Press, Atlantic Highlands, New Jersey, 1976); M. E. James, 'Obedience and Dissent in Henrician England: The Lincolnshire Rebellion 1536', *Past and Present*, 48 (1970), 3–78.

[62] Margaret Bowker, *The Henrician Reformation: The Diocese of Lincoln Under John Longland, 1521–1547* (Cambridge University Press, Cambridge, 1981); David G. Hey, *An English Rural Community: Myddle Under the Tudors and Stuarts* (Leicester University Press, Leicester, 1974); James E. Oxley, *The Reformation in Essex to the Death of Mary* (Manchester University Press, Manchester, 1965).

reorganization that institutionalized the Reformation in England was well in progress by the end of Henry's reign.

Thus in all three cases – the Rhineland corridor, Scandinavia, and England – the growth of commerce had an impact on the Reformation, not simply in the towns, but in the territorial or central regimes. Chiefly, it created an expanded array of options for dealing with the reformers while removing or at least temporarily quieting the voice of the landed aristocracy. The various magistrates, princes, and kings who participated in deciding religious policies that affected the Reformation were, therefore, in a position to move, often gradually and unwittingly, in a direction that favored the commercial interests, the reformers, and their own bureaucracies and treasuries. The critical factor was not so much a less authoritarian style of government – the Tudors could scarcely be accused of abandoning authoritarianism – or even a less centralized regime, but rather a shift in the balance of power that reduced the state's fiscal and administrative dependence upon the landowning elite.

The Reformation failed to achieve the same kind of backing in Poland, France, and Spain, despite its popular appeal in some towns, at least partly because the states remained much more heavily dependent upon the landowning elite. This dependence was, to recall Fox's thesis, due in part to geographic factors that limited the growth of revenues from commerce, particularly in Poland, where commerce consisted chiefly in locally grown agricultural commodities rather than an entrepôt trade in luxury goods. France was also less favorably situated than either the Rhineland corridor or the Baltic waterways to take advantage of commercial expansion. Much of the economic growth it experienced during this period was located in agriculture. Approximately 90 per cent of the population continued to live on the land, and the wealthier elites did not transfer much of their assets to the cities.[63] In Spain a similar deficiency was evident both in the development of an indigenous

---

[63] Frederich Lutge, 'Economic Change: Agriculture', in *New Cambridge Modern History*, vol. II: *Reformation*, pp. 45–6; Guy Fourquin, *Les Campagnes de la Region Parisienne a la Fin du Moyen Age au Milieu du XIIIe siecle au Debut du XVIe siecle* (Presses Universitaires de France, Paris, 1964), pp. 523–4; James B. Wood, *The Nobility of the Election of Bayeux, 1463–1666: Continuity through Change* (Princeton University Press, Princeton, 1980), p. 106; Marc Bloch, *French Rural History: An Essay on Its Basic Characteristics* (University of California Press, Berkeley, Calif., 1966), p. 125; Elizabeth S. Teall, 'The Seigneur of Renaissance France', *Journal of Modern History*, 37 (1965), 131–50.

merchant class and in the persistence of agricultural dominance over local markets as well as major sectors of the export trade.[64]

But the persistence of noble influence was not simply a function of geography. It was also interwoven with regimes' fiscal and administrative policies. Spain provides the clearest example, for it was in a sense the state that gained the most from commerce and thus might have been expected on the basis of geography alone to have extricated itself effectively from the rural aristocracy. In large measure because of Spanish conquests in the New World, royal revenues rose thirty-fold during the last quarter of the fifteenth century.[65] In the sixteenth century approximately 40 per cent of all American bullion flowed into the royal treasury – an amount that multiplied about forty times over the course of the century.[66] Despite these increases the state remained heavily indebted to the landed aristocracy. Lacking an indigenous bourgeoisie (other than the Genoese), incurring increasingly unfavorable trade balances, and suffering huge costs from efforts to control its vast dynastic holdings, the state had to rely heavily on taxes and loans from the landed sector. Toward the end of Charles V's reign only 10–15 per cent of the crown's income came from American bullion, while about 50 per cent came from taxes on land, and most of the remainder from loans from the nobility.[67] Administratively the state also remained largely in aristocratic hands as high officials were required to be recruited from the nobility, and tax measures as well as major legislative acts required approval by the aristocratically controlled *cortes*.[68]

The central regimes in France and Poland remained dependent upon the landed elite nearly to the same extent. In France the nobility retained virtual control over local and provincial government as well as over the military, kept the central bureaucracy understaffed and ineffective, and

[64] Glamann, 'Changing Patterns of Trade'.

[65] Stanley G. Payne, *A History of Spain and Portugal*, (2 vols, University of Wisconsin Press, Madison, 1973), vol. I, p. 178.

[66] Earl J. Hamilton, *American Treasure and the Price Revolution in Spain, 1501–1650* (Harvard University Press, Cambridge, Mass., 1934), p. 34; Parry, 'Transport and Trade Routes', p. 210.

[67] Payne, *History of Spain and Portugal*, p. 283; Miguel Angel Ladero Quesada, 'Les Finances Royales de Castille a la Veille des Temps Modernes', *Annales ESC*, 25 (1970), 775–88.

[68] J. R. L. Highfield, 'The Catholic Kings and the Titled Nobility of Castile', in *Europe in the Late Middle Ages*, eds. J. R. Hale, J. R. L. Highfield, and B. Smalley (Northwestern University Press, Evanston, Ill. 1965), p. 377.

played the dominant role in royal finances through loans and tax policies.[69] Poland's central regime became increasingly subject to the nobility, almost in direct proportion to the nobility's success in reviving serfdom in the countryside. Parliament, dominated completely by the nobility, exercised broad prerogatives over state policy, including the right to control taxation, to convene without royal summons, and to elect the monarch.[70]

Thus in all three countries the regime supported the nobility's propensity to abort the Reformation. Lacking the autonomy that the rulers in England, Denmark, Sweden, Saxony, or Hesse enjoyed, the central regime either tacitly or actively followed the landed elite's policies. In Poland anti-Hapsburg sentiment as well as a relatively weak degree of Catholicization in the eastern provinces led some of the nobility to favor the Calvinist reforms and thus to lobby for religious toleration. But the dominant response to the Reformation included local indifference, repression of popular uprisings in the towns, royal edicts against reformed teachings, and an increasingly close alliance between the church and the nobility.[71] In France the reformers were greeted with official repression, which included book burnings, heresy trials, executions, and forced oaths of allegiance.[72] Not until the internecine struggles among the upper nobility broke into open civil war did Protestantism gain a political voice, and even then it remained a minority voice. Similarly, in Spain, despite some early converts among the royal council, the new religious doctrines were soon rooted out. Both the state and the nobility exercised powerful control over religious life and deployed this control to uphold the established patterns.[73]

[69] J. Russell Major, 'The French Renaissance Monarchy as Seen through the Estates General', in *Government in Reformation Europe, 1520–1560*, ed. H. J. Cohn, (Macmillan, New York, 1971); J. Russell Major, *Representative Government in Early Modern France* (Yale University Press, New Haven, 1980); P. S. Lewis, *Later Medieval France: The Polity* (St Martin's Press, New York, 1968), p. 195; R. J. Knecht, 'The Early Reformation in England and France: A Comparison', *History*, 57 (1972), 1–16; Alain Guéry, 'Les Finances de la Monarchie Français sous l'Ancien Régime', *Annales ESC*, 33 (1978), 216–39.

[70] Betts, 'Constitutional Development', p. 465.

[71] Bogucka, 'Towns in Poland'.

[72] Knecht, 'Early Reformation'; David S. Hempsall, 'Martin Luther and the Sorbonne, 1519–21', *Bulletin of the Institute of Historical Research*, 46 (1973), 28–40.

[73] M. L. Bush, *Renaissance, Reformation and the Outer World, 1450–1660* (Blandford Press, London, 1967).

CONCLUSION

Returning then to the questions posed at the outset – which towns adopted the Reformation and why – it appears evident that an adequate answer must include not only the role of commerce but also the broader social and political context in which commerce was embedded. Protestant theology may have held certain intrinsic attractions for the rising merchant class that made up the new 'trade diaspora' of northern Europe: an ascetic ethic, greater individuality, fewer ritual obligations to the local community.[74] But its appeal was neither restricted to the merchant class nor sufficient in itself to evoke official sanction for the Protestant cause. The towns that gave Protestantism this sanction tended to consist of long-distance commercial centers rather than local trading hubs, yet even the most pronounced commercial towns were sometimes hostile or indifferent to the Reformation. The critical factor was the balance of power that developed between the indigenous elites of the towns and the landowning elites who influenced policies locally or in the central regime. Especially important was the capacity of regimes, either municipal or central, to extricate themselves from financial and administrative dependence upon the nobility. Those able to gain such autonomy, generally through the new resources supplied by commerce, had greater freedom to pursue options that violated the traditional interests of the church.

This interpretation obviously differs from standard sociological explanations of the Reformation. It suggests that the Reformation was not simply a function of expanding horizons leading individuals to favor new ideas. Nor was it strictly a function of the production by commerce of a new elite that needed to legitimate itself. Commerce was important to the Reformation, but its effects were mediated in conjunction with other social factors. The commercial elite did not operate in isolation from the landed nobility or the state. A conjuncture of commercial and state power as well as relative autonomy from the nobility was needed for the Reformation to succeed. Commercial elites and heads of state often had a personal interest in the Reformation. Sometimes they wished

[74] P. D. Curtin, *Cross-Cultural Trade in World History* (Cambridge University Press, Cambridge, 1984); Fernand Braudel, *Civilization and Capitalism, 15th–18th Century* (3 vols, Harper and Row, New York, 1983), vol. II, *The Wheels of Commerce*, pp. 569–71.

it to advance, at other times they were ambivalent or hostile. Seldom, however, did they set out with a clear, rationally calculated vision of furthering the Reformation for their own interests. Instead they pursued short-term policies by selecting among the options available at the time. The outcome – often unforeseen – of these decisions was in some cases to favor the Reformation and in others to hinder it. One of the crucial differences was attributable to the constraints set by governing units' relations to the landed sector. Commerce interacted with a web of pre-existing social arrangements to set the structural conditions under which Reformation policies were pursued.

Finally, in the spirit of Fox's work, we may ask what may be gained from this reconsideration of the Reformation so far as the more general relation between geography and ideology is concerned. If the present conclusions are any indication, geography's impact on ideology is mediated by social institutions rather than being primarily a direct factor in the shaping of individuals' ideologies. Persons who happened to live near waterways may have adopted Protestantism because it seemed psychologically compatible with their increasing participation in commerce. But that possibility – largely untestable – tells only part of the story. Late medieval religion was not only an individual belief system but a firmly established institution. Powerful resources were required to supplant it. Geography influenced the spatial distribution of these resources. But it was often the regime that determined the balance of power. The rise of commerce not only created new economic resources and a new merchant class; it also opened a deep cleavage within the governing class – between its commercial and agrarian fractions – that ultimately affected the regimes' capacity to rule.

3

Towns, Transport and Crown: Geography and the Decline of Spain

DAVID RINGROSE

THE QUESTION OF DECLINE

In the years after 1550 the King of Castile and Aragon nominally ruled an empire uprecedented in history. Charles V was sovereign in most of Italy, Austria, Hungary, Germany, and the Low Countries, while his son had just married the Queen of England. He appointed Viceroys to govern from Mexico to Chile as rulers of two conquered American empires and their immensely wealthy silver and gold mines. A generation later some of the European holdings had pulled away, but Phillip II had acquired Portugal, the Portuguese empire in South America, Africa, and Asia, and the Philippine Islands. Yet a century after 1550 this great power structure was in a shambles, many of its regions impoverished, its military apparatus destroyed, and its European prestige dissipated. Despite a modicum of recuperation in the eighteenth century, Spain never recovered from the crises that precipitated that ruin.

The explanations for this dramatic decline are many and complex. Indeed, their content depends as much as anything on the assumptions of the historical analyst. Many of the numerous explanations have substantial validity, but we still do not have a clear idea of how some of the mechanisms of decline actually worked. At the risk of advancing yet another monocausal interpretation, I suggest that within the Iberian peninsula the collapse of the regional economy and population was closely linked with the rise of Madrid as a major European capital. This powerful new center for consumption disrupted the regional economy, pre-empted valuable co-ordinating services, and forced the countryside toward economic stagnation. This neglected feature of the 'decline of Spain' suggests that the success of the empire, which depended on centralized government, was linked to a capital city that simultaneously undermined the economy necessary for long-term fiscal stability. It would be simplistic and illogical to argue that the rise of Madrid 'caused' the economic collapse of Castile. Rather, many forces, decisions, and trends reached interior Spain via Madrid, and in passing though its urban economy, they acquired a negative impact on the Castilian economic world that had been constructed during the sixteenth century. The great difficulty has always been to find an effective way of explaining this urban–regional interaction in a manner that relates geo-economic limitations to historical action.

The Spanish empire was a complicated, dynastically united coalition of regional societies that encompassed large parts of Europe and America. The ability of its Hapsburg rulers to control and tax local economies varied tremendously from one domain to another and was best developed in the Kingdom of Castile. Historians have offered several explanations of Spanish 'decline', all of which suffer when reduced to a few sentences.[1]

One explanation blames decline on an autocratic clique out of touch with changing reality.[2] Consequently, the Hapsburg system disintegrated while its operators tilted at windmills. An alternative explanation emphasizes the fiscal constraints of the monarchy. Trends created by population growth and Atlantic expansion combined with an inflexible tax structure to reduce the purchasing power of tax revenue.

[1] J. H. Elliott, 'Self Perception and Decline in Early Seventeenth-Century Spain', *Past and Present*, LXXIV (1977), pp. 41–61; J. I. Israel, 'A Conflict of Empires: Spain and the Netherlands 1618–1648', *Past and Present*, LXXVI (1977), pp. 34–74; Henry Kamen, 'The Decline of Spain: A Historical Myth?', *Past and Present*, LXXXI (1978), pp. 24–50; Charles Jago, 'The 'Crisis of the Aristocracy' in Seventeenth-Century Castile', *Past and Present*, LXXXIV (1979), pp. 60–90; John J. TePaske and Herbert S. Klein, 'The Seventeenth-Century Crisis in New Spain: Myth or Reality?', *Past and Present*, XC (1981), pp. 116–35; J. I. Israel, 'The Decline of Spain: A Historical Myth?', and rejoinder by Henry Kamen, *Past and Present*, XCI (1981), pp. 170–85. See also J. H. Elliott, 'The Decline of Spain', in *Crisis in Europe, 1560–1660*, ed. Trevor Aston (Anchor-Doubleday, Garden City, New Jersey, 1967).

[2] J. H. Elliott, *Imperial Spain, 1469–1716* (Edward Arnold, London, 1963), pp. 299–303, 375–8; Lawrence Stone, *The Crisis of the Aristocracy, 1558–1641* (Clarendon Press, Oxford, 1965), pp. 303–33.

Philip II imposed new taxes, but revenues still fell short of paying for continual wars. By 1600 the main revenue sources were America and Castile, but thereafter silver receipts declined and the Castilian tax base collapsed. While the revenue system was collapsing the crown undertook ever larger international commitments, with disastrous results.[3] A third explanation emphasizes the self-destructive nature of the government's fiscal practices. In its perennial need for cash, the crown repeatedly imposed new taxes, manipulated the coinage, 'borrowed' private bullion, and suspended its payments. The consequent ruin of Spain's merchant-bankers only prompted additional expedients that further damaged the economy.[4] A fourth explanation focuses on the political repercussions of improvisation and reform. Various attempts at administrative consolidation led to revolts in Granada and the Netherlands in the 1560s, and in Aragon in the 1590s, and culminated in a devasting series of revolts in Vizcaya, Catalonia, Portugal, and Naples after 1630. These internal political failures used up scarce military resources and left the empire vulnerable.[5]

These explanations, while useful, do not explain Castile's failure to maintain the 'high population equilibrium' achieved in areas as diverse as England and Languedoc in the same period. Despite growing poverty and inequity, Languedoc maintained local specialization, cross-regional trade, and inter-regional market activity, forestalling demographic collapse.[6] In England, rural society avoided crisis by transforming itself

[3] This combines Hamilton's view and that exemplified by Hammarström. Earl J. Hamilton, *American Treasure and The Price Revolution in Spain, 1501–1650* (Harvard University Press, Cambridge, Mass., 1934); Ingrid Hammarström, 'The "Price Revolution" of the Sixteenth Century: Some Swedish Evidence', *Scandinavian Economic History Review*, 5, (1957), pp. 118–54. On conscription, Antonio Domínguez Ortiz, *La Sociedad Española del siglo XVII*, vol. I (CSIC, Madrid, 1963).

[4] The notorious example is the *medio general* of 1577, a settlement that crippled Castilian commercial life. Felipe Ruiz Martín, *Lettres Marchands Échangées entre Florence et Medina del Campo* (SEVEPEN, Paris, 1965), p. lii. J. H. Elliot, *Imperial Spain, 1469–1716*, pp. 279–85.

[5] J. H. Elliott, 'Revolts in the Spanish Monarchy', in *Preconditions of Revolution in Early Modern Europe*, eds. Robert Forster and Jack P. Greene (Johns Hopkins University Press, Baltimore, 1970), pp. 109–30.

[6] Ortiz, *La Sociedad Española*, discusses the manpower costs of warfare, but they coincide with the decline itself, rather than with the conditions which precipitated decline. Emmanuel LeRoy Ladurie, *The Peasants of Languedoc*, tr. John Day (University of Illinois Press, Urbana, Ill., 1976), pp. 213–30.

to supply the needs of a booming market in London.[7] Under similar conditions, Castile's regional economy maintained its equilibrium until around 1610, but then disintegrated rapidly.

CITY SYSTEMS AND REGIONAL ECONOMIES

Before we can pursue an explanation of that collapse we must review some of the propositions developed by economic geographers regarding urban development and urban–rural interaction. One set of abstract models ignores the limitations of geography and transport; the other, represented by E. W. Fox, points to the social and economic implications of difficult transport.

However small and isolated the communities of a rural society, they are invariably part of a network of towns with more distant commercial and administrative contacts. At the same time, the apparent dichotomy between 'urban' and 'rural' history has been dissolved by anthropologists and geographers, who have shown that the countryside and its towns constitute an integral social and economic system. Disruption of either kind of interdependence will alter an entire regional economy in far-reaching ways.

Towns receive supplies and population from their hinterlands through various exchange mechanisms. Some exchanges are spontaneous arrangements between neighboring peasant communities, while others are market induced or administratively coerced transfers imposed from outside the local society.[8] Town populations reflect the number of people able to live outside agriculture even though they serve an agricultural economy. Townspeople provide marketing, administrative, and professional services; transform goods into useful products; constitute a market themselves; and increase regional productivity. Thus they link rural communities, towns, and the larger world.[9]

[7] E. A. Wrigley, 'A Simple Model of London's Importance in Changing English Society and Economy, 1650–1750', *Past and Present*, XXXVII (1967), pp. 44–70.

[8] Edward Whiting Fox, *History in Geographic Perspective: The Other France* (W. W. Norton, New York, 1971), pp. 37, 47.

[9] On local trade and urban hierarchies, see Brian J. L. Berry, Edgar C. Conkling and D. Michael Ray, *The Geography of Economic Systems* (Prentice-Hall, Englewood Cliffs, New Jersey, 1976), pp. 226–42. The literature is discussed in Richard E. Blanton, 'Anthropological Studies of Cities', *Annual Review of Anthropology*, V (1976), 249–64,

Since the ratio of people to land changes continually, the relation is never static. When the population increases, scarcity forces peasant communities to specialize, to produce surpluses, and to depend upon outside suppliers and markets. Such exchanges may remain secondary to the peasant economy, but they create a system of identifiable market and service centers.[10] That network offers openings for external political and commercial interests to redirect part of the rural output into transactions over long distances. Whether collected as rents and taxes or in exchange for other goods, the flow of basic supplies can be directed to or attracted to large and complex cities. An apparently self-sufficient peasant economy can thus be one of the mainstays of an urban system. Town-based elites and merchants elaborate the system further as they contact distant economies and extend their influence into the rural exchange system. Their activity intensifies contact between rural society and the wider world, inducing commercialization.[11]

These abstract propositions acquire important social and cultural dimensions as we come to terms with E. W. Fox's observations regarding the crucial role of transport costs in determining the complexity of a regional society and economy. In his stimulating *History in Geographic Perspective*, Fox offers several generalizations that have implications far beyond his discussion of France. Among the more suggestive are his insistence on the differences between trade, commerce, and communication.[12] The distinctions invite endless discussion, but they have considerable explanatory power for the pre-industrial era because of the differences between the cost and speed of land and waterborne transport.

High cost (land) transport encourages local isolation and economic self-sufficiency supplemented by short-range trade.[13] External contacts

---

and Carol A. Smith, 'Economics of Marketing Systems: Models from Economic Geography', *Annual Review of Anthropology*, III (1974), 167–201. Carol A. Smith, ed. *Regional Analysis*, (2 vols, Academic Press, New York, 1976) is a good introduction.

[10] Networks suggestive of France and Spain also existed in China and Guatemala: Stuart Plattner, 'Rural Market Networks', *Scientific American*, CCXXXII (1975), 66–79.

[11] Fox outlines this relation in *History*, pp. 47–52. Note that the money is as important in mobilizing wealth as are transfers of goods, and that inland states are very aggressive in exploiting this device. See also Edward Whiting Fox, 'The Range of Communications and the Shape of Spatial Organization', *Communication*, V (1980), p. 283.

[12] Fox, *History*, pp. 14–15, 28, 34, 45, 49–51. These ideas are presented in a broader context in Fox, 'The Range of Communication', 275–87.

[13] Fox, *History*, especially ch. 2, pp. 33–53; Fox, 'The Range of Communication', p. 277.

depend upon commerce in expensive luxury goods and on transfers of information. Isolation reduces markets to a marginal role in decisions about production and encourages local economic autonomy. Conversely, if exposed to cheap (maritime) transport and external commerce in staple products, peasants can become market-oriented farmers, and regional societies can exploit their comparative advantages.

Where transport costs are inherently high, orders and information can still be distributed with a relative ease that permits the social and political integration of a governing elite based on dispersed real resources and centralized command. But such a hierarchical communication system requires arbitrary and militaristic authority that can raise armies for defense and social control through forced redistribution of resources despite adverse market conditions. The result is an authoritarian society with a tendency to rural self-sufficiency and militaristic values. Alternately, cheap waterborne transportation allows longdistance interdependence, which requires rule by law and recognition of contracts. Governance, oriented toward maintenance of the commercial network, rests on the consensus of the important commercial and productive elements. Militaristic values and arbitrary authority conflict with the orientation and social base of society.[14]

In delineating this vision of parallel political and economic cultures within Europe, Fox borrows heavily from the same central place theory used in this essay. His characterization of areal and linear societies is a brilliant, coherent blend of spatial concepts from Christaller, Lösch, and Skinner, and societal concepts from Sjoberg, Weber, and Braudel.[15] This conceptual schema bridges the static central place models of geographers and the realities of many pre-industrial settings. Used properly, it allows us to grasp dynamic processes in a way that neither geographers nor historians do separately. To do so, we must articulate Fox's propositions carefully, and expand his ideas about forms of regional integration.

Several factors determine the nature and location of towns in a region. Every service or commodity that a town provides has an optimal distribution area, which varies with the source of the service or commodity, the availability of substitutes, and the cost of distribution. The last of these reflects the technology and location of transport; thus

[14] Fox, *History*, pp. 54–60; Fox, 'The Range of Communication', pp. 278–81.
[15] Fox's most succinct statement is in *History*, pp. 38–9.

the siting of transport facilities influences the location of towns. A commodity that is expensive to transport will be provided by many distribution points, each of which serves a small area. A commodity that can be distributed cheaply will be distributed from a few towns, each of which serves a large area. The larger distribution area generated by the second commodity will encompass many of the small service zones that provide the first commodity. The larger area will thus contain one two-function town and several (usually smaller) one-function towns. The availability of a particular commodity also depends upon the amount of capital necessary for its production. An expensive facility is hard to duplicate, especially in a capital-poor society, and will have to service a large area even if delivery costs are high.

Political and professional services in particular can be distributed to large areas from a few centers since they rely on the exchange of information.[16] Letters and orders are easy to transport compared with most commodities. A town that provides the political services that depend upon communication may also become a center for distribution of easily transported commodities with large distribution areas and for production of capital-intensive goods. Concurrently, such a 'political town' serves as residential center for regional or national elites and facilitates integration of the ruling class.[17]

Where production and distribution operate under relatively open market conditions, the central place system that results will include towns with a predictable variety of size and complexity.[18] Under specified conditions, the presence of a regular rank–size distribution demonstrates a complex network of interdependency. Given these conditions, the second-largest city is half to two-thirds the size of the first, while third-level towns are typically half to two-thirds the size of the second center. As many

---

[16] Fox, *History*, p. 25.

[17] Chauncy D. Harris and Edward L. Ullman, 'The Nature of Cities', in *Cities and Society* eds Paul K. Hatt and Albert J. Reiss (Free Press, New York, 1957), pp. 237–47; Edward L. Ullman, 'A Theory of Location for Cities', in Hatt and Reiss, *Cities and Society*, 227–36. The first of these appeared in 1945, the second in 1941.

[18] The basic work is Walter Christaller, *Central Places in Southern Germany*, tr. Carlisle W. Baskin (Prentice-Hall, Englewood Cliffs, New Jersey, 1966: first pub. 1933), esp. pp. 51–3, 96, 101, 110–20. On the durability of this framework: Berry, Conkling, and Ray, *Geography of Economic Systems*, ch. 12.

as seven levels with decreasing town size and complexity have been suggested, although the distinctions are sometimes hard to see.[19]

In the world that Fox set out to discuss, therefore, towns are crucial to rural well being and a regular rank – size hierarchy suggests efficient regional use of resources. Here Fox's formulation may contain an overstated dichotomy. Inland areas with pre-modern transport do not inevitably lack cities and commerce. The difference is one of degree. A landlocked area will at best see a modest part of its gross product or population embodied in its urban sector, but even where transport is primitive and peasants are oriented to self-sufficiency, towns allow local specialization, exploitation of comparative advantages, and alternatives for landless countryfolk. Within those general constraints a developed central place system can make a material contribution to living standards or to the size of the population a landlocked region can sustain.[20]

[19] Smith, *Regional Analysis*, I, 28–9. On the seven levels, see: Gilbert Rozman, *Urban Networks in Ch'ing China and Tokugawa Japan* (Princeton University Press, Princeton, 1973), pp. xiv, 14. Economic geographers disagree about this rank – size model, and about the sort of economy that produces a regular hierarchy. The rank – order concept is discussed in Brian J. L. Berry and William L. Garrison, 'Alternate Explanations of Urban Rank – Size Relationships', *Annals of the Association of American Geographers*, XLVIII (1958), pp. 83–91; John B. Parr, 'City Hierarchies and the Distribution of City Size: A Reconsideration of Beckmann's Contribution', *Journal of Regional Science*, IX (1969), pp. 239–53; Martin J. Beckmann and John C. McPherson, 'City Size Distribution in a Central Place Hierarchy: An Alternative Approach', *Journal of Regional Science*, X (1970), pp. 25–33; and Robert Higgs, 'Central Place Theory and Regional Urban Hierarchies: An Empirical Note', *Journal of Regional Science*, X (1970), pp. 253–5. James E. Vance, *The Merchant's World: The Geography of Wholesaling* (Prentice-Hall, Englewood Cliffs, New Jersey, 1970), pp. 140–3, considers it a special case caused by relative isolation. Nevertheless, the model works for self-contained pre-industrial regions in which conditions approximate Christaller's original assumptions. See: Vance, *Merchant's World*, p. 19. The difficulty arises from the absence of the pattern in developing, export-oriented economies typical of contemporary Third World societies. The hierarchy reappears where economic development has become general, but on a larger geographic scale. See: E. A. J. Johnson, *The Organization of Space in Developing Countries* (Harvard University Press, Cambridge, Mass., 1970), p. 28.

[20] The contrast between land and sea freight rates is clear everywhere. T. S. Willan, *The Inland Trade, Studies in English Internal Trade in the Sixteenth and Seventeenth Centuries* (Manchester University Press, Manchester, 1976), pp. 4–11, suggests overland rates of 4d to 12d per ton/mile and water-borne rates of 0.1d to 1d per ton/mile in England. Similarly, rates across New York fell from $.19 per ton/mile to less than $.01 per ton/mile when the Erie canal opened. See Harvey H. Segal, 'Canals and Economic Development', in *Canals and American Economic Development*, ed. Carter Goodrich (Columbia University Press, New York, 1961), p. 227. Willan also comments, however, that overland transport

The larger world, in the pursuit of its own goals, may impose exchanges that alter this intra-regional development without necessarily benefiting the local population. Middlemen encourage the production and export of selected commodities, while gaining control of the price paid to the producer. Consequently, distant markets encourage a 'dendritic', tree-like pattern of regional trade that links many villages directly to one center.[21] Under such circumstances, the foreign goods received by the rural world are consumed directly, villagers come to depend on foreign suppliers, and the import-export pattern reduces opportunities for cross trading between rural communities. Orientation to distant markets and suppliers encourages primate cities that specialize in the export of commodities extracted from a world of isolated and dependent rural communities. Such cities buy most of what they consume with export earnings not passed on to their hinterlands, even though local resources could provide much of what they need. Thus they fail to stimulate the economy of their own rural hinterlands. Instead of criss-crossing the regional economy, goods leave the farms along branch-like routes to a few large centers and bring little return trade. As this situation evolves, the primate city attracts regional elites and the professionals, merchants, and artisans who serve them. In consequence, the economic life of the secondary towns, which once provided central place services throughout the region, is undermined. A region with an older, market-inspired central place network suffers a species of deurbanization and a narrowing of economic opportunity in rural society.

TRANSFORMATION OF A CENTRAL PLACE SYSTEM

Fox couched his ideas with reference to France, but the decline of Spain offers a parallel story. It is one in which another successful state, based on similar assumptions of royal sovereignty, imposed itself upon a regional economy. That economy, despite the limitations of overland

---

was used for a variety of purposes and that the comparative costs are sometimes difficult to ascertain. The capacity of carts and animals was the same as in Spain. See also David R. Ringrose, *Transportation and Economic Stagnation in Spain, 1750-1850* (Duke University Press, Durham, North Carolina, 1970), pp. 43-8.

[21] Johnson, *Organization of Space*, pp. 83-92, discusses the separation of local and export trade. On wholesale trade: Vance, *Merchant's World*, pp. 148-55.

transport, had developed a lively urban–rural interaction and a complex central place system.

Indeed, the Castilian economy of the sixteenth century included sophisticated craft industries, regional markets, and export trades in silks, woolens, ceramics, weapons, wool, and agricultural products from Segovia, Guadalajara, Cuenca, Avila, Toledo, Talavera, Valladolid, and Burgos. Merchants from Toledo, the largest interior city, bought and sold domestic and imported merchandise throughout the southern two-thirds of Spain and in the southern and eastern ports.[22] With Toledo as co-ordinating center, Burgos organized trade to the Atlantic north, and Seville did the same in the Atlantic south. Intermediate centers included cloth towns like Cuenca and Segovia, agricultural towns like Soria and Salamanca, and administrative towns like Valladolid and Granada. These towns maintained surprisingly complex inter-regional exchanges that supported a network of thirty-five regional fairs in New Castile alone.[23] The vitality of the fairs is illustrated by that of Tendilla, a town of 3000 inhabitants sixty-five kilometers east of Madrid, where cloth was sold from Segovia, Cuenca, Aragon, and the Rioja, merchandise from Portugal, Flanders, and Vizcaya, as well as goods presented by the '*mercaderes gruesos*' of Toledo and Madrid.[24] Despite economic difficulties after 1575, this regional network was still functioning in 1600.[25]

These towns exhibited a rank-size hierarchy predictable for an autonomous region with open markets. Toledo, with 65,000 people, dominated New Castile and co-ordinated exchanges with Valencia,

[22] Michael Weisser, 'Les Marchands de Tolède dans l'Économie Castillane, 1565–1635', *Mélanges de la Casa de Velazquez*, III (1971), pp. 223–36.

[23] To give one example, Cuenca traded its woolens with Seville, Medina del Campo, Medina de Rioseco, and Villalón, and in fairs at Torrijos, Alcalá de Henares, Mondéjar, Tendilla, and Pastrana. Martín, *Lettres Marchandes*, pp. xxxv–xxxviii.

[24] Noël Salomon, *La Vida Rural Castellana en Tiempos de Felipe II* (Planeta, Barcelona, 1973), pp. 96–117 and app. X. In French: *La Campagne de Nouvelle Castille à la Fin de XVIe siècle d'après les 'Relaciones topográficas'* (S.E.V.P.E.N. Paris, 1964).

[25] José Gentil da Silva, *En Espagne: Développement Économique, Subsistance, Déclin* (Mouton, Paris, 1965), pp. 1–57; Fernand Braudel, *The Mediterranean and the Mediterranean World in the Age of Philip II* (2 vols, Harper and Row, New York, 1973), I, pp. 293–4, 404–8; Salomon, *La Vida Rural Castellana*. On population: Jaime Vicens Vives, *Manual de Historia Económica de España* (5th ed., Ed. Vicens Vives, Barcelona, 1967), pp. 301–2; Ortiz, *La Sociedad Española*, p. 113. On population trends, Gentil da Silva, *En Espagne*, pp. 21–2; Salomon, *La Vida Rural Castellana*, pp. 45–6.

Cartagena, Seville, Burgos, and Bilbao. Valladolid, with 40,000 people, ranked second. An administrative center, it provided many services for Old Castile, but depended on Toledo, Burgos, or Bilbao for more distant mercantile and financial connections.[26] Below Toledo and Valladolid in the central place system were a number of cloth towns of 15,000–30,000 (such as Segovia, Avila, Guadalajara, Cuenca, and Salamanca), smaller entrepôts (Medina del Campo, Burgos, Astorga, and Talavera), and district centers with a limited range of services (León, Ciudad Real, Albacete, Soria, Trujillo). All were linked to the regions's periodic fairs.[27] As the seventeenth century approached, this urban system facilitated local specialization and inter-regional exchange as Castile's expanding population struggled to compensate for lagging agricultural output.[28]

Thus, within the constraints imposed by overland transport, Castile had developed an urban network and an elaborate market system to compensate for the growing tension between rising population, static technology, and declining productivity in agriculture. As of 1600 one could not say that the economy was prosperous, but it was still functioning. The rapid rise of Madrid, especially after 1600, threatened this precarious situation with increasingly sharp economic distortions. The results were not happy, and it is here that our model of urban–rural interdependence speaks to the larger problem of decline.

The growth of the capital from 35,000 inhabitants in 1560 to 175,000 in 1630 appears analogous to that of London, but, lacking coastal communications, Madrid was poorly suited to be an entrepôt and exported few products of its own.[29] In Madrid, principally a residential center for bureaucracy and aristocracy, disposable income was concentrated in the hands of a small elite. The largest sector of the work

---

[26] Bartolomé Bennassar, *Valladolid au Siècle d'Or* (Mouton, Paris, 1967), pp. 99–102, 116–19; Bennassar, 'Medina del Campo: Un Example des Structures Urbaines de l'Espagne au XVIe Siècle', *Revue d'Historie Économique et Sociale*, XXXIX (1961), p. 492.

[27] Weisser, 'Marchands de Tolède'.

[28] The 'Malthusian' cycle is best documented for Segovia: expansion, 1530–80; decline, 1600–50; expansion, 1700–60; stagnation, 1760–1814. Angel García Sanz, *Desarollo y Crisis del Antiguo Régimen en Castilla la Vieja: Economía y Sociedad en Tierras de Segovia de 1500 a 1814* (Akal Ed., Madrid, 1977) pp. 24, 75.

[29] For more detail, see Ringrose, *Transportation and Economic Stagnation*; T. S. Willan, *River Navigation in England, 1600–1750* (Frank Cass, London, 1964); Willan, *The English Coasting Trade, 1600–1750* (Augustus Kelly, New York, 1967); Willan, *Inland Trade*.

force consisted of domestic servants, and the availability of unskilled labor kept wages very low. The city included relatively few middling elements with moderate amounts of discretionary income and an appetite for domestic artisanal goods and specialized agricultural products. The market for middle-range commodities and craft products stagnated even though the population grew; that stagnation deprived the regional exchange network of an essential segment of demand. As Madrid supplanted earlier urban centers, urban demand was increasingly polarized between a burgeoning subsistence class and an import-oriented elite. The corresponding decline of urban demand for specialized regional products upset the regional exchanges that had sustained the Castilian economy.

The impact of Madrid involved more than shifts in urban demand. It also implied changes in relative commodity prices and aggravated the instability of regional commodity markets. The case of wine and wheat illustrates the impact of relative price changes derived from the polarization of urban demand. Wine was a widely used commodity bought with discretionary income. Prior to 1590 wine prices rose faster than cereal prices; hence, many towns specialized in wine and depended on the market for foodstuffs. As Madrid began to overshadow Toledo during 1590–1610 period, wheat prices soared by 90 per cent while wine prices fell by 20 per cent. This price spread undermined local economies that had come to depend on exchanging wine for foodstuffs. Meanwhile, the same increase in wheat prices pushed labor costs up in the cloth towns and undermined their competitive position.[30]

Agricultural societies with poor transport are inherently subject to unstable commodity markets. But beginning with the 1590s there is clearly a connection between the growing volume of consumption in Madrid and the increasing severity of price fluctuation during the recurrent supply crises normal to such an economy. During the thirty years of declining agricultural output after 1600, Madrid's consumption of olive oil doubled, while its consumption of wine, meat, and wheat

[30] Gentil da Silva, *En Espagne*, pp. 19–26; Salomon, *La Vida Rural Castellana*, pp. 42–5; Bennassar, *Valladolid*; Braudel, *La Méditerranée*, I, pp. 245–52; Jose Deleito y Piñuela, *Solo Madrid es Corte*, pp. 69–70; J. M. Houston, *The Western Mediterranean World* (Longmans, London, 1964), pp. 114–15; Helmuth Hopfner, 'La Evolución de los Bosques de Castilla la Vieja en Tiempos Históricos', *Estudios Geográficos* 15, no 56 (1954) pp. 415–30; Jean Vilar Berrogain, *Literatura y Economía: La Figura Satírica del Arbitrista en el Siglo de Oro* (Revista de Occidente, Madrid, 1973).

trebled.[31] The prices of basic foodstuffs became extremely volatile, and the epidemics at the close of the century do not account for all of the variation.

Simultaneously, the countryside was exposed to frequent and far-reaching administrative interference in the supply market, which imposed more and more transfers of produce to Madrid. Given the nature of Madrid's market and its lack of entrepôt or industrial capacity, these became one-way transfers that precluded the reciprocal exchanges essential to the economic equilibrium of the central place network of the sixteenth century.

The development of a new primate city within Castile's already complex regional economy precipitated a striking transformation of the regional central place system. The imposition of a supply system dominated by a single large city upon a central place network based on relatively open markets entailed relocation of urban functions and forced the countryside toward economic stagnation. This neglected feature of the 'decline' of Spain suggests that Madrid's success in integrating an empire contributed directly to the decline of Castile, to the crown's growing fiscal instability, and to the long-term stagnation of the Spanish interior.

As Madrid grew, it used the power of the crown to organize a one-way flow of resources to supply its population in the face of high overland transport costs. This intervention had many aspects. Corvée-like supply obligations were imposed on towns near Madrid and prices were adjusted to attract goods to the capital. Grain purchases were subsidized in times of dearth, and the royal government had far more resources for such subsidies than any municipality. In accordance with the quality of the harvest for a given commodity, yearly embargoes were imposed that extended 75 and 100 miles from Madrid and in time of shortage blocked the shipment of supplies to markets in other cities.

The impact of such interference was magnified by the nature of the Castilian transport industry. The entire Spanish interior depended on overland transport for, despite efforts by Phillip II and, two centuries later, Charles III, there was no significant waterborne transport to provide cheap bulk haulage. The industry included three groups of

---

[31] David R. Ringrose, 'The Impact of a New Capital City: Madrid, Toledo, and New Castile, 1560–1660', *Journal of Economic History*, XXXIII (1973), pp. 761–91; Gonzalo Anes Álvarez, 'Tendencias de la Producción Agrícola en Tierras de la Corona de Castilla (siglos XVI a XIX)', *Hacienda Pública Española*, XLV (1978), p. 100.

transporters: long-haul professional carters; an elite of professional – and expensive – muleteers (the Federal Express of Castile); and a large pool of part-time transporters who entered the industry as a supplement to farming, much as other peasants engaged in handicraft industry on the side. By its nature this transport was slow and seasonally scarce. Manpower was limited by the seasonal needs of agriculture. The animal power was limited by the seasonal availability of roadside grazing. The ability to move anything was limited by the weather and the state of the roads. The elite muleteers, with trains of pack animals, could travel from Bilbao to Madrid in three to five days, delivering delicacies like fresh (?) fish and personal baggage. The professional carters, however, worked with ox-drawn carts limited to 500–1000 pounds capacity by the state of the roads. Traveling little more than 10 miles a day, and limited by seasonal factors, a typical cart could make no more than about six long hauls a year, moving perhaps 3 tons of goods an average distance of 200 miles. Generally speaking, it was not surprising to see transport costs double the price of wheat within 100 miles of its origin.

The professional transporters of Castile included a series of royally chartered regional organizations. As the crown became more concerned to supply Madrid, the transporters' regulations and privileges were reorganized, special royal protection provided, and access to roadside grazing guaranteed. In return, transporters were obligated to abandon other customers when summoned by the crown, usually to supply the capitol.

Given the intricate interdependence between transporters, regional comparative advantages, and the conditions that affected the industry, arbitrary reallocation of transport services was more destructive than it first appears. It not only disrupted established commercial exchanges, but wasted transport capacity. Since Madrid was not an entrepôt or source of saleable goods, transporters rarely found cargoes that were leaving Madrid for other destinations. Of 800 transport transactions charted for the 1750s, half involved Madrid and only two mentioned cargoes that were leaving the city. Cartage to Madrid precluded cross-regional traffic, and carriers who were visiting the city traveled long distances with empty carts and loadless animals.[32] In effect, diversion of one ton of goods to the supply of Madrid deprived the older exchange network of two tons of transport capacity.

[32] Ringrose, *Transportation*.

Nevertheless, as the crown concentrated patronage and royal resources in the capitol city, Castilian aristocrats, professionals, rentiers, and merchant-bankers settled at court, bringing with them the services and income once dispensed in provincial towns. Concentration in Madrid provided the counterpoint to the well-known decline of the fairs of Old Castile. With urban services concentrated in a distant capitol city, and crippled by an increasingly erratic supply of transportation, secondary central places ceased to function as links between local and long-distance exchange. The resultant drift to self-sufficiency reduced regional productivity.[33]

The major Castilian towns were transformed. From 1570 to about 1610 Toledo had a stable population of 65,000, while Madrid reached that size around 1600. At that moment, Castile was supplying 130,000 people in Madrid and Toledo in addition to the rest of the urban system. The extreme instability of food prices suggests that the region had reached the limits of its ability to support a non-agricultural population. By 1630, however, Madrid alone had 175,000 people. Given the weak technology and dense population of the region, it could only be supported by usurping the supply markets of other cities – a usurpation that hastened their decline and, in the process, upset the market-dependent demographic equilibrium.[34]

As the stability and integration of local and long-distance exchange broke down, Toledo and Valladolid collapsed. High local costs shut Toledo out of distant markets, while her entrepôt function declined as the surrounding communities were caught between falling prices for their products and rising food prices. Recurrent interference in the food supply deprived Toledo of respite, and much of its business community moved to Madrid. Toledo declined to barely 20,000 people in 1630 and 15,000 in 1669.[35] Similarly, Valladolid reached a population of 40,000 by 1591[36] and was momentarily spurred by the return of the Court in 1602–6. Thereafter it collapsed and in 1688 the population was between

[33] Smith, *Regional Analysis*, I, pp. 31–7.

[34] David R. Ringrose, *Madrid and the Spanish Economy, 1560–1850* (University of California Press, Berkeley, Calif., 1983); 'Impact of a New Capital City'.

[35] Ringrose, 'Impact of a New Capital City', Ringrose, *Madrid and the Spanish Economy*.

[36] Bennassar, *Valladolid*, pp. 125, 132–5, 141–4, 185; Michael Weisser, 'The Decline of Castile Revisited', *Journal of European Economic History*, 12–3 (1973) pp. 614–40.

15,000 and 20,000.[37] Toledo became a provincial capital enhanced by Spain's metropolitan see, while Valladolid became a provincial capital enhanced only by the *Chancillería* (Court of Appeals for the north half of Castile).

The fate of third-level cities is illustrated by Segovia, which grew to 21,000 inhabitants by 1591. The population then declined by 50 per cent in a generation, while the number of looms fell from 600 in 1591 to 300 in 1620 and to 159 in 1691.[38] The smaller specialized centers had more varied fates, but all declined substantially. One good example is Astorga, on the road from Madrid to Galicia, and home of a large group of long-distance muleteers who linked Old Castile with the ports of Galicia.[39] Astorga counted 650 *vecinos* in 1591, but as Castilian commerce reoriented toward Madrid, their business declined; by 1659 Astorga counted only 200 *vecinos*. The story recurs in Talavera, but with a difference. On the route between Madrid and Extremadura and Portugal, Talavera grew rapidly to 2,000 *vecinos* by 1591. Despite plague and subsistence crisis the town lost only 25 per cent of its population by 1632. Talavera achieved relative stability because it became a clearing house for Madrid's supplies and a stopping place on the route between Madrid and Andalucía and Portugal. But then Madrid itself declined, and so did Talavera: by 1646 Talavera's population had fallen below 1000 *vecinos*. Even so, Talavera fared relatively well, thanks to its relation to the capital.[40]

---

[37] Adriano Gutiérrez Alonso, Juan José Martín González, Jesus Urrea, Lorenzo Rubio González, and María Antonia Virgili Blanquet, *Valladolid en el siglo XVII* (Ateneo de Valladolid, Valladolid, 1982), pp. 40–9, give the higher figure, based on a ratio of 4.7 inhabitants per *vecino* – a ratio that seems too high. Also, Bennassar, *Valladolid*, pp. 347–8; Ortiz, *La Sociedad Española*, I, pp. 137–8.

[38] Sanz, *Desarrollo y Crisis*, pp. 45–8, 215–17; Ortiz, *La Sociedad Española*, pp. 150–1. Cuenca had a similar woolens industry, with peninsula-wide distribution. Market tax revenues peaked around 1580, fell 25 per cent by 1600, and 60 per cent between 1600 and 1635 as the population declined by two-thirds. Paulino Iradiel Murugarrén, *Evolución de la Industria Textil Castellana en los Siglos XIII–XVI* (Universidad de Salamanca, Salamanca, 1974).

[39] Valentín Cabero Diéguez, *Evolución y Estructura Urbana de Astorga* (Universidad de Salamanca, Salamanca, 1973), pp. 35–8; Jaime García-Lombardero, *La Agricultura y el Estancamiento Económico de Galicia en la España del Antiguo Régimen* (Siglo XXI, Madrid, 1973), ch. 3.

[40] María C. González Muñoz, *La Población de Talavera de la Reina, Siglos XVI–XX* (Diputación Provincial, Toledo, 1975), pp. 95, 131–3, 180–90, 245.

Near the bottom of the central place hierarchy were the centers that served agricultural regions directly and had modest connections to the larger network. Here regional rather than long-distance conditions predominated. In places like León in the north west, population was stable during the late sixteenth century, although its economy adjusted to diminishing returns in agriculture by developing craft industry and regional exchanges. By 1600, with 4000 people, León was a modest regional capital. The subsequent collapse of the urban system affected León less seriously than larger centers involved in inter-regional services, and the population fell only 30 per cent by the 1640s.[41] León was clearly less vulnerable than higher-order central places to the breakdown of inter-urban exchanges.[42] More dependent upon local than inter-urban life, the smaller central places experienced less decline than the larger ones that depended more heavily on the services and resources pre-empted by Madrid.

In the twenty years after 1606, the central places that had sustained Castile's commercial life into the seventeenth century collapsed. The magnitude of change in the urban network is evident in the redistribution of urban population. In the 1590s, Madrid and ten other interior cities contained 300,000 people, 20 per cent of them in Madrid. By the later 1600s, the same cities counted only 200,000 people, 60 per cent of whom were in Madrid. An urban hierarchy that had integrated specialized agriculture, craft industries, local trade, and long distance commerce had been dismantled. Castile was left with rudimentary regional centers, few middle-range urban services and an oversized primate city fed by a 'commerce' that consisted of administered and subsidized transfers of staple commodities. The drift of the interior toward subsistence was inevitable.

[41] Valentina Fernández Vargas, *La Población de León en el Siglo XVI* (Universidad de Madrid, Madrid, 1968), pp. 139–47, 162–3; Gentil da Silva, *En Espagne*, pp. 28–30, 82; Ortiz, *La Sociedad Española*, p. 150.

[42] Other examples include Albacete and Ciudad Real, where market tax revenues declined after 1581. This reflects declining agricultural yields and disruption of markets; its gradualness the stability of local activity relative to long-distance commerce. This trend is echoed in the baptismal records of Ciudad Real, where population and baptisms leveled off around 1570 but did not fall until after 1600. Subsequently they stabilized as early as the 1620s. Carla Rahn Phillips, *Ciudad Real, 1500–1750* (Harvard University Press, Cambridge, Mass., 1979), pp. 22–3, 30.

LEGACY OF THE REDISTRIBUTION OF URBAN ACTIVITY

The debased central place system that evolved by the mid-seventeenth century was part of a regional economy that became resistant to change. Castilian stagnation is conventionally attributed to a shopping list of factors that includes sheepraising, uneconomic attitudes, clerical mortmain, private entail, the resultant narrow market in land, and the lack of credit with which to finance improvement. Such observations are not wrong, but they frequently treat symptoms as causes and do not perceive the problems precipitated by the rise of the state and the concomitant investment in a major capital city. Observers long have commented on Madrid's parasitism, but they have not examined how its presence shaped the regional economy.

One way of glimpsing the significance of Madrid is to compare the Castilian central place network before and after the city became a major metropolis. In 1575–79 the crown carried out a detailed survey of the towns in New Castile, collecting data on population and other indicators of central place function. In 1787, the monarchy took the first modern census of Spain, collecting information on both population and occupational structure. Both dates coincide with moments in which the regional economy, at the end of a period of demographic and agricultural expansion, shows signs of a Malthusian crisis – declining agricultural productivity, land hunger, and worsening problems of cyclical mortality. In the first period, Madrid was not a central feature in the regional economy. In the second, 150 years after the crisis of the Castilian central place system, Madrid was the largest city in Spain and ten times as big as any city within interior Spain – the capital contained 120,000 people in 1700 and grew by 70 per cent to 200,000 in 1800. The renewed potential for competition between urban supply and regional development is clear.

The results can be seen in two different places in the regional central place system: the population of the larger Castilian towns as the region evolved, and the structure of the central place system at the lower and local levels of the central place hierarchy. Population estimates indicate that the only interior towns to recover from the wreck of the seventeenth century were places that facilitated the flow of resources toward Madrid. Municipal tolls and market duties, which in the general expansion of the sixteenth century produced corresponding increases in revenue, only did so in the eighteenth century if associated with traffic to the capital. Other market indicators, even in provincial capitals, actually drifted downward after 1720 despite the gradual expansion of the rural economy. The trend is echoed by stagnation and even a net decline in the population of the cities of the interior. The cloth towns of Segovia and Palencia, for example, seem to have expanded slightly in the first half of the century, but actually lost population between 1751 and 1787.[43] Despite brief prosperity induced by the unsuccessful *Compañía de Comercio de Toledo*, Toledo contained 15,000 people in 1669, 15,400 in 1787, and 14,800 in 1842.[44] Ciudad Real and Albacete show expansion until 1750 and stagnation thereafter.[45] In 1797 Madrid and fifteen other principal interior cities counted 323,000 people – 60 per cent of them in Madrid. During the preceeding century Madrid had grown by 70 per cent, while the combined population of the other fifteen towns remained virtually unchanged.[46]

Thus while the rural economy expanded during the first two-thirds of the eighteenth century, except for Madrid the larger cities of the central place system did not. Without the urban services they had provided in the sixteenth century, a more efficient exchange network could not develop. Most indications of growing long-distance commerce bear, not on inter-regional exchanges, but on sea-port to Madrid traffic. The muleteers of Astorga, for example, shifted their activity to Madrid-bound cargo, Talavera doubled in size as co-ordinator of the meat supply from Extremadura, and increased traffic at Arganda and Albacete reflects commerce from the Mediterranean to Madrid.[47]

[43] Eugenio Larruga, *Memorias Políticas y Económicas sobre los Frutos, Comercio, Fábricas y Minas de España* (45 vols, Madrid, 1787–1800), vol. XXXIII, pp. 119–31, 170, 186; Sanz, *Desarrollo y Crisis*, pp. 45–8, 215–17. Gonzalo Anez Alvarez and Jean Paul Le Fiem, 'Las Crises del Siglo XVII: Producción Agrícola, Precios e Ingresos en Tierras de Segovia', *Moneda y Crédito*, XCIII (1965) pp. 3–55.

[44] Michael Weisser, *The Peasants of the Montes* (University of Chicago Press, Chicago, 1975); Larruga, *Memorias*, VII; James C. LaForce, *The Development of the Spanish Textile Industry, 1750–1800* (University of California Press, Berkeley, Calif., 1965).

[45] Phillips, *Ciudad Real*, pp. 17–35.

[46] Miguel Capella Martínez and Antonio Matilla Tascón, *Los Cinco Gremios Mayores de Madrid* (Cámara Oficial de Comercio e Industria, Madrid, 1957), pp. 42–3, 210–15, on commercial interests in Madrid. Official census for 1797.

[47] Diéguez, *Evolución y Estructura*, pp. 38–9, 47; Muñoz, *Población de Talavera*, pp. 189–257, 340–67; Ringrose, *Madrid and the Spanish Economy*, part III; Ringrose, 'Perspectives on the Economy of Eighteenth-Century Spain', *Historia Ibérica* (Las Américas/Anaya, New York and Salamanca, 1973), pp. 59–101.

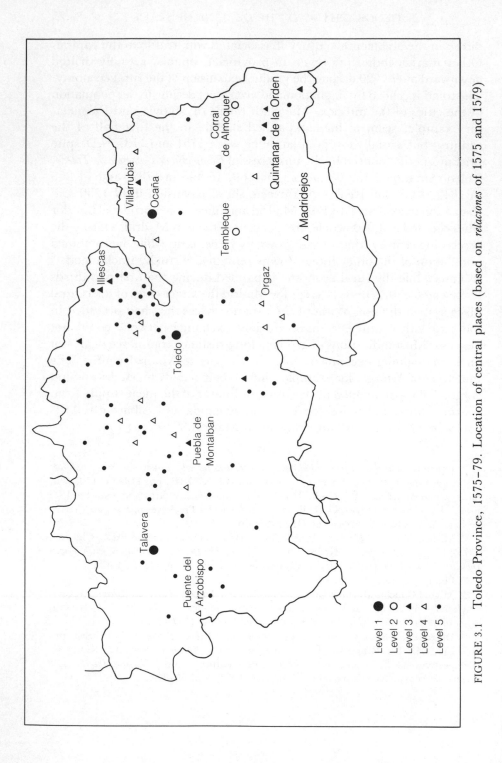

FIGURE 3.1 Toledo Province, 1575–79. Location of central places (based on *relaciones* of 1575 and 1579)

The persistent weakness of the regional central place system is also apparent if we look beneath the level of provincial capitals and compare networks at the local level in 1575 and 1787. To illustrate the change, I constructed a crude 'index of centrality' for each town in the Province of Toledo for each date. The indices reflect population, but were weighted to take account of the presence of commercial activity, production for extra-local markets, and administrative functions. The two data sets are slightly different, but they contain enough comparable variables to establish comparable central place systems. Individual town index numbers were ranked on five-step scales intended to allow rough comparison of central importance. Thus an index number that falls into group one for either date indicates a major center, while those in group five reflect minimal external contact. Figure 3.1 shows the location of towns at various levels of centrality in the 1570s, Figure 3.2 for 1787.[48]

Although Toledo province is only part of a central place system, the comparison is instructive. Table 3.1 compares the central place distribution by rank for the province on the two dates in question.

TABLE 3.1   Toledo Province, Distribution by Rank of Central Places, 1575–79 and 1787

Rank or level	Number in 1575–79	Number in 1787
1	3	1
2	2	1
3	11	4
4	14	28
5	58	61

Including Toledo itself, the sixteenth-century province included five towns in the two highest index groups. After Toledo's 65,000 inhabitants, the next largest towns counted 12,000 and 8,000 people. In 1787 the same province included only two centers in the two highest groups, one of which was Toledo itself, now hardly larger than its sixteenth-century satellites. At the third level on my improvised scale, the sixteenth-century

[48] The data for 1575–9 is based on the *Relaciones Geográficas* of the period as tabulated by Salomon, *La Vida Rural Castellana*. Figures for 1787 from village responses in the *Censo de Floridablanca*, Real Academia de la Historia, Madrid. All towns have been rearranged to correspond to modern boundaries.

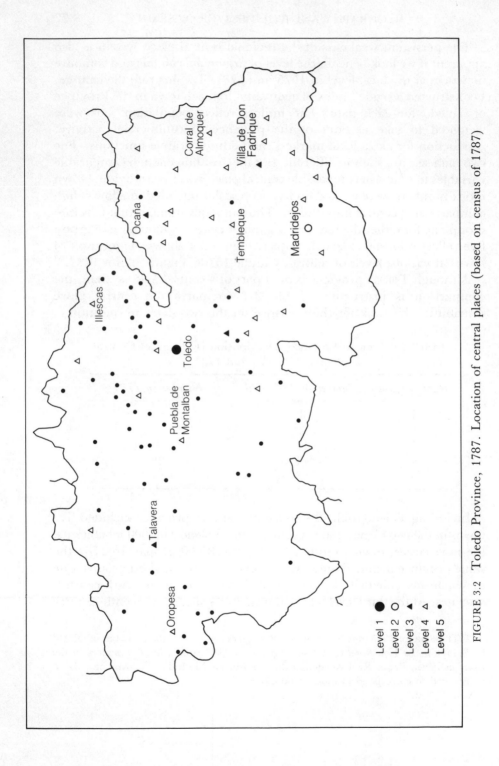

FIGURE 3.2 Toledo Province, 1787. Location of central places (based on census of 1787)

Level 1 ●
Level 2 ○
Level 3 ▲
Level 4 △
Level 5 ●

province counted eleven towns with significant central place functions, while in 1787 there were only four. Thus the town system of the 1570s included sixteen centers that were clearly part of a provincial market network, while in 1787 the same system had only six.

Moving down to the modest level four centers, the numbers are reversed. Towns with indices of centrality in this range contained a very modest amount of market-related activity, most of it associated with inter-community exchanges integral to local subsistence economies. The network in the earlier period contained fourteen such centers, while in 1787 there were twenty-eight. Since the later census represents a more complete list of small towns, the contrast may be exaggerated, but even so, the provincial central place network was far less complex in 1787 and reflects a much less integrated regional economy than that of the sixteenth century. The most striking change in the regional central place system, meanwhile, was the rise of the capital city and the massive supply system that evolved to provision it. Thus the stagnation of other Castilian towns and cities reflects the permanent concentration of income and economic services and implies a corresponding reversion of the countryside to greater self-sufficiency.

By the second half of the eighteenth century, the disparity between Madrid and any other interior town was overwhelming. With a retail market that approximated in value half of all goods and silver reaching Cadiz, Madrid dominated the long-distance commerce of the interior and monopolized services that earlier had been dispersed throughout a hierarchy of central places. This situation lasted past the middle of the nineteenth century and began to change only after the railroad system was completed. In 1860 the population of Madrid and fifteen other interior cities totaled 463,000, but 70 per cent of them were in Madrid.[49] Only Valladolid and Burgos had begun to develop again, as the new railroads began to reorient their hinterlands to the northern and eastern ports.

In the terms of our central place model, new urban functions associated with political and aristocratic centralization were acquired by a tertiary town in the sixteenth-century central place system. Linked to an empire outside the Castilian interior, the new functions (policy making, administration, and elite integration) required a large investment in the facility – a capital city – needed to produce them. In a capital-poor

[49] See n. 46 and the census of 1860.

economy with a tendency toward self-sufficiency, this investment produced a disproportionately large primate city. Other central places were able to retain only low-order functions with restricted fields of influence. The shift of societal priorities, to creation of a home for the state bureaucracy and royal court represented a permanent commitment of social resources. The large fields of influence inherent in administrative functions, combined with systematic distortion of regional commodity markets, helped to transform the older urban hierarchy. In its place there arose a macrocephalic one that became a permanent feature of Spanish life.

In the process, agriculture was left with a single large urban market that depended on the crown and its Atlantic empire and was thus destined to fluctuate in response to conditions external to the realities of the interior. The basis for the redistribution of goods in the interior had changed from a 'market principle' embodying solutions to the problems of regional society, to a 'traffic principle' in which coercion and politically sustained subsidies directed most traffic toward a single collection point.[50] With urban services available only in Madrid, if at all, and limited to supplying agricultural staples to the capital city, the eighteenth-century countryside lacked a central place system capable of providing even the services of the sixteenth century.[51]

Thus, the resources of an empire, used to sustain a governing center, created a dendritic pattern of one-way commodity flows around Madrid, impoverished Castile, and locked it into an inefficient system of production and exchange. In Fox's terms, administered distribution that minimized incentives for improving regional productivity had replaced market-driven redistribution. This administered distribution took place within a landlocked regional economy that could never have reached the level of development epitomized by the Italian or Dutch town systems. Even so, it offered a large enough tax base to play a major role in Hapsburg 'greatness'. In the event, another essential part of Spain's 'greatness', its administrative capital, helped destroy that regional system and as a result played a part in Spanish 'decline.' In the centuries after the rise of Madrid, the price of a centralized state in Spain included persistent Castilian backwardness.

[50] Johnson, *Organization of Space*, pp. 128–31, 137.

[51] The implications of an inadequate central place system are in Johnson, *Organization of Space*, pp. 171–4.

4

A Geographic Perspective in Microcosm: An Artisanal Case Study

P. S. SEAVER

That history has a geographic dimension is obvious, even if we historians customarily neglect it. That the exchange of goods and the transmission of messages have different dimensions seems evident even today when the movement of goods and messages has become so much more rapid. Messages cross continents and oceans almost instantly by satellite relay, but bulk goods still travel most economically by water at speeds little more than twice or thrice that of the sailing ships of the eighteenth century. Edward Fox's hypothesis rests on these undeniable distinctions. Here we shall see what light it sheds, not on large-scale regional exchanges of trading or commercial centers, but on the exchanges of goods and messages of a single individual – a London artisan of the early seventeenth century.

Grant that before the industrial revolution and the revolution in land transport that accompanied it, the presence of waterborne transport created societies and cultures radically different from those of land-locked communities. Grant also that seventeenth-century London, already the most rapidly growing metropolis in Western Europe, was well on the way to becoming the nodal point of a seaborne empire the growth of which rested on the economic advantage of seaborne trade.[1] The

---

[1] The following may be a useful introduction to London and the growth of London and the seaborne empire: F. J. Fisher, 'London as an "Engine of Economic Growth,"' in *The Early Modern Town*, ed. Peter Clark (Longman, London, 1976), pp. 205–15; F. J. Fisher, 'London's Export Trade in the Early Seventeenth Century,' in *The Growth of English Overseas Trade in the seventeenth and eighteenth Centuries*, ed. W. E. Minchinton (Methuen,

question here is what difference all this made in the life of an ordinary artisan whose market was necessarily local, composed, so far as we can tell, entirely of other Londoners. Obviously, some artisans – weavers for example – might produce for the export market, but they constitute a special case not under consideration here.

Nehemiah Wallington, the object of this case study, was chosen less because of any purported typicality – although he may well have been representative of the majority of small masters – than because of his accessibility to modern scrutiny, for it is possible to know more about him than perhaps any other artisan in early modern England. Wallington, who was born in 1598 and remained a resident in London until his death in 1658, was raised a Puritan and, convinced that godliness required the discipline of self-examination, filled some fifty notebooks with religious reflection, autobiographical detail, and political comment. Six of these notebooks survive and provide the basis of this study.[2]

As a Puritan, Wallington was atypical in that he belonged to a religious minority, but for our purposes he was even more unusual in that he died in the tiny parish of St. Leonard's Eastcheap, a hundred yards or so north of London bridge, in the same parish in which he had been born sixty years before. London was a city of migrants; in fact, its spectacular growth – its population doubled from 200,000 to more than 400,000 in Wallington's lifetime – was due to immigration, for the mortality rate within the City was higher than the birth rate.[3] E. A. Wrigley has estimated that in the century after 1650 at least 8,000 migrants must have entered the City every year. The number could not have been much less in the previous generation, for it has been estimated that some four to five thousand apprentices were bound to masters in the City guilds and companies each year by 1600, and the Carpenters' and Turners'

London, 1969), pp. 64–77; Ralph Davis, *English Overseas Trade 1500–1700* (Macmillan, London, 1973); David B. Quinn and A. N. Ryan, *England's Sea Empire, 1500–1642* (Allen & Unwin, London, 1983).

[2] For a description of the corpus of Wallington's writings, see P. S. Seaver, *Wallington's World: A Puritan Artisan in Seventeenth Century London* (Stanford University Press, Stanford, 1985), chapter 1 and the Appendix.

[3] Roger Finlay, *Population and Metropolis: The Demography of London 1580–1650* (Cambridge University Press, Cambridge, 1981), p. 51; for a slightly higher estimate, see Lawrence Stone, 'The Residential Development of the West End of London in the Seventeenth Century,' in *After the Reformation*, ed. Barbara C. Malament (University of Pennsylvania Press, Philadelphia, 1980), p. 168.

Company records suggest that only about ten per cent were London born.[4] Although Nehemiah Wallington's mother was a Londoner, the daughter of Anthony Hall, Citizen and Skinner, Wallington's father had come to the City in the 1570s, when he bound himself apprentice to a turner in the neighboring parish of St. Andrew's Hubbard. Wallington's wife, Grace Rampaigne, does not appear to have been London-born, and the marriage he arranged for his daughter, Sarah, in 1647, was to a young master turner, Jonathan Houghton, the son of a Bedfordshire yeoman who had come to London and bound himself apprentice to a master turner ten years earlier.[5]

Economic opportunity drew the young from all over England. Between 1604 and 1625, twelve per cent of the turners' apprentices came from the North and Wales, and the lethal environment of the City constantly made room for the newcomers. In the first decade of the seventeenth century in St. Leonard's Eastcheap the parish clerk recorded the date and age of all those buried in the parish; of those recorded as being buried, sixty-four per cent had not yet reached the age of twenty-one at the time of death. John and Elizabeth Wallington, Nehemiah's parents, had a dozen children before Elizabeth's death in 1603, but only four were still alive when their father, by then an ancient patriarch, died at the age of eighty-six. Nehemiah's older brother, John, and his wife Mary Valentine, had four children baptized in St. Leonard's Eastcheap, none of whom survived to adolescence. Of Nehemiah and Grace's five children, only one, Sarah, survived. Not only was life terribly brief and transitory for most Londoners, but a corollary of the high mortality was necessarily a high degree of geographic mobility. Of the forty householders listed as resident

[4] E. A. Wrigley, 'A Simple Model of London's Importance in Changing English Society and Economy 1650–1750,' in *Towns and Societies*, eds Philip Abrams and E. A. Wrigley (Cambridge University Press, Cambridge, 1978), pp. 216–20; Finlay, *Population and Metropolis*, p. 66. Between 1604 and 1625 the Turners Company bound 500 apprentices, 50 of whom were London born; between 1620 and 1630 the Carpenters Company records the binding of 334 apprentices, 23 (6.8 per cent) of whom were Londoners. The percentage of London born apprentices increased: between 1640 and 1684 about 25 per cent of the Turners' apprentices were London born. Guildhall Library [henceforth GL], MS. 3302/1, Turners Company Apprentice Bindings 1604–1694; GL, MS. 4329/4, Court Book of the Carpenters Company August 1618–September 1635.

[5] For Wallington's father's apprenticeship, see Folger Library, MS. V.a.436, pp. 202–3, for Nehemiah Wallington's copy of a memoir written by his father concerning his early years in London; for Jonathan Houghton's apprenticeship, see GL, MS. 3302/1, entry dated December 15, 1637.

in the two precincts of St. Leonard's in 1654, only five had been Wallington's neighbors twenty years earlier, and one of the five was his own brother, John.[6] None of Wallington's own apprentices were London born: One of the nine came from as close as Lambeth, Surrey, across the river from Westminster, but the others came from as far away as Warwick, Norfolk, Cheshire, and even Ireland.[7] Although a native Londoner and a small artisanal master whose horizons were necessarily limited by his trade, Wallington could not have been oblivious to the larger world that provided both a constant stream of visitors to England's only major metropolitan center and, even more important, a constant stream of immigrant labor.

The geographic dimension of Wallington's trade seems nonetheless to have been narrowly restricted. As a turner, Wallington made a variety of wooden objects on his wood turner's lathe – spoolwork stools and chairs, wooden bowls and trenchers, pails and wash tubs, pulleys and deadeyes, and a variety of other small household and industrial items, mostly of slight individual value. Like the carpenters, the turners must have bought their timber from the wholesale timber merchants on the Thames side.[8] Although the turners obviously manufactured most of their goods on their own shop floors, they also bought finished products – chairs, spade handles, scoops – made elsewhere and brought up to London by traveling chapmen.[9] An order of the Turners Company of February 20, 1615–16, suggests that this trade in foreign goods was extensive, for it ordered that all 'chairs that are made at Colchester [some 50 miles to the northeast of the City] and other farther parts from London' be brought to Company Hall for inspection, that the price of such chairs be regulated, and that the Master and Wardens of the Company 'shall divide their chairs among the shop keepers of the Company' – clearly a measure designed to prevent a small number of

[6] The precinct lists for St. Clement Eastcheap are found in the records of Bridge Ward Within, Wardmote Inquests, etc., GL, MS. 3461/1.

[7] For Nehemiah Wallington's apprentices, see the Turners Company Apprentice Bindings, GL, MS. 3302/1.

[8] For the Thames side timber merchants, see Carpenters Company Minute Book, GL, MS. 4329/1, entry dated February 9, 1572/3.

[9] For Wallington's mention of chapmen, see, e.g., British Library [henceforth BL], Additional MS. 40,883, fo. 170r-v; for a recent study, see Margaret Spufford, *The Great Reclothing of Rural England. Petty Chapmen and Their Wares in the Seventeenth Century* (Hambledon Press, London, 1984).

masters from monopolizing the cheaper foreign goods.[10] Some goods may have come overland much greater distances, for a letter from Wallington's friend, Francis Wilsmore of Nottingham, some 120 miles to the north of London, apologizes for the 'hard bargain that you had of me (through the dishonesty of the chapman of whom I had the ware).'[11] Whatever the origin of the goods he sold, Wallington himself remained a sedentary shopkeeper in St. Leonard's Eastcheap, never, so far as he tells us, venturing farther outside the City to trade than to go to Bartholomew Fair in Smithfield and Walton Fair, some fifteen or so miles up the Thames on the Surrey side of the river.[12] It was not impossible for artisans to enter London's long distance trade. Wallington's older brother, John, and a close friend and business associate, John Gace, both of the livery of the Turners Company, became war contractors, supplying spades and shovels to Cromwell's army in Ireland. But most turners must have been limited in their economic exchanges to their own neighborhoods in the fast-growing City.[13]

Wallington's own sense of the territory with which he was familiar – his sense of community and neighborhood – cannot be defined with any precision, but his writings do provide fragmentary evidence from which his small urban world can be partially reconstructed. He must have been acquainted with, in fact have known well, the inhabitants of his tiny parish of St. Leonard's, all of one and four tenths acres, the residence of some seventy-three households, according to the tithe valuation made in 1638.[14] Those were the people he saw regularly, not only in his shop but also at Morning and Evening Prayer and on lecture days; those were the people (or the godly minority of them) whom he and his brother John represented as Presbyterian elders in the Fourth London Classis from the autumn of 1646 until age and illness incapacitated them in the

[10] Turners Company Minute Book, GL, MS. 3295/1, entry dated February 20, 1615/16.

[11] BL, Sloane MS. 922, fo. 5r.

[12] For mention of Walton Fair, see GL, MS. 204, p. 9; for Bartholomew Fair, see GL, MS. 3295/1, entry dated January 19, 1625/26.

[13] For warrants for payment on such contracts to John Wallington and John Gace, see *Calendar of State Papers, Domestic, 1651*, pp. 557, 564, 584, 587; *Calendar of State Papers, Domestic, 1651–52*, pp. 587, 591, 595, 618.

[14] T. C. Dale, *The Inhabitants of London in 1638* (London, Publ. for the Society of Genealogists, 1931), vol. I, pp. 88–9.

late 1650s.[15] The parish was necessarily an intimate community, and the only members of the City elite whom Wallington alludes to – Alderman Thomas Adams and Captain Thomas Player, the commander of one of the London regiments – were both fellow parishioners. How claustrophobic this tiny London parish must have been and how intimately neighbors must have known the doings of their fellow parishioners are demonstrated in a letter Wallington wrote 'in love' to his neighbor Constance Waddington in 1640, whom he charged with deceitful trading, of 'selling of your ware' in 'the breach of the Lord's day,' and 'of sleeping in church,' presumably not all on the same sabbath. Wallington also noted that such reprehensible behavior in his neighbor was surprising, 'forasmuch as I have heard you many times at prayer and sometimes at reading,' and 'I do much marvel what comfort you can find in those duties, when your conscience (if it be not seared) cries guilty of the many abominations you live in.'[16]

The parish must have been a face-to-face community, and neighbors can have had few secrets from each other. Such intimate knowledge of one's neighbors must nevertheless have been limited in this densely populated, highly mobile City. Wallington was active in his ward, Bridge Ward Within, which encompassed twelve precincts in the parishes of St. Olave's Southwark, St. Michael's Crooked Lane, St. Martin's Orgar, St. Magnus Martyr, St. Margaret's New Fish Street, St. Leonard's Eastcheap, St. Benet's Gracechurch, and Allhallows Lombard Street, an area of fewer than 20 acres (17.2 acres if one excludes the London Bridge and the part of St. Olave's Southwark included in the ward). There Wallington had served in the onerous office of constable in 1638 and 1639 and had later (1643, 1645, 1649, and 1655) served as a member of the ward's grand jury.[17] Despite his local civic activism, Wallington could not have had anything like an intimate knowledge of the inhabitants of the ward, for the seven parishes north of the river

[15] For Wallington's comment on his election to the eldership, see BL, Sloane MS. 922, fos 153r–154r; for his and his brother's activity in the Fourth Classis, see *The Register Book of the Fourth Classis in the Province of London, 1646–59*, ed. Charles E. Surman (Harleian Society Pubs., vols 82–83, London, 1953), *passim*.

[16] For Adams and Player, see BL, Sloane MS. 922, fos 4v, 153r–154v; for Constance Waddington, see *ibid.*, fos 134v–137v.

[17] For Wallington's 'very troublesome' service as constable, see Folger Library MS. V.a.436, p. 60; for his service as grandjuryman, see Bridge Ward Within, Wardmote Inquests, etc., GL, MS. 3461/1.

had 752 households in 1638 and a population in the neighborhood of 4,600.[18]

Wallington records an incident that took place in 1631 that illustrates how quickly the face-to-face community of the parish gave way to the anonymity of the City. At six on an August evening his daughter Sarah, not yet four years old, had been playing by the shop door with a neighbor's child. She had then wandered off down Eastcheap and Tower Street through Barking to Tower Hill, no more than five or six hundred yards from her father's shop door. There she had stumbled 'and hit herself sore on the forehead.' A woman passer-by had picked her up to comfort her and had just started to carry her into Wapping, supposing she had come from that riverside parish, when a passing servant recognized Sarah as a Wallington from Eastcheap and returned her to her home. Later that evening Wallington reflected that but for the happy circumstance of the passing servant, Sarah might have been lost to them forever, 'for it might have been that we should have seen her no more, . . . and then what strange, distractful thoughts we should have had, and how could we eat or have slept that night with thinking what is become of our poor child.'[19]

If close familiarity extended no more than a couple of hundred yards from his shop door, kinship and friendship gave Wallington a wider acquaintance with the City and its environs. Wallington's youngest sister Sarah lived after her marriage in Lewisham, Kent, across the river about five miles southeast of London Bridge. In 1625 a visit to Lewisham turned out to be a memorable occasion, for, making a family outing of it, Wallington and his wife and two children, his maid Ruth, and his half-sister Patience, all set out by water, and the boatman 'rowed his boat over the cable rope of a ship, which as we all do think was two feet above the water, and it was the great mercy of God that the boat did not overwhelm us all.'[20] Even after the death of his sister, Wallington continued to make family excursions to Peckham fields on the Surrey side, a part of the south shore he must have come to know on his visits to Sarah. When their last child Samuel did not flourish, the Wallington's put him out to a wet nurse in Peckham, where he died on a rainy October

---

[18] The population estimate is arrived at by multiplying the households listed in the 1638 tithe survey by 6.1 person per household, which gives a total for the ward of 4,587. See Finlay, *Population and Metropolis*, pp. 74, 168–170.

[19] GL, MS. 204, pp. 435–436.

[20] *Ibid.*, p. 408.

day in 1632.[21] Much earlier in life when Nehemiah was still living at home, he had on several occasions run away, once as far as Colchester, some sixty miles to the northeast of the City, from which he then returned on the road to London, stopping at Ingatestone in Essex for a fortnight 'to learn to work.'[22] Wallington's best friend, James Cole, was a resident of Whitechapel, the large parish to the east of London between the walls and Stepney, and Wallington's son-in-law, Jonathan Houghton, moved his young family in the early 1650s five miles up river to the country village of Fulham.[23] Nearer at hand Wallington was evidently acquainted with Westminster, for in 1638 he had been summoned to answer charges there before the Court of Star Chamber for possessing illegal books – a thoroughly frightening experience. Three years later in the midst of the revolutionary excitement of the spring of 1641 he had again gone to Westminster, this time with the London mob to surround Parliament and to cry for 'justice! justice!' against the Earl of Strafford.[24]

Had Wallington been illiterate and an unquestioning member of the Established Church, there might be little more to tell. Restricted by his trading interests to his immediate neighborhood in the City, limited in his friendships and kinship to London and environs – to Peckham and Lewisham, Fulham and Whitechapel, for there is no evidence that he ever visited 'brother' Cross in Chelmsford – Wallington might have lived out his life, as most ordinary folk must have done in the seventeenth century, only intermittently aware of the great events that were taking place around him. But Wallington was literate, and his literacy enabled him to enter the quite different world of transmitted messages. As Edward Fox has noted, the rules that governed the exchange of messages are radically different from those which govern the exchange of goods, for the advantages that riverine and oceanic transport give to the movement of bulk commodities hardly exist for the movement of messages, which are comparatively cheap to transmit and which even during

[21] BL, Additional MS. 40,883, fo. 83r; see also fos 144v, 150r. For Samuel's being put to nurse in Peckham, see GL, MS. 204, pp. 431–2.

[22] Folger Library MS. V.a.436, pp. 7–8.

[23] BL, Sloane MS. 922, fo. 98r; for the move to Fulham, see Folger Library MS. V.a.436, p. 213.

[24] For Wallington before the Star Chamber, see GL, MS. 204, pp. 445–6; for Wallington's presence in Westminster, May 3, 1641, see Folger Library MS. V.a.436, p. 190.

the seventeenth century were limited in speed of transmission only by
the state of the existing technology. Letters sent by pack horse or cart
moved slowly, but messages were not to move much faster until the
employment of steam trains in the nineteenth century, a generation or
two before the telegraph and the wireless. Hence, Wallington was able
to correspond in the 1620s and 1630s with his clerical brother-in-law,
Livewell Rampaigne, whose pastoral livings were the remote Lincolnshire
parishes of Burton and Broxholme.[25] And while there is no evidence
that Wallington ever wrote to his other brother-in-law, Zachariah
Rampaigne, an Anglo-Irish planter, there is evidence that after
Zachariah's death at the hands of Brian Maguire's Irish troops in the
opening weeks of the Irish rebellion in October 1641 both Nehemiah
and Grace wrote to Zachariah's widow, Dorothy, to persuade her to
entrust their surviving nephew to the Wallingtons, who promised to take,
and subsequently did take, young Charles Rampaigne as an
apprentice.[26]

Wallington's correspondence was not limited to his immediate kin.
At some point during the 1630s Wallington formed a friendship with
a fellow Puritan, Francis Wilsmore of Nottingham. Wallington carefully
copied Wilsmore's anxious letters about his two sons whom Wallington
had helped to City apprenticeships and later, after the meeting of the
Long Parliament, equally anxious letters about the fate of the godly cause
and of his sons, now soldiers in the Parliamentary army. The
correspondence between these two kindred spirits evidently continued
until the untimely death of Wilsmore in 1643, when he was struck down
by a stray bullet fired by the Parliamentary garrison in Nottingham
castle.[27] In these years Wallington maintained contact with even more
distant friends. Letters were exchanged with Edward Brown, a former
neighbor in St. Leonard's Eastcheap and a fellow turner who had
emigrated to Ipswich in the Massachusetts Bay colony. Wallington
continued to correspond with his closest friend, James Cole of
Whitechapel, who had also emigrated in the middle years of that troubled
decade and had settled in Hartford, Connecticut. Their exchange of

[25] For Livewell Rampaigne's livings in Lincolnshire, see *Alumni Cantabrigienses. A
Biographical List of all Known Students, Graduates and Holders of Office at the University of
Cambridge, from the Earliest Times to 1900*, ed. John and J. A. Venn (4 vols, Cambridge
University Press, Cambridge, 1922–7), vol. III, p. 416.

[26] The letters to Dorothy Rampaigne are in BL, Sloane MS. 922, fos 155v–159v.

[27] *Ibid.*, fos 116r–17v, 120v–21v, 126v–28v.

letters, slowed by the many months it took for letters to pass back and forth across the Atlantic, continued at least until 1650.[28]

Both Wallington's literacy and his correspondence were heavily conditioned by his Puritanism. Puritanism, as a religion preeminently of the Book, required literacy of its adherents. Literacy permitted the godly adept to reinforce his peculiar form of religiosity by the continual reading of printed sermons and edifying tracts, and it permitted a religious minority to maintain a sense of community among its scattered members. Those whom Wallington seems to have written to with some regularity were all fellow saints: his brother-in-law, Livewell Rampaigne, until his death in the mid 1630s, Francis Wilsmore until his death in 1643, Edward Brown and James Cole across the Atlantic at least until 1650. In his letter book Wallington copied exemplary letters by such famous Puritan preachers as Edward Dering and Paul Baynes, letters not addressed to Wallington personally but evidently in circulation within the community of the godly.[29] Ideology also seems to have determined the inclusion of a letter by Thomas Weld, written from Boston, Massachusetts in 1633 and addressed to his former parishioners of Terling, Essex. The letter described Boston as a Puritan paradise in which, unlike London, 'the greater part are the better part,' and in which 'our ears are not beaten, nor the air filled with oaths, swearers and ranters, nor our eyes and ears vexed with the unclean conversations of the wicked.'[30] Wallington also included a letter to his neighbor, Captain Thomas Player, urging him to take on the onerous but godly task of a parish elder in the Fourth London Classis, the presbyterian system authorized by the Long Parliament and instituted in parts of London in late 1646. And there is another letter to a 'Goodman' Cox, an acquaintance who was a 'Prayer Book' Christian and whom Wallington urged for the sake of his soul to seek the spiritual nourishment provided by the sermons of the godly preachers.[31]

Literacy, the capacity to participate in the network of written communication formerly limited to the clerical and administrative élites, was in Wallington's case determined less by occupation or class than by an ideology based on the sacred Word that gave to its adherents a consuming interest in the fate of their co-religionists and of the godly

[28] *Ibid.*, fos 94r–107v, 173r–76v.
[29] *Ibid.*, fos 23r–30v, 52r–68v.
[30] *Ibid.*, fos 90r–93v.
[31] *Ibid.*, fos 153r–54v, 142r–44r.

cause in general. Hence, Wallington treasured and copied a letter by his nephew, John Bradshaw, who, as a seaman, had witnessed the last terrible stages of the siege of the Huguenot stronghold of La Rochelle, a siege the English fleet under the Duke of Buckingham had failed to lift.[32] The same preoccupation led Wallington to note the fortunes of Gustavus Adolphus, the Swedish Lion of the North, during the Thirty Years War and to fill a number of notebooks with news of the Long Parliament's efforts to bring about the long-awaited godly reformation. Later notebooks recorded the fortunes of the Parliamentary armies during the first Civil War.[33] The Parliamentary cause and the rising English commerce centered in the great port of London were evidently tightly connected, at least in the early 1640s, but as a small trader, Wallington was linked to this larger world not by economic interest but by ideology.[34] The world of which Wallington was aware beyond parish, neighborhood, and City was the world of an embattled Protestantism that stretched from the Palatinate on the Rhine in the East to Massachusetts and Connecticut in the West. By the 1650s the Navigation Acts testify to an awareness of the connection between Protestantism, empire, and commercial expansion, but this was a nexus that largely escaped Wallington's ken.

Perhaps nothing better illustrates the differing geographic perspectives of Nehemiah Wallington, London artisan, and Nehemiah Wallington, Puritan ideologue, than an incident that took place in the mid 1630s. For reasons never explained, James Cole, Nehemiah's close friend, became a bankrupt in the summer of 1634, fled the City to escape his creditors and sought refuge initially in the Puritan community of Ipswich in Suffolk. From there he wrote to his family and friends, acknowledging the moral ambiguity of his flight, admitting that he could not in consequence 'escape much reproach and much revilings,' but expressing the determination not

[32] *Ibid.*, fos 87r–89v.

[33] For Wallington's prayer for the success of Gustavus Adolphus, see GL, MS. 204, p. 493; for his notebooks on the Civil War period, see Folger Library MS. V.a.436, preface 'To the Christian Reader,' and BL, Additional MS. 21,935.

[34] For the complex relationships between the London mercantile community and the parliamentary cause in the early 1640s, see Robert Ashton, *The English Civil War. Conservatism and Revolution 1603–1649* (Weidenfeld and Nicolson, London, 1978), pp. 85–97; Robert Ashton, *The City and the Court, 1603–1643* (Cambridge University Press, 1979); Robert Brenner, 'The Civil War Politics of London's Merchant Community,' *Past & Present*, 58 (1973), pp. 53–107; Valerie Pearl, *London and the Outbreak of the Puritan Revolution* (Oxford University Press, Oxford, 1961); and Leonard Hochberg, 'The English Civil War in Geographical Perspective,' *Journal of Interdisciplinary History*, 14 (1984), 729–50.

to return and face prison for debt until he was able to 'make them restitution.' Nehemiah's father wrote to him to urge his return, for 'the chief care of a child of God is and must be still to glorify God in the place and calling wherein God set him' – a conception of 'place and calling' that went far beyond the usual vocational meaning of the term. When letters failed to move Cole to return, Nehemiah set out to visit him. Nehemiah describes quite matter-of-factly his setting out from London down river to Woolwich, where he took ship for Harwich on the coast of Essex, where he arrived at midnight. He then took a small boat up the River Orwell to Ipswich where he disembarked 'near two o'clock on the Lord's day in the morning,' found 'my brother Mr. Cole and went into the field and conferred together.' Never very confident in his own powers of persuasion at the best of times, Wallington sought reinforcement and urged Cole to seek the advice of Samuel Ward, the well-known Puritan town lecturer. Like the rest of the godly community, Ward evidently advised Cole to return home, 'so betimes on Monday morning we set forth on foot from Ipswich toward London and scarce rested till I was there, my brother Cole parted from me at Elton [Eltham] and went to Barking till his wife came to him, but I went home and upon Tuesday morning at five o'clock I was in my chamber by my wife's bedside very weary.' It seems evident that, although he never mentions having been there before, Wallington was familiar with the passage to Ipswich, knew where to take ship at Woolwich beyond the Pool of London, and knew where to tranship at Harwich for the journey up the Orwell. The way back by land must also have been familiar in part, for it lay through Colchester and was the same road he had traversed when he had run away from home as a young man some fifteen or so years earlier.

Cole did not remain long in Barking, and Warwick, where he next sought refuge, was evidently unfamiliar territory. For from there Cole wrote to Wallington in evident surprise that 'with us where I do now sojourn there be two congregations that is in two great men's hands, where is neither crosses, nor surplices, nor kneeling at the Sacrament, nor the Book of Common Prayer, nor any other behavior but reading the Word, singing the Psalms, prayer before and after sermon with catechism, which I did think it had not been in any congregation in the kingdom.' One of the 'great men' was undoubtedly Robert Greville, the second Lord Brooke, and the other may well have been William Fiennes, Lord Say and Sele, for shortly after writing to Nehemiah, Cole wrote to his wife that 'my Lords' desire is to employ me in

New England,' and he was shortly off to the Say-Brooke plantation in Connecticut.[35]

It seems evident that East Anglia – Harwich, Ipswich, and the Colchester road – were familiar even to a London tradesman who normally never travelled so far in the way of business, but who evidently knew how to travel into those parts both by sea and by road. Although Warwick was not much farther from London than Ipswich – about 90 miles northwest of London by road through Oxford and Banbury, compared to 70 miles to Ipswich – Warwick was not within the main trading system of the City. Essex and East Anglia supplied the metropolis with cereals and cloth and even its turners with rush-seated chairs made in Colchester.[36] Warwick on the Avon, although connected by road to London, looked southwest down the Avon valley to Tewksbury, the Severn river, Gloucester, and the port of Bristol. Although it was the county town of Warwickshire, its market was of little more than local importance.[37] Lords Brooke and Say were as committed to colonial plantation and empire as Robert Rich, the second Earl of Warwick, whose seat was in Essex, but the town of Warwick, Lord Brooke's seat, was at best a sleepy county town.[38] For Wallington and his friend Cole, Londoners as well as Puritans, Essex and Suffolk were familiar territory and Samuel Ward, the Puritan preacher of Ipswich, a known quantity. The Puritan connection, a message system that encompassed but was not limited to the rising world of commerce centered in London, enabled Cole to find his way to safety in Warwick, but neither he nor Wallington knew what to expect in that unfamiliar setting. As an artisan, Wallington's world was confined to parish and neighborhood, a subset of the bustling metropolis of London. As a Londoner, Wallington was familiar with that principal artery of London's economic influence that ran up the east coast of Essex and East Anglia. But Puritanism and the literacy that gave even an artisan

[35] BL, Sloane MS. 922, fos 94r–98v.

[36] J. A. Chartres, *Internal Trade in England 1500–1700* (Macmillan, London, 1977), pp. 14–25, 27–8.

[37] A. L. Beier, 'The Social Problems of an Elizabethan Country Town: Warwick, 1580–90,' in *Country Towns in Pre-industrial England*, ed. Peter Clark (Leicester University Press, Leicester, 1981), pp. 48–53.

[38] For Lords Brooke and Say and the second Earl of Warwick, see A. P. Newton, *The Colonizing Activities of the Early Puritans* (Yale University Press, New Haven, 1914), pp. 64–7, 83–4; William Hunt, *The Puritan Moment. The Coming of Revolution in an English County* (Harvard University Press, Cambridge, Mass., 1983), pp. 161–6, 263–6.

access not only to the Bible but to the Puritan message system opened up a much wider world that stretched from the remote reaches of Lincolnshire to Massachusetts and included Nottingham and Warwick, important for their godly communities if not for their trade with the powerful metropolis.

5

The Scribe-Ethnographer, Pierre Prion of Aubais

EMMANUEL LEROI LADURIE *AND*
OREST RANUM

Two Frances? Seen with the hindsight of the late twentieth century, it is evident that across the centuries, at least down to World War I, an agrarian and village economy, society, and culture lived cheek by jowl with a commercial, urban, and cosmopolitan society and culture in the hexagon that is France. The hypothesis of two distinct Frances tempts anyone who has sought to understand the French in some more fundamental way than by merely recounting the surface change of political regimes.

The France of wheat fields, vines, olive groves, and pastures certainly exists, and has existed for centuries. Its families and communities have sought to raise all the food needed for life and have hoped to have a surplus after paying tithes, rents, and taxes.

The France of Paris, the provincial capitals, and Marseilles, with their squares of high-built merchant houses and markets, also exists, and has existed for centuries. Networks of merchants have traversed the realm, Europe, and the colonial empires to buy and sell raw materials, manufactured goods, and exotic products. Artisan communities long formed the support structure for these mercantile elites, for whom money itself was the principal product to be hoarded, bought and sold.

Nuances and exceptions immediately come to mind to shade the bright contrast in the peasant–merchant, rural–urban dichotomy. Artisans drew

This contribution first appeared as Emmanuel LeRoi Ladurie and Orest Ranum *Pierre Prion Scribe* (Paris, 1985).

on rural sources for their leather, wood, and wool; farmers added to their income by spinning and weaving cloth that would be sold in town; and rich merchants almost invariably invested in rural property, which brought them immediately into contact with the rural population. But these nuances and exceptions are not the heart of the matter. No one would deny that there was frequent and steady contact of goods and foodstuffs between the two Frances. The flow of rural jobless youths into the city in search of jobs also tempered the strictly urban character of city life. The value of Edward Fox's concept of the two Frances lies elsewhere.

The economic and geographic delineations of the two Frances spawned two richly developed, variegated, and quite autonomous social realities and cultures. Exchange does not necessarily bring about a sharing of values, aims, and perspectives. In fact, quite the opposite may result. The social distances that separated the two Frances were not only nourished by economic and geographic conditions; over the centuries they also sometimes prompted deep feelings of misunderstanding, hostility, and repugnance. For the rural French, the townspeople were often synonomous with fraudulent cheats who tricked anyone they could in purchasing wheat or wine, or selling merchandise of inferior quality at high prices. And for the townspeople the rural French were ignorant, stubborn, sometimes seemingly beastly people who could not be trusted. What is particularly interesting, however, is not the analysis of how rural and urban perspectives differed when in direct *ad hominem* confrontation. The deeper cultural phenomenon of being literally unable to perceive the 'other' is still more significant. Did this form of cultural blindness exist? Here, we explore this question and offer some evidence that it did, as refracted in autobiographies in the eighteenth century.

The jotting down of personal observations and experiences occurred very rarely among artisan and peasant social groups, and yet at these levels of the population the evidence must be found for the study of cultural perspectives and blindness. The recent publication of the autobiography of the Parisian artisan glazier, Ménétra, offers a unique insight into popular urban attitudes during the late eighteenth century.[1] As a young skilled artisan Ménétra made several extensive trips around France, working along the way. The cabarets, especially those kept by housemotherly wives of artisan glaziers or their relatives, are noted here

[1] *Journal de ma Vie*, ed. Daniel Roche (Montalba, Paris, 1982).

and there. Ménétra even fell in love with a Huguenot widow down in the south, and he expressed joy at living with her for a few days in the *délices* of her country place. But never once in all the minute detail about his work and travels did peasant society and culture come into his purview. Ménétra was Parisian, and he noted that others remarked his Parisian accent. Although often destitute, lost, and waylaid by bandits on the terrible roads and rivers of eighteenth-century France, his only perspective remains focused on the cities he visits. Ménétra loved Paris, knew his neighborhood, and reveled in walking and drinking all over it with his fellow artisan companions. Ménétra was so *urban* that while he traveled and no doubt saw and spoke with the 'other France' he was entirely blind to it. Further research may well bring to light autobiographies of other artisans who had a more qualified urban perspective than Ménétra, but the 'thick description' of urban France by the man of the people, Ménétra, will always be a powerful confirmation of the hypothesis that born city dwellers who lived in artisan communities were culturally blind to life on the land.

What of the perspective of the rural French on city life? Here again it is difficult to unearth sources that are ethnographic in a deeply personal way. The more literary traveler, educated priest, or nobleman must be avoided. His education has exposed him to any one of several literary tropes – the most prevalent derived from Vergil's *Georgics* – that fix their gaze in the direction of the bucolic country and the vice-ridden city. Only recently, however, has the manuscript of a mid-eighteenth century obscure servant and copyist from southern France been unearthed and published. Pierre Prion traveled widely and had several extended stays in the capital, but the perspective of the modest boy born in remote, isolated Réquista, the province of Rouergue, remains southern and small-town. Let us explore Prion's life through his autobiography in order to elucidate how he perceived the geographic and social worlds around him.

Though the author of several historical compilations and a lengthy autobiography, Pierre Prion made no claims, at least directly, to be a man of letters. he traveled around southern France, and even made trips to the north, on foot, on a donkey's back, and by coach and barge.

Prion's upright character and solid elementary education started him toward developing familiarity with many more things than might usually be expected of someone who had no secondary education. Still, partly because of his attitude and sense of place in society, Prion remained unaware of, and even ignorant of, many areas of learning. If we are to believe him, he lacked a high degree of intelligence, but this may have been a pose or genuine modesty.

From May, 1712, he lived in Aubais, in the Vaunage country, now in the Gard department, not far from Nîmes. He lived in the chateau, and his principal duty was to copy manuscripts for the *châtelain*. In addition, Prion was asked to do various other chores, including the supervision of the demolition of part of the village to make way for a new wing on the chateau, the construction of that wing, the supervision of the wine cellar and olive harvesting, and even cooking for the Marquis of Aubais, who spent his time doing research on the history of his family and locality. In 1759, the year when Prion stopped writing his autobiography, he was still living in Aubais castle, but his stay there had been interrupted frequently by trips to Paris, Savoy, Guienne, Catalonia, and Provence.

Born in Réquista on 11 October, 1687, in what was called the province of Rouergue before the French Revolution, and what is now the Aveyron department, Prion's godparents were a blacksmith and the wife of a prosperous farmer. His father, Etienne Prion, was a royal notary in Réquista. A distant relative had served in Marshal de Gassion's army, and an uncle was an activist parish priest who sought to convert the Huguenots, and who ended his career with the high rank of canon.

Pierre Prion was born at the end of the grape harvest – 'bare-headed and without a caul' – a sure sign that he would never become rich. Still, as a child in a notarial family, Prion would be familiar with some wealth and education, though it would be easy to exaggerate both for notaries in Rouergue in the eighteenth century.

During the seven years of some type of schooling, Prion learned the rudiments of grammar and arithmetic from a M. Valette, teacher, phrase-maker, and great pupil-punisher who was 'brusque, violent, and more dangerous than Emperor Charles V's giant – beating children with scourges, a big club, and a whip, until the blood flowed'. Valette appears to have trained Prion well, for once the boy needed a job he could become a copyist or hired secretary right away without further training. At the age of eleven Pierre Prion participated in the battles organized among the forty pupils of his class. He divided the group into two bands that would fight one another. His education in reading and writing placed Prion in a slightly higher echelon in local society, for the Rouergue of his day still contained many who were illiterate among the lowest ranking social groups. As a child Prion visited both Rodez and Albi, the one being the center and the other the gateway to the province of his birth.

In spite of the boy's resistance his father placed him to work out of the house when he reached the age of twelve, first copying for a lawyer, and then for a judge who lived in his town. These legal professionals worked for the seigneurial judge of the County of Verdalle, seated in Réquista. In the next year, 1700–1, a short stay in Toulouse working for a lawyer displeased him so strongly that he returned home. When about fourteen, Prion spent some time as a shepherd and fruit harvester, but he barely alludes to these activities, though we can imagine him carrying a shepherd's crook and having a knapsack on his shoulders. As a shepherd he witnessed the sun's eclipse in 1706, and sought first to calm down his flock, and then also the credulous neighbors in Réquista who had gathered in terror on the public square, convinced that the end of the world was upon them.

It appears that Prion lost his father and mother at almost the same time. His father's will bequeathed his property to a sister, Pierre Prion's aunt, who unambiguously turned over the entire estate to her niece, Pierre's sister. Thus the four boys including our author, were left entirely disinherited. In acting in this way the aunt no doubt confirmed her own preference, but she in no way violated the categorical and imperious Roman law of inheritance in force in Rouergue, as manifested in the king's highest court in the region, the Parlement of Toulouse. Roman law sustains a testator who wishes to favor only one child, male or female, while leaving the other children nothing.

The four brothers were left with only one thing to do: they left the family house in Réquista. In fact they may have been thrown out *in manu militari* by their own sister and aunt. A younger brother 'croaked' in 1712. A still younger brother, in a typical Rouerguat effort to find a job, went down into Languedoc, where he learned to be a cobbler, and then returned north to marry. The couple died in the terrible year 1746. The youngest brother, Raymond, married, but had no children. The sister-heiress, Marguerite, died in 1737, as did her husband. The harsh reality was that the sons had no choice but to set out to look for work, and our author did so along with his brothers.

As the servant boy of the Abbot Vernet in Coupiac he cooked, made the bed, tended the horse, chopped firewood, and collected the tithe tax in grain. The amount of wine provided by the abbot to his young valet seemed appropriate, but the cooking was middling at best. The abbot was a great drinker and arguer himself, but he was not without his good qualities. He gave food to the limit of his budget to the starving migrants who came his way during the famine of 1709. Prion recorded his impressions of that terrible winter, particularly of the aged dressed in rags, and the children that he helped to bury – 'their composure as beautiful as that of the angels', and their mouths sometimes still full of the grass that they had tried to chew up as they attempted to survive the terrible famine.

Since there was nothing to keep him in his home country, Prion set out in 1710 along the traditional itinerary of migrants from Rouergue. He walked down the steep Pas de l'Escalette toward the Mediterranean on the way toward the vaguely mentioned Lodève and Montpellier. A detachment of royal troops, in need of more men because of the War of the Spanish Succession, captured him and impressed him into the army. In the town of Pellissanne he managed to desert his military captors by hiding in the steeple of a local church. Under cover of the night he climbed over the ramparts of the town with the help of someone there whom Prion did not know. He lost almost all his clothes in this escapade.

In the spring of 1711, Prion went to Arles, where he managed to enter the service of the Marquis of Saint-Véran, but later in the same year he returned home to Rouergue, not far from the Roquefort caves (which are still used to age the cheese), to begin work for the Marquis of Saint-Véran-Mélac. After being the unwilling witness to a killing in a duel, Prion decided again to leave Rouergue in the direction of Montpellier. Thanks to Saint-Véran's good offices, Prion found work as a copyist for the Marquis of Aubais in 1712, the employment he was to keep for the rest of his life. The Marquis was virtually the same age as Prion, married, and proud of his Italian aristocratic lineage in the Baschi family. Though nominally Catholic, both the Marquis and his wife had Huguenot ancestors and were tolerant of those on their estates and in their social orbit who still held heretical doctrines. The Marquis was a cultivated man, and there is little doubt that he appreciated the talents of his copyist, Prion.

Employment stability does not necessarily mean staying in one place. One of Prion's principal tasks in his youthful years was to accompany his master on his research jaunts. In 1712 they went off to Provence. Prion visited Manosque as well, where the natives were still talking in fearful tones about the earthquake that had occurred the year before.

The strong anti-Protestant sentiments in Provence also impressed Prion, as did their almost joyful willingness to rebel in defense of the local principal court, the parlement. In Aix-en-Provence he noted that there were two leaders of the local youth bands: the 'king of the lawyers', who had the young clerks and prosecutors as a following; and the 'prince of love', who presided over the sporting of the young nobles. Later, in Avignon, Prion addressed doggerel verses to the inkeeper's wife, who charmed him. From there he accompanied his master to Savoy, where the Marquis took the waters at Aix-les-Bains. They then returned south via Lyon. In that city Prion was 'shaken down' by the inkeeper's wife, who took his money at 50 per cent of its value. The ride down the Rhone that followed occurred in a cabin boat, in the company of a colonel, who had brought his valets and horses on board with him. From the water's edge the customs officers fired shots at them – real bullets from muskets. Prion dropped flat on his stomach in the bottom of the barge, and got off at Viviers, to the south. After observing some strange goings-on by what were perhaps Huguenot convulsionaries (1713), whom Prion calls 'parpaillots', and their competitors, some Sulpician priests, he finally made it back to Aubais by way of Bourg-Saint-Andéol, where he found commoner women inclined to speak in dialect and the ladies in French. In Uzès Prion waxed eloquent about the exotic underclothing worn by both the local males and females under their trousers and dresses to shield them from the mistral.

The following year, and in mid-winter, Prion set off again from the Gard region for Paris, and on foot. He there joined the Marquis of Aubais, who had come by coach. On the trip Prion narrowly missed being impressed into the army for a second time after passing through the papal territory around Avignon, and after some striking eating and dancing episodes. On the Tarare coast Prion feared he would freeze to death, which is what happened to a young pharmacist who was making the trip with him – killed outright by the cold. Prion pulled himself through, he believed, by a judicious use of the brandy flask that he took with him wherever he traveled. At Roanne he climbed into a boat on the Loire with fifteen other people, one of whom was a swarthy Indian. Each passenger had to row in turn, fights occurred, and the Indian came down with diarrhea as a result of having drunk the river water. Leaving their boat at Briare, the little group visited the chateau of Fontainebleau on their way to Paris.

In the capital, Prion drank beer for the first time, and concluded that it was washwater. He was also robbed by the 'cartouchiens', the adepts of the famous bandit Cartouche. On a visit to Versailles Prion reflected on the sunset of the Sun King's long reign and observed the magnificent arrivals of the ambassadors of Venice and Savoy. Later that evening he saw the brilliant spectacle of fireworks in honor of the Peace of Utrecht.

This trip to Paris was followed by an uneventful return to Aubais, and six years of copying old papers without interruption, in the chateau, in his tiny garret room. In 1720 Prion described the distant but real effects of the plague in Marseille. The panic that occurred in Aubais was not followed by an outbreak of disease. The troops stationed along the border between Languedoc and Provence to prevent persons from Provence from leaving may have helped contain the disease. Of all the regions to the west only the Gévaudan suffered some epidemic, but fear remained strong everywhere. Women in Aubais undertook various preventatives in almost feverish activity. They rubbed themselves with garlic, ceaselessly swept the streets, burned the horns of bulls, and placed toads in baskets, believing they would drink up the infectious venom as it spread. The men posted themselves on the hastily built, mortarless walls around the town that the municipal elite – consuls, seigneurial judge, and court clerk (Prion) – had had built around the village.

Though only a propertyless immigrant, Prion climbed up to the rank of notability in Aubais. His learning as a copyist brought him selection as village secretary, and in this capacity he wrote out the health certificates that permitted villagers to leave the town despite the quarantine prompted by the plague in Marseille. Prion let a young woman, presumably quite attractive, out to visit other communities in the region, because she was certified as uninfected by plague. In 1722 another plague outbreak prompted the Marquis and his copyist to go down to Perpignan. There the picayune manners of the Catalans prompted unfavorable observations by our author.

Moving up to the Albigeois region, Prion copied manuscripts about the wars of religion for his master. They stayed at Brassac, in the residence of a judge from Toulouse. Prion observed that the local country people raised ducks and lived on corn bread. And even well-born women wore wooden shoes. These ladies spoke a sort of half French, and the churchmen a half Latin. In Toulouse itself, a city full of pedants and monks, Prion admired the Midi Canal that joins the Mediterranean and Atlantic, and he claims to have submitted some verses in a competition for the poetry prize of the Jeux Floraux. By May 1722 he was in Gascony, in the chateau of Esclignac, where the rats ate part of his trousers. This time he made the trip to Paris in the company of various noble families who were going up the western side of France. In June 1722 Prion started out by boat on the Garonne toward Agen, by Bordeaux, reaching Jonzac. Not withstanding his pro-papal convictions, he observed the incontrovertible evidence of courtesy among the Huguenots.

By this time Prion had become the trusted servant of the Marquis, and this new trip was made in more comfortable ways than the preceding ones. Via Poitiers Prion reached the Vienne River, which he crossed at Châtellerault. There the ladies spoke good French, and they did not wear wooden shoes.

As an amateur ethnographer and tourist curious about people and places, Prion took time out to visit the celebrated battlefields of the Middle Ages and the seventeenth century. He also saw sacred trees that were reputed to cure the insane. As he and the other travelers came along the Loire, they saw the loading docks and the cave dwellings or troglodyte houses in the Amboise area. Via Tours, Etampes, and the Hurepoix region Prion reached Paris in late June 1722. He observed the insane in the Bicêtre Hospital, and the astronomical observatory with its portrait of Copernicus. Finally, after reading up on the subject and participating in debates on astronomy in Aubais, Prion decided in favor of Copernicus's heliocentric theories. He also expressed curiosity about the attitudes of Parisians toward women, particularly those in the guilds of washerwomen and sewers, and he noted the unpopularity of the former finance minister and sometime wizard with money, John Law, as it came to be expressed in typical anti-British feeling.

On 26 August Prion started back toward the south again, on his master's orders, traveling this time by coach or on horseback. These comforts certainly confirmed his rise in the hierarchy of the Marquis's domestic servants. In Castres, a town with a large Protestant community, some Jansenists, and 'no Free-Masons', he undertook the copying of old books and the compilations of various inventories, all of which irritated him because they included so many grammatical errors.

After finally returning to Aubais, he did not budge for the next ten years. In 1730, when Prion was forty-three, the Marquis shifted him away from his copying in order to have him supervise the masons and laborers who were rebuilding the chateau in a more grand and modern style. They built a drawbridge, new wings, a walled grove of trees, a library, and a stable. In order to carry out all these projects forty houses and a part of a cemetery had to be pulled down, which prompted strong protest from the other villagers. A riot developed that Prion says had an inclination to kill him. And as if this were not enough, the workers laid a trap for him that might have killed him in an 'accident' of rocks placed to fall on him. All this did not impede Prion, the demanding supervisor, from continuing the work, and acquiring the muscles and calluses that only hard labor brings. Prion loaded sand carts and drove the beasts that pulled them; he supervised the harvesting of olives, the replanting of grape vines, and the harvesting of grain. In order to undermine the hatred of the villagers he restored an isolated chapel that had fallen into ruins. While regaining the good graces of the neighbors by such activities, he nonetheless harbored bitterness toward them because of their pride and insulting manners. He characterized the Languedocians as extremely susceptible to offence; hence one had always to take off one's hat when speaking to them, even if they were only common soldiers, lackies, or peasants.

In 1732 Prion had the very special honor of conducting the chatelain's seven-year-old daughter, Mademoiselle de Marissargues, to the remote convent of Montfleury in Grenoble. The lovable child had to spend some time there as a resident in order to study. Upon arriving in Grenoble she, her two servants, and Prion stayed at the Coupe d'Or, the local first-class inn. Then there occurred the formal reception of the girl into the convent and cloisters of Montfleury. Forty nuns constituted the elite of that community, most of them of noble origin from the Dauphiné and close by. Each nun had her own 'stove' for cooking, and two chambermaids to attend them. There were eighteen residents en pension, one of whom was little Marissargues.

On the return trip the flask of brandy came in handy in the usual way when two servant women and Prion got shut up in a light carriage in a blinding downpour. The following summer (1733) a second trip to Grenoble was required to pick up the girl, and this time the Marquise accompanied Prion to visit her daughter. Prion was charged with distributing generous gratuities wherever the noble lady went – a still more evident sign of his own rank in the household.

While on this trip Prion went off to visit the great Carthusian monastery – the Grande Chartreuse – nearby. He recorded his visit in detail, and as usual, remarked on the quality of the local wines served. A friendly encounter with the valet of the superior-general permitted him a deeper observation of the community of silent monks and the brothers who served them, and who also served as shepherds for the abbey's cattle herds. Prion noted a bit of local folklore – the angel that brought food to St Bruno and his companions high up in the mountains, as they built the first great Carthusian monastery in the eleventh century. Indeed, this hagiographic belief about Bruno was widespread. As a visitor Prion was given what we have come to think of as a Breton-style closet bed in which he was locked up for the night, a rather terrifying experience.

Indeed, during this fearful night of being locked into a bed an abrupt change occurred in the way he was writing about his own life. In the first part, written entirely in 1743–4, he wrote as if all the events described confirmed his horoscope, supposedly written by the notary in Aubais, Valz, in 1687, the year of Prion's birth. This part, as well a horoscope might be, is written in the future tense and in the third person singular, for example, 'Prion will do such and such.' Suddenly, in one paragraph, the writing slips to the first person singular and the past definite tense, for example, 'I went straight to the church, I said goodbye to the valet.'

Having survived a very disagreeable encounter with two wolves up near the Chartreuse, Prion, who was still the chateau scribe, took up teaching a chambermaid to read in at least four lessons a day. She had come from a region further west of Languedoc, like many other servants in the household. The lessons ended in a noisy quarrel between teacher and pupil. Was Prion accused of having sought to seduce his pupil? Whatever happened, he was ostracized by the rest of the servants, including those previously friendly to him. The Marquise, who spoke in the familiar *tu* form to him, intervened to patch up the quarrel.

Since the Marquis and, more important, his cook, were off in Paris when a group of unannounced noble guests fell upon the chateau, Prion assumed the duties of cook and supervisor of the kitchen servants. With a napkin artfully wrapped around his head and a knife stuck in his belt, he set about making the meal. Later in his career he was to become his master's wine steward.

Thus it is as a jack-of-all trades, or more accurately, a complete man, that we meet Prion the traveler, writer, thinker, horseman, architect and mason, farmer, cook, and even Enlightenment figure in the broad, non-Voltairian sense of that term. He was also a devout Catholic, a believer in Copernican heliocentrism, and a learned worthy who was familiar with the history of many times and places in France. In some ways he may be taken as representative of an unknown and unstudied group of village thinkers in the eighteenth century. Nobles, high ranking servants in their chateaux, rural magistrates, clerks, and parish priests like Abbé Fabre – that great Languedocian writer of the early modern centuries, and for a time the vicar to the priest of Aubais – constituted an elite of sorts. It was through such men as Fabre and Prion that elite culture from the century of Louis XIV, and perhaps some of that of his successor, Louis XV, was refracted or in some sense filtered into rural and small-town society.

From just this period of his life, that is the 1730s, the beginning of the personal reign of Louis XV, Prion became interested in the manners and customs of his neighbors, the Aubais villagers. Their social and cultural life was to be the principal subject of the second part of his work, the still unpublished *Chronologiette*. With an ethnographer's eye he recorded details of everyday life that very few of his contemporaries 'saw' or took the trouble to record. For example, he noted that at meal times the men in the region ate sitting at their tables, while the women ate on their balconies in the summer or in the corner of the fireplaces in the winter. In other words, couples did not eat together. The Marquis's servants, by contrast, imitated their noble master by dining together, not differentiated by sex. Each formed, in a kind of bourgeois style, a common table of male servants on one side, and female servants and chambermaids on the other, all in the great kitchen of the chateau.

Events in the village and in the countryside around it also attracted Prion's attention. He was called upon to draw up the legal record of a bloodless *cruentation*. A shepherd from the Gévaudan region (yet another migrant worker from a mountainous region) was accused of murdering a local herd boy. The local seigneurial justice – or as Prion calls it, not without a touch of irony, the 'famous judicial tribunal of Aubais' – consisting of a judge, prosecutor, clerk, and marshal, forced the accused shepherd to spread himself out on top of the boy's corpse in order to try to discern whether he was innocent of the crime. It was believed that the color of the face of the accused would change in the presence of the deceased. After this 'trial' the accused was put in the seigneurial prison, having had the buttons and laces of his breeches cut off, the perennial precaution against escape. Later the accused would be judged innocent by a royal court in Nîmes, after which he fled back up into his native province without returning to Aubais to collect his pay.

In 1738 Prion reflected without nostalgia on what he calls his life of slavery and bondage, of happy submission and poverty. Slaves never get rich, he says, without a tone of rebelliousness. As the eldest son of a notary, he considered himself *déclassé* because he had been deprived of his inheritance. A devout Catholic, Prion was not at all superstitious. He was not an ardent pilgrim either. He kept his distance from Jansenism as if it were a plague and signed the statement that rejected its tenets. Thus, Prion accepted his mediocre social condition with a sense of fate, with humor, and with occasional good cheer. He did not chafe against his social decline from being a son of a low-ranking, modestly fortunate family to being a high-ranking domestic servant. Should we feel sorry for him? The answer is unclear.

With his mania for statistics, Prion counted up all the Marquis's servants of every rank that had worked with him in his forty-seven years in the chateau. There were exactly 288: an average turnover of sixty-one per decade. The greatest number came from the low-ranking servants – the lackies and chambermaids. This evidence is important for social history. The paternalism of the nobility – much discussed by historians – did not extend very far down among their servants. The constant change among the low-ranking servants was the rule in the great seigneurial households of the past. The low wages in Languedoc in the eighteenth century permitted the large-scale employers to sustain, if only marginally and momentarily, hundreds of persons spread out over several decades. Prion, however, did not belong to this large floating group. The nucleus of privileged servants was small, and thanks to their intelligence, docility, and talent they became indispensable to the master and mistress of the household. These privileged servants benefited from stable employment, a de facto permanency in the household.

While Prion's father had been a notary, he was a secretary, the occupation of writing not being all that different in the two cases. What differentiated them was the shift from his father's ownership of a small amount of capital in the office of notary to his own meager salary in money, room, and board. In several respects Prion's example illustrates what occurred in the eighteenth century: the number of workers on salary tended to increase. Prion may have been somewhat degraded socially, but because of his personal vitality he came to enjoy a low-level niche in society that was not entirely lacking in comfort and rewards in the form of self-esteem.

In turning back to the chronological account of Prion in 1738, the striking event was his departure for Paris, his last trip to the capital. He crossed the Rhone at Pont St Esprit, a habitual crossing place for

travelers and something of a 'tourist' center. He traversed the Comtat
Venaissin – the papal territory encircling Avignon from south to north –
and saw Valence, with its decadent university. The doctorate was no
longer awarded at discount fees in Prion's day. The fine wines of the
region had a way of mitigating life's difficulties, and thus for our traveler
the region was to be 'remembered for well-balanced people with good
taste'.

Once in the Dauphiné, Prion mounted a fat donkey that carried him
all the way to the Guillotière suburb of Lyon. Then via Tarare, Moulins,
Nevers, and Montargis he reached Paris, and as usual he was very much
inclined to count everything that seemed curious and particularly
Parisian. And on this visit he was robbed by an alcoholic Norman
innkeeper. Near the gates of the Louvre, Prion again imbibed beer in
the summer season, and this time was attacked by two soldiers of the
watch, with the lady tavernkeeper as the ruffians' accomplice. The
summer heat of 1738 became so intense that Prion finally began to drink
Seine water, since he lacked the money to buy wine. The bacteria in
the water gave him a terrible case of diarrhea. Soon after recovering
he took up with a peasant girl born in or near Rodez, the capital of his
native province. She worked as a servant for a tyrannical Parisian woman.
Prion even received a marriage proposal through the good offices of an
innkeeper, but he peremptorily declined on anti-feminist pretexts and
out of deep feelings of poverty.

Did he keep a diary in this period – out of which he would write the
autobiography in 1747? Probably. On folio 107 of the manuscript he
wrote: 'Having *today* taken leave of the city of Paris in order to return
to Aubais . . .' – which strongly suggests an excerpt from a diary.

After attending the festivities that Louis XV offered on the occasion
of the marriage of Madame de France with the Spanish heir-apparent,
Prion set out for Languedoc by the typical route through Champagne,
Burgundy, then Sens, Joigny, Chalon-sur-Saône, Mâcon, and Lyon.
Among the descriptions of cities that he made on this trip that for
Villefranche-sur-Saône merits summary. Prion mentioned that it was
a city without noble residents, which was exceptional for cities in the
eighteenth century, since most were controlled by well-to-do notables
and nobles. And Prion noted the twelfth-century seigneurial privilege
of giving husbands the right to beat their wives until the blood flowed.
As if this were not enough medieval custom, he also recorded that the
inhabitants with little or no money had the right to harvest grain wherever

they wished, but only on the condition that they take only the tenth sheaf. Was this, in fact, a survival of a communal custom from the Middle Ages?

Over the next five years (1740–4) Prion did little else but copy, or as he puts it, 'pounding notebook on notebook with writing as small as the foot of a fly on lines as tight as sardines packed into a crate'. He pulled together various manuscripts on the geography and history of the French monarchy from the earliest period of history for the Marquis. In this way the *Pièces Fugitives* were assembled on the history of Rouergue, Languedoc, the Cévennes region, and on Protestants. Out of the impetus to increase his income, and friendship, he took up teaching sons of the local notables and lesser bourgeois part time. Some of his pupils were to do very well for themselves later on as lawyers in Nîmes.

In 1744, at the age of 57, Prion completed his work on his autobiography. At the end he recapitulates the festive occasions he had witnessed, the coats of arms of noble houses with which he was familiar, the battles fought during his lifetime. He also inserted some interesting excerpts from his own 'fieldwork' – about the Huguenots for example, particularly on whether they were of the convulsionary type, and/or sincere devout Protestants from the isolated region in which they held clandestine prayer meetings.

He would carry on his duties of writing for about fifteen more years, until 1759, the year of his death. Thus, during the mature years of Louis XV's reign, Prion kept a regular and perhaps even daily journal – the *Chronologiette* of the events and customs of the village of Aubais, including life in the chateau. The specifically autobiographical features were relegated to second place, perhaps because his advancing age impeded travel. He scarcely left the village in his later life and observed only the community and the seigneury. His own self, his own destiny, seems to have interested him less than it did in the past. He noted, as something now quite personal, that in August–September 1744 he assumed a double responsibility, which revealed the Marquis's great confidence in him. On 3 August 1744 the keys to the chateau cellar were given to him, and then in September the responsibility for the Marquise's correspondence. Scarcely a year later Prion complained of an ache in a knee, perhaps from a boil or a swollen joint. Nine years later in 1754, the copyist, nearly seventy years old, suffered from an attack of apoplexy from which he also recovered, but only after having sweated so much that his shoes filled up with water.

Some time before his death, Prion lost control. His style and thought weakened in the last pages of his manuscript, and, in consequence, the purely autobiographical elements of the *Chronologiette* are marginal. Curiously, however, Prion mentions the existence of his 'spouse' and also his daughter, Angélique Prion. Until further research is done there is no proof of marriage. The ribald contexts in which his wife is mentioned raise doubts about her existence. Young Angélique may also have been only imaginary, or an illegitimate daughter, or perhaps simply a pretty girl from Rouergue, the daughter of a brother or cousin. Whatever she was, she occupied a soft spot in Prion's heart. Some passages from the *Chronologiette* reveal this affection, although the principal subject of that work is the seigneury and village of Aubais.

Prion offered a lengthy portrait of his master, Charles de Baschi, Marquis of Aubais (1686–1777), and his wife Dianne de Rozel, who was of Calvinist descent. They, in effect, tolerated the heresy of the Huguenots in some of the seigneurial villages. They had four children who survived infancy, Jean-Francois de Baschi, Marquis du Cayla, and three daughters, all of whom married noblemen from the region.

The Marquis was well educated and created a library in his chateau of at least 20,000 volumes. Immediately after his death it was sold. The other properties were considerable, though nowhere near as immense as some that belonged to the royal tax farmers. Charles de Baschi received 30,000 livres a year in income, which amounts to an estate of about a million in capital. Of this income, 8.500 livres came from the produce and rents of the fields, barns, vines, and sharecropped lands in Aubais and nearby, and 13,000 more from the Cayla, a superb estate in the Camargue where the Marquis kept numerous herds of horses and other livestock under the careful supervision of keepers and managers. The rest of his income came from rents on land located in various parts of France, but mostly in the south. Of his total annual income, the feudal dues, as strictly defined, amounted to only 387 livres! In other words, the seigneur Baschi d'Aubais was rich and influential from his land and from his seigneurial justice, which was conducted for him by the magistrate, Batifort.

As a historian and writer, the Marquis needed the inspiration that came from Paris. He 'went up' to the capital often. The trip from Aubais would take about twenty-two days. Altogether he spent several years in Paris, always accompanied by copyists and, of course, his lackies. Temperamental and playful, Madame la Marquise did not accompany her husband on his trips. She preferred to tour the south on her own. Late in life the old Marquis, a widower and over eighty, suffered occasional bouts of love-sickness over various women.

In the main, the household servants did not have secure employment, but Prion, by good fortune and talent, became a household fixture. Understandably, he mentions most frequently those other servants who had the same degree of employment security. These were also firmly entrenched in the aristocratic household. Rouaud, the principal secretary, held a position different from that of the 'linguists, librarians, geometers, and secretaries'. His wife, Madame Rouaud, or *de* Rouaud, as Prion mockingly refers to her because of her pretentious manners, was the intendant of the chateau. Indeed, the Rouauds and the maître d'hôtel, Bouchet, were rather prestigious persons on the local scene. Their children became part of the local notable elite without difficulty. The cooks, scullery boys, coachmen, lackies, chambermaids, grooms, and cleaners, not to mention Chaplin Coteron, gave a certain vitality to the massive residence. Indeed, the size of the residence was partly explained by the need to house all these servants here and there in the attics and cubbyholes to which each was assigned. The Marquise and her sons-in-law, their families, local and other nobles, bureaucrats from Nîmes, provincial officials, English and Scandinavian travelers, endless churchmen, and begging nuns, stopped by and were all put up in the chateau. All the guests admired the great staircase and, of course, the library. Protestant ministers also made clandestine visits, and they were not reported by the Marquis's Catholic servants. Whether out of fear of the Marquis, or whatever, they kept silent.

Bourgogne, the village priest, and his family with him, enjoyed a fair income. The vicars, however, changed often, and rarely had any money. Often made fun of by the richer, half-Protestant villagers, the vicars nonetheless carried on their roles. A real hermit also lived on the edge of town, in the St Nazaire chapel that Prion had rebuilt.

While the Marquis and the local clergy had higher rank in society than the commoners, the latter were sometimes not all that common. Judge Batifort and his family were well off. A certain fiscal prosecutor, not insignificantly named Gruvel-le-Paysan, brought cases before the seigneurial court presided over by Batifort. The duties of clerk of court were often carried out by Prion at the Marquis's request. Finally, there was also the surgeon (a Huguenot but nonetheless friendly with the clergy), a schoolmaster and a schoolmistress. Together these people made up the administrative and educated cadre of the village, the influential group in a population of from 800 to 1000 inhabitants. Despite La Bruyère's suggestion that the more educated classes abandoned the peasantry, it is clear from the example of Aubais that these educated and trained persons were important in enriching the cultural life of the villagers. Only one professional role was missing, that of the physician. There was one living in the nearby town of Sommières, close to Nîmes, but neither he nor others wished to venture residence in the 'obscure hole' that was Aubais. He came out only to bleed or to purge the high-born inhabitants of the village, the first of whom was Charles de Baschi himself.

While learned or scientific cultural elements were much stronger in the cities, they were not absent in the villages. The male children of the local judge and notary went off to study in Toulouse and Montpellier, and one of them became a lawyer in Nîmes – all signs of a certain openness toward professionalism and education beyond the three Rs. We have not only Prion's testimony, but also that of Abbé Fabre. The culture that they brought to rural society was precisely defined; it was proper and learned Catholicism in the sense that it rejected Protestant 'heresy', Jansenist deviations, and sacreligious innovation of the philosophic-Voltairian type. True, their education resulted in a distancing of this group from the folk customs and popular story-telling of the villagers, though there no doubt was some familiarity with them. The *Jean-l'ont-pris* by Fabre is a brilliant literary adaptation of a story in the Oc of Languedoc that had previously only been part of the oral literature of the Vaunage region.[2]

The Catholicism of Febre, and more especially of Prion, was open to influences of the Malebranchian theology that was influential in the Gallican Church at that time. Prion's beliefs includes Copernicus's thought, and above all that of Descartes. Scientific discovery was not rejected by all elements in the church. So, Copernicus and Descartes – but not Newton, Voltaire, and Fontenelle just yet. The best educated of the bona fide residents in the village were therefore behind the times, but just because they were not familiar with the latest expressions of eighteenth-century learning did not mean that they were unreceptive to the higher expressions of seventeenth-century learning, and rationalism in particular.

---

[2] See Emmanuel LeRoi Ladurie, *Love, Death and Money in the Pays d'Oc*, tr. Alan Sheridan (Braziller, New York, 1982).

Still, the educated villagers we have met so far were only partially representative of the educated culture as a whole, and this was largely the result of Louis XIV's discriminatory legislation. The elite was only recruited from among Catholics. The Huguenots were excluded from the educated milieu in the village, despite their constituting about half the population. The Huguenots were forced to stay with the strictly working occupations – artisanry, farming, shopkeeping – and they did well. In Aubais, as in Millau, the Calvinists were the richest among the villagers, or to put it more accurately, the least poor. With this village as something of a statistical sample, and a sample that is telling, it is evident that Max Weber's thesis that the Protestant ethic favors capitalism is confirmed in Aubais. Though now a fervent papist, the Marquis had not entirely forgotten the beliefs of his Protestant ancestors. He took Protestants under his wing, and they benefited from having a seigneur who was generous to them. Indeed, the Marquis let his estate managers take a slice from his revenues for themselves. An example was Delort, the general manager of the seigneury, who became very wealthy and who was Protestant. The principal valet of the chateau was also a Huguenot. Prion says that he had accused this man in a friendly way of being a republican, that is to say, a wordy protestor against the established social and religious ways of doing things. This did not mean, of course, that either the monarchy or the seigneurial order that reigned supreme in Aubais was threatened.

The economic activities of the village included raising grain crops, grapes, olives, and silkworms, and the making of woolen cloth. The last was one of the principal sources of dispute in the village. The farmers who were well off, those called *ménagers*, had their orchards and harvest watched by the village keeper. The local cloth-makers, who were all very small producers who owned little land, tended to steal from their richer neighbors' crops. This small transgression in proper behavior was a source of one of the principal divisions in the community.

What might be called the bourgeois or, more accurately, the petty bourgeois elite, consisting of wig-wearing males and ladies and dressing-gown-wearing damsels, held themselves as well as they could above the commoners. The commoners gave the impression of poverty but in fact were certainly better off than the destitute families that could be found in Rouergue.

A few community activities continued to attract various segments of the population despite religious differences. The principal ones were, of course, the *fêtes*, especially those which included marriages, and particularly ones that joined Catholics and Protestants. A marriage in one of the well-off families brought cavalcades and fireworks in which all the young people joined together. On occasion, if the newly weds declined to make a 'gift' to the youth group because they were old or tight with their money, there would typically be an uproar or black charivari in which poor boys and shepherds would also participate.

Let us return to the question of heresy. In the nineteenth century the Protestants in the region and in the nearby Cévennes isolated themselves as much as possible from Catholicism by withdrawing into what became their own counter-society. In the eighteenth century, if Prion can be trusted, the Protestants tried to maintain ties with their Catholic neighbors by organizing gala dinners that would take place at almost any hour of the day, including the morning. These social occasions pulled together the 'high society' of the region, which really consisted of the lesser notables from both religious communities in the village, well-off commoners, and the clergy. At these galas the Marquis's top domestic servants would be present, the priest and his vicar, the estate manager, the judge, the prosecutor (who was really a well-off peasant), their relatives and acquaintances, and their children, many of whom would eventually marry each other. The collective purging through liberal doses of Euzet mineral water also brought the same groups together, for another type of gala – one which turned on the elimination of foodstuffs instead of their consumption. And there were fishing, swimming, and, above all, hunting together, despite the seigneurial monopoly on game which was more or less enforced. A few ladies put up lotteries that entertained the locals. The schoolmaster put together religious plays with his best pupils as the actors and itinerant jugglers joining in. The Lenten carnival and spring love festivals, such as the dances around the Maypole, were also occasions for much feasting that filled the local clergy and commoners with food. On such occasions expressions of deference were given to the seigneur. Indeed, the undercurrent of animosity and protest were scarcely expressed in the carnival and Maypole festivals, but they did appear in the charivaris and in other little incidents in daily life. When the local youth group put together a special entertainment they sometimes worked up a special crop of silkworms to finance the occasion.

In early September the local festival centered on sports. Every age group was mobilized, and male–female rivalries came out in the races and competitions between children, men, boys, and women. The winners almost always belonged to the more well-to-do segment of Aubais society, referred to by the honorific title of *monsieur*, or at the minimum, *sieur*. The time of branding the bulls in the swampy Camargue with a hot iron was also a time for a wild but bloodless race. The skills of the commoner boys were recognized on these occasions as the large crowds of people came out of the valleys and hamlets to watch.

When we look for what would be defined later as delinquency or crime, in the general meanings of those terms as they might be applied to the behavior of individuals in a period which at least in theory was more strict than ours, it is interesting to note that sexual activity only rarely included rape. It ended much more frequently in premarital pregnancy, that is of children born before eight months of marriage, or in downright illegitimacy, that is to say, children born out of wedlock. Adultery seems not to have been widespread since it was contrary to family honor and feminine self-esteem. Prion, who was always after the tiniest bit of gossip, only mentioned one case of betrayal of the marriage bed, though he gives plenty of evidence of disputes within families. Drunkenness or, more accurately, heavy drinking, remained marginal in Aubais, as is always the case in the wine-producing Midi. By contrast, the petty theft of fruit and harvests constituted the customary revenge of the propertyless on their landed neighbors. The illegal traffic carried out by specialized dealers in contraband salt was not unknown in the village. Mandrin's tricks on the customs and tax officials produced reverberations throughout the Vaunage. Prion also noted numerous cases of assault and battery, and disturbances of the peace, poaching, and, finally, murder. Quarrelsome women took after each other by pulling off *coiffes* and tugging at each other's hair. Old disagreements often lurked beneath these incidents of violence, and, therefore, some Protestants settled accounts with their neighbors by violence in retaliation for the state and church oppression under which they lived.

Village politics, in the sense of communal participation, was rather intense, though it was regulated by the seigneurial judge, Batifort. The 'general assembly' of the notable inhabitants consisted of about thirty heads of households. Sometimes women were admitted. The meetings were infrequent. Whether elected or selected by co-option, the village council (in many respects like the municipal council in France today) carried out its labors under the leadership of two consuls, one a notable, the other a peasant, and occasionally even an illiterate one who also distinguished himself by covering his increasing baldness with a pretentious wig. By law the consuls had to be Catholic, which reduced the democratic representation in Aubais by about half. Royal taxes were lighter in Aubais than they had been in the past as a result of the improved conditions in the eighteenth century compared with what they had been a hundred years earlier. Protest in the village over taxes was infrequent in the eighteenth century. Noisy discontent turned instead on local religious, legal, and political matters – challenging the authority of the seigneurial judge and his clerk rather than daring to criticize the Marquis himself.

Little news reached the villagers from the world outside except for military battles, deaths, births, and marriages in the royal family, all of which were marked by appropriate celebrations improvised by the Aubaisians for the occasion. The Wars of the Austrian Succession and the Seven Years' War struck hard during 1744–59, the years covered by the *Chronologiette*. The royal army made its presence felt by requesting one or two militiamen from each village, a rather gentle but not easily accepted form of military service enforced at the time. There was no general conscription during the *ancien régime*. The officials whose duty it was to represent the intendant, the principal royal official in the province, rarely appeared in Aubais, but they did oversee the selection of men to serve in the militia.

Young men of both poor and well-off families eager to serve in the army were rather numerous, since it was a way of escaping the humdrum careers and occupations in the village. The mustering-in pay given to those who signed up provided the bait. One of the volunteers who had signed up under Louis XIV and had risen to the rank of officer returned after his year of service to an easy retirement in Aubais.

Religious activities were certainly a demanding but not a monopolistic part of community life. The priest was made fun of, but he nonetheless remained an arbiter in disputes. He was listened to and respected. The processions and ceremonies held to obtain bountiful crops were occasions when the whole Catholic population of the village filed by, like some gigantic caterpillar, by rank, headed by the clergy, magistrates, well-off commoners, and, as Prion says, 'peasantized' people, schoolboys, other boys, girls, and women. The rivalry between the priest and the hermit who lived at the Saint-Nazaire chapel was intense but difficult to elucidate from our source. The confraternity came together from time to time in the village church, joining the papist villagers, presided over by the priest, the prosecuting attorney with peasant origins, and the judge, the last two of whom were related. This organization administered the parish finances and supervised the ushers. In essence it constituted a sacred pendant to the municipal government that handled the secular affairs of the village. The faithful, including the parish poor, pressed the confraternity for specific things. During the Lenten season they demanded a preacher from outside the village who would give the number of homilies for which he had been paid.

The Protestants were the obscure other side of local society. In Aubais they had the Marquis's protection, but in the neighboring seigneuries, notably the seigneuries held by two ladies, Marquise de Galargues and Comtesse de Fontanes, the Calvinist vassals were continually harassed. In the sixteenth century and during the first half of the seventeenth century the Huguenots in Aubais remained tolerant of the Catholics in the village. The Catholics responded in a similar fashion even after they were given powers to oppress their 'heretical' neighbors by the Revocation of the Edict of Nantes. Relations between the two groups thus remained good, and on occasion even cordial. Nonetheless outbursts of some sort of 'fanaticism' inspired by the prophetic local traditions nourished in the Cévennes would come from the Protestant side from time to time down to 1750. The persecutions that emanated from the central government in Versailles were a pendant to these outbursts, and continued to have a negative effect on the little independent Protestant community in the region for which Aubais served as one of the centers. In 1746 Pastor Désubas, or 'de Juba' as he was called, was hanged. Prion cracked some jokes about this that were in bad taste. The years 1750–4 were particularly tense, since the lieutenant general of the province, the Duc de Richelieu, unleashed arrests, repression, executions, and forced rebaptizing upon the Protestants. In 1756 the Duc de Mirepoix, who replaced Richelieu, after a brief period of harshness turned to more gentle methods of repression. As early as 1757 the Protestants took heart and even became audacious in expressing their faith. The 1760s were ones of de facto toleration; official toleration came on the eve of the French Revolution.

The death of Prion in 1759 and that of the old Marquis in 1777 marked the end of an era on the local level. The tacit compromise that had held the communities together no longer seemed necessary. Just in this period the Huguenots ceased to suffer persecution, and hence they no longer needed seigneurial protection. The Marquis's heir came from the D'Urre family, which lost the support of Huguenots. Then the Batifort family, which had controlled the magistracy of the seigneury and had been Catholic, was thrown out of office by the D'Urre. As a result the Batiforts became leaders of a sort of pre-revolutionary Catholic opposition against the seigneury. Indeed, the Batiforts went so far as to call for a revolt against the seigneury – a revolt against the despot by the slaves. This divisive climate presaged the 1789 revolution, and it certainly would have irritated Prion, the admirer of Descartes who seems not to have read Rousseau. Or did he choose to ignore Rousseau? Aubais was to join the regions in rebellion, and things really became quite violent in the revolutionary decade. The chateau was set afire and badly burned in April 1792.

Prion's observations have given us evidence about life in a large village prior to the Revolution. Poverty did not bear down heavily on the inhabitants. While it is important to avoid evoking Aubais as some sort of perfect place to live, it is clear that the poor were able to maintain some self-esteem and a positive attitude, and to participate in the work, crimes, village holidays, and even the intense moments of piety that came forth occasionally from the two religious communities.

Prion differed markedly from his near contemporaries who also came from the lower classes and who wrote. Jamerey-Duval was more of a questioning philosopher, Rétif more of a socialist-leaning Jansenist and freethinker, and Ménétra more of a sex maniac who also had revolutionary inclinations. Prion, by contrast, remained an open-minded Catholic imbued with Copernican astronomy. He stayed chaste and conservative despite the vague traces of prudent anti-clericalism and anti-seigneurialism that he expressed. Since he was so conservative and chaste does he support the frequently-made contention that French southerners were behind the northerners in evolving toward more contemporary attitudes?

Throughout his life, that is from the age of twelve to that of seventy-two, Prion worked away at his career as it was defined early on. He wished to be a copyist, and that is what he became in Aubais, as in Rouergue, the writer-observer of the village and of himself. He visited the great cities of France, but he certainly was not of them. Nor did he particularly understand or express the attitudes that dominated the merchant classes that created urban society and culture. Like Amiel, who had a quieter life than Prion, he wrote and talked about himself. Like Saint-Simon, who was his near contemporary, Prion started out as the observer and then became the voyeur of a tiny society. Instead of scrutinizing a thousand courtiers at Versailles, Prion observed a thousand peasants who lived in the diocese of Nîmes.

6

Transportation and the Geographical Expression of Capitalism

JAMES E. VANCE, JR

Few today would neglect systems of economic activity in their consideration of the cultural evolution that is history. Few would accept the once prevalent separation of economic concerns from such matters as dynastic, military, and religious history. During the nineteenth century and up to the Second World War economic explanation held a central role in geography, but the subsequent virtual disappearance of empirical economic geography and of political geography have left consideration of the spatial impact of the economy confined to a rather neo-scholastic and abstract debate between Marxists and non-Marxists. Yet the general concerns for the economy that have influenced social science research in recent years apply equally to geography, understood in a broader way than is common today.

Political and economic systems must be understood within a clearly delineated economic geography. The recent work of Fernand Braudel has examined the historical expression of that delineation, with its examples of 'world economies'.[1] Here my purpose is to consider the specifically geographical expressions of world economies in the context of some of my earlier work and its direct application to a geography of the transportation that ties the core to the periphery – which are normally the principal areal elements within the world economies envisaged by historians. As Braudel has it, 'Geographical space as a source of

[1] Fernand Braudel, *Civilization and Capitalism: The Perspective of the World, 15th-18th Century* (Harper and Row, New York, 1984), p. 22.

explanation affects all historical realities, all spatially-defined phenomena: states, societies, culture and economies.'[2]

Until fairly recently the view that medieval economies were parochial and geographically enclosed was widely held. On such a base it was very difficult to explain the burst of European economic activity that carried traders to the Americas in the sixteenth century and to Africa and Asia in the seventeenth. In seeking to solve this, among other problems of distant trading, some years ago I proposed a series of successive stages in the historical geography of mercantile activity.[3] A clear contrast between the endogenic and exogenic forces present in economies should be drawn and full attention paid to the presence of exogenic forces even during the Middle Ages. The critical points made were two: that economic history has stages in which the roots of future developments are planted and grow and that there has always been an exogenic force at work, though it has gained greater importance with the passage of time.

In the spread of European mercantile activity, the sixteenth and seventeenth century merchants were directly applying medieval experience to an emergent economic geography delineated during the age of discovery. The great cities of the Middle Ages were rooted in distant trade; so would be the developing nation states.

History does not furnish much evidence as to the stages of economic-geographical evolution in the Middle Ages, but the modern era gives us much information on which to establish tentative stages drawn from extra-European expansion.

The first was an exploratory stage during which the physical nature of newly discovered lands was partially established. As the projection of European trade to new lands was certainly the most important objective of the voyages of discovery, the appraisal of the economic potential of an area found in that geographical search was immediately undertaken.

A second stage was reached when the initial exploratory efforts at trade, carried out from Europe without any permanent distant settlement of Europeans, was followed by the planting of Europeans in 'factories' and entrepôts on distant coasts, to secure more control of the trade than might be gained through the efforts of occasional passing ships. In particular this planting of people, the original meaning of the 'plantations', was

---

[2] Ibid., p. 21.

[3] James E. Vance, Jr, *The Merchant's World: The Geography of Wholesaling* (Prentice-Hall, Inc., Englewood Cliffs, New Jersey, 1970).

intended to facilitate the transport of goods in trade. Mercantilist theory fully appreciated the earnings to be gained from the conduct of the carrying trade, seeking, therefore, to control the navigation from Europe and rapidly striving to improve and direct transport inland from the entrepôt.

The third stage was reached when control of the entrepôt and its inland transport was seen as insufficient for gaining the greatest economic return; instead actual 'occupation' of the distant land took place, either through widespread European settlement (as in North America, parts of Latin America, South Africa, Australia, and New Zealand) or through European colonial administration (as in much of Africa and Asia). Economic control remained vested in Europe, though the colonizing and settling powers might decentralize much day-to-day administration to the entrepôts. The leading force in these events was the establishment of trade, and then its enlargment through the increasing application of capital and the expanding settlement of Europeans. This represented the final stage of the European economic expansion overseas as long as colonial control was maintained. Other stages followed with the independence of the European dependencies, though those stages tended to replicate internally, for the now independent entrepôts, the same pattern of ecumene and economically dominated area that had characterized the colonial extra-European expansion.[4]

The staged evolution of the relations between the European ecumene – and later, after independence in the United States and other new lands, their national ecumenes – and a vast dominated area resulted in considerable measure from the development of long-distance trade within a capitalist system. Private capitalists undertook their investments in shipping, entrepôt founding, internal transportation construction, agricultural, forestry, and mining development in a serial fashion, each development suggesting the profitability of a successively more distant and more material investment. The mercantile expansion of Europe into the world outside evolved alongside the capitalist system. The control of the carrying trade with the colonies, as evidenced by the British Navigation Acts, was for the benefit of private shipping industry though

[4] The matters of endogenic and exogenic forces shaping economic geography and of the stages in that evolution are discussed in Vance, *Merchant's World*. The relations of the ecumene and dominated area are analyzed in James E. Vance, Jr, *Location in A System of Global Extent*, University of Reading Geographical Papers, No. 81, 1982.

that growth began as a part of mercantilist thought. Once the third phase in the mercantile mode was reached, it was the search for profit that brought funds from the homeland to the colonies to build railroads to open the interior to economic development.

Under a now largely capitalist system there was an obvious symbiosis between the development of production in agricultural, forest, and mineral products and the private provision and conduct of transportation. Profit motivated all these acts, but there were public benefits to be gained from them. The cultural benefits of a continuing tie between an economically simple dominated area and a complex ecumene should not be belittled. Social advantages gained from a broader human interaction have proven themselves over the years. The instruction and experience in efficient production secured by a colony, even under economic domination, was considerable. And, finally, the capitalist investment coming from the ecumene bestowed a permanently valuable infrastructure on the dominated area. Capitalism certainly sought a profit, but it could not continue to gain it in increasing volume without providing varied and often permanent benefits to the dominated area. Transportation was the most obvious beneficiary, and I wish here to analyze its staged evolution and to note at the outset the parallelism of the mercantile model of settlement I proposed some years ago[5] and the evolution of transportation here outlined.[6]

A STAGED MODEL OF TRANSPORTATION AND ECONOMY

For the interaction of economic system and transportation development a simple staged model may be used to examine: (1) the relation in the Middle Ages before the full emergence of capitalism; (2) that under the mature capitalism of the nineteenth century; and (3) that in prospect in the post-capitalist countries today.

The Middle Ages

The relatively autarkic and natural medieval economy suffered regional disintegration and a low utilization of transportation. The accompanying

[5] Vance, *Merchant's World*, pp. 138–67.

[6] A detailed discussion of the evolutionary stages of transportation is contained in James E. Vance, Jr, *Capturing the Horizon: The Historical Geography of Transportation Since the Transportation Revolution of the Sixteenth Century* (Harper and Row, New York, 1986).

feudal system sought to provide the infrastructure for movement in a fashion characteristic of contemporary institutions; through the imposition of a servile obligation, the corvée, locally organized and directed and thereby normally parochial in its accomplishments. One suspects that the range of a good that Walter Christaller found so powerful in shaping Bavaria's settlement was as strongly influenced by the construction attitudes of the corvée as by any general 'economic' principles of distance decay such as he proposed.[7] The local corvée normally had little interest in distant travel so it tended to repair roads near the settlement and to let those which led to neighbor settlements revert from the earlier Roman thoroughfares to difficult and indistinct forest tracks.

To break out of the narrow region, medieval traders had, in the absence of broader economic organization, to turn either to nature or to the one seemingly 'universal' institution, the church. Nature contributed waterways, coastal or riverine, which required little or no investment in improvements. The church contributed to long-distance trade indirectly, through its improvement of routes for easing the pilgrimage and the flow of church business and tithes. In this highly adventitious provision of long-distance routes a great focusing of trade might be expected, of the sort Edward Fox has shown for the Rhenish corridor that left France to the west and Bavaria to the east much more agricultural and economically disintegrated than those areas which grew up along the route beside western Europe's most naturally navigable stream. The general medieval economy did not initiate or advance this trade. Nature, the church, and a group of persons often held in pariah status (Jews and 'Orientals') created it. Not only were those wandering merchants socially apart from the settlement of their times, but they were distinctive in being the only group engaged in the provision of transportation over any appreciable distance. The combination of these two basically geographical qualities generated a sharp discordance between the provision of transportation infrastructure, based on the local corvée, and the undertaking of transportation service, largely the activity of strangers from a distance. The corvée seldom provided an adequately integrated system of long-distance routes, so the traveling merchants were forced to turn to natural water routes to gain distant objectives.

[7] Walter Christaller, *Central Places in Southern Germany* (Prentice-Hall, Inc., Englewood Cliffs, New Jersey, 1966).

Nature may have provided the route, but it remained for the mobile traders to give it competence, defined – as in hydrology – as the scale of the item that may be transported. Under initial natural conditions only small items, and those in a modest aggregate, could be moved in distant trade. The merchants expanded that competence by investing in vessels and vehicles, and possibly by providing dams and locks to deepen waterways for larger loads. The investments of the merchants of the Lübeck salt trade made Europe's first watershed canal, on the upper Stecknitz in the fourteenth century, a work of more than local significance. In Flanders and the Po Basin contemporaneous modest works integrated the often interrupted natural waterways in the interests of extending trade beyond the region. These works suggest an alternative source to the corvée in the provision of infrastructure by plowing back some of the mercantile profits into those facilities and into the vessels that might profit from their use. This practice foreshadowed capitalism's projection of support for a transportation development well beyond the boundaries of the immediate seat of the merchants. But during the Middle Ages most development of transportation facilities remained local and produced geographically disconnected patterns that clearly displayed their endogenic origins.

The coastal as well as potamic (riverine) base for extended medieval trade introduced a problem of recovering such early mercantile investments in long-distance facilities. To the extent that the works directly benefited those who paid for their construction, as had occurred when the corvée provided the general transportation infrastructure, financial recovery may have been unnecessary. But in works more likely to be used by aliens it gained importance. At locks, dams, and places at which obstacles might have been removed, tolls became common. On the sea coast the difficulty in enforcing user charges encouraged the growth of laws of cabotage that restricted coastal trade to denizen vessels. Establishment of a route monopoly could generate the funds invested in improvements – docks, tidal gates, lighthouses, channel markings – that might not be directly recoverable through tolls.

In sum, the economy of transportation in the Middle Ages had strong endogenic shaping forces, though with hints of a more exogenic system possible in the future. The long dominating corvée was paired with an increasing use of private capital for the provision of specialized facilities for distant trade. The rise of that trade was encouraging the private effort to enlarge the competence of transportation to match any possible extension of its service to encompass larger geographical areas.

The Transportation Revolution

Capitalism remained recessive under the regional disintegration of feudalism and its natural economy: it became dominant with the rise of the integrated state and its support for the outward expansion of national interests. In the specifically European context, the integrated state had to give attention to long-distance domestic transportation to survive politically, and it had to think of extended sea transport to grow economically. As the nation state was emerging, northwestern Europe was quickly adopting and advancing the effort toward pelagic navigation that had begun in the Mediterranean. By the beginning of the sixteenth century ships were available for ocean sailing, and the necessary nagivation was becoming adequate to allow trade to be projected across wide seas.

Efforts to improve on the natural land routes proceeded more slowly. Italy and the Low Countries had begun to develop canals by the thirteenth century, but mainly for drainage or irrigation rather than for transportation. Only slowly could those canals be made traversable by boats – through the development of the pound lock, which reached its full development only in the sixteenth century. National interest in roads arose also in that century and led to initial efforts at improvement. By the seventeenth century a national route system radiated from Paris. So long as France envisaged public investment it had few followers, but by the seventeenth century capitalism had sufficiently evolved to allow private funds to be tapped for improvements in transportation facilities: for example, investments from the Dutch cities in *Trekvaarten* canal improvements, creation of the public–private co-operation in the turnpike trusts of England, and the joining of personal and royal fortunes in the undertaking of the Canal de Briare and the Canal du Midi in France. These efforts required a prior quickening of trade to offer reasonable prospects for toll collections adequate to repay the private investment.

The link reveals the functional harnessing of transportation and capitalism. Under medieval conditions there had also been a tie between political economy and transportation technology, but the rise of capitalism represented a major geographical revolution of utmost significance to transportation. Where the medieval economy had emphasized the parochial, the early modern sought geographical extension. Efforts were strong toward the integration of the economic activities within an entire nation and beyond that newly enlarged ecumene was a considerable mercantile push overseas, where market enlargement could come with greater ease than in Europe. To facilitate either of these geographical changes, shifts in transportation were essential. Within the nation state the natural route that had been the backstay of the medieval economy proved inadequate. There had to be some broader conception of route structure and some instrument for accomplishing national improvements. Use of the corvée came into question in most places, though in France it persisted until the Revolution mainly through the creation of a professional planning and engineering office to guide it into national works. In England the goal of a national transportation system more directly advanced the rise of capitalism. At first the English employed the corvée as the French did, but with one important difference: already in the seventeenth century public–private turnpike trusts of local origin and purview became the instrument of change, rather than some equivalent of the national supervision of the Corps de Ponts et Chausée. In this way English private capital was introduced into the provision of infrastructure, and money tended to be most readily available where the demand was greatest. Capitalism provided the demand for infrastructural improvements and furnished the wherewithal for its accomplishment. And as economies expand so does the transportation that provides their backstay.

The other geographical extension brought by the onset of the mercantile economy, that by ships overseas, also yoked capital and transportation. In the fifteenth century the Atlantic fringe of Europe had been developing the ocean ship, highsided and more boxlike, with smaller sails that permitted economical manning, and had been devising the system to control it in pelagic navigation. Capital could be concentrated on the vessel alone, so, through use of the natural route of the sea, far greater extensions of the national trading system could be gained quickly than was possible on land. This contrast in employment of capital helps explain how there could be parts of France or England beyond the national ecumene while ships from their ports contested in India, the West Indies, and on the St Lawrence. When capital provided the funds and determined the location of improvements, the next most significant enlargement of the geography of integrated transport tended to be bought by each successive increment of investment. In this way the transportation revolution of the sixteenth, seventeenth, and eighteenth centuries more fundamentally transformed human movement than had efforts during the entire classical and medieval periods.

The three centuries of the transportation revolution saw the establishment of two national policies intended to enhance returns from investments in ocean shipping. The first was the 'discovery that economic growth can be used *in the national interest* under mercantilism', as John Hicks tells us, by projecting outward 'national objectives of all sorts, including the pursuit of influence over other nations, of prestige and of power'.[8] And second was the discovery that, by controlling trade, a nation could capture the carrier's part of profits from long-distance trade – an effort encouraged under the new laws of cabotage that reserved the coasting trade of a nation and its offshore political dependencies to the ships of the nation itself. Jointly, these policies clearly recognized that the nation was made wealthy by the long-distance carrying trade that had necessarily become an important component of the 'common wealth' as fixed capital in vessels, docks, and navigation improvements increased.

Mature Capitalism

The economic ascendency of Britain during the eighteenth century assured a virtually unmixed use of capitalism to secure the necessary improvements in the transportation infrastructure. The corvée and public initiative were largely confined to pre-revolutionary France and the Continent. For example, in England the early provision of lighthouses was joined to the older pilotage duties of Trinity House and fell as a charge on master mariners and shipping owners. The maintenance of what we would consider coastguard coastal lifesaving activities was, and remains, a private undertaking. In many other ways, on land as well as on the sea a direct tie existed between the accumulation of mercantile capital and the provision of the facilities that made trade, and later manufacturing, possible.

The existence of an improved system of roads and waterways permitted England to experience the first industrial revolution. The enlarged competence of canal barges and ships, which opened wider and larger markets to growing factory industry, stemmed from the specifically capitalist provision of transportation. Profits in transportation stemmed directly from the volume carried and the efficiency with which greater loads could be handled. Any seasonal interruption of movements, any clogging of flow by bottlenecks in the facilities, or any constraints on

---

[8] John Hicks, *A Theory of Economic History* (Oxford University Press, Oxford, 1969), pp. 161–2.

the geographical availability of service on canals and waterways, tended to affect the profitability of trade, and thereby of the profit-oriented manufacturing and carrying companies that supported trade.

The locational needs of the new factory industry put great pressure on the traditional, natural provision of transportation infrastructure. Ports and trading towns commonly had arisen in relation to that system of natural routes, but industry frequently did not. As a result, the Industrial Revolution greatly magnified the need for constructed routes. Questions arise about the source of funds to provide them. Britain, as the hearth of industry, and the United States, as one of the earliest to follow, were among the first to discern the need for a new form of transportation, in the railroad, and the possibilities for a new financial provision of transportation facilities under the conditions of capitalist conduct of trade and manufacturing. Those railroads held out hope for year-round, more competent, easily extensible, and, particularly, more functionally financed transport than had previously been possible on land.

The tie of capitalism and railroad building is clearly shown by the contrast between British and American construction. In Britain the railroad was introduced into a rapidly developing industrial-trading society in which the previous construction of turnpikes and canals had only partially met transportation needs. The immediate success of the Stockton and Darlington (1825) and the Liverpool and Manchester (1830) encouraged successful promotion of a great variety of lines and the Railway Boom of the 1840s. These lines were constructed by private capital, usually at a high standard, that has required little improvement even for the running of today's high-speed trains. In the United States trade expansion and manufacturing were well under way but hardly dominant in the national economy when the earliest lines opened in the first half of the 1830s. The South Carolina Railroad of 1834 was the world's longest, 134 miles, but perhaps one of its least substantial, and Boston, though the world's first railroad junction city in 1835, was served by lines of modest physique. Iron strap-on wooden stringers sufficed as rails on most American lines. The American system of railroad construction had the most primitive facilities that could be provided and still maintain a working connection. Entrepreneurs hoped that a market would develop to repay initial costs, allow capital accumulation to finance further construction, and make the railroads sturdy enough to survive. Significantly in this capital-poor time the American railroad promoters made an investment decision similar to that characteristic of the earlier years of capitalist provision of transportation: they opted for building superbly strong vehicles, depending upon their strength to cope with the wretched infrastructure on which they had to operate. In other words, they made a stingy nature provide a railed-way as cheaply as could be built by constructing the best locomotives that ingenuity could devise, even at a considerable investment cost. In the absence of a fully evolved industrial economy, land development held out to speculators' towns and pioneer farmers hope for recovering risky investments even within the first generation of American railroading. The developers rationally appraised existing markets, the prospective for repaying their investment, and the geographical railroad strategy.

Americans quickly adopted an exogenic pattern of railroad construction. In contrast road-building in America continued under the traditional corvée, persisting in some towns in New Hampshire down to the Second World War, and thereby was shaped to a highly endogenic and unintegrated pattern until state highway departments began to be established at the turn of the century. But from the beginning the railroads used private investment to cheapen construction and make it geographically pioneering. Lines were pushed beyond the developed ecumene and even beyond the settlement frontier, so there had to be both an expectation of rapid market development and a participation in speculative rewards for those making correct geographical predictions. When British investors faced an uncertain economic geography and a problematic market, as they did overseas, as good capitalists they tended to adopt American railroad-building practices. The three-feet-six-inch gauge of South African railroads still shows this adoption, as do the narrow gauges of many Indian, Australian, and other formerly 'colonial railways'. And in a number of cases British investors reluctantly had to abandon the beloved but overtaxed British locomotives in favor of Brother Jonathan's more powerful products, or at least his designs.

The exogenic nature of railroad planning and construction, in Britain as well as America, gave investors an instrument that facilitated the spread of international commerce. If Argentina was to send meat to feed the British working class, furnishing in return a market for British manufacturers, railroads had to connect the Pampas at the end of the steamship lines and thereby the River Plate to Britain. Private British investment furnished both the railroads to the Pampas and the freighters to British ports. In similar fashion, Americans interested in mining in the Andes had to finance the railroads that would climb to the heights at which the ores were found. The geography of railroad transportation in the nineteenth century largely reflected world trade as then practiced or in reasonable prospect. It commonly projected outward from a few centers of trade and manufacturing that were accumulating capital and that could appreciate the need to integrate transport over great distances. Here we see Braudel's capitalist city or state at work in providing a transportation infrastructure even where political control was indirect.

There were two functional parts to the world of transportation: (1) the vast basic production areas of agricultural, forest, fish, and mineral commodities that had existed sometimes for millennia and had been commonly constrained by parochial transport to local consumption; and (2) the mercantile and industrial regions of the national ecumenes integrated first regionally and then nationally by the advent of exogenic provision of transportation facilities mainly through capitalist investment. As economic development at home advanced, those nations which had learned the values of exogenic provision began to apply them on a global geographical scale. In that way long-distance trade could be established and, through it, externally generated integration of much of the world's transportation could be achieved. The specific geography of that transportation tended to reflect the objectives of those distant trader-capitalists, but as time passed, and earnings (sometimes handsome) flowed back to the investors, they found virtue even in the construction of facilities in distant lands intended only for the domestic demand found there.

At that point transportation could become a specifically capitalist undertaking divorced from its earlier tie to the older, more specialized long-distance mercantile activity. Thus, we find such unpredictable associations as the heavy participation of Canadian capital in Brazilian trolley lines. This geographically detached investment in transport construction, more developed in the British Empire and Commonwealth than elsewhere, brought great economic benefit to Britain. Profits from the provision of service on trade routes centered in Britain or other trading nations might combine with simple investors' returns on facilities built entirely to satisfy domestic needs in the distant land. In consequence, transportation frequently represented the largest economic interest an investor nation might have in another country. Ultimately, the sundering of colonial ties and the decline in external control over the production of basic commodities in areas of primary production has tended to dry up traditional core-region sources of private investment in distant transportation, and forced the newly independent peripheral country to rely on often inadequate domestic capital to maintain and improve its inherited transportation infrastructure. In such cases there has been a tendency to revert to the more primitive state in which capital is concentrated in the provision of vehicles rather than of facilities, and, increasingly, nature is left to provide the minimum requisite infrastructure.

Incipient Post-Capitalism

In the century before 1939 the geographical scope for capitalist investment in transportation seemed universal, when to a considerable degree it was merely imperial. With so much of the poorly industrialized world held in colonies of European powers, investment was exogenic geographically but still internal to the political unit in conformity to the longstanding mercantilist notions that Braudel specifies. Only the Americas displayed considerable purely capitalist investment. Railroad development in the United States had benefited in its early years from foreign funds, but by the turn of the century the United States could have financed its own infrastructure if it had so wished. The economic disruptions of the First World War removed Europe as a significant source of capital just when the private provision of transportation had reached its peak and was to experience a strikingly rapid economic decline. Briefly, the electric traction industry, which had risen after 1890 to provide a locally oriented transportation system through private investment, collapsed spectacularly. 'Few industries have arisen so rapidly or declined so quickly, and no industry of its size has had a worse financial record. The inter-urbans were a rare example of an industry that never enjoyed a period of prolonged prosperity; accordingly, they played out their life cycle in a shorter period than any other important American industry.'[9]

The collapse of the electric traction industry shows clearly the economic limitations to the private provision of transportation. In addition, the political part of the economy began to establish limits. Just as the First World War sapped European capital, the Second World War initiated the geographical constraints that are evident today. At the close of that war two transformations began: European imperialism largely disappeared

---

[9] George W. Hilton and John F. Due, *The Electric Interurban Railways in America* (Stanford University Press, Stanford, 1960), p. 3.

and economic nationalism burgeoned. As a result, the exogenic forces in transportation development declined rapidly. Countries became more inward looking in their planning and resistant to private, let alone foreign, control of facilities or service. Significant transformation was made possible by the rise of civil aviation, which reintroduced an enlarged dependence upon the natural provision of the infrastructure of the route. That return to earlier practices accompanied the 'Five Freedoms' adopted at the Chicago Convention of 1944 on civil aviation, which largely assured the internationalization of air space – with the exception of the Soviet Union's – that encouraged practical long-distance routing and the formulation of bilateral treaties to encourage a national pairing on those routes. From that pairing came the notion of 'national prestige' as a basis for the creation of an economic geography of transportation. Since the airways were largely free, an investment could be concentrated in vehicles, ease of entry fully transformed the conduct of long-distance transportation, particularly from the late 1930s, as equipment became virtually standardized outside the Soviet bloc through the domination of the aircraft industry by American builders.

Capitalist provision of transportation faced this postwar advent of state enterprise and nationalism by turning its attention much more to manufacturing investment, by creating the multinational corporation as an outlet to investment, and by restricting private participation in transportation largely to ocean shipping. Even in ocean shipping, nationalism encouraged the foreign registry of vessels to take advantage of flags of convenience. But in most of the world's transportation the long period of exogenic provision of transportation was over after 350 years as the primary force in shaping an integration of the long-distance movement of people and goods.

Exogenic provision did not disappear; it was internationalized. Many developing countries still needed external funds, but nationalism, and frequently socialism, ruled out private investment as their source. Instead the policy of financing and controlling transportation infrastructure by public sources required that external sources must also be 'public' and furnish monies as grants or long-term public loans rather than investments. The recent challenge of the American dominance in aircraft manufacturing by the European Airbus consortium has demonstrated the ultimate politicizing of what seemed the last remnant of the long tradition of private external investment. France perhaps never gave up its belief in the rectitude of public participation in transport despite the

Revolution and the reluctant abandonment of the corvée. Having built the railroad infrastructure at public expense during the nineteenth century, well before those railroads were actually 'nationalized' in 1938, France led the way in the use of diplomatic pressure to sell Airbuses and in public subventions to finance their sale. Even where such direct national efforts are avoided, external funds are funneled through the World Bank and other multinational agencies. In geographical terms, the net effect of this return to endogenic planning of transport has been to make the nationally parochial purpose once again dominant. Hence, the concentration on distant connections, which was so much in the forefront of developers' minds until the Second World War, has sharply declined. The notion of a Cape-to-Cairo railroad seems quaint today, and its replacement by air service creates only a tenuously thin topological routing of national pairings of carriers on that still important route.

A STAGED MODEL OF THE ECONOMY OF TRANSPORTATION

The evolution of the relation between capitalism and transportation provides the historical base for a model of the economy of transportation as broken down into three broad stages of development. It thereby provides a model of historical geography. Assuming that transportation development has been continuous since the Middle Ages, if sharply different in timing and geographical reach, we may begin those historical-geographic stages with one termed 'medieval'. From perhaps the twelfth century until the sixteenth, transportation was local in the provision of infrastructure and parochial in its lack of effective distant integration. Thus, change was endogenic, based on local efforts of a corvée that shared with the other medieval institutions inputs mostly of labor rather than of capital. From that labor base sprang much of the geographical discontinuity of the transportation system, for labor was geographically immobilized under feudalism and scarce or plentiful in relation to a highly regionalized, if not even more parochialized, factor endowment. The manorial economy could subsist under those conditions, but long-distance trade was severely repressed by them.

The rise of capitalism concerns us here only in its effect on transportation. In that narrower context there was a direct tie between the advent of capitalism and the creation of integrated long-distance transportation: one required the other, and capitalism could provide the

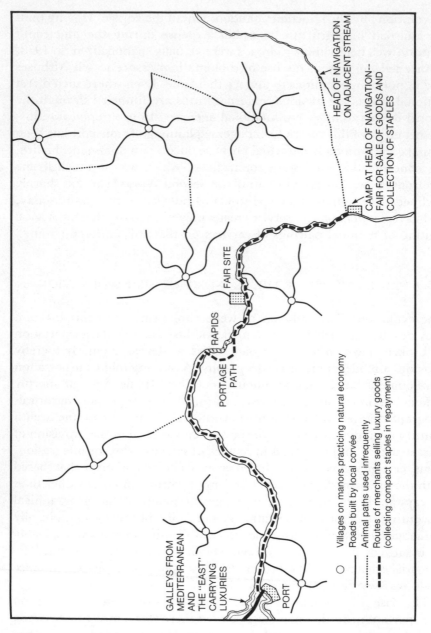

FIGURE 6.1 Transportation in the medieval stage

GALLEYS FROM
MEDITERRANEAN
AND
THE "EAST"
CARRYING
LUXURIES

PORT

PORTAGE
PATH

RAPIDS

FAIR SITE

CAMP AT HEAD OF NAVIGATION—
FAIR FOR SALE OF GOODS AND
COLLECTION OF STAPLES

HEAD OF NAVIGATION
ON ADJACENT STREAM

○ Villages on manors practicing natural economy
—— Roads built by local corvée
······ Animal paths used infrequently
▬▬▬ Routes of merchants selling luxury goods
(collecting compact staples in repayment)

integrating geographical links in a way the medieval political economy could not. And capital was geographically mobile in a way that labor was not, certainly until the social disruptions of the sixteenth and seventeenth centuries. The earliest capital was mercantile, and its growth required an integration of local infrastructure into distant-trading routes. Thus, capitalism supplied two decisive elements for the creation of an extensive network of routes: it was itself mobile in a way that servile labor had not been, and it could benefit more than most other institutions from an integration of transportation.

The contemporaneous rise of the nation state and of capitalism must have been in part due to mutual benefits. Economically mercantile capitalists sought and prospered from distant routes; politically the nation state, in direct competition in many cases with local political units, burgeoned by their integration.

We may appropriately designate an initial stage of capitalist provision of transportation as extending from the sixteenth to the early nineteenth century. During that period the mercantilist economy expressed an economic-geographical concept that elevated transportation to a dominating role in the shaping and support of the state. But capital was still scarce, so improvements had to be made selectively, with first investments drawn from sectors in which the smallest amount of money would gain the greatest incremental benefit. Turnpike trust improvement on roads, the dredging, blasting, and damming of rivers in 'navigations', and the construction of the earliest watershed canals all maximized those investment returns. A third stage was reached only later, as capital became more plentiful from the returns on investment and more particularly from the quick growth of the mercantile activity they fostered. Under it manufacturing, based on the capital from the earlier activities, grew rapidly and the demands on transportation increased. Manufacturing introduced a strongly marked geographical division of labor that particularly enlarged the demand for distant transport, so that a new competence and comprehensiveness of connections was needed.

The mature capitalist stage of transportation was characterized by the creation of the first essentially ubiquitous system of land transportation – the railroad. Less controlled by terrain and climate than had been waterways, with their mixed natural and constructed provision, railroads could be expanded in capacity to meet growing movement and in comprehensiveness to meet geographical enlargements in the market. To the surprise of early promoters, the railroad proved as useful in the

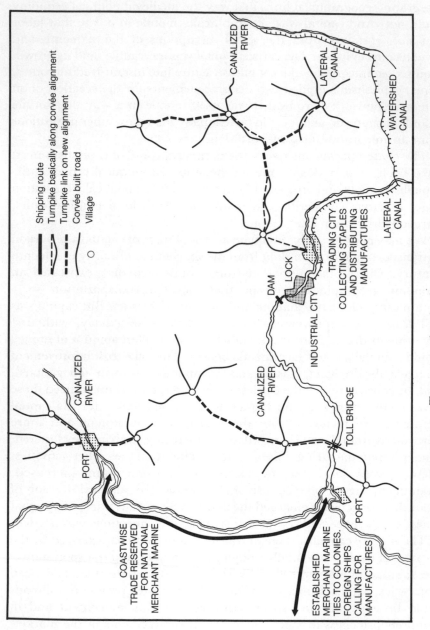

FIGURE 6.2 Transportation in the early capitalist stage

movement of people as of freight, so it seemed to meet virtually all demands for movement felt during the nineteenth century. In less than a hundred years more than a million miles of railroad were constructed, largely through private investment, with the greatest density in western Europe, and the largest national system, a quarter of the total mileage, in the United States. This railroad era represented the epitome of capitalist provision of transport, with its direct linking of transportation to the growth of large manufacturing and commercial cities. In an interesting fashion, particularly in North America, the railroad nurtured the growth of such great mercantile-industrial cities as Boston, Philadelphia, Baltimore, Toronto, and Chicago, the capital accumulation of which began to create 'Empires of Domination' within North America similar to the political empires Braudel cites as having spread from European 'City States'.

So great was that level of urbanization that for the first time a need to provide transportation within cities and their environs, and almost entirely for the movement of people, was perceived. From that perception came the rapid rise of the electric traction industry in a period of about twenty years (1889–1909), which absorbed huge amounts of capital, with such inter-regional and international transfers as American investment in London's tube lines playing a major role in shaping exogenic change.

The mature capitalist stage declined nearly as rapidly as it had arisen. The decline began between the two World Wars, both in Europe and America, when earnings on investments in transportation facilities lagged. The Depression of the 1930s worsened the prospects, so that by the latter part of that decade public provision of improvements was bruited and outright municipalization or nationalization began to take place. The French National Railroads (SNCF) came into being in 1938, and London Transport had actually been formed even earlier, in 1933. The general confusion of the Depression probably masked this structural change by making it seem the result of a broader collapse of capitalism, but the rejuvenation of the capitalist economy during and after the Second World War did not restore the use of private investment to maintain transportation, local, national, or international. Only air transport, with its emancipation from the provision of infrastructure, seemed to belie this generalization, though in our time even it seems at least to have wilted selectively.

The critical geographical feature of this capitalist provision of transportation infrastructure was its exogenic quality. Capital could be

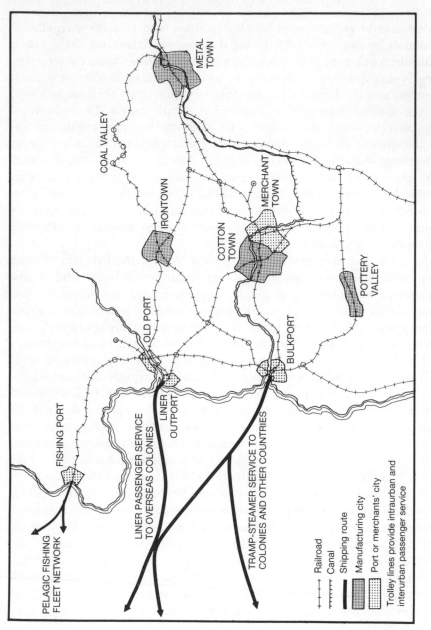

FIGURE 6.3 Initial post-capitalist stage

moved world wide, and with that injection of funds, even in wilderness areas, the labor constraint that had so hampered the integration of parochial systems in the Middle Ages could be removed. The great influx of Chinese laborers to build the North American transcontinental railroads provides a case in point. Undoubtedly, during the capitalist stage world parochialism declined rapidly. But as with an exogenic provision of capital there was sometimes inadequate attention paid to the local needs that had dominated the previous stage. Where those needs held hope for sound returns on private capital, as in the Canadian investment in Brazilian trolley lines, exogenic provision did not fail the native population; where they did not, investors tended to turn rapidly to more handsome prospects. The result was a strong feeling that the capitalist provision of transportation had served its own, often foreign but in most cases at least distant, interests. The Granger movement in the economically dominated area within the United States showed that populist belief. Thus, even during the last century, there was a none too recessive idea that capitalist provision of transportation was fundamentally against the popular, and in some cases the national, interest. For colonies such a conclusion seemed inescapable, and independence led almost automatically to the domestication of transport. Even in the investing countries the seemingly self-serving nature of capitalist investment, when viewed geographically, was such that local concerns on occasion advocated a similar parochialization of service to accompany public ownership. The rise of socialism, as originally a municipal-level notion of political economy, quickly led to the adoption of the idea of public, and thereby endogenic, provision of transportation.

The destruction and transformation that came with the Second World War ended the capitalist stage of transportation provision. The war destroyed the colonialism that had become the geographical expression of mercantilism; it freed long-distance trade and reduced the influence of exogenic provision. Bombing and combat operations destroyed much of the European infrastructure of transportation, and a trend toward nationalization, as in the France of 1938, became virtually universal – witness British Railways in 1947. The earlier dominant mercantile capital had been displaced by manufacturing capital, with a reduction of the direct feedback to transportation. Even more important, the scale of necessary investment for rebuilding and modernizing transportation facilities proved too great for any rational expectation of acceptable repayment of the costs of private capital. And philosophically, state

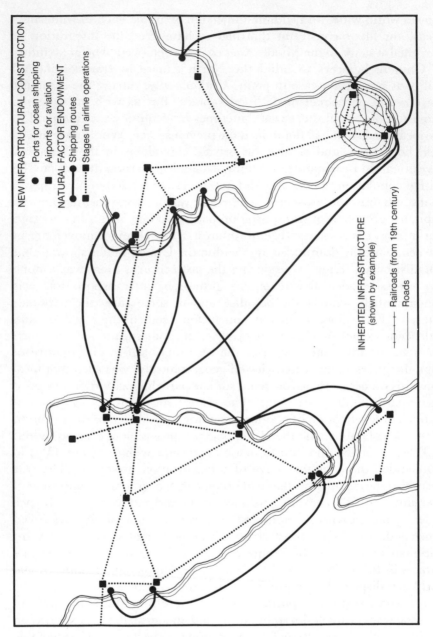

NEW INFRASTRUCTURAL CONSTRUCTION

● Ports for ocean shipping
■ Airports for aviation

NATURAL FACTOR ENDOWMENT

●━━━━● Shipping routes
■┄┄┄┄■ Stages in airline operations

INHERITED INFRASTRUCTURE
(shown by example)

━┼┼┼━ Railroads (from 19th century)
━━━━ Roads

FIGURE 6.4 Full capitalist stage

planning and socialism strongly suggested public ownership and operation of the 'elements of production', most notably transportation. As the end of the European dominance of the world economy became obvious such European political-economic thinking was rapidly adopted by colonies as they became independent, and by politically independent but formerly economically dependent countries in Asia and Latin America.

This incipient post-capitalist stage, ushered in during the two decades after 1945, remains with us today. Exogenic provision of transportation virtually disappeared, through nationalization of facilities and the assumption of domestic operation and direction. The labor contribution has become dominant in the less developed countries, as it was in Europe during the Middle Ages. Less wide ranging goals determine the location of improvements. Nationalism has shut off the little private investment there would have been, and has created a new and potentially dangerous situation wherein capital-poor countries, having rejected capitalist provision, have had to turn to institutionalized public borrowing to maintain and improve transportation facilities. One wonders how much of the current vast debt of the less developed world was incurred in gaining infrastructure that capitalists provided, at least in part, before 1945. Private debts can be washed away by bankruptcy; public repudiation is not readily forgiven.

The nationalization of transportation and its provision has placed a further burden on the poorer countries by entanglement with questions of 'national prestige'. Highly nationalistic former colonies, and countries freed from previous economic domination without actual political control, have found it 'necessary' to undertake international airline operations that incur additional international borrowing and often annual subsidies for operating costs. Certainly, returns now flow to the country itself rather than to outsiders, but in an industry characterized by insubstantial profits and sometimes disastrous risks, that is poor fare indeed.

The costly burden of the nationalized airline is paired with the costly nature of nationalized general transportation. Lest this seem a hidden argument for 'privatizing' these activities, as proposed by the present British government, it should be noted that times have changed: type of ownership is probably not the determinant of profit or loss in transportation.

Today only those forms of transportation that gain some sort of 'free ride', through tremendous subventions in facilities or labor, seem able to operate at a profit, either privately or publicly. Different kinds of transportation can be operated at a profit as much by public as private companies: trucking and intercity busing in the United States, where they were provided with the splendid Interstate Highway network in the post-war period at little actual cost to operators; airlines, where labor costs and terminal charges can be kept low; ocean shipping, where flags of convenience keep labor costs down and the sealanes are free; and inland navigation where tolls and lockage charges are omitted. Aside from these instances private and public operators prove equally unprofitable today. Those who, in the United States, single out Amtrak as a peculiarly subsidized rail passenger system merely show their ignorance of world conditions. In any place in which the facilities and services are at all adequately related to the demand for transportation, enormous subsidies accompany passenger transportation. These are normally much greater than those furnished to Amtrak, and privatization holds no promise of change. Prime Minister Thatcher has 'privatized' British Airways; she sees improvement of British Railways only through 'abandonment'.

As this stage of incipient post-capitalism in transportation progresses it seems increasingly clear that, for reasons that cannot be analyzed here, the exogenic provision of transportation that came under capitalism, with its ability to shift some costs away from transport to mercantile and manufacturing capital, probably accustomed us to budgeting too little for transportation, and to devaluing its provision excessively. In other words, we have until recently lived in a time of cheap energy, cheap labor, cheap provision of infrastructure, and unduly sanguine assumptions about actual costs of the provision of service; in consequence, we have evolved most of our thinking in a context of subsidized transportation. Today, though we have nationalized and parochialized, we can no longer command that capitalist subsidy. Transport labor, controlling such a vital service, is probably the most overpaid in our society, as the recent ferment among America's airlines attests. Energy is no longer cheap and is not likely to be so again. And capital comes at a bargain price no longer.

We are faced with fundamental problems. We have created a geographical integration of transportation, and thereby a vast growth in the world economies and their political modularity, through an exogenic provision of facilities, but today there is no way to spread those costs geographically, save through what increasingly seems unrepayable borrowing, whether by New York City for subways or by Third World countries for airlines.

Our choices include: (1) returning to geographical parochialism, with a low-cost localization of transportation; (2) discovering a new source of exogenic subvention; and (3) reducing the scale of mobility for people and goods that we expect to secure in the future.

We have become accustomed to long and strong 'internal links and exchanges' that have created modern, capitalist world economies, even in areas no longer capitalist. Braudel's notion that the historical geography of the last half-millennium is mainly explicable in the context of these increasingly larger world economies and the forces that shape them must, in conclusion, be examined in the light of the radical change in transportation provision. In Braudel's studies there has been an ever-increasing enlargement of the geographical scale of those economies, and certainly the rise of the multinational corporation seems to confirm the unidirectional nature of geographical links under capitalism. The spread of manufacturing has maintained those 'internal links' mainly by using sea and air connections that may depend heavily on the free provision of facilities by nature.

For the trade in primary products that must move by land the picture is grimmer. In a number of former colonial areas railroads have existed that no longer serve, as the inability of the Sudanese Railroads to handle famine relief shows, and expansion of land transportation to agricultural developments often proves difficult. Have we then arrived at the point at which the historical direction of geographical changes has been reversed? Are we about to see the constriction of the world economies in a 'discriminatory geography' that will sharpen the distinctions between the capitalist cores and the non-capitalist peripheries? The answers to these questions are not yet clear, but for the half-millennium under consideration, the tie between capitalism and the provision of the internal links of world economies has been both direct and fundamental.

7

France: A Special Case?
A World-Systems Perspective

IMMANUEL WALLERSTEIN

The intellectual conundrum that surrounds the understanding of France's role in the modern world has often, explicitly or implicitly, taken the form of a query: why did France do 'less well' than England? There are at least two assumptions in this intellectual query. The first assumption is that France did in fact, by some criteria, do 'less well' than England over a period of say 500 years. (Perhaps 1450–1950 would serve as well as any set of dates). The second assumption is that, if so, it is in some sense surprising. For if from the outset any reasonable scholar would assume the comparison to be implausible, it would scarcely be worthwhile to pursue the matter as intensely and as extensively as world scholarship has done.

By and large, the respondents to this query have focused heavily on certain elements of the internal structure of the two 'countries' in order to develop plausible hypotheses. Explanations have been located in political history, dominant value systems, demographic patterns, economic resources, the organization of work, and the presumed degree of inventiveness of innovators.

Edward Whiting Fox has insisted, however, that if we neglect 'the geographic dimension of history' we will not be able to understand coherently either the observed historical trajectories or the contemporary constraints within which people and groups operate. This is a truism, but one largely ignored in practice. Geography by definition concerns space, and hence, more perhaps than most perspectives, forces us to think about relational processes.

Let me therefore rephrase the query. In early modern times France was the largest European state in population and area under the authority of a single ruler. It was a locus of relatively high economic production and wealth. It had a wide commercial network. It had at many points in time, if not all, the strongest army in Europe and a powerful navy. For its time it had a strong, centralized bureaucracy. It was overall perhaps the strongest locus of cultural activities and cultural attractiveness in Europe. And yet, as the story goes, the nineteenth – and twentieth – centuries passed France by. It was England that had the 'first industrial revolution'. It was England that enshrined its hegemony in the Pax Britannica. Further back, it was around Amsterdam, and, earlier still, around Venice or Antwerp – but never around Paris – that the nascent European world-economy built its structures. And going forward in time to the twentieth century, it was the United States that replaced Great Britain as the hegemonic power. And if there had been in the early twentieth century any formidable challenger to the United States, it was Germany rather than France.

Yet at no point during the past 500 years could it ever have been said that France was an unimportant or minor state in the constellation of geopolitical forces or in the world-economy's division of labor. In contrast the role of other 'countries' underwent much greater fluctuations. In some ways, it could be argued, France's role has remained constant, forever a sort of brilliant second. Is this a plausible characterization? And if it is, what could account not only for France's never having become in some sense hegemonic in the world-system, but simultaneously never having slipped out of a sort of inner circle of powerful states?

Perhaps if we allied one simple observation with the basic conceptual antinomy of Edward Fox, we would go a long way towards explaining this phenomenon. The simple observation is that France is the only country in Europe that embraces, and is more or less equally divided between, its two major climatic regions.[1] This observation correlates with a long French literature on the line St. Malo-Geneva[2] and on the cultural-political dichotomy of the Langue d'Oïl and the Langue d'Oc.[3]

---

[1] See B. H. Slicher van Bath, "Agriculture in the Vital Revolution", in *The Cambridge Economic History of Europe* (7 vols, Cambridge University Press, Cambridge, 1941–78), vol. V: *The Economic Organization of Early Modern Europe*, eds. E. E. Rich and C. H. Wilson (1977), p. 61.

[2] See Roger Chartier, 'Science Sociale et Découpage Régional: Note sur Deux Débats 1820–1920', *Actes de la Recherche en Sciences Sociales*, 35 (Nov. 1980), pp. 27–36.

[3] See Emmanuel Le Roy Ladurie, 'Occitania in Historical Perspective', *Review*, 1 (1977), pp. 21–30.

Fox's basic conceptual antinomy, as we know, is that between the centralization of the state and the development of (non-local) commerce.

How shall we conceptualize the relation of these two vectors – the strengthening of state structures and the commodification of everything? In fact, there have been two major theoretical positions concerning this relation: one that sees the two vectors as going in quite different directions, so that if the one is emphasized, the other is undone; and another that sees the two as going in the same direction and therefore mutually reinforcing. This difference of viewpoint has been the focus of debates about national policy in almost every modern state, and it has always been particularly vigorous in France. Indeed, France has consistently been divided on this issue and may be said never to have definitively terminated the internal debate on it.

I believe the issue has been falsely presented as a political and intellectual clearcut choice – free trade versus mercantilism, laissez-faire versus *dirigisme* – when the reality has been much more flowing and complicated. For neither the creation of centralized state structures nor the steady commodification of everything are processes that can be analyzed in themselves, independent of each other. They are both key elements in and expressions of the continuing structuring of a capitalist world-economy.

All accumulators of capital take one fundamental position vis-à-vis state structures. They favor anything the state does to help them, in particular to further the possibilities of accumulation, and they oppose anything that hurts their interests. Two problems complicate every assessment by a particular set of accumulators of capital: over what length of time one makes one's assessment; and the degree to which one is able to take into account the consequences of indirect state action – what is usually termed political and cultural action as opposed to strictly economic action. And there is a further complication: the pressure in the short run of encrusted stereotyped assessments or what is usually termed the effect of ideology. But in the middle run, accumulators of capital are cold-heartedly self-interested in their assessments of state action and stand on no abstract principle.

What can a state that operates inside the capitalist world-economy and is subject to the constraints of the interstate system do for accumulators of capital who are located or are operating inside its frontiers? There are three main points at which state policy regularly touches directly the interests of accumulators of capital. The state tightens or loosens frontiers and thereby adjusts the ease with which goods, capital, and labor cross these frontiers. The state both taxes and disburses. The state makes rules as to the operations of social life within its frontiers. In each of these arenas, the attitude of accumulators of capital is, and can only be, pragmatic. Free flows across borders benefit some groups at certain times and do harm at others. A given taxation disbursement equation may or may not be beneficial, not only directly but also indirectly through its effect on competitors. And the state's efforts to maintain order and political stability may advance, but also may retard, the possibilities of profit for given groups of accumulators. The accumulators of capital have two ways of affecting such state action. They may operate within the political structure of the state or they may operate against the structure of the state in what might be called antinational activity. Patriotism is a calculation.

Conversely, the state has a similarly ambivalent attitude to accumulators of capital. First, there is no single social entity, 'the state', any more than there is a single entity, 'national capital'. There are multiple groups with varying degrees of control over state policy, frequently in considerable rivalry with each other. Groups that control state power have the same pragmatic attitude toward accumulators of capital as the latter do toward the former. From the point of view of those who control the state-machinery, enterprises are important sources of state wealth and are both directly and indirectly essential for the creation of the necessary tax base. State wealth is obviously related to the stability of the state structure and to the ability of the state-machinery to meet the multiple political demands placed upon it.

In addition, particular groups of state officials may owe short-term or even medium-term allegiance to particular groups of accumulators of capital, for reasons that range from venality to communal ties to the maintenance of a political base. But the immediate purpose of those who control state power is to retain that state power, just as the immediate purpose of accumulators of capital is to accumulate capital. To ensure the maintenance of internal order, those who control the state may, at various moments, have to make concessions to groups to which they hold either no or a lesser allegiance. Thus, just as given sets of accumulators of capital may turn against those who control the state-machinery, so may the reverse occur. Indeed, those who control the state-machinery may themselves have recourse to external, 'antinational' forces in their efforts to curb given sets of accumulators of capital.

Thus, for the world-economy as a whole, the strengthening of state structures and the commodification of everything are both long-term parallel but not necessarily harmonious trends, certainly not within the boundaries of given states. The pairing of the trends generates a continuous tension, reflected in considerable zigzagging of policy positions. This zigzagging constitutes a large part of the story of the continuing short-term political life of the world-system. The emphases in the policies of any given state are, furthermore, in large part a function of its role in the world-system and therefore of the range of options available both to those who control the state-machinery and to those within its jurisdiction who seek to accumulate capital.

All this is by way of prelude of analyzing what has or has not been special about France. In the beginning France suffered from being the heir of Charlemagne and Joan of Arc. In some sense, one can conceive of feudal Europe less as the outcome of the disintegration of the Roman Empire than as the outcome of the disintegration of the (putative) Carolingian world-empire. Its political disintegration did not go as far as it might have. In the Albigensian crusades, followed by the Hundred Years War, the area that is now France was seriously threatened with division into multiple enduring political entities. Joan of Arc incarnated – and hence symbolizes today – the politico-military counterthrust that prevented just such a political redefinition of France's state boundaries.

Thus, when the modern world-system began to be constructed in the second half of the fifteenth century, including as it did the creation of the first modern sovereign states through the agency of the so-called 'new monarchies', the boundaries of France were not much different from those of today. But the basic problem of the France of 1450, indeed of the France of 1750, was that it was too big.

It might have been better if France had lost its thirteenth-century battles. As has been frequently noted, France was the largest country in the European world-economy of early modern times – largest in area, and in population, and largest by a big margin. Consequently, France alone encompassed in a significant way the two prime geographical zones of Europe – the more northern cereals-producing zone and the more southerly wine-producing zone.

The French state was a complicated juridical amalgam with one basic structure that covered most of the northern part of the country and various other structures that covered many zones of the southern half as well as the Ponant in the west.[4] But this in itself was not unusual.

---

[4] The New Cambridge Modern History (14 vols, Cambridge University Press, Cambridge, 1970), vol. XIV: *Atlas*, eds. H. C. Darby and Harold Fullard, maps 112b, 113a, 113b.

The same could be said of Spain. As for the northern Netherlands (the United Provinces), its constitution was in some ways an absurdity. But such 'absurdities' were all part of the shaking down that marked the transformation of the multiple overlapping partial jurisdictions of a feudal system into the sovereign states that were being created within an interstate system. That England largely, although not entirely, escaped having one of these awkward state structures was due primarily to its late and top-down introduction of feudal forms, for, in consequence, the English feudal monarchy was already the most centralized of all in the pre-modern period. Thus, when we talk of 'absolute monarchies' – and the France of Louis XIV remains the exemplar of this genre – we are talking more of rhetoric than of reality, more of aspiration than of realization, more of weakness than of strength.

In addition to size, the other significant geographical feature was location. Given the boundaries of the European world-economy as it came to be constituted in the period 1450–1750, France had the nearest thing to a central location. Important members of the system were to be found on all its frontiers. It stood astride both the Atlantic and the Mediterranean, but was nonetheless very much a continental power. No other country combined all these features. They served France well in some ways, but meant inevitably that no interstate conflict could be without immediate consequence to her. France was never really at liberty to remain neutral for long.

In making the now inevitable comparisons between England and France, one should remember two things. First, France was four times the size of England and twice the size even of Great Britain. And second, England's size was approximately the same as that of the Five Great Farms, the truly comparable unit. Comparison of the Five Great Farms with England reveals that between 1450 and 1750 their differences were minimal: aproximately the same area without internal customs barriers, and hence one internal 'market'; the same cereals-based large agricultural units, the same trend towards 'disappearance' over time of the larger direct producer (yeoman farmer/*laboureur*), the same emergence of intermediate large-scale managers/rentiers, the same kind of textile industries that were undergoing comparable shifts from urban to rural and then back to urban locations. There was, however, one enormous difference: the Five Great Farms were located within a much larger political entity called France. Paris governed Nantes and Toulouse as well as Orléans and Beauvais. The Five Great Farms were not only a zone of internal free trade; they were a barrier to economic flows as well. Brittany and Languedoc were cut off from, far more than they were united with, the Ile de France. And from this reality many decisions flowed.

The English version of mercantilism, which provided the framework within which England laid the base in the seventeenth and eighteenth centuries for its economic triumphs of the nineteenth century, was much tighter and much more efficacious than the rival version that France, first under Richelieu and then under Colbert, tried to build. France was never mercantilist enough.[5] The explanation is political, and the underlying factor in the politics was the geography.

The consequences of this basic reality can be seen in three fundamental policy decisions, or more exactly policy outcomes, of the continuing internal debates between 1450 and 1815 – and beyond – which determined the place and patterns of France in the nineteenth and twentieth centuries.

1   France was less oriented than England to the development of settler colonies in the Americas.

Why? The creation of settler colonies, by no means an easy proposition, required considerable energy and expense, both for the governments and for the individual participants. No doubt some of the latter had immediate motives that made them wish to be settlers, but in general settler colonization was an uphill battle which the force of inertia, so to speak, was against. In this case, we should pose the historiographic question: did it offer sufficient social value for a given country to warrant the effort?

One of the significant advantages over time of the creation of settler colonies was the widening of markets for the products of the home country. If we start with England and the Five Great Farms as comparable units, where could external markets be found and secured? For both there was continental Europe. For England there was Scotland, with the Union of the Crowns of 1603 followed by the more important Union of Parliaments of 1707, and the settler colonies in Ireland and North America. For the Five Great Farms, there was the rest of France. Simply put, the efforts aimed at creating the internal economic unification of France, which was only fully achieved by the Revolution, was the

[5] See Charles H. Wilson, *England's Apprenticeship, 1603–1763* (Longmans, London, 1965), p. 65.

social equivalent for the period of the sixteenth to eighteenth centuries of England's creation of Great Britain plus England's settler colonization. It made no sense for France's central government to seek to construct a settler North America before 'absorbing' Languedoc and Brittany.

One might even say that England's option of settler colonization was a *pis aller*. Lacking the size of France's potential home market, England was forced into this less desirable alternative. But having been so forced, England obtained some hidden benefits. The English had to develop their navy and merchant fleet. To do this, they needed access to supplies of naval stores and thus had to concentrate on developing an export trade that made it possible to purchase them. Participation in an expanded Atlantic trade led to the development of a re-export trade to dispose of the surplus of tropical products, and hence served to create a powerful internal group whose interests were anti-mercantilistic. Finally, in precisely this period, sea transport became significantly less dear than land transport. What had originated as a response to England's weakness vis-à-vis France became over three centuries a source of strength.

2   The French state's geopolitical option was an orientation towards land power; that of England's was towards sea power.

The geographical basis was obvious. France was a great land power, and it occupied the heartland of the interstate system as it existed in the sixteenth to eighteenth centuries. England was spatially marginal, an island, and committed to the development of the North Atlantic link. Once again, this was France's relative strength. It occupied the center of the checkerboard and had the demographic and financial base to mount a large army. Once the Hapsburg rival structure broke into two, there was no obstacle to the French moment of 'preponderance' on the European continent.[6]

England could not rival France on land. Both England and France recognized early that neither could afford both land and sea as serious military expenditures. In England, there ensued a long debate in which the 'Maritime School' won out over the 'Continental School'.[7] In France no comparable debate took place. The definitive decision for both

---

[6] See A. de Saint-Léger and Philippe Sagnac, *La Préponderance Française* (F. Alcan, Paris, 1935).

[7] See C. Ernest Fayle, 'The Deflection of Strategy by Commerce in the Eighteenth Century', *Journal of the Royal United Service Institution*, 68 (1923), pp. 281–90.

seems to have occurred during the first great Anglo-French wars of
1689–1713, which included the decisive French naval defeat at Barfleur
in 1692.[8] The absence of a debate in France comparable to the one in
England demonstrates that, to France, France's choice seemed obvious.
It was dealing from strength and had only to follow the logical course
of action. England, given its spatial positioning in the world-system,
was dealing from weakness and had to opt once again for a *pis aller*, which
would once again turn out to have hidden advantages.

France's decision to orient her strategy to continental Europe had large
consequences. The strategies of the French and British states within the
interstate system came to diverge sharply. Given the mixture of interests
of those who controlled the state-machinery and those accumulators of
capital located in that state, and given the inevitably ambiguous relation
between the two groups, two alternate strategies were possible: to move
toward changing the capitalist world-economy into a world-empire; or
to move toward achieving hegemony in this capitalist world-economy
and its interstate system. They were – and are – radically different options
that resulted in different internal and external political alliances.

A move toward a world-empire requires the direct absorption of the
foreign elites, first through dynastic links, then through subordination,
eventually through conquest. A move toward hegemony in the interstate
system requires creation of conditions in which the foreign elites, kept
politically and culturally at a distance, find it in their own interest to
operate in the interest of the hegemonic power. One is a policy of intense,
hot links with passion, sympathy, and hatred. The other is a policy of
intricate, impersonal, cool links with mild distaste and interested
indifference. Compare the relations of France to Spain in the period
from Louis XIV to Napoleon with the relations of England to Portugal
during that same period. The former set of relations was imbued with
the spirit of a *Pacte Familial*, which culminated in Joseph Bonaparte on
the throne of Spain. The latter was marked by the deeply unequal
exchange relations instituted by the Treaty of Methuen and consecrated
in the nineteenth century by Ricardo's use of the example to demonstrate
the presumed beneficence of specialization in the international division
of labor through free trade. The same difference of strategy would repeat

[8] See John Ehrman, *The Navy in the War of William III, 1689–1697* (Cambridge
University Press, Cambridge, 1953); Geoffrey Symcox, *The Crisis of the French Sea Power,
1688–1697* (Martinus Nijhoff, The Hague, 1967).

itself in a later era when Germany and the United States would struggle for top position, and the roots were once again in the alternatives available to those in more and less central locations in the world-system.

The structure of a capitalist world-economy contains powerful forces hostile to its conversion into a world-empire, as both Louis XIV and, even more spectacularly, Napoleon would learn. Even clothed in universalist and egalitarian language, the imperial thrust cultivates its own opposition. The pay-off in the end is not worth the cost. Only in the absence of a viable choice does one enter the slower, more subtle, arduous path of constructing a hegemonic order within the framework of a universalist ideology that is more technocratic and less social. But it is the fable of the tortoise and the hare. When hegemony arrives, it pays off handsomely. Once, through careful long-term state action and monopolistic protection of one's 'secrets', one has obtained the true, if momentary, competitive edge, one can impose free trade à la England rather than trade constraint à la Continental Blockade, and end up on top. France's initial strengths once again proved her middle-term disadvantage.

3   The French state was more subject than the British to centrifugal forces, and hence the French state never grew as strong as the British state.

In France's political structure the northern heartland of the Five Great Farms, containing the capital city, controlled the country's policy. The outlying regions – the west, the south, the northeastern borderlands – lay outside, not merely geographically but juridically, culturally, and even linguistically. They were further disadvantaged in the taxation–disbursement equation, suffering higher taxation and lower disbursement,[9] but they were not outside the main currents of the economic life of the capitalist world-economy. The south via the Mediterranean, the Ponant via the Atlantic, the northeast borderlands via the long-existing trade routes of Europe's 'dorsal spine' were well situated to develop commerce and industrial production.

If we now return to Fox's two vectors, that of the centralization of the state and that of the development of non-local commerce, we can see clearly

[9] See René Pillorget, *Les Mouvements Insurrectionnels de Provence entre 1596 et 1715* (A. Pedone, Paris, 1975), p. 879.

how the different geography of the two countries led to different internal political alliances. In France, because of size, basic economic strength, and above all diversification and dispersion of production, the forces that supported state centralization had their base in the Five Great Farms and the forces that supported the development of non-local commerce had their base primarily in the outlying regions. In Great Britain the geographical periphery did not provide a primary impetus for either the movement to centralize the state or the movement to develop non-local commerce. (The somewhat in-between status of Lowland Scotland led to its rather inconsistent politics.) For these reasons the strains of capitalist development made it possible to arrive at earlier and more solid constitutional compromises in Great Britain than in France.

Those who controlled the economic and political structures in Great Britain enjoyed a greater degree of national harmony than their French counterparts did. They could build a much stronger state structure than the French could during the seventeenth and eighteenth centuries. The most important feature was that the British state could tax more – tax not only the aristocracy but the middle classes as well.[10] Since the British had a stronger state structure, they could also have a less costly direct tax-collecting system in contrast to France's *affermage* or tax-farming; they thus got a higher yield from the harvest of surplus-extraction.[11]

In consequence, the British state had the ability to aid significantly in the elimination of the stratum of small but independent cultivators – the so-called yeoman farmers/*laboureurs*. The economic process that undermined their survival were similar in England and France, particularly in France's cereal-growing zones in the Five Great Farms; but in the last great thrust to push out the hard core of resistants in the late eighteenth century, Britain's Enclosure Acts worked and similar legislative attempts in France were abortive or inadequate. There were

[10] See Roland Mousnier, 'L'Evolution des Finances Publiques en France et en Angleterre pendant les Guerres de la Ligue d'Augsbourg et de la Succession d'Espagne', *Revue Historique*, 205 (1951), pp. 1–23; Peter Mathias and Patrick O'Brien, 'Taxation in Britain and France, 1715–1810. A Comparison of the Social and Economic Incidence of Taxes Collected by the Central Governments', *Journal of European Economic History*, 5 (1976), pp. 601–50.

[11] See Pierre Léon, 'Les Nouvelles Élites', in *Histoire Economique et Social de la France*, eds. Fernand Braudel and Ernest Labrousse (4 tomes, Presses Universitaires de France, Paris, 1970–82), tome II: *Des Derniers Temps de l'Age Seigneurial aux Préludes de l'Age Industriel (1660–1789)*, eds. Ernest Labrousse et al. (1970), pp. 623–4.

many reasons for greater French political resistance to the division of the commons and the abolition of collective servitudes (obligatory *vaine pâture, droit de parcours*). French landowners had a greater scattering of landholdings than the English did[12] – the result in large part not of geography but of different inheritance systems. In France the advantages to large landowners of such land clearance was often ambiguous, for collective rights could sometimes also serve the large landowner well. But there was a second factor: the greater strength of French property rights – that is, the lesser juridical, and hence moral and political, right of those who controlled the state-machinery to interfere with those who controlled economic structures (even the small controllers such as the *laboureurs*).[13] The rights of property against the state were stronger in France than in Britain.

The weaker French state led to a stronger French peasantry, more able to resist the destructive consequences of the development of capitalist forces. This had two important results. In the seventeenth and eighteenth centuries, the numerous peasant uprisings could ally with various anti-centralizing forces in the French state, giving all these uprisings, whatever their religious or cultural clothing, a profoundly regionalist flavor that further weakened the state. The effect was cumulative. Second, when the last great and finally successful attempt at state centralization was made between 1789 and 1815, the peasantry was politically able to defend its interests effectively, and therefore effect a partial but significant redistribution of the capitalist pie.

If Colbertism, to use a generic name, did not succeed, it did not fail either. All the gigantic effort put into creating a centralized bureaucracy (the *intendants*) and into encouraging economic development (the *manufactures royales*) – an effort that resulted from the French state's relative weakness – were enough to hold the fort. When the Ponant began to relinquish its industrial base, to become more of a conveyor-belt of the Dutch,[14]

---

[12] See Jean Meuvret, *Études d'Histoire Économique* (A. Colin, Paris, 1971), p. 196.

[13] See Marc Bloch's comment: 'Natural in a country where the largest segment of landholding had not at all been able to achieve perpetuity, was [enclosure] conceivable in France? The economists, the administrators did not even envisage the possibility.' *Les Caractères Originaux de l'Histoire Rurale Française* (2 vols, A. Colin, Paris, 1952–6), vol. I (1952), p. 236.

[14] See Pierre Boulle, ' "Failed Transition", Lombardy and France: General Comments', in *Failed Transitions to Modern Industrial Society: Renaissance Italy and Seventeenth-Century Holland*, eds. Frederick Krantz and Paul M. Hohenberg (Interuniversity Centre for European Studies, Montreal, 1975), p. 73.

Colbertism reconstructed other industry elsewhere. The net balance many have been zero. But, as shown by the experience of Portugal in this same period, a net balance might well have been negative. From one perspective, the French Revolution was a 'go-for-broke' of Colbertism. From that perspective, especially in view of the consequences of twenty-five years of struggle in which the gap of French–British economic strength widened considerably to France's detriment, Lévy-Leboyer was right: the French Revolution was a 'national catastrophe'.[15] But from another perspective, it provided the structural adjustment that made possible an economic growth in nineteenth-century France without many of the 'disamenities' of British economic growth. 'Nor is it at all obvious that the path of economic development taken by France from 1780 to 1914 was inferior to the vaunted British model.'[16]

All these three differences between England and France from 1450 to 1750 derived in one way or another from their different geographies: England's greater investment in settler colonies, its geopolitical stress on sea rather than on land, and the regional correlation of economic and political forces that led to a weaker state structure in France. In combination, these differences explain England's ability to achieve during the eighteenth century, before the so-called 'cluster of innovations',[17] the succession of minor edges that permitted the breakthrough vis-à-vis the France of 1792–1815. France was the victim of its own early economic strength and seemingly central location in the first centuries of the capitalist world-economy. It suffered the great negatives this combination brought in its train – the two Frances of Edward Fox. England benefited from its tighter structure and its more marginal location during the sixteenth, seventeenth and eighteenth centuries, as Portugal had from its tighter structure and more marginal location during the fourteenth, fifteenth and sixteenth centuries.

But in the long run France benefited from its 'failures' vis-à-vis Britain, as did we all. French liberalism, which has always been a bit shrill, has traditionally been the expression of those who feared that France has failed, that is had needed in some sense to 'catch up' first with England,

[15] Maurice Lévy-Leboyer, *Les Banques Européennes et l'Industrialisation Internationale, dans la Première Moitié du XIXe Siècle* (Presses Universitaires de France, Paris, 1964), p. 25.

[16] Patrick O'Brien and Caglar Keyder, *Economic Growth in Britain and France, 1780–1914* (George Allen & Unwin, London, 1978), p. 196.

[17] Phyllis Deane, *The First Industrial Revolution* (2nd ed., Cambridge University Press, Cambridge, 1979), p. 106.

then with the United States. But the French liberals have never prevailed for very long. Witness the short-lived glory of 'grain liberalism' from 1763 to 1770,[18] brought to its knees by the *guerre des farines*.[19] French nationalism has constantly reasserted itself and has always found its realization in setting constraints on the hegemonic power – as much intellectually and culturally as politically or economically. France could not have played this role had it not had the particular geography of the 'two Frances', which it did have in early modern times, and which made it the *terre d'élection* of the life work of Edward Fox. What has been interpreted by too many as France's 'anomalous' history turns out rather to be perfectly explicable within a world-systems perspective, and indeed provides a key to understanding the complex history of the workings of the modern world-system well beyond the simplistic and ideological theorizing of nineteenth-century history and social science.

---

[18] See Steven L. Kaplan, *Bread, Politics, and Political Economy in the Reign of Louis XV* (2 vols, Martinus Nijhoff, The Hague, 1976).

[19] 'Against a crazy price of cereals regulated by supply and demand which was what the Physiocrat Turgot wanted, the mass of ordinary workers (*manoeuvriers*), especially the artisans, demanded in the name of "the moral economy of the crowd", a just price.' Emmanuel LeRoi Ladurie, 'De la Crise Ultime à la Vraie Croissance, 1690–1789', in *La Histoire de la France Rurale*, ed. Georges Duby (4 vols, Seuil, Paris, 1975–6), vol. II: *L'Age Classique des Paysans, 1340–1789*, ed. E. LeRoi Ladurie (1975), p. 388.

8

The Geography of European Statemaking and Capitalism Since 1500

CHARLES TILLY

OTHER FRANCES AND OTHER EUROPES[1]

TABLE 8.1   The basis of Fox's argument

	Communications/Control	Commerce
Land	easy	hard
Water	hard	easy

[1] I am grateful to the National Science Foundation for financial support. Participants in the North American Labor History Conference (Detroit, October 1984) gave me useful criticism of one portion of the argument. Wim Blockmans and R. Bin Wong provided valuable comments on an earlier draft of this paper. In addition to the items cited in the following notes, the general literature on which this paper draws includes: Risto Alapuro, 'Regional Variations in Political Mobilisation: On the Incorporation of the Agrarian Population into the State of Finland, 1907–1932', *Scandinavian Journal of History*, I (1976), pp. 215–42; Philippe Aydalot, Louis Bergeron, and Marcel Roncayolo, *Industrialisation et Croissance Urbaine dans la France du XIXème Siècle* (Centre de Recherches Historiques, École des Hautes Études en Sciences Sociales, Paris, 1981); Paul Bairoch, *Taille des Villes, Conditions de Vie et Développement Économique* (Éditions de l'École des Hautes Études en Sciences Sociales, Paris, 1977); Paul Bairoch and Maurice Lévy-Leboyer, eds., *Disparities in Economic Development since the Industrial Revolution* (Macmillan, London, 1981); Maxine Berg, Pat Hudson, and Michael Sonenscher, eds., *Manufacture in Town and Country Before the Factory* (Cambridge University Press, Cambridge, 1983); Grethe Authen Blom, ed., *Urbaniseringsprosessen i Norden* (3 vols, Universitetsforlaget, Oslo, 1977); Charles Bright and Susan Harding, eds., *Statemaking*

Edward Fox implicitly organized the argument of his stimulating *History in Geographic Perspective* around a four-fold table, shown in Table 8.1. Thus before the railroad era European places that stood at any distance from navigable waterways but within the range of demanding states were, he argued, likely to live parochial lives. State fiscal demands played a dominant part in the modest commercialization experienced by inland cities. Port cities, in contrast, escaped partially from state control and throve on their commercial contacts with centers elsewhere. Writing about Europe in general but concentrating on France, Fox drew from his neat distinctions a portrait of two contrasting social worlds, an account of

---

and Social Movements (University of Michigan Press, Ann Arbor, 1984); Harold Carter, *An Introduction to Urban Historical Geography* (Arnold, London, 1983); Hugh D. Clout, ed., *Themes in the Historical Geography of France* (Academic Press, London, 1977); Paul Combe, *Niveau de Vie et Progrès Technique en France (1860–1939). Contribution à l'Étude de l'Économie Française Contemporaine. Postface (1939–1949)* (Presses Universitaires de France, Paris, 1956); R. A. Dodghson and R. A. Butlin, eds., *An Historical Geography of England and Wales* (Academic Press, London, 1978); R. H. Dumke, 'The German Zollverein as a Model for Economic Integration', paper presented to the International Conference on Economic Integration in the 19th and 20th centuries, Schloss Rausch-Holzhausen, 1983; S. N. Eisenstadt, *The Political Systems of Empires: The Rise and Fall of the Historical Bureaucratic Societies* (Free Press, Glencoe, Ill., 1963); Edward Whiting Fox, *History in Geographic Perspective: The Other France* (W. W. Norton, New York, 1971); Rainer Fremdling and Richard Tilly, eds., *Industrialisierung und Raum. Studien zur Regionale Differenzierung im Deutschland des 19. Jahrhunderts* (Klett-Cotta, Stuttgart, 1979); David Friedman, 'A Theory of the Size and Shape of Nations', *Journal of Political Economy*, 85 (1977), pp. 59–78; John Gooch, *Armies in Europe* (Routledge & Kegan Paul, London, 1980); R. D. Grillo, ed., *'Nation' and 'State' in Europe: Anthropological Perspectives* (Academic Press, New York, 1980); F. E. Ian Hamilton, ed., *Contemporary Industrialization: Spatial Analysis and Regional Development* (Longman, London, 1978); John Hobcraft and Philip Rees, *Regional Demographic Development* (Croom Helm, London, 1979); Étienne Juillard and Henri Nonn, *Espaces et Régions en Europe Occidentale* (Éditions du Centre National de la Récherche Scientifique, Paris, 1976); Herman Kellenbenz, *The Rise of the European Economy: An Economic History of Continental Europe from the Fifteenth to the Eighteenth Century* (Weidenfeld and Nicolson, London, 1976); Kellenbenz, ed., *Agrarisches Nebengewerbe und Formen der Reagrarisierung im Spätmittelalter und 19./20. Jahrhundert* (Gustav Fischer, Stuttgart, 1975); Peter Kriedte, *Peasants, Landlords and Merchant Capitalists: Europe and the World Economy, 1500–1800* (Cambridge University Press, Cambridge, 1983); Witold Kula, 'Secteurs et Régions Arriérés dans l'Économie du Capitalisme Naissant', *Studi Storici*, I (1960), pp. 569–85; W. R. Lee, ed., *European Demography and Economic Growth* (Croom Helm, London, 1979); Pierre Leon, François Crouzet, and Raymond Gascon, eds., *L'Industrialisation en Europe au XIXe Siècle. Cartographie et Typologie* (Éditions du Centre National de la Récherche Scientifique, Paris, 1972); Yves Lequin, *Les Ouvriers de la*

French political distinctions, and reinterpretations of a number of major transitions. *History in Geographic Perspective* constitutes an effort to grasp the contrasting spatial logics of statemaking and capitalism.

Since the publication of *History in Geographic Perspective*, important new works by Eugen Weber, Yves Durand, and others have joined in Fox's

---

Région Lyonnaise (1848–1914) (2 vols, Presses Universitaires de Lyon, Lyon, 1977); Margaret Levi, 'The Predatory Theory of Rule', in *The Microfoundations of Macrosociology*, ed. Michael Hechter (Temple University Press, Philadelphia, 1983); Jack S. Levy, *War in the Great Power System, 1495–1975* (University Press of Kentucky, Lexington, 1983); Georges Livet and Bernard Vogler, eds., *Pouvoir, Ville, et Société en Europe, 1650–1750* (Ophrys, Paris, 1983); Alf Lüdtke, 'Genesis und Durchsetzung des Modernen Staates: Zur Analyse von Herrschaft under Verwaltung', *Archiv für Sozialgeschichte*, 20 (1980), pp. 470–91; Eric Maschke and Jurgen Sydow, eds., *Stadt und Umland. Protokoll der X. Arbeitstagung des Arbeitskreises für sudwestdeutsche Stadtgeschichtsforschung*, Veröffentlichungen der Kommission für Geschichtliche Landeskunde in Baden-Württemberg, Reihe B, 82 (Kohlhammer, Stuttgart, 1974); Franklin Mendels, 'Des Industries Rurales à la Protoindustrialisation: Historique d'un Changement de Perspective', *Annales: Économies, Sociétés, Civilisations*, 39 (1984), pp. 977–1008; John M. Merriman, ed., *Consciousness and Class Experience in Nineteenth Century Europe* (Holmes & Meier, New York, 1979); Jean Meyer et al., *Études sur les Villes en Europe Occidentale* (2 vols, Societé d'Edition d'Enseignement Supérieur, Paris, 1983); Alan S. Milward and S. B. Saul, *The Economic Development of Continental Europe, 1780–1870* (George Allen & Unwin, London, 1973); F. J. Monkhouse, *A Regional Geography of Western Europe*, 4th edn (Longmans, London, 1974); Daniel Noin, *Géographie Démographique de la France* (Presses Universitaires de France, Paris, 1973); John Patten, *Rural-Urban Migration in Pre-Industrial England*, Occasional Papers, No. 6 (School of Geography, Oxford University, Oxford, 1973); Norman J. G. Pounds, *An Historical Geography of Europe, 1500–1840* (Cambridge University Press, Cambridge, 1979); Norman J. G. Pounds and Sue Simons Ball, 'Core-Areas and the Development of the European States System', *Annals of the Association of American Geographers*, 54 (1964), pp. 24–40; E. A. G. Robinson, 'Location Theory, Regional Economics and Backward Areas', in *Backward Areas in Advanced Countries* (Macmillan, London, 1969); William Rowe, 'Approaches to Modern Chinese Social History', in *Reliving the Past*, ed. Olivier Zunz (University of North Carolina Press, Chapel Hill, 1985); Gilbert Rozman, *Urban Networks in Russia, 1750–1800, and Premodern Periodization* (Princeton University Press, Princeton, 1976); Josiah Cox Russell, *Medieval Regions and their Cities* (David & Charles, Newton Abbot, 1972); C. T. Smith, *An Historical Geography of Western Europe before 1800* (Longmans, London, 1967); Carol A. Smith, 'Analyzing Regional Systems', in *Regional Analysis*, ed. Carol A. Smith (2 vols, Academic Press, New York, 1976), vol. 2: *Social Systems*, pp. 3–20; Arthur L. Stinchcombe, *Economic Sociology* (Academic Press, New York, 1983); Jan Sundin and Eric Soderlund, eds., *Time, Space and Man: Essays in Microdemography* (Almqvist & Wiksell International, Stockholm, 1979); Francis X. Sutton, 'Representation and the Nature of Political Systems', *Comparative Studies in Society and History*, 2 (1959), pp. 1–10; Louise A. Tilly, 'Industrial Production and portrayal of interior France as fragmented and isolated.[2] Simultaneously, however, inconvenient facts have come more clearly into view: the extensive population mobility of the eighteenth century, the eighteenth-century expansion of manufacturing in many rural regions, the formation of something like a national grain market well before the railroad, and more.[3] Guy Arbellot writes of a 'great change'

and the Redistribution of Capital and Labor in Nineteenth Century Lombardy', in *Habiter la Ville. XVe–XXe Siècles*, eds. Maurice Garden and Yves Lequin (Presses Universitaires de Lyon, Lyon, 1984); Clive Trebilcock, *The Industrialization of the Continental Powers, 1780–1914* (Longman, London, 1981); *Villes en Mutation XIXe–XXe Siècles. 10e Colloque International. Actes* (Credit Communal de Belgique, Brussels, 1982); Jan de Vries, *The Economy of Europe in an Age of Crisis, 1600–1750* (Cambridge University Press, Cambridge, 1976); Jan de Vries, 'Barges and Capitalism: Passenger Transportation in the Dutch Economy, 1632–1839', *A. A. G. Bijdragen*, 21 (1978), pp. 33–398; Aristide R. Zolberg, 'Strategic Interactions and the Formation of Modern States: France and England', *International Social Science Journal*, 32 (1980), pp. 687–716.

[2] Yves Durand, *Vivre au Pays au XVIIe Siècle. Essai sur la Notion de Pays dans l'Ouest de la France* (Presses Universitaires de France, Paris, 1984); Eugen Weber, *Peasants into Frenchmen: The Modernization of Rural France, 1870–1914* (Stanford University Press, Stanford, 1976).

[3] Maurice Aymard et al., eds., *Les Migrations dans les Pays Méditerranéens au XVIIIe et au Début du XIXe* (Centre de la Méditerranée Moderne et Contemporaine, Nice, 1974); Serge Chassagne, 'Aspects des Phénomènes d'Industrialisation et de Désindustrialisation dans les Campagnes Françaises', *Revue du Nord*, 63 (1981), pp. 35–57; Abel Châtelain, *Les Migrants Temporaires en France de 1800 à 1914* (Publications de l'Université de Lille III, Villeneuve D'Ascq, 1976); Bernard Chevalier, *Les Bonnes Villes de France du XIVe au XVIe Siècle* (Aubier Montaigne, Paris, 1982); Hugh D. Clout, ed., *Agriculture in France on the Eve of the Railway Age* (Croom Helm, London, 1980); Colin Heywood, 'The Role of the Peasantry in French Industrialization, 1815–80', *Economic History Review*, 2nd series, 34 (1981), pp. 359–76; Steven Laurence Kaplan, *Provisioning Paris: Merchants and Millers in the Grain and Flour Trade during the Eighteenth Century* (Cornell University Press, Ithaca, New York, 1984); Peter Kriedte, Hans Medick, and Jurgen Schlumbohm, *Industrialisierung vor der Industrialisierung. Gewerbliche Warenproduktion auf dem Land in der Formationsperiode des Kapitalismus* (Vandenhoeck & Ruprecht, Göttingen, 1977); Jan Lucassen, *Naar de Kusten van de Noordzee. Trekarbeid in Europees Perspektief, 1600–1900* (privately published, Gouda, 1984); Ted Margadant, 'Proto-urban Development and Political Mobilization during the Second Republic', in *French Cities in the Nineteenth Century*, ed. John M. Merriman (Hutchinson, London, 1982); Kevin McQuillan, 'Modes of Production and Demographic Patterns in Nineteenth-Century France', *American Journal of Sociology*, 89 (1984), pp. 1324–46; Franklin F. Mendels, 'Seasons and Regions in Agriculture and Industry during the Process of Industrialization', in *Region und Industrialisierung. Studien zur Rollen der Region in der Wirtschaftsgeschichte der Letzten zwei Jahrhunderte*, ed. Sidney Pollard (Vandenhoeck & Ruprecht, Göttingen, 1980),

in French roads during the eighteenth century. Between 1765 and 1780 alone, a combination of improved surfaces and accelerated coaches halved the travel times between Paris and a number of interior cities. Some examples are shown in Table 8.2. Times to cities along the older main roads, such as Lyon (4–5 days), Valenciennes (1–2 days), and Rouen (less than one day), changed little during the same period.[4] Thus an already fairly effective system of land communication ramified and intensified.

Water transportation likewise linked France's interior cities more effectively than Fox's scheme implies. Bernard Lepetit's analysis of French land and water connections in 1835 shows the northern two-fifths of the French interior strongly connected by navigable waterways and likewise assigns Paris a powerful position within the entire system.[5] Lepetit's findings undermine the sharp distinction of ports from all other places. So do recent studies of population mobility before France's capital-

---

pp. 177–89; Leslie Page Moch, *Paths to the City: Regional Migration in Nineteenth Century France* (Sage, Beverly Hills, 1983); Michel Morineau, *Les Faux-semblants d'un Démarrage Économique. Agriculture et Démographie en France au XVIIIe Siècle*, Cahiers des Annales, 30 (Armand Colin, Paris, 1971); William N. Parker and Eric L. Jones, eds., *European Peasants and Their Markets* (Princeton University Press, Princeton, 1975); Abel Poitrineau, *Remues d'Hommes. Les Migrations Montagnardes en France, 17e–18e Siècles* (Aubier Montaigne, Paris, 1983); Jean-Pierre Poussou, *Bordeaux et le Sud-Ouest au XVIIIe Siècle. Croissance Économique et Attraction Urbaine* (Éditions de l'École des Hautes Études en Sciences Sociales, Paris, 1983); Roger Price, *The Economic Modernisation of France* (Croom Helm, London, 1975); Vernon W. Ruttan, 'Structural Retardation and the Modernization of French Agriculture: A Skeptical View', *Journal of Economic History*, 38 (1978), pp. 714–28; Louise A. Tilly, 'The Food Riot as a Form of Political Conflict in France', *Journal of Interdisciplinary History*, 2 (1971), pp. 23–57; David M. Weir, 'Markets and Mortality in France, 1600–1789', paper presented to the Cliometrics Twenty-Fifth Anniversary World Congress, 1985.

[4] Guy Arbellot, 'La Grande Mutation des Routes de France au Milieu du XVIIIe Siècle', *Annales: Économies, Sociétés, Civilisations*, 28 (1973), pp. 765–91.

[5] Bernard Lepetit, *Chemins de Terre et Voies d'Eau. Réseaux de Transports, Organisation de l'Espace* (Éditions de l'École des Hautes Études en Sciences Sociales, Paris, 1984); see also André Rémond, *Études sur la Circulation Marchande en France aux XVIIIe et XIXe Siècles* (Rivière, Paris, 1956), vol. I: *Les Prix des Transports Marchands de la Révolution au Premier Empire*; François Roubaud, 'Partition Économique de la France dans la Première Moitié du XIXe Siècle', *Institut d'Historie Économique et Sociale de l'Université de Paris I Panthéon-Sorbonne. Recherches et Travaux*, 12 (1983), pp. 33–58; Louis Thbaut, 'Les Voies Navigables et l'Industrialisation du Nord de la France', *Revue du Nord*, 61 (1979), pp. 149–64.

TABLE 8.2 Days' travel to Paris

From	1765	1780
Limoges	9	3-4
Cahors	13	5-6
Dijon	5-6	2-3
Nancy	7-8	2-3
Sedan	5	1

intensive industrialization, which show that areas bound by land transportation frequently supported large systems of temporary migration to areas of more intensive wage-work and trade. Such regions overcame the limits on their food supply by exporting mouths and bellies.[6] Accumulating evidence, in short, challenges the sharp distinction between ports and interior cities that *History in Geographic Perspective* proposes.

Nevertheless, Fox's analysis gives a fresh look to old, important problems. At a European scale, water-transport and land-transport economies did contrast sharply until the nineteenth century. Water transport and intensive commercialization did reinforce each other. Landlocked cities – Madrid and Berlin are the most salient examples – faced severe practical limitations to their food supplies and grew only by exercising very extensive control over the food production of their hinterlands.

In the case of Madrid, David Ringrose describes the paradoxical process by which the city's demand for wheat dominated the commercialized production of a hinterland 150 to 200 miles in diameter, called up a 'corps of purchasing agents [who] . . . traveled throughout Castile buying up the output of the two or three major farmers and rentiers in each village and dealing with resident brokers in the principal market towns', eventually encouraged those wealthier suppliers to take up idle residence in Madrid and thus compound the tight interdependence of city and hinterland, but had relatively little transforming effect on small peasants' production.[7] On the whole, Ringrose portrays Madrid as a bureaucratized parasite that impeded Spanish economic expansion

[6] See especially Châtelain, *Les Migrants Temporaires en France*; Lucassen, *Naar de Kusten van de Noordzee*; and Poitrineau, *Remues d'Hommes*.
[7] David R. Ringrose, *Madrid and the Spanish Economy, 1560–1850* (University of California Press, Berkeley, Calif, 1983), quotation from p. 190.

and did not even stimulate the establishment of efficient agriculture in its own drawing area until nineteenth-century transport changes brought costs down. Compared to sister cities on coasts and navigable rivers, landlocked centers such as Madrid only supplied themselves at the cost of extensive organization and coercion.

In a similar way, the combination of low transport costs, commercialized agriculture, and long-distance trade significantly affected the fiscal policy of a city or state and the consequences of that policy.[8] Maritime England, Holland, and Denmark drew large shares of their governmental revenues from customs and excise taxes without building bulky bureaucracies for tax collection. That policy had less promise for inland Poland or Prussia. In Europe's German regions, city states survived on customs and excise so long as they could monopolize important trade routes, but they never succeeded in dominating more than their immediate hinterlands. On the whole, bulky state structures grew up on a base of taxes drawn from land-linked grain farming. All these historical realities, and more, suggest that Fox's four-fold distinction touches important divisions within the European experience.

The remainder of this essay conducts another search for those divisions at a European scale. Starting from Fox's problem, it lays out arguments and historical speculations about the social processes that produced the correlations Fox observed. The core argument follows a simple line: the formation of national states and the development of capitalism were the dominant processes that transformed Europe from 1500 onward. Each had a distinctive spatial logic – a logic that changed to some extent as a function of alterations in the predominant activities and organizations within statemaking and capitalism. The relative position of any locality within the two dominant processes strongly affected its social structure. The spatial distribution of different kinds of localities therefore changed systematically in the course of statemaking and the development of capitalism. This essay will simply explore some of the implications of that argument and illustrate them by means of broad observations on changes in European political and economic geography since 1500.

Students of Europe have often thought about the encounters between commercial systems and political systems, between merchants and

---

[8] See Rudolf Braun, 'Steuern und Staatsfinanzierung als Modernisierungsfaktoren: Ein Deutsch-Englischer Vergleich', in *Studien zum Beginn der Modernen Welt*, ed. Reinhard Koselleck (Klett-Cotta, Stuttgart, 1977).

statemakers. Alexander Gerschenkron saw the variable relations between capitalists and managers of states as a key to the diverging patterns of European industrialization.[9] Stein Rokkan tried to capture the covariation of economies and political systems in a giant 'conceptual map' of Europe.[10] Michael Hechter and William Brustein have divided the continent of a thousand years ago into sedentary pastoral, petty-commodity, and feudal modes of production, then argued that only the feudal regions served as effective bases for the construction of large national states.[11] None of these schemes, however, adequately represents the partial independence and continuous interaction of the two regional systems built around coercion and extraction or production and distribution. European statemaking and capitalism constituted two sides of a dialectical process. Analyses of the European experience must deal fully with the construction, destruction, interaction, and change of both sides: state systems and regional modes of production.

ACTIVITIES OF STATES

As of 1300 or so, identification of the most powerful organizations in Europe remains debatable; churches, major cities, leagues of cities, conglomerate monarchies, and states all wielded considerable power. By 1700, national states had clearly become dominant. To define these: a national state is a relatively centralized, differentiated, and distinct organization that controls the principal concentrated means of coercion within a contiguous and clearly bounded territory. In this strict sense, national states are rare historical phenomena. Different parts of the world have much more often organized themselves in more or less autonomous bands, lineages, leagues, and empires than they have in national states. Yet after 1400 such organizations greatly

[9] Alexander Gerschenkron, *Economic Backwardness in Historical Perspective* (Harvard University Press, Cambridge, Mass., 1962).

[10] Stein Rokkan and Derek W. Urwin, eds, *The Politics of Territorial Identity: Studies in European Regionalism* (Sage, Beverley Hills, 1982); Per Torsvik, ed., *Mobilization, Center-Periphery Structures and Nation-Building: A Volume in Commemoration of Stein Rokkan* (Universitetsforlaget, Bergen, 1981).

[11] Michael Hechter and William Brustein, 'Regional Modes of Production and Patterns of State Formation in Western Europe', *American Journal of Sociology*, 85 (1980), pp. 1061–94.

increased in strength; they began to divide up the entire territory of Europe into separate terrains.

Agents of the sorts of states that have prevailed in Europe since 1500 have carried on six major activities in varying combinations:[12]

1 Warmaking: eliminating or neutralizing their own rivals outside the territories in which they have clear and continuous control.
2 Statemaking: eliminating or neutralizing their rivals inside those territories.
3 Protection: eliminating or neutralizing the enemies of their clients, both inside and outside the territory in which they, the agents, have clear and continuous control.
4 Production: creating goods and services (both individual and collective) by transforming labor, land, capital, and/or raw materials.
5 Distribution: allocating goods and services, both individual and collective.
6 Extraction: acquiring the means of carrying out the previous five activities: warmaking, statemaking, protection, production, and distribution.

These activities, to be sure, overlap and depend on each other. To the extent that the external enemies of state managers and of their clients coincide, for example, warmaking and protection combine. Warmaking,

[12] Edward Ames and Richard T. Rapp, 'The Birth and Death of Taxes: A Hypothesis', *Journal of Economic History*, 37 (1977), pp. 161–78; Bertrand Badie and Pierre Birnbaum, *Sociologie de l'État* (Bernard Grasset, Paris, 1979); Richard Bean, 'War and the Birth of the Nation State', *Journal of Economic History*, 33 (1973), pp. 203–21; Pierre Birnbaum, *La Logique de l'État* (Fayard, Paris, 1982); Samuel E. Finer, 'The Morphology of Military Regimes', in *Soldiers, Peasants, and Bureaucrats: Civil-Military Relations in Communist and Modernizing Regimes*, eds. Roman Kolkowicz and Andrzej Korbonski (Routledge & Kegan Paul, London, 1982); Metin Heper, 'The State and Public Bureaucracy: A Comparative and Historical Perspective', *Comparative Studies in Society and History*, 27 (1985), pp. 86–110; Peter Mathias and Patrick O'Brien, 'Taxation in Britain and France, 1715–1810. A Comparison of the Social and Economic Incidence of Taxes Collected for the Central Governments', *Journal of European Economic History*, 5 (1976), pp. 601–50; William H. McNeill, *The Pursuit of Power: Technology, Armed Force, and Society since AD 1000* (University of Chicago Press, Chicago, 1982); George Modelski, 'The Long Cycle of Global Politics and the Nation-State', *Comparative Studies in Society and History*, 20 (1978), pp. 214–35; Barrington Moore, Jr, *Social Origins of Dictatorship and Democracy* (Beacon Press, Boston, 1966); Gianfranco Poggi, *The Development of the Modern State: A Sociological Introduction* (Standord University Press, Stanford, 1978).

in most states, sets the large rhythms of extraction: taxation, borrowing, conscription, and similar extractive activities rise and fall with war and preparation for war. The labels are, nevertheless, more than different words for the same thing. The relative inportance of these various activities changes over time, and varies from one state to another. The contrasting histories of warmaking Prussia and protection-lending Switzerland – at least after Swiss conquests ended, early in the sixteenth century – make the point clearly.

Warmaking, statemaking, and extraction dominated the early centuries of statemaking; their coercive core established the priority of states over all other organizations in their vicinities. Protection gained in relative importance up to a point as, on average, the protected proportion of the population rose; the establishment of police forces distinct from the national military capped that development. In the last century or so all states have carried on increasing amounts of production and distribution. So far, however, they have varied more in the extent of their involvement in those activities than with respect to warmaking, statemaking, protection, and extraction.

Each activity has spatial implications. Warmaking, especially on land, gains from and promotes the creation of a large, contiguous, defensible, and clearly bounded home territory; that is more true of land warfare than of seafaring. Success in warfare implies expansion and consolidation of national territory.

Statemaking benefits from the establishment of hierarchical, geographically dispersed grids of surveillance and control through the national territory, as well as from the creation of correspondence between national boundaries and lines of cultural heterogeneity. In Europe, statemaking occurred, broadly speaking, in two major phases. During the first, the central powers eliminated, subdued, supplanted, co-opted, or bought out regional power-holders, through whom they continued to rule indirectly. During the second, beginning with the French Revolution, European states began to rule directly, extending their surveillance and control into local communities and daily life. (It would, of course, be perfectly compatible with this summary to discover that in the process states became subservient to capitalist interests; everything depends on the terms of accord between capitalists and statemakers.)

Protection has more variable implications for space, depending on the character and location of the state's clients. To the extent that they are traders who operate abroad, as Frederic Lane showed for Venice, agents of a state have incentives to build mobile, wide-ranging means of surveillance and military intervention.[13] More generally, protection calls for a distribution of coercive resources that corresponds to the geographical distribution of clients. The correspondence operates both nationally and locally: rural areas, in which a high proportion of all territory falls into private space, require a different style of policing from that required by urban areas, in which the majority of all space is public or readily accessible from public space. As countries urbanize, therefore, shifts toward routine patrolling, police-initiated apprehension of offenders, and public order offenses tend to occur.

Production and distribution likewise vary in geographical implications, in accordance with goods, services, producers, and consumers. Until the later nineteenth century European states generally concentrated their direct productive activity on capital-intensive items having military or fiscal significance, such as cannon, ships, salt, and tobacco. Meanwhile, they aimed their distributive activity at food and fiscally crucial items. The production piled up in a few well-defended locations, but the distribution required a wide net of inferior agents.

Extraction of food, men, services, draft animals, and money to support warmaking, statemaking, and protection favored the creation of hierarchical systems of surveillance and control spread throughout the national territory but especially dense where those resources were richest. In European statemaking, the formation of regular systems for conscription, supply, and, especially, taxation to support warmaking shaped the state's basic structures: treasury, debt, central bureaucracy, representative institutions. The bulk of those structures, however, depended on the interaction between the volume of extraction, the organization of extraction, and the mobility of the extracted resources. At one extreme, the Dutch state taxed the trade of its highly monetized economy without building a huge apparatus. At another, Russia created a cumbersome bureaucracy in the effort to extract revenue from its vast but little-commercialized lands.

---

[13] Frederic C. Lane, 'Force and Enterprise in the Creation of Oceanic Commerce', *The Tasks of Economic History*. Supplemental issue of the *Journal of Economic History*, 10 (1950), pp. 19–31; Lane, 'Economic Consequences of Organized Violence', *Journal of Economic History*, 18 (1958), pp. 401–17; Lane, 'The Economic Meaning of War and Protection', in *Venice and History: The Collected Papers of Frederic C. Lane* (Johns Hopkins University Press, Baltimore, 1966; first published in 1942); Lane, 'The Role of Governments in Economic Growth in Early Modern Times', *Journal of Economic History*, 35 (1975), pp. 8–17.

In general, nevertheless, states moved in the same direction. The expansion of warmaking, statemaking, protection, production, distribution, and extraction promoted the creation of large, contiguous, bounded, socially homogeneous territories divided into hierarchically controlled administrative areas that differed somewhat in organization as a function of proximity to the capital, to frontiers, and to resources suitable for state activities. Warmaking, statemaking, protection, production, distribution, and extraction, in short, built national states.

CAPITALIST SPACE

The spatial structure of a capitalist economy obviously depends on more than one factor. Distribution of raw materials, mix of goods and services produced, prevailing technologies of production and distribution, spatial pattern of labor supply, location of markets, costs of shipment and communication interact to produce a complex geography. Yet on the large scale and in the long run three factors dominate the system: the location of capital, its mobility, and the distribution of markets for the goods and services produced under its control.

Over the centuries after 1500, the geographic distribution of European capital shifted several times, and significantly. On an international scale, Fernand Braudel and Immanuel Wallerstein have called attention to the successive centers of capital accumulation: Genoa, Antwerp, Amsterdam, London, New York.[14] As hegemony shifted from one to the next, the relative importance of the networks of cities that were most closely connected with the capitalist headquarters likewise shifted; Seville, Madrid, Milan, Lyon, Paris, Bruges, Augsburg, Danzig, Kiev, and other regional metropolises likewise had their moments of sun and shade.

At a smaller scale, capital eventually concentrated; a system in which many scattered merchants each deployed enough capital to keep households and shops producing gave way to one in which a few hands held the major part of the capital. Late in the process, the mobility of capital declined as its owners and managers fixed it in buildings, machines, mines, raw materials, stocks, and payroll funds. The

[14] Fernand Braudel, *Civilisation Materielle, Économie, et Capitalisme, XVe–XVIIIe Siècle* (3 vols, Armand Colin, Paris, 1979); Immanuel Wallerstein, *The Modern World-System* (2 vols, Academic Press, New York, 1974 and 1980).

concentration and immobilization of capital, in their turn, promoted a general implosion of production: deindustrialization of the countryside, clustering of labor in and around major cities, increasing separation of workers from control of the means of subsistence and of production, and, therefore, accelerated proletarianization. In agricultural areas, a less visible but no less insistent logic of concentration worked itself out, as enclosures, capitalization of farming, and elimination of common rights squeezed tenants, squatters, and householders into agricultural and industrial wage-labor, and finally off the land entirely.

The distribution of markets for goods and services likewise changed drastically over the centuries. The establishment of national and international markets for food, the growth of regional textile industries that were oriented to American, African, and Middle Eastern consumers, and the demand engendered by the great urban concentrations of wage-earners and their separation from production of food and clothing all bespoke increases in the scale and regional differentiation of markets, not to mention alterations in the relative importance of different market centers.

We might summarize these many changes in the geography of European capitalism as two distinct phases:

1 From 1500 to 1800 or so, merchant capital remained mobile and dispersed. A large portion of production went into food and textiles, and increases in production generally occurred through the multiplication of small, dispersed, merchant-connected units of production such as households and shops. Capital frequently moved to the location of labor rather than vice versa. Consequence: a finely articulated hierarchy of markets from local to international, with local markets that corresponded to the geography of labor.

2 The nineteenth and twentieth centuries brought expansion and concentration of capital, fixing of capital in a limited number of (mainly urban) locations, movement of labor to those locations, increasing commercial production of consumer durables and services, and a sharpening division between agricultural countryside and service plus industrial production in cities. Consequence: radical urban implosion, simultaneous expansion and simplification of the market system, increasing organization of the system around large cities.

Did these transformations of capitalist economy spell themselves out as clear geographic shifts at the scale of Europe as a whole? If so, how?

PRODUCTION, COERCION, SPACE

From the fifteenth century onward, the map of Europe reorganized in two contrasting ways: cities multiplied and crowded together, while states expanded, consolidated, and dwindled in number. The number of cities greatly increased; as a consequence the hinterland served or dominated by the average single city diminished. Let us take the land area of Europe west of Russia as 1.9 million square miles, imagining each city and its hinterland as a circle with the city ensconced exactly in the center. Jan de Vries's recent compilation of evidence concerning European urbanization since 1500 makes possible some simple but telling computations.[15]

	1500	1600	1700	1800	1890
Number of cities of 10,000 or more	154.0	220.0	224.0	364.0	1,709.0
Population in cities of 10,000 or more (millions)	3.4	5.9	7.5	12.2	66.9
Percentage of population in cities of 10,000 +	5.6	7.6	9.2	10.0	29.0
Square miles per city (thousands)	123.0	86.0	85.0	52.0	11
Radius of circle with city at its center (miles)	198.0	165.0	164.0	129.0	59

During the twentieth century, the barrier of 10,000 lost its meaning. By 1980, a full 390 cities had 100,000 inhabitants or more. In fact, the 1980 statistics showed 34.6 per cent of the population in places of 100,000 or more.[16]

---

[15] Jan de Vries, *European Urbanization, 1500–1800* (Harvard University Press, Cambridge Mass., 1984), pp. 29–48; see also Peter Hall and Dennis Hay, *Growth Centres in the European Urban System* (Heinemann, London, 1980); Paul M. Hohenberg and Lynn Hollen Lees, *The Making of Urban Europe* (Harvard University Press, Cambridge Mass., 1985); H. Schmal, ed., *Patterns of Europe Urbanization since 1500* (Croom Helm, London, 1981).
[16] de Vries, *European Urbanization*, p. 47.

The numbers describe an interesting, and partly unexpected, sequence. Notice, for example, the period from 1600 to 1700: almost no increase in the sheer number of larger cities, declining rate of growth (as compared with the previous century) in the absolute population of those cities as well as their share of the entire population. During the following century, a time of rapid general population growth, we witness a sharp increase in the total number of urban places, a significant rise in total urban population, but a further slowing of gains in the urban share of the total population. In the nineteenth century, implosion: five-fold increase in the number of larger cities, quintupling of their population, tripling of the proportion urban. Only in the nineteenth century do the figures identify the larger city as the predominant site for production, consumption, and proletarianization.

Over the entire period from 1500 to 1890, as the population in cities of 10,000 or more increased twenty-fold, such cities became around twelve times as thick on the ground. The great acceleration of urban growth came after 1800, with the nineteenth-century concentration of capital, increase in scale of workplaces, and creation of mass transport. But through most of the period after 1500, the exclusive hinterlands available to most cities were shrinking in size.

States, on the other hand, diminished in number and increased in area. The European map of 1500 assigns substantial zones to Spain, France, England, Sweden, Poland, Russia, and the Ottoman Empire, but also marks off hundreds of duchies, principalities, archbishoprics, city states, and other miniature states. The roughly 500 formally autonomous European political entities of the time controlled an average of 3,800 square miles – the order of today's Cyprus, Lebanon, or Jamaica. Europe's population of approximately 62 million in 1500 divided up into an average of some 125,000 persons per state.

During the next four centuries, many peace treaties and a few deliberate federations drastically reduced the number of European states. During the nineteenth century, the number stabilized. At the beginning of 1848, for instance, Europe hosted from 20 to 100 states, depending on how one counts the 39 members of the German Confederation, the 17 papal states, the 22 technically autonomous segments of Switzerland, and a few dependent but formally distinct units such as Luxembourg and Norway. The full alphabetical list then began with tiny Anhalt-Bernburg, Anhalt-Dessau and Anhalt-Kothan before getting to more substantial Austria, Baden, and Bavaria.

Major consolidations occurred with the formation of the German Empire and the Kingdom of Italy. By the start of 1890, the roster had declined to about 30, of which 9 were members of the German Empire. At the end of 1918, the list included about 25 separate states. Although boundaries changed significantly with the settlements of World Wars I and II, the number and size of European states did not change dramatically during the twentieth century. If, following Small and Singer, we count only those states large enough to make an independent military difference, we actually detect a slight twentieth-century reversal of the long-term trend: 21 contenders at the end of the Napoleonic Wars, 26 in 1848, and 29 (including Malta, Cyprus, and Iceland) in 1980.[17]

In contrast to the 3,800 square miles of 1500, the 30 states of 1890 each controlled an average of 63,000 square miles – in the class of today's Nicaragua, Syria, and Tunisia. Instead of the 124,000 inhabitants of 1500, the average state of 1890 had about 7.7 million. Imagined as circles, states rose from an average radius of 35 to 142 miles. Furthermore, although such micro-states as Andorra (175 square miles), Liechtenstein (61), San Marino (24), and even Monaco (0.7) survived the great consolidation, inequalities of size declined radically over time.

The last major region of Europe to consolidate into substantial national states was the Rhineland corridor, a band of city states from northern Italy to the Low Countries. The successive unifications of Germany and Italy brought those prosperous but cantankerous little municipalities and their hinterlands under national control. It is as if Europeans discovered that under the conditions prevalent since 1800 or so a viable state required a radius of at least 60 miles, and could not easily control more than a 250-mile radius.

The diverging trends of cities and states changed some critical ratios. In 1500, Europe had only one city of 10,000 or more inhabitants for every three or four states. In 1890, the mythical average state had about six cities of 10,000 or more. Today, there are more than 15 cities of 100,000 per state, and they contain more than a third of the average European state's population. That change alone implies findamental alterations in the relations between rulers and ruled: altered techniques of control, altered fiscal strategies, altered demands for services, altered

[17] Melvin Small and J. David Singer, *Resort to Arms: International and Civil Wars, 1816–1980* (Sage, Beverley Hills, 1982), pp. 47–50.

politics.[18] The general establishment of uniformed, salaried, bureaucratized police forces, the shift of police forces toward patrolling, surveillance, and anticipation of criminal and collective action, the declining importance of land taxes, the creation of employment services, and the rise of the demonstration as a means of political communication all reflect, in their ways, the altered relationships between the geographies of states and of capitalism.

Europe's thinning states and thickening cities pose a fascinating historical problem: why, how, and with what consequences did the changes in scale occur? The question recalls Edward Fox's initial problem.

FROM EUROPE TO CHINA TO EUROPE

The European changes also recall an important contribution to Chinese history by G. William Skinner.[19] Skinner portrays the social geography of imperial China as the intersection of two sets of central-place hierarchies. The first, constructed largely from the bottom up, emerged from economic transactions; its overlapping units consisted of larger and larger market areas centered on towns and cities of increasing size. The second, imposed mainly from the top down, resulted from imperial control; its nested units comprised a hierarchy of administrative jurisdictions. Down to the level of the *hsien*, or county, every city had a place in both the commercial and the administrative hierarchy. Below that level, even the mighty Chinese Empire ruled indirectly through its gentry. In the top-down system, we find the spatial logic of coercion and extraction; in the bottom-up, the logic of production and distribution.

In some regions imperial control was weak relative to commercial activity; there, cities generally occupied higher ranks in the order of markets than in the imperial order. Elsewhere (especially at the empire's periphery, where regions were typically more valuable to the empire

---

[18] Jacques Aubert et al., *L'État et sa Police en France (1789–1914)* (Droz, Geneva, 1979); Stanley Cohen and Andrew Scull, eds., *Social Control and the State: Historical and Comparative Essays* (Martin Robertson, Oxford, 1983); Clive Emsley, *Policing and its Context, 1750–1870* (Macmillan, London, 1983).

[19] G. William Skinner, 'Cities and the Hierarchy of Local Systems', in *The City in Late Imperial China*, ed. G. William Skinner (Stanford University Press, Stanford, 1977), pp. 275–351.

for security than for revenue), imperial control placed a city higher than did commercial activity. Skinner sketches some interesting correlates of a city's relative position in the two hierarchies; for example, imperial administrators who were assigned to cities that occupied relatively high positions in the market hierarchy accomplished more of their work by dealing with 'parapolitical' networks of merchants and other prospering notables than did their colleagues in less well-favored areas. The regions that included those major market cities, furthermore, financed more than their share of candidates for the imperial examinations that led to careers in the bureaucracy. Many other consequences flowed from that interplay of the top-down and bottom-up systems.

Skinner is describing China, and not the world at large. He points out, for instance, the division of city systems into nine well-defined physiographic regions, but denies any strict geophysical determinism. 'Nonetheless', he concludes, 'knowing in advance the extent of the domain within which the Chinese were destined during the imperial era to achieve and sustain both numerical and political dominance, one is struck by the overwhelming importance of physiographic structure in shaping regional economies and regional social systems.'[20] Thus the Chinese system, in its wondrous complexity, conforms to the Chinese landscape.

Skinner's questions and distinctions deserve exploration in Europe. Europe never hosted an empire of the scale and scope of China's at its prime. After the fragmentation of Rome's domains, Europe never felt the rule of another empire worthy of the name. Yet even after the Roman Empire's disintegration, Europe experienced in its own more segmented way the interplay of the two processes Skinner detects in China: the bottom-up building of regional hierarchies based on trade and manufacturing, the top-down imposition of political control. At times, the continent also experienced the complementary processes of unbuilding and slackening control – although a crucial question for European historians is whether the two systems waxed and waned together to the same degree that they seem to have in an imperial China repeatedly riven from top to bottom by crisis, decay, and rebellion.

R. Bin Wong's comparison of struggles over food in Europe and China suggests some important Skinnerian parallels between the experiences

[20] G. William Skinner, 'Introduction: Urban Development in Imperial China', in Skinner, *The City in Late Imperial China*, p. 12.

of the two continents.[21] Despite significant differences in structure, people in both regions seem to have been especially likely to seize food forcefully in times of shortage or high prices where and when the gap was widening between the extent of food marketing and the degree of governmental control over food supply. Poor people who depended on local markets for their food substituted themselves for authorities who no longer enforced the locality's claims to food stored, marketed, or shipped within its perimeter. In eighteenth- and nineteenth-century China imperial control declined while markets held their own or even expanded. Local people blocked shipments, bullied merchants, or seized stored grain to enforce their claims to the supply.

In eighteenth- and nineteenth-century Europe, marketing of food expanded even faster than the local strength of governments; European people seized grain to enforce claims that their officials would no longer respect.[22] No one has done a sufficiently broad geography of grain seizures in Europe or China to determine whether they followed an appropriately Skinnerian pattern. In Europe, the marked tendency of grain seizures to ring major cities and ports does suggest such a pattern. China's banditry, rebellion, and other forms of collective conflict also showed marked regional differences that bear at least a rough correspondence to the joint distributions of imperial and mercantile activity. Hence we might reasonably search for similar geographic inequalities within Europe.

[21] R. Bin Wong, 'Les Émeutes de Subsistances en Chine et en Europe Occidentale', *Annales: Économies, Sociétés, Civilisations*, 38 (1983), pp. 234–58. See also R. Bin Wong and Peter C. Perdue, 'Famine's Foes in Ch'ing China', *Harvard Journal of Asiatic Studies*, 43 (1983), pp. 291–332. It is only fair to point out that Wong concentrates on *differences* between Europe and China, and thereby raises doubts about conventional explanations of European struggles over food.

[22] See John Bohstedt, *Riots and Community Politics in England and Wales, 1790–1810* (Harvard University Press, Cambridge, Mass., 1983); Andrew Charlesworth, 'A Comparative Study of the Spread of the Agriculture Disturbances of 1816, 1822 and 1830', Working Paper No. 9, Liverpool Papers in Human Geography (Department of Geography, University of Liverpool, Liverpool, 1982); Charlesworth, ed., *An Atlas of Rural Protest in Britain, 1548–1900* (Croom Helm, London, 1983); Rémi Gossez, 'A Propos de la Carte des Troubles de 1846–1847', in *Aspects de la Crise et de la Dépression de l'Économie Française au Milieu du XIXe Siècle, 1846–1851*, ed. Ernest Labrousse (Imprimerie Centrale de l'Ouest, La Roche-sur-Yon, 1956), vol. 19, *Bibliothèque de la Révolution de 1848*. Tilly, 'The Food Riot as a Form of Political Conflict',

The patterns of political co-variation Skinner describes also have likely European counterparts: the administrative capitals in regions of scanty commerce in which a viceroy held power through direct military control but could produce little revenue for the king, the lower ranking royal officials surrounded by prosperous landlords and merchants with whom they had no choice but to negotiate. Consider the contrast between eastern Prussia, where the state's administrative apparatus tended to overwhelm merchants in favor of great landlords, and western Prussia, where a similar apparatus almost dissolved in the region's commercial activity.

As Gabriel Ardant has pointed out, the correspondence between fiscal system and regional economy determines the cost and effectiveness of attempts to tax.[23] In an area with little market activity, for instance a land tax based on estimated value and levied in cash in likely to cost a great deal to collect, rest on inequitable assessments of value, miss a good deal of potential revenue, and incite widespread resistance.

Ardant did not observe, however, that high levels of commercial activity are likely to give merchants considerable political power with which to prevent the creation of a state that would seize their assets and cramp their transactions. In Europe, the extent of commercial activity strongly affected the viability of the various tactics used to build their strength. Indeed, one of Europe's most salient contrasts recalls Skinner's distinctions: the remarkable difference between city-state Europe from northern central Italy through the Rhineland to Flanders, where capitalists prospered, statesmen borrowed, and large national states were extremely slow to form; and the flanks of that corridor, regions of less active commerce and manufacturing that hosted substantial national states.

To be sure, we must not press parallels too far. Over most of the time for which we have workable records, a single empire, more or less unified, dominated the great mass of China; that fact in itself defined a different relationship between statemaking and economic change in China. In historic times, external wars played a relatively small part in Chinese statemaking, and an enormous part in European statemaking. On the other hand, recurrent massive rebellions against the central authority

---

[23] Gabriel Ardant, *Théorie Sociologique de l'Impôt* (2 vols, SEVPEN, Paris, 1965). See also Ardant, 'Financial Policy and Economic Infrastructure of Modern States and Nations', in *The Formation of National States in Western Europe*, ed. Charles Tilly (Princeton University Press, Princeton, 1975).

shook the successive Chinese empires. The early creation of a relatively
effective and centralized system of food supply under imperial
control sets off the Chinese experience from the European. Considering
its size and geographic diversity, the Chinese empire enjoyed
or produced a remarkable cultural unity. The next round of
analogies and comparisons must take precisely those differences
into account.

In one fundamental regard, indeed, the analysis of differences between
China and Europe will surely yield more return than the search for
fugitive similarities. Representative institutions of various sorts – city
councils, Estates General, legislatures, guild assemblies and many more –
had a remarkable vitality over nearly a millennium of European history.
Yet their forms and fortunes fluctuated. In Europe, representative
institutions seemed to have formed and gained power in two very different
ways: first, they came into being as instruments of local self-government,
often oligarchical self-government, but gained importance as interlocuters
with outside powers, especially when those outside powers were
conquering states; second, they emerged from the bargaining with power-
holders and subject populations over the yielding of taxes, labor power,
and the means of war. In such regions as northern Italy, Flanders, and
the Rhineland, the prior existence of widespread local representative
institutions, however oligarchical, presented statemakers with very
different strategic problems from those faced by princes who sought to
subordinate rival princelings in regions of feudal control. But in both
sorts of regions the struggle over the wherewithal of warmaking,
statemaking, and protection eventually brought into being some sorts
of representation of the entire population at a national scale. No doubt
analogues of these struggles occurred at various times in China. The
long existence of an empire that was far more extensive and powerful
than any possible coalition of local powers, however, seems to have
produced a fundamentally different process of state penetration and
control in China. If Europeans did not struggle more, they struggled
differently.

REVOLUTION AND EMPIRE AS NATURAL EXPERIMENTS

In that perspective, the French Revolution and Empire performed
an enormous, fascinating natural experiment in Europe's spatial

structure.[24] Three French actions altered relations between the commercial and administrative hierarchies. First, revolutionaries sought to extend direct rule within France from Paris down to individual communities. Not only did they impose a uniform administrative structure on localities throughout France, but also they turned local administrators, including priests, into state officials. In three decisive and related moves, they abolished venal offices, eliminated most tax exemptions based on status or office, and absorbed the debts of municipalities into the national debt.

At the start, the administrative reform met obstacles: bitter competition among municipalities for priority in the administrative hierarchy, struggle against the Civil Constitution of the Clergy, resistance by the privileged. The revolutionary government overcame the obstacles by encouraging the formation of revolutionary committees and militias with strong ties to the government, by using the widespread personal and commercial networks of revolutionary bourgeois, and eventually by organizing coercion in the name of an endangered country; those strategies converged and peaked in the Terror. Subsequent governments little by little supplanted that risky system by installing a firm, centralized administrative hierarchy backed by specialized police and increased military force. Much of that centralized system survived the Restoration of 1815.

Second, the new national administrative hierarchy had a peculiar feature. The Old Regime's major administrative divisions, the

---

[24] Geoffrey Best, *War and Society in Revolutionary Europe, 1770–1870* (Fontana, London, 1982); Iain A. Cameron, 'The Police of Eighteenth-Century France', *European Studies Review*, 7 (1977), pp. 47–75; Richard Cobb, *Terreur et Subsistances, 1793–1795* (Clavreuil, Paris, 1965); Owen Connelly, *Napoleon's Satellite Kingdoms* (Free Press, New York, 1965); Philipe-J. Hesse, 'Geographie Coutumière et Révoltes Paysannes en 1789', *Annales Historiques de la Révolution Française*, 51 (1979), pp. 280–306; Ernst Hinrichs, Eberhard Schmitt and Rudolf Vierhaus, eds, *Vom Ancien Regime zur Französischen Revolution. Forschungen und Perspektiven* (Vandenhoeck & Ruprecht, Göttingen, 1978); David Hunt, 'Peasant Politics in the French Revolution', *Social History*, 9 (1984), pp. 277–99; Lynn Hunt, *Politics, Culture, and Class in the French Revolution* (University of California Press, Berkeley, Calif., 1984); Colin Lucas, *The Structure of the Terror: The Example of Javogues and the Loire* (Oxford University Press, London, 1973); Patrick Schultz, *La Décentralisation Administrative dans le Département du Nord de la France, 1790–1793* (Presses Universitaires de Lille, Lille, 1982); André-Jean Tudesq, 'Les Influences Locales dans l'Administration Centrale en France sous la Monarchie de Juillet', *Annali della Fondazione Italiana per la Storia Amministrativa*, 4 (1967), pp. 367–86.

gouvernements and *généralités*, varied in scale and administrative structure and numbered about twenty. The revolutionary government of 1790 divided the entire territory into almost ninety regions – the *départements* – which were much more similar in area and population than the Old Regime's major divisions had been, which had direct representation in the national legislature, and whose senior officials reported directly to superiors in Paris. That tremendous flattening at the top of the hierarchy placed once mighty Lyon at the same level as puny La Roche-sur-Yon. In a Skinnerian logic, we might expect it to enhance the power of merchants and capitalists with respect to functionaries in such major commercial centers as Lyon. Combined with the institution of direct rule, however, we might expect it to have a different effect in places (such as La Roche-sur-Yon) that occupied low positions in the commercial hierarchy: a general increase in the advantage of administrators, and in the likelihood of coercive rule. French experience during and after the Revolution seems to bear out those expectations.

Third, as French armies conquered much of Europe, they set up administrations that resembled those France had already adopted: relatively small and uniform administrative regions, a clear hierarchy of administrative centers, highly centralized national administrations, attempts at direct rule. The thoroughness of these steps depended on the circumstances and duration of French conquest; they went farther in Belgium, for example, than in the volatile satellite kingdom of Spain. But in Belgium, Italy, and elsewhere, many features of French administration survived the shaking off of French rule.

Thus the conquering French performed an incredible experiment, quickly building similar administrations in vastly different conditions of production and trade. In modern European experience, only the formation of the Zollverein, the consolidation of the German Empire, and the unification of Italy rivaled that experiment. Clearly, the variable political experiences of French-occupied regions deserve closer attention than they have received so far. Skinner's ideas should help us organize the inquiry.

REGION, STATE, CAPITAL

Finally, Skinner's analysis of Chinese social change recalls a repeated discovery of European economic history: from the perspective of production and distribution, the units that typically shared an interdependent fate were neither national states nor individual communities, but regions consisting of a dominant urban cluster and its hinterland: Milan and Lombardy, Lyon and the Lyonnais, Zurich and its Oberland. Some regions (for example, much of southern Italy) did deindustrialize during the nineteenth century. A few others (such as the Borinage) industrialized from one end to the other. Yet more commonly manufacturing, earlier dispersed among many towns and villages, concentrated within the same interdependent region in a few central sites, while the remaining areas turned to cash-crop agriculture and sent off much of their industrial population to the cities. The concentration of capital in urban centers induced a major redistribution of labor.

Here, no doubt, the relative strengths of officials and merchants affected the extent to which officials could shape the redistribution to their own needs for revenue and control. One might speculate that deindustrialization went farther, *ceteris paribus*, where capitalist power stood greatest relative to governmental power. Thus Skinner's treatment suggests a way of thinking through broad economic changes and their connections with political transformations without simply shoving the economic changes into boxes defined by the boundaries of national states. The logic of coercion and the logic of capital interacted to produce hierarchies of places that both contradicted and reinforced each other.

PART II

Europe and the Atlantic World

9

A Geographical Transect of the Atlantic World, *ca.*1750

D. W. MEINIG

In 1971 Edward Fox opened his incisive book on 'the other France' with a blunt statement:

> History and geography were once assumed to be sister sciences so close in method and focus as to verge on representing two aspects of a single subject. Today they share nothing, not even regrets for what had been looked upon as a particularly promising alliance.[1]

He went on to demonstrate that, properly understood, 'history in geographic perspective' does not mean an exposition in environmentalism but an exploration of how history is bound up with the ways in which the human world is anchored in locality and organized spatially as sets and systems of places.

Since that time the appearance of monumental works of 'history in geographic perspective' in one form or another – one thinks immediately of the English translation of Fernand Braudel, *The Mediterranean*, and of Immanuel Wallerstein, *The Modern World-System* – as well as invited programmatic statements suggest that there may be a growing number of scholars who regret what Robert S. Lopez, in a review of Fox's book, called 'the murder of geography' and 'its expulsion from history'.[2]

---

[1] Edward Whiting Fox, *History in Geographic Perspective: The Other France* (W. W. Norton, New York, 1971), p. 19.

[2] Fernand Braudel, *The Mediterranean and the Mediterranean World in the Age of Philip II*, tr. Siân Reynolds (2 vols, Collins, London, 1972); Immanuel Wallerstein, *The Modern World-System: Capitalist Agriculture and the Origin of the European World-Economy in the Sixteenth*

There are now numerous signs of mutual interest, even collaboration; the emergence of historical geography as a distinct discipline, nurtured in geography but increasingly recognized and welcomed in history, provides the most substantial evidence.[3]

Nevertheless, the kind of alliance demonstrated by Fox, and implicit in Wallerstein, proceeds haltingly because, among other obstacles, it is difficult to show how the world is organized and operates as a set of spatial systems. This difficulty confronts any effort to build an encompassing geographic view of the European penetration and colonization of North America. An immense literature bears upon the topic, but little is given explicit geographical formulation. The simple and obvious geographic structure of a Europe and an America separated by the Atlantic is recognized and signified in various ways. Pairs of terms, such as homeland and colonies, metropolis and frontier, center and periphery, and variations thereof, are loaded with meaning, carrying as they do implications of old and new, dominance and subordinance, innovation and diffusion. But even where some such meaning is specified these crude bi partite structures provide no real basis for geographical analysis. Such concepts are fundamental but insufficient. To generalize in such broad terms requires a clear understanding of what we are generalizing from. We need to penetrate this simple dualism and identify a more intricate set of geographic parts if we are to bring such a vast transoceanic creation into clearer view. Consider, for example, the over-arching European-initiated systems that by 1750 had created a single great geographical field extending from the seats of imperial and commercial power in London and Paris to the deep interior of North

---

Century (Academic Press, Inc., New York and London, 1976); Donald W. Meinig, 'The Continuous Shaping of America: A Prospectus for Geographers and Historians', *American Historical Review*, 83 (1978), pp. 1186–217; Carville Earle, 'Comments [on "The Continuous Shaping of America"]', *American Historical Review*, 83 (1978), pp. 1206–9; Robert S. Lopez, *American Historical Review*, 77 (1972), p. 1086.

[3] These opening comments refer to the specific American situation. The relation of geography and history has been marked by strong national peculiarities. The situation in France is discussed by Alan R. H. Baker, 'Reflections on the Relations of Historical Geography and the *Annales* School of History', in *Explorations in Historical Geography: Interpretative Essays*, eds. Alan R. H. Baker and Derek Gregory (Cambridge University Press, Cambridge, 1984), pp. 1–27. And a new program for British geography is argued in the remainder of *Explorations in Historical Geography: Interpretative Essays*.

America. One could with only minor modifications illustrate the system that extended from Madrid to New Mexico as well.[4]

The commercial system, with its opportunistic search for profits, offered the most effective instrument of expansion of these empires, which represented the outreach of commercial capitalism from the culture hearth in the maritime states of Northwest Europe. That was especially true of the English and of their Dutch rivals, less fully so of the French – as Fox has clarified – where Huguenot commercial initiatives could never get free of repressive imperial strategies. Our inventory of geographical parts begins (Figure 9.1) with the headquarters in the capital city, the seat of management, control of financial resources, commercial intelligence, and marketing systems. And in these two cases, major Atlantic ports often served as primary bases for the actual procurement of ships and of trading goods and tools. The hinterlands of these ports developed industries specifically in response to American needs, such as blankets from the factories at Stroud and iron tools and utensils from forges in the Forest of Dean. On the westernmost fringes of Europe, such as Brittany, Devon, and southern Ireland, Atlantic outports provided last-stage provisions and manpower for the oceanic voyage.

On the American side, if we assume for simplicity the most direct route to the mainland colonies – Newfoundland or the West Indies were outports on some important circuitry – the colonial port had complementary functions to that in Europe. It received, disassembled, stored, and arranged for distribution. It drew upon the European colony in its own hinterland for food and other materials and perhaps for additional trading goods, especially alcohol from local distilleries. Near the inland edge of this colonized area was the frontier entrepôt, seat of the principal traders and various specialists who served the interior economy, such as gunsmiths, blacksmiths, boatbuilders, cartwrights, and the main point of periodic contact with Indian leaders. Further inland were outposts staffed by local traders: the Indian core area of the powerful intermediary tribes who fostered procurement from a wide hunting hinterland and tried to control distributions of trade goods to the most remote participants.

[4] Since this essay is adapted from portions of a book in press on Atlantic America, a geographic study that traces this European outreach and its consequences to the year 1800, no attempt will be made here to provide documentation for these illustrations. Excerpts and diagrams are used by permission of Yale University Press.

EUROPE

ATLANTIC	OUTPORT	ATLANTIC PORT	HINTERLAND	CENTER
	IRELAND DEVON	BRISTOL	FOREST OF DEAN STROUD	LONDON
	BRITTANY	LE HAVRE LA ROCHELLE	NORMANDY ATLANTIC FRANCE	PARIS
company and contract shipping	oceanic provisioning recruitment of seamen and laborers	shipping services boat-building marketing	iron utensils, weapons, blankets, cloth, foodstuffs	headquarters entrepreneurs state & corporate systems commercial intelligence
Ocean vessels		riverboats, wagons coastal and river vessels		

AMERICA

EXPLOITATION AND INDUSTRIAL HINTERLANDS	INDIAN CORE AREA	OUTPOSTS	FRONTIER ENTREPÔT	COLONY	COLONIAL PORT	ATLANTIC
OHIO MISSISSIPPI VALLEY	ONONDAGA COWETA	OSWEGO	ALBANY AUGUSTA	NEW YORK SOUTH CAROLINA	NEW YORK CHARLESTOWN	
VILLAGE CLUSTERS						
GREAT LAKES		DETROIT	MONTREAL	CANADA	QUEBEC	
trappers and hunters	Indian middlemen	local traders gunsmiths and blacksmiths	Chief traders	Euro-American agriculture	mercantile leaders marketing	company and contract shipping
preparation of furs and skins		Indian provisionmen		local industry distilling	warehousing local capital	
canoes and porters	canoes and pack trains		riverboats, wagons, pack trains		ocean vessels	

FIGURE 9.1   The commercial system

The Atlantic was a distinct area that required special shipping services. A supplemental way of defining such a set of areas would be to identify the transport facilities (as shown in the bottom band of Figure 9.1), the particular vessels and vehicles, pack trains and lines of human porters, and the actual set of contracts in this intercontinental exchange. The deep penetrations of North America afforded by the St Lawrence, Hudson, and Great Lakes, are obvious and famous; less so was the largely overland network of commerce that reached inland from Charleston.

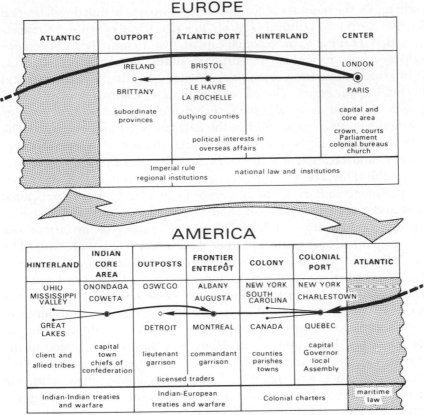

FIGURE 9.2   The political system

Since our main purpose is geographical rather than economic, the diagram draws attention to the furthest reaches rather than to the greatest volumes of this traffic. It illustrates the fur trade rather than the far larger volume of commerce between Europe and the colonies on the American seaboard. Such a simple transect cannot display the complexities of transatlantic and intercolonial traffic, but it can help organize our thinking about economic relations.[5]

Focus on the political system (Figure 9.2) reveals many of the same centers and areas but somewhat differently connected and less far

---

[5] The mercantile model of settlement in James E. Vance, Jr, *The Merchant's World: The Geography of Wholesaling* (Prentice-Hall, Inc., Englewood Cliffs, New Jersey, 1970) offers an explicitly geographic formulation of this economic system.

reaching, for the tentacles of European commerce penetrated well beyond effective European political control. The trunk line of empire connects the imperial capital to the colonial capital, overarching the local center–periphery patterns within the European states. Britain, especially, had an internally complex geopolitical structure relating to Scotland and Ireland, but our concern here is only with those features directly bound up with the larger imperial system, such as those special political interests in American affairs generated in the Atlantic ports and outports. The imperial trunk line was actually several strands of administrative, military, and ecclesiastical links. Technically, the French system was a geopolitical hierarchy of military officials, from the Crown and heads of departments in Paris to the Governor-General in Quebec, to regional commandants as at Montreal, and lieutenants in outlying districts, although Louisbourg and New Orleans, as centers of distinctive and widely separated areas, also had some direct connections with Paris. The British empire seems in comparison hardly a system at all. In 1750, fifteen political jurisdictions on the mainland south of the Gulf of St Lawrence varied greatly in size, origins, and political character. Each colony was unique in the details of local government, and there were differences in the bundle of connections each had with various departments in London. Most important, each colony was directly connected to the imperial capital (Figure 9.3). There was no governor-general for the American colonies, although there had been an attempt to establish one for the northern colonies in the abortive Dominion of New England during 1685–8, and from that time on New York City served as the principal military base and the seat of important imperial officials. Later, the British would establish two Superintendents of Indian Affairs with a direct line of authority from London that bypassed colonial governors. Such complexities preclude simple diagrammatic representation, but note in this transect the connection and overlap of the European political system with that of the Indians. Rival European powers laid sovereign claim to all the lands of their Indian allies, but the Iroquois chiefs who periodically assembled at the central council fire at Onondaga or the Creeks who gathered at Coweta would have been contemptuous of such assertions. They had not been conquered, and they held sway over their own geopolitical systems, which included an array of confederated, allied, subordinated, and client tribes.

These several areas were bound together through various colonial charters, administrative decrees, and treaties. But again, such a simple

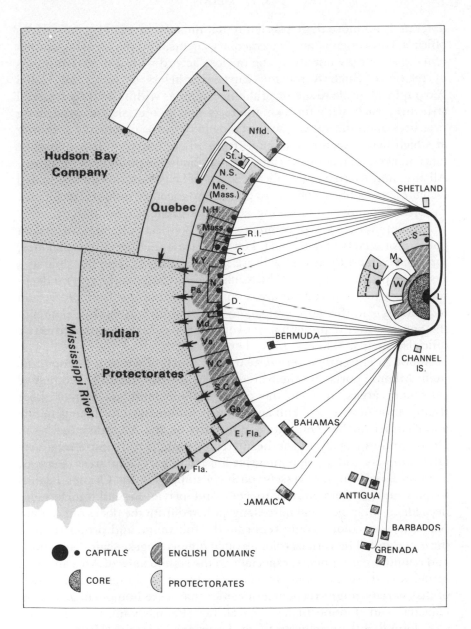

FIGURE 9.3 A conspectus of the British Atlantic Empire

diagram is no more than a skeleton that must be vivified by the various officials, constituents, and intermediary agents, and the actual operation of the system may not always be in close accord with formal definitions of relations. Such a scheme can nevertheless serve as an initial geographical guide to the several kinds of areas within such an imperial structure, each with its own interests and potentials for generating pressures upon the system, and a guide to those local points of authority at which decisions are made and from where coercive action may be taken in event of trouble. It can call attention to the position of Montreal, Albany, and Augusta as de facto centers of large laboriously negotiated bicultural geopolitical complexes that bound together Indian associations, European colonies, and a king across the great sea.

Implicit in these sets of commercial and political parts are concordant patterns of society (Figure 9.4). Here we face some special complexities, for 'society' and things 'social' are not so readily comprehensible as a system of points and parts. The terms may encompass the several deep-rooted societies of particular areas, migrations of people from one region to another, and the variety of sojourners stationed at various points in the political and commercial networks for a period of assigned duty: officials, agents, soldiery and other operatives.

Although emigrants were drawn from much of western Europe, the main Atlantic ports and their hinterlands, usually the most productive catchment areas, became the principal homeland anchors of those transatlantic networks of kith and kin which were most likely to generate and channel further emigration. Outports on the Atlantic edge, as in Devon and especially in southern Ireland, might contribute relatively large numbers and develop intensive links with particular areas overseas. Hudson Bay Company vessels routinely stopped in the Orkney Islands to pick up laborers inured to cold and privation and much more dependable than the usual miscellany gathered from the docks of London. No American colony could replicate the full range and proportions of the homeland. The various colonies often differed markedly in their ethnic and religious components, especially in the significance of Africans, and in the way these components were structured. A simple classification of that variety might recognize societies that were homogeneous (as in Canada and Connecticut), pluralistic (Pennsylvania), segmented (Newfoundland), racially stratified (Louisiana), biracial (Virginia), and complex (New York and East New Jersey). These classifications refer to the main body of the colony, but there may be special features

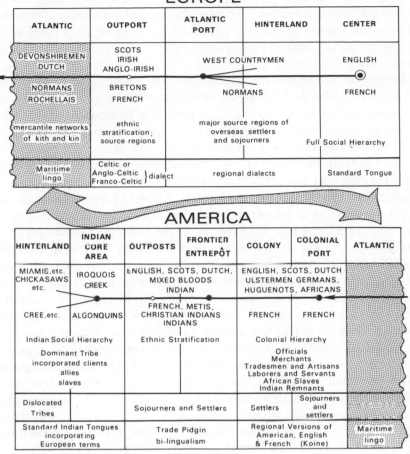

FIGURE 9.4 Ethnic and social patterns

associated with particular points recognized in our scheme of geographical parts. A characteristic result of imperialism is the social complexity derived from the sustained encounter between the invaders and the invaded. Major frontier entrepôts, such as Montreal, Albany, Augusta, and nearby districts, included a varied assortment of Europeans, Indians of the powerful tribes who were partners in this intercontinental system, refugee Indian groups, new associations formed of remnants of shattered tribes, Christian Indians, and detribalized mixed bloods, all in complex stratifications and segregations. Some such variety might be found in many localities scattered over the entire Europeanized area, and in many colonies the importation of Africans and subsequent consequences of miscegenation, emancipation, and escape created further social complexities.

Another important feature of these imperial colonies is the coexistence, but different roles and diverging interests, of sojourners and settlers. The settlers, derived increasingly not just from emigrants but from the American-born, made up the bulk of the population, and, by definition, were spread over the whole colonized area. The sojourners were to be found at operational points in the imperial networks, most prominently in the colonial port and capital and in the frontier entrepôt and outposts. Distinctions sometimes were blurred. As a colony developed, an increasing share of the offices and agencies on the American end of these networks would likely be held by American-born persons rather than Europeans on colonial assignment, and many an agent sent over for a tour of duty elected to stay as a permanent settler. A differentiation between these two groups of colonial residents nonetheless remained and became critically important when the empire was brought under internal stress. This kind of geographic view of the parts and points in the imperial system is essential to effective analysis of the patterns of loyalism during the American revolution. Once the people who operated the empire are identified, it is much easier to bring into focus the various religious, ethnic, and political groups that resisted imperial dismemberment.

As an example of another way of looking at society in such a geographic scheme we might look at language, analogous in a way to transport, each a medium of communication that links these sets of peoples and social areas. Such a view would not only take note of the variety of languages and dialects in these several parts but bring into focus those areas and points of contact characterized by bilingualism, translators, and trade pidgin in a network that spanned the great geographical and cultural separation between the dominant tongue of the imperial capital and the unaltered tongue of the most remote American Indian participants. Such a simplified momentary transect can no more than hint at the dynamics of linguistic change induced by these encounters and associations, migrations and separations.

Thus by looking more closely we can penetrate any simple core–periphery or metropolis–frontier concept of empire and identify almost a dozen geographic parts, each with its own characteristic peoples, activities, and patterns of settlement. Ideally, these several topical patterns should be lined up on the same chart to relate the economic, political, and social characteristics of any one geographic part, or set of parts. In that way we provide context for the consideration of particular elements or processes, anchoring them within particular types of geographic areas. And we may attempt to envision this whole span of areas as a system, with arteries that pulsate with circulations of persons, goods, money, messages – a network that connects a series of stations in which decisions are made, policies applied, transactions negotiated, goods exchanged. It was not a simple system of centralized authority and subordinate parts but several systems, interlocked in various ways and degrees and complicated by numerous subsystems. In the British case, especially, the political and commercial systems were relatively autonomous and often discordant with one another, and some of the concomitant social changes went unmanaged, unforeseen, and unwelcome to London authorities.

We can also try to envision this transect as a spectrum of gradations in power, intensity of interaction, and social character. In general, imperial power declined with distance from the European capital until it became feeble and indirect in the interior of North America, where it was represented by European seasonal agents and Indian allies. And we might project an analogous cultural gradient from, say, a basic 'Englishness' as defined by a social elite in London, through many shadings and transitions until it fades to the faintest evidence of things 'English' and disappears in the still strong 'Indianness' of the American Interior. Such terms suggest a European view of Americans as fading versions of European archetypes, although a different view would prevail on the American colonial side. The most directly opposite view would be to stand with those as yet barely affected Indians of the Interior and look with fear and wonder at the apparent precipitous gradations of 'Indianness' as one goes eastward.

A feature implicit in the inclusion of both the British and the French empires in this example deserves emphasis: the value of such a framework for comparative studies. Empires may be classified by geographical types.[6]

---

[6] Donald W. Meinig, 'A Macrogeography of Western Imperialism: Some Morphologies of Moving Frontiers of Political Control', in *Settlement and Encounter: Geographical Studies Presented to Sir Grenfell Price*, eds. Fay Gale and Graham H. Lawton (Oxford University Press, Melbourne, 1969), pp. 213–40.

As displayed in this specific transect these empires were combinations of riverine and settler types. In both cases commercial extension along waterways deep into the continent preceded any extensive European colonization, although for New York the Dutch created and the English took over that system. Thus the same geographic parts apply, broadly, to both empires, with due attention to a few differences in detail. The basic applicability of these generic areas permits annotation of each, with the similarities and differences, and thereby strengthens comparative work.

Thus these simplistic diagrams bring complex topics into geographic focus. Consider briefly two important matters that require some such perspective.

The need to integrate Indians and Europeans within the same history to a degree we have yet to achieve is becoming well recognized. One of the most difficult obstacles had been the deeply-entrenched concept of the frontier as a point or line of contact between the two peoples, 'the meeting point between civilization and savagery', whereas there was in fact a shared zone of joint occupancy, interlocking interests, and interacting influences.[7] Our transect makes this immediately apparent. We can identify within the general overarching system a European-dominated sector and an Indian-dominated sector, the two joined at what is commonly called the 'frontier' (Figure 9.5, top shaded band). But the two peoples shared a broad extent of territory that spanned several zones (Figure 9.5, second shaded band), and they would continue to do so even as the specific geography, the systems that bind them together, and the kinds of areas appropriate to any such continental transect changed over the centuries. After all, Indians are still present in Quebec, New York, and South Carolina, as well as in New England, Virginia, and other areas of the American seaboard, although their proportionate positions have changed.

It would be appropriate to recognize three types of areas as gradations in the relative impact of this great encounter between Europeans and Indians (Figure 9.6): a coastal zone of conquest and encapsulation, a second zone–partly coastal, mostly inland – of articulation and interdependence, and a third zone deeper in the interior beyond sustained

[7] Frederick Jackson Turner, 'The Significance of the Frontier in American History', *Annual Report of the American Historical Association for the Year 1893* (1893), pp. 199–227; Howard Roberts Lamar and Leonard Thompson, *The Frontier in History: North America and Southern Africa Compared* (Yale University Press, New Haven and London, 1981).

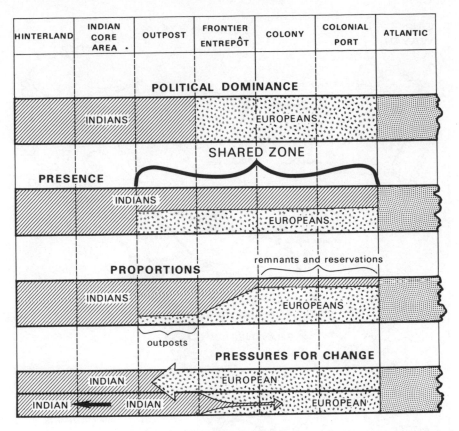

HINTERLAND	INDIAN CORE AREA ·	OUTPOST	FRONTIER ENTREPÔT	COLONY	COLONIAL PORT	ATLANTIC

FIGURE 9.5   Indian and European territory

massive contact but markedly affected by it. By 1750 in the seaboard zone of European conquest and colonization the Indians had been drastically reduced and mostly confined to tiny enclaves. The intensity of relations differed. In some districts they huddled on tracts of forest, swamp, or shore with as little outside contact as possible; in others they lived adjacent to towns in close dependence upon Europeans. In many cases they had traders, missionaries, and others in their midst who provided daily interaction and pressures for social change. Even where there was little regular interaction adaptations had to be made. Confinement altered economies and ecologies: European tools became necessities, European clothing and housing gradually more acceptable, European languages indispensible to tribal leaders who coped

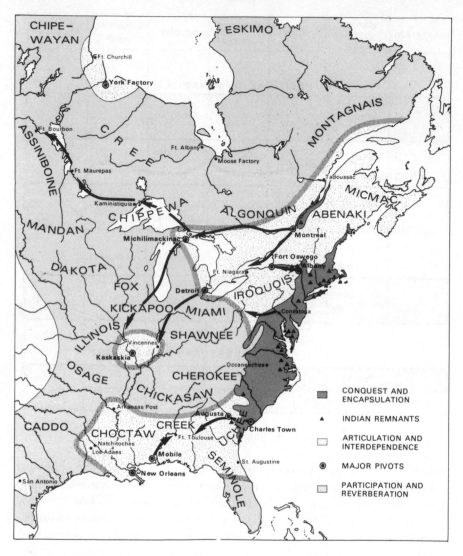

FIGURE 9.6   Zones of encounter, *c.* 1750

with the encompassing imperial society. Even though they persevered as discrete local ethnic societies, these Indians were clearly captive remnants within a conquest completed. No longer a threat and with too little land left to covet, such people were outcasts, generally treated with contempt and for the most part ignored, especially in the English colonies. Only in French and Spanish areas where European – Indian racial mixtures were more openly accepted and Catholic missionaries had had some success did such people have a recognized place in European-dominated American societies.

But west of this colonized area relations were sharply different. Here lay the critical points of articulation at facilities geared to European – Indian relations, such as district headquarters, garrisons, entrepôts, and outposts, with an array of specialists geared to this intercultural system: traders, packers, warriors, teachers, missionaries, translators, diplomats, provisioners, craftsmen, and a wide variety of hangers-on. In this zone of obvious interdependence and greater equality, European intentions and assertions might be no less imperial than they had been on the seaboard, but here Europeans were dealing with as yet unconquered peoples who were still in a position to demand recognition as equals. Formal relations were established through laboriously negotiated treaties; European agents could safely venture farther inland only on the sufferance of local tribes; trading protocol was largely by Indian custom; and the terms of exchange were defined by astute bargaining by both sides.

Still farther inland lay the main centers of Indian power and intertribal commerce. Here Europeans were few and sporadic; the commercial system was operated mainly by Indian trappers, hunters, carriers, traders, and various production specialists across a broad span of tribal territories. Although this zone was as yet beyond the effective reach of imperial power, it resounded with political reverberations that rolled inward from the collision of cultures. Relative power among tribes had been altered, alliances rearranged, factionalism magnified, warfare intensified. It was in some ways the most volatile, unstable zone of all.

Any sustained encounter between two peoples will produce culture change. The entire economic system depended upon the labor, skills, and co-operation of Europeans and Indians alike, and such intense and sustained interaction inevitably produced changes in both. Some were simply utilitarian, such as Indian adoption of iron utensils, weapons, and blankets and European adoption of moccasins, snowshoes, and canoes; some were more complex and mutual such as the development of pidgin as a language of negotiation, and of modes of warfare used by both sides – usually by forces made up of both Indians and Europeans – which combined in various ways Indian stealth and woodlore and European disciplined movement and attack. Inevitably, miscegenation became widespread, but the status of mixed-blood offspring varied greatly and depended especially upon whether such persons were raised within Indian or European communities. Intermarriage of Europeans and Indians had been advocated by a few European spokesmen as an obvious means of ameliorating the collision of cultures, but this was not widely acceptable in colonial societies, although most traders resident in Indian lands lived with Indian women, often for political as well as more personal advantage. It was an important characteristic of this zone of articulation that the offspring of such unions had greater freedom of action and often played prominent roles as leaders and intermediaries, whereas they would generally be pressured toward the lower levels of the social hierarchy in the more fully Europeanized districts.

The very nature of empire, the intrusion of one people upon the territory of another, must have profound but asymmetrical effect, usually felt far more heavily by the invaded than the invader. While most of the Europeans in the North American interior were commercial or political agents or opportunists who, unlike Christian missionaries, had no interest in effecting change in the Indians beyond that needed to secure some minimal level of co-operation or subordination, the cumulative impact of the European invasion was apparent well beyond the regular presence of Europeans. Dislocations from conquest of the seaboard, decimations by disease, deformation of the ecology of Indian life, and disruptions of older political relations had reverberated over a vast interior zone. Still, the expansion of the system and the changes that it brought resulted from powerful forces of attraction as well as of destruction and domination. This imperialism continued to penetrate ever more deeply into North America in part because many Indians as well as Europeans readily participated. The ominous feature for the Indians was that even though they might establish relations with Europeans for mutual advantage, they could not be on equal terms in a larger sense. Europeans and Indians were interdependent within the commercial system they had together created but they were not equally dependent on that system. Europeans could shift to trading opportunities elsewhere or settle down within a diversifying European colony, whereas Indians could not go back to old ways, for they had lost lands and skills and could never again insulate themselves from European pressures and dangers. They were caught within a world system.

Broadly, the amount of change generally accorded with the intensity and comprehensiveness of contact. But the evidence of 1750 indicated that even where Indians were encapsulated remnants under the heaviest pressures of acculturation they were not simply absorbed; they did not become European facsimilies; their societies were not variously proportioned composites of Indian and European elements. Indians showed little interest in becoming Europeanized, and wherever their societies survived at all they were contemporary versions of their particular Indian culture, displaying through their multivarious adaptations the continuous vitality of Indian life. That is how they had survived decades and centuries of encounter up to 1750, and that is how they would survive as Indian societies for centuries thereafter. At the southern edge of the city of Syracuse, New York, lies the Onondaga Reservation, a small pocket of poverty and pride, former capital and still home to a thousand Iroquois for whom imperialism exists as everpresent reality.

The pattern of Indian influence upon Europeans seems much more limited and abrupt. East of the 'frontier' one finds utilitarian adoptions of many Indian crops and enrichment of the colonial diet, a few tools and techniques, a good many Indian words and thousands of place names, but no obvious alteration of basic European patterns of life. The disastrous impact of this encounter upon the Indians, reinforced by continuing immigration, rapid natural increase, and organization of large coherent societies, ensured European dominance. But we must resist seeing the European success as a 'march of civilization' that relegated the Indians to a colorful but ephemeral role as an obstacle to be removed. In simple but long-neglected truth, Indians critically participated in the creation of every European mainland colony. As Francis Jennings has stated, Europeans did more than fight their way into America, they entered into 'symbiotic relations of interdependence with Indians (and Africans), involving both conflict and cooperation. . . . Every European "discovered" had Indian guides. Every European colonizer had Indian instruction and assistance'.[8] Adding the critical Indian participation in the vast harvest of resources and mercantile system that was the great instrument of this European penetration, we might well conclude with Jennings that 'what America owes to Indian society as much as to any other source, is the mere fact of its existence'. Such interpretations are bound to be controversial, but this simple device of a geographic transect

[8] Francis Jennings, *The Invasion of America: Indians, Colonialism, and the Cant of Conquest* (University of North Carolina Press, Chapel Hill, 1975), pp. 173–4.

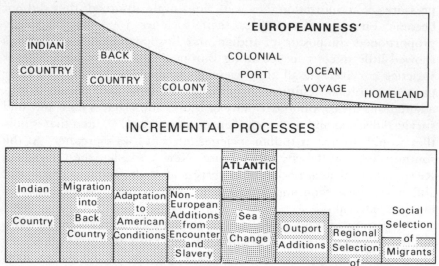

FIGURE 9.7   Cultural divergence

both forces the topic upon our attention and provides one useful means of considering it carefully.

Similarly, when we shift our focus to the European-dominated sector of this panorama we see another set of complexities in another kind of culture change, which arises from the very act of migration and colonization. The cultural divergence between mother country and overseas colonies lies at the very heart of American history. At the simplest geographic level this divergence appears as a function of distance, or perhaps of 'effective distance', which takes into account the decreasing efficiencies of transport as Europeans moved farther and farther away and ever less closely in touch with the full force of their homeland culture (Figure 9.7). Notwithstanding much complexity and the obvious results of the United States case, differentiations that arise from transoceanic movement and colonization may not prove culturally or politically disruptive. Such overseas colonies begin as European enclaves and may long develop as simply additional regional versions of the homeland culture – as distant provinces not essentially different in kind from counties on the homeland fringes of such composite kingdoms as England and France (Figure 9.3).

To see such a spectrum of change as a 'distance decay' effect does not explain anything. One has to examine the actual processes of change in the constituent elements of the system, and here again we can bring a large and rather nebulous topic into much sharper focus by a geographical view, which would immediately suggest a set of processes each primarily related to a specific type of area that would tend to produce an incremental divergence from center to periphery (Figure 9.6). To summarize: cultural differentiation begins with the very act of emigration, for every shipload is a skewed sample, a selection of only a limited range of social types, often primarily of those already uprooted and mobile and drawn more from some regions than others. Additions from the outports added to the variety. The pressurized association of diverse peoples on the long ocean voyage may in some cases ease, in others intensify, social differentiations. In many areas of America the presence of Indians and Africans, as well as subsequent immigrations of different Europeans, created social patterns that had no counterpart in Europe and that thereby further empowered the forces of change. And in all colonies the need to domesticate new ground and new environmental and locational conditions required special adaptations. Migration into backcountry districts further strained the connections with the homeland culture. Here we refer not just to a transitory pioneer phase of differentiation between metropolis and frontier, but to a divergence that arose from new environments and experiences, new problems, and a new sense of future possibilities. At any stage and in any of these zones the results of such changes take on special meaning when selfconsciously asserted by the peoples themselves, when emigrant and stay-at-home, colony and mother country, backcountry and seaboard, begin to declare their differences and even cultivate a sense of separateness that transforms colonists into nationalists and frontiersmen into regionalists, and thereby gives geopolitical expression to distance and divergence.

Any analysis of these processes of divergence must take into account those systems of spatial interaction that bound center and periphery together and thus countered pressures toward separation. Since such changes underlie the disintegration of empires, a cultural geographic analysis ought to contribute significantly to our understanding of the American Revolution as well as of the Canadian evolution. We must not let dramatic political rupture or slower but seemingly inexorable divergence blind us to the connections that endured or were renewed or initiated later. There is, after all, still an over-arching North Atlantic relation, with its systems and spectrums, and circulations and concatenation of geographic parts, that remains a challenge to geographic analysis of our own time.

Thus our geographic transect has produced a simple framework, adaptable to any kind of core–periphery, metropolis–frontier, imperial or world-system view of historical relations, that provides the combination of control and flexibility needed for analytical and comparative studies of such macrogeographic topics. Such frameworks help us to define manageable sub-topics, guide us to points of entry, and display a set of logical connections to other topics. They force us to bind the content of areas and relations between areas together. They encourage the development of a coherent body of work without demanding conformity in philosophy or style. More broadly, by their steady focus upon places, types of places, and connections among places, such devices declare the general importance of geography and the kind of contribution that geographers might make to some topics of common interest. Substantial work along such lines might even revive hopes for 'a particularly promising alliance' between history and geography.

10

High Altitude Andean Societies and their Economies

JOHN V. MURRA

The comparative study of high altitude, mountain societies acquired a new, unexpected dimension in 1931, when Carl Troll, a geographer at Bonn, published his map and analysis of Andean civilization.[1] A mountaineer by upbringing, Troll conducted field work in his native Alps, the Himalayas, East Africa, and the Pyrenees, as well as the Andes. The Andean phenomena engaged much of his attention because of the unique features he found there.

The Western observer, familiar with geographic and statecraft conditions studied elsewhere, finds in the Andes the improbable circumstance of dense populations and high productivity at just under 4,000 meters. In fact, modern development technicians – agronomists, planners, nutritionists – wonder aloud and in print about the reasons for folk's insisting on living in conditions that to the Europeans, eastern or western, seem impossible. Even where the archeological evidence of cities, highways, and temples at such altitudes cannot be denied, the modern, well-meaning expert manages to separate past glories from present-day destitution and continuous outmigration.

Troll's map (Figure 10.1) distinguishes the high *puna* from surrounding mountain chains, most of them covered with snow the year around. It also isolates the *puna* from the more distant coastal desert to the west, and the Amazon rainforest to the east. Free of artificial, European-imposed, and republican borders, it stresses the relevance of the *puna*,

---

[1] Carl Troll, 'Die geographische Grundlagen der Andinen Kulturen und des Inkareiches', *Ibero-Amerikanisches Archiv*, V (Berlin, 1931).

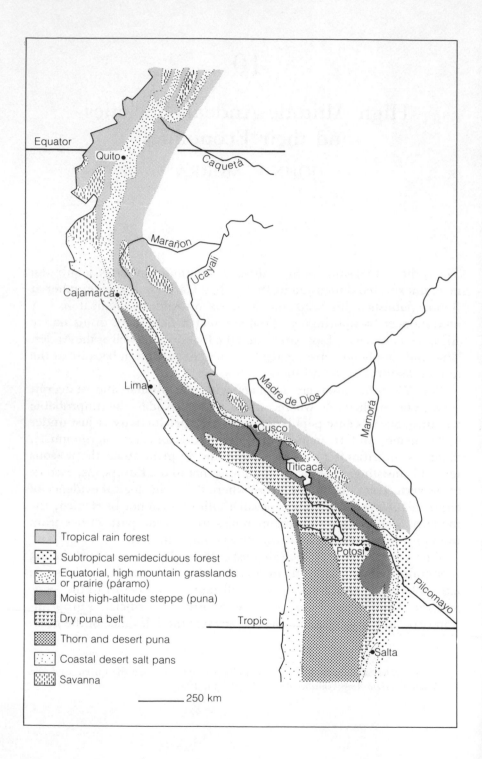

	Tropical rain forest
	Subtropical semideciduous forest
	Equatorial, high mountain grasslands or prairie (páramo)
	Moist high-altitude steppe (puna)
	Dry puna belt
	Thorn and desert puna
	Coastal desert salt pans
	Savanna

——— 250 km

Equator

Quito

Caquetá

Marañon

Ucayali

Cajamarca

Lima

Madre de Dios

Cusco

Titicaca

Mamoré

Potosi

Pilcomayo

Tropic

Salta

both north and south of Lake Titicaca, located at 3,800 meters. This narrow belt has contained the highest population density in both pre-European and modern times. In pre-industrial, pre-capitalist times, a high population constituted a sound indicator of productivity, although until very recently no agronomist would have agreed since no antecedent for such density at high altitudes has existed elsewhere. Fortunately, the 1960s produced a generation of agricultural experts and veterinarians concerned with the development of the Andean achievement and not only with the application of alien technologies.[2]

Cultivation of almost 100 crops above 3,400 meters and the husbandry of two varieties of camelids above 4,000 were achieved over the millennia to take advantage of tropical, if high altitude, conditions. As the archeology of the region becomes better known, we notice the continual effort, through conscious selection, to raise the ceiling at which tubers will produce a crop.[3] Some cultivars (maize, cotton, sweet potatoes) provide a bridge to areas elsewhere in the continent, but the vast majority are locally domesticated, hardy, highly adapted tubers and seeds – a separate, unique, native agricultural system.[4] In recent years we have also learned to stress the importance of high altitude herding[5] and the gathering of uncultivated plants from land and sea.

Of special significance is the 'domestication' of frost. Since the Andean region is wholly within the tropical zone, days are uniformly warm – 'summery', to use a northern hemisphere term. But nights are uniformly

[2] Ana María Fries, ed., *Evolución y Tecnología de la Agricultura Andina* (Instituto Indigenista Interamericano, Cusco, 1983).

[3] John Earls, 'Evolución de la Administración Ecológica Inca', *Revista del Museo Nacional*, XLII (Lima, 1978), pp. 207–45; John Earls and Irene Silverblatt, 'Sobre la Instrumentación de la Cosmovisión Inca en Moray', in *Runakunap Kawsayninkupaq Rurasqankunaqa*, eds. Heather Lechtman and Ana Maria Soldi (Universidad Nacional Autónoma de México, Instituto de Investigaciones Antropologicas, Mexico, 1981).

[4] Carl O. Sauer, 'Cultivated Plants of South and Central America', *Handbook of South American Indians*, VI (1949), pp. 487–543.

[5] Jorge Flores Ochoa, *Pastores de Puna – Uywamichiq Punarunakuna* (Instituto de Estudios Peruanos, Lima, 1977).

FIGURE 10.1 *(opposite)* The landscape belts of the tropical Andes (based on Carl Troll, 'Die geographische Grundlagen der Andinen Kulturen.') Reproduced from *Anthropological History of Andean Polities*, eds., John V. Murra, Nathan Wachtel and Jacques Revel (Cambridge, Cambridge University Press 1986).

cold, and frost can be expected in inhabited places as frequently as 250 and even more nights a year, particularly from May to August. A 50°C difference can occur within twenty-four hours.

In one sense the bulk of the food came from the top level, for freeze-dried tubers were everyone's staple. The tubers themselves can be grown anywhere, much as potatoes can be grown at all levels. But *ch'uñu*, one of the many tuber preserves, cannot be manufactured without the alternation of 'summer' and 'winter' every twenty-four hours. Even today, potato cultivators at lower reaches bring the 'seed' from the uppermost tier. And preference and status intervened, for tubers and their derivatives may have been the staple, but everyone preferred the luxury maize. Most warehouses were silos that stored *ch'uñu* or maize. So quantitatively, tubers formed the bulk and were essentially high altitude products. 'Experimental stations' were located in the highlands, and an effort was made to raise the ceiling of cultivation up to 4,000 meters and beyond.

There have always been bad years in which nothing was harvested. The constant processions to beg for rain and the measures taken to prevent severe frosts indicate anxiety over the fate of the crops, but the primary sources contain few references to famine. Friedrich Katz has drawn attention to the contrast with Meso-America, where most historical events were dated in relation to a given, named famine. The Andes have no such period markers.

Dense populations and statecraft in such circumstances required more than just endurance. The polities had to find ways to turn what in other continents would seem lethal into positive advantages. The sharp oscillation in temperature between 2PM and 2AM became an asset once they discovered that the contrasts allowed them to freeze dry and store all animal and vegetal tissues. With time, such survival tactics developed into an infrastructure that permitted the maintenance of an army in the field for years at a time,[6] the building and maintenance of more than 25,000 kilometers of road,[7] the construction of cities like Cusco, Machu Picchu, or Huánuco Pampa, and other feats of political and economic organization admired by tourists if not by planners.

These technological achievements do not exhaust Andean exceptionalism. Given the broken mountain terrain occupied by the many

[6] John V. Murra, 'La Guerre et les Rebéllions dans l'Expansion de l'Etat Inka', *Annales:Economies, Sociétés, Civilisations*, no. 6 (1978), pp. 927–35.

[7] John Hyslop, *The Inka Road System* (Academic Press, Orlando, 1984).

polities of the pre-1400 Andes, each of the ethnic groups – some as small as 500 households and others as large as 20,000 – attempted to defeat the threats of high altitude by distributing landholdings over as wide a geographical range as its armies could defend. Given the tiered nature of the Andean landscape, such territories can be held at sea level; at 500 meters in either the wet country east of the Andes or the desert near the Peruvian coast; at 1,500 meters and elsewhere, all the way up to 5,000 meters, where the alpaca herds thrive best. Each polity made an effort to control a maximum of such tiers; its fortunes rose and fell over centuries, but in certain highly desirable pockets several polities tolerated truces that permitted multi-ethnic access by permanently settled outliers. While the bulk of the population continued to live at the high altitude nucleus, the seat of power, some households were resettled in a wide variety of microclimates.

Such a sprinkled distribution of the population, over distances of four, seven, even ten days' walk away from the center, is sometimes called an 'archipelago', sometimes just 'ecological complementarity'.[8] The outliers had a permanent population, cultivating, fishing, or timbering on behalf of the home polity. They were kinfolk of the lords who lived at the nucleus and maintained religious, marriage, or political rights at the center, though their permanent residence may have been at a lower tier. Hence, the ethnic map of any such polity was a widely dispersed territory, limited only by the radius that could be physically enforced and by the truces that could be negotiated.

Some would stress the unstable nature of such dispersed polities. All the polities competed to give their caravans as wide a range as possible. Temporary hegemonies emerged, oscillated, and could get knocked out, but the periphery, whether on the arid coast or the Amazonic forest, remained multi-ethnic. At times, over-arching state formations emerged. The Inka, invaded by the Europeans, are only one example and that very recent. Andean history reveals smaller polities with widely dispersed territories.

One feature of the archipelago compels our attention here: the llama caravans that connected the nucleus at 3,800 meters with the coastal oases or the rain forest were not commercial expeditions. There were

---

[8] John V. Murra, 'El "Control Vertical" de un Máximo de Pisos Ecológicos en la Economia de las Sociedades Andinas', in *Formaciones Económicas y Políticas del Mundo Andino*, ed. John V. Murra (Instituto de Estudios Peruanos, Lima, 1975), pp. 59–116.

no markets or fairs, and no traders like the *pochteca* in pre-Columbian Mexico or the *mindala* of southern Colombia and northern Ecuador. The caravan connected kinfolk who cultivated or fished at the periphery with their original settlements. The outliers produced for the warehouses at the nucleus and received high altitude staples as a matter of complementary rights, not as commercial exchange.[9]

The early observers were especially impressed with the wealth found in storage: 'The Christians took all they wanted,' as one of them put it, 'and it looked as if nothing had been touched.' Much of the total social effort of the society went into processing food, with the centers of population on the top levels, where they did the processing. Edward Fox has reminded us that in seventeenth- and eighteenth-century France, an estimated 80 per cent of the population fed themselves and the other 20 per cent. In contrast, the Altiplano produced food with less than 80 per cent and provided ample nourishment from this relatively small part of the population.

Even more impressively, people owed the state not only the cultivation of state acreage, but roadwork, military service, and portaging. Although they had burden-bearing llamas, most of the carrying had to be done on human backs since the animals were small and could not be used in tandem. All timber, for example, had to be hauled by human beings to the Altiplano, thirty or forty days walk away.

Goods traveled enormous distances. High-status maize, for example, was sometimes carried for hundreds of kilometers on both llama and human backs, since a given variety was the only one appropriate for sacrifices or for ritual beer-brewing. This maize was generally used ceremonially and not, as in Meso-America, as a staple. The first step was to ensure daily tuberous bread. But soon after, the need for beer became manifest. Consider one of the few cases for which a quantitative statement can be made. A minor local lord, ruling only a few hundred houses, is reported to have had four wives – brewing was a major feminine activity – and four retainers, distributed according to the archipelago pattern: one in the high country with the herds; two at the village level, where potatoes could be grown but not processed; one far below in the forest and the coca leaf.

---

[9] The differential rights in such exchanges of the ethnic lords deserve special study, which, given our sources, cannot be undertaken now.

Thus, the ratio of eighty to twenty, cited for France, appears much higher than that for the Altiplano. The fed group probably fell below 20 per cent. The principal group that did not cultivate – apart from royalty and the lords – consisted of soldiers. But even there, most were peasants who were fed on campaign but then returned to their villages, where their acreage was worked by kinfolk. Only in the last few decades of Cusco rule did 'professional' armies appear. Even in Cochabamba, where Altiplano polities had to send their people to cultivate faraway maize fields, each 'quarter' of the landscape contained two strips out of sixteen to produce food for the workers. The warehouses remained untouched.

The symbolic and physical indicator of dispersed territoriality was the highway, the *qhapaq ñan*. It is still visible today in the republics of Ecuador, Peru, Bolivia, Chile, and Argentina, where yesterday's American-sponsored and financed roads are falling apart. According to Hyslop's measurements, it was the largest civil engineering work of the pre-capitalist world. The road was Cusco's flag, flying all over the territory, but unlike such public works elsewhere, it did not always connect inhabited places. Most of the time the road led from one state administrative center to another, as if to avoid populated centers. No matter how isolated the wilderness, at the end of each day's march there was a *tampu* – a way-station with barracks and storage and feeding facilities.

The warehouses, which held hundreds of thousands of cubic meters of storage space, have revealed a multiplicity of shapes and functions.[10] The army on the march, the bureaucracy, the priests, and whoever else used the roads were issued food, clothing, weapons, and benediction as they needed by the resident custodians, some sent from the capital but most people from the surrounding region. In the early years after the European invasion, foreign observers noted how quickly such administrative centers became overgrown with weed and neglected. Once Cusco rule had collapsed, no one resided there or took care of them.

The warehouses were as diagnostic an indicator of the Andean system as the highway. In fact, separating the two is probably our distortion: before 1532 the two had formed a single system that allowed quick connection between the nucleus and the periphery and permitted an army

[10] Craig Morris, 'Tecnología y Organización Inca del Almacenamiento de Víveres en las Sierra', in Lechtman and Soldi, *Runakunap*, pp. 327–75.

or the porters to remain in the field beyond a single agricultural cycle. The system of warehouses and highways visibly demonstrated Cusco's rule over hundreds of quite different polities. Both were built and maintained by nearby ethnic groups that rotated their services.

Before or during Inka rule, goods in the Andes were produced by people who frequently came from far away. The product was then moved hundreds of kilometers to the appropriate storage facilities. None of these transactions was commercial. In the absence of trade and markets the state did not collect taxes or tribute in kind. The household or the ethnic group owed nothing to the state from their own granary – a fact they kept explaining to the invading Europeans.[11]

A fundamental distinction must be drawn between ethnic traditional lands and those which produced the state's revenues. Royal acreage on the state's side was used to feed members of the royal lineages, which included the mummies of dead kings and their retainers, all fed from this major category. Similarly, on the ethnic side, lands were used by the local lords and their kinfolk to produce sacrificial food for the mountain shrines. Many more categories may be distinguished as better primary sources are discovered. Ecological complementarity enters here: probably, different rights in land would prevail if a peripheral coca-leaf-producing oasis was multi-ethnic. Some ways of ensuring sharing must have existed, but we still lack the details. Similarly, the high altitude range was governed by grazing rules for the many kinds of herds.

As a new polity was incorporated into the over-arching Inka state, it lost some of its acreage – the proportion remains unknown – which the Cusco bureaucracy alienated for its own use. These state plantations mostly produced maize. Sometimes the new authorities sponsored new terraces and irrigation works. The harvest was usually placed in the warehouses along the royal road.

The state assumed all risks. Since it now controlled fields at all latitudes and altitudes, a bad harvest in any one place could be compensated for elsewhere. Eventually, just before the European invasion, the Inka took a completely new step: instead of alienating some of the land in the Cochabamba Valley, they deported the whole population and worked this fertile maize-producing region with highlanders who were not

[11] John V. Murra, 'The Mit'a Obligations of Ethnic Groups to the Inka State', *The Inca and Aztec States, 1400–1800: Anthropology and History*, eds George A. Collier et al. (Academic Press, New York, 1982), pp. 237–62.

resettled but came on rotation to plant and harvest, much as they had worked on the road.[12]

A single highway connected the archipelago from one end to the other and enabled the state to control the areas between the administrative centers. Before the Inka unified the country, the ethnic lords enjoyed dispersed territoriality, which presumably became a nuisance after 1438. Measures such as the establishment of the maize plantations of Cochabamba must have reduced the lords' spheres of influence, while the long and distant wars limited the lords' initiatives in given years. We hear also of rebellions.

Lines of communication had to be kept open, but the road was cut frequently. Since there are numberless chasms of the San Luis Rey kind described by Thornton Wilder, the rope bridges were frequently cut by retreating armies or caravans. Local people knew of more than one route; they also knew how reweave the bridge. Even more frequent than the cutting of communication lines were piratical attacks on caravans. Oral tradition, recorded by the Andean writer Waman Puma, talks of a period just before the Inka which was *awqa runa* time (the enemy era), when all fought against each other. Both piracy and the cutting of communication lines must have led, from time to time, to truces, some imposed from above, some achieved at the conference rug.

The building of the roads facilitated primarily the movements of the army and of the groups in charge of major public works. The Cusco rulers did not interfere in the local ethnic governance beyond carving out some acreage for themselves. The local ethnic lords continued to rule in local matters in accordance with traditional patterns. There was never a large 'federal' bureaucracy. Unfortunately, the information at this local level is not satisfactory. Some scholars project a Cusco-centric system (Zuidema, Duviols), while others stress the vitality of the incorporated polities.

Cusco's imposition of Pax Inkaica changed some of the settlement patterns. In the Lupaqa kingdom, for example, the Aymara-speaking people, at least 100,000 strong, were moved by the Inca to the Lakeshore, along the royal road to Chile and Argentina. The Lupaqa had many outliers, east and west, but the effects of resettlement can only be guessed at, although they are the best-described ethnic group in the Andes. The

[12] Nathan Wachtel, 'The *Mitimas* of the Cochabamba Valley: The Colonization Policy of Huayna Capac', in Collier et al., *The Inca and Aztec States*, pp. 199–235.

European sources were not much interested in their archipelago, except for their nucleus by the Lake.

From the point of view of the Cusco rulers, the country was in continuous 'rebellion', since peripheral groups were reported to have tried to break out of the Inka realm. For the Inka, as for the Ashanti, as recorded by Kwame Arhin or Ivor Wilks, rebellion was a built-in structural feature. Thus, some of the ethnic lords welcomed the Europeans. As in Meso-America, the invasion was supported by local lords who saw the Europeans as allies against Cusco. In the area I know best from field work, Huánuco, it took the Europeans ten years to break down local resistance – ten years during which they traversed many thousands of miles southward. But in Huánuco it took the help of the Wanka, a friendly polity, to put an end to resistance.

Yet the sources for Andean studies are only marginally historical. The accounts of the European eyewitnesses of the invasion are not numerous. Prescott already had most of them at his disposal. Only rarely do we hear the voice of an Andean observer.[13] In such circumstances archeology has frequently been co-ordinated with written sources, particularly administrative accounts, censuses, and notarial protocols kept by the colonial regime.[14] Since Andean languages are still spoken by close to ten million people in the five republics, and since peasant activities, if not macro-organizational features, reflect strong continuities in these exceptional circumstances, contemporary ethnography is also proving especially useful.[15]

Foreign scholars rarely do this research well. In recent decades local scholars have frequently recognized that in the Andes the past has a special immediacy. Since most imported efforts to 'develop' the countryside at close to 4,000 meters have failed, there is a growing interest in fathoming how wealth and technological advances had been achieved in the past.[16] Since in three of these republics the Andean population is still in the majority, such efforts may turn out to be relevant not only for scholarship but for the effective future.

---

[13] An exception is Waman Puna de Ayala, *Nueva Coronica y Buen Gobierno* [1650], eds John V. Murra and Rolena Adorno (Siglo Veintiuno, Mexico, 1980).

[14] John V. Murra and Craig Morris, 'Dynastic Oral Tradition, Administrative Records and Archeology in the Andes', *World Archeology*, VII (1976), pp. 269–79.

[15] Gary Urton, 'Chuta: el Espacio de la Práctica Social en Pacariqtambo, Perú', *Revista Andina*, II (1984), pp. 7–56.

[16] John V. Murra, 'Derechos a las Tierras en el Tawantinsuyu', *Revista de la Universidad Complutense*, XVIII (1980), pp. 273–87.

11

Cultural Continuity and the Shaping of the American South

FORREST McDONALD

With a few notable exceptions, the history of British North America before 1776 has been written with scant attention to the culture that immigrants brought with them from Europe to the New World. As Mark Kishlansky pointed out in a review article in 1980, even 'the intensive New England town studies published in the early 1970s were conceived, researched, and written with only the most casual reference to the habits of English life.'[1] To be sure, a number of scholars have explored the European origins of American legal and political institutions and thought, and others have studied the European sources of American religious traditions and practices.[2] But these are examples of what cultural anthropologists call diffusion – the spread of characteristics from one

---

[1] Mark A. Kishlansky, 'Community and Continuity: A Review of Selected Works on English Local History', *William and Mary Quarterly*, 37 (1980), pp. 139–46.

[2] See, for example, Julius Goebel, Jr, *History of the Supreme Court of the United States* (Macmillan, New York, 1971), 2 vols, vol. I: *Antecedents and Beginnings to 1801*; Douglass Adair, '"That Politics May Be Reduced to a Science": David Hume, James Madison, and the Tenth *Federalist*', *Huntington Library Quarterly*, 20 (1957), pp. 343–60; Bernard Bailyn, *The Ideological Origins of the American Revolution* (Harvard University Press, Cambridge, Mass., 1967); H. Trevor Colbourn, *The Lamp of Experience: Whig History and the Intellectual Origins of the American Revolution* (University of North Carolina Press, Chapel Hill, 1965); J. G. A. Pocock, *The Machiavellian Moment: Florentine Political Thought and the Atlantic Republican Tradition* (Princeton University Press, Princeton, 1975); Garry Wills, *Inventing America: Jefferson's Declaration of Independence* (Doubleday, Garden City, New York, 1978); Sydney E. Ahlstrom, *A Religious History of the American People* (Yale University Press, New Haven, 1972); Forrest McDonald, *Novus Ordo Seclorum: The Intellectual Origins of the Constitution* (University of Kansas Press, Lawrence, 1985).

people to another – and not of the persistence of Old World traits in the New. Apart from Sumner Chilton Powell and David Grayson Allen, I know of no American colonial historians who have given this persistence much systematic thought and study, though some modern urban historians have done so.[3]

The neglect is understandable. In part it is attributable to the belief of Americans in their uniqueness as a people – a belief that for a long time was reinforced historiographically both by the myth of the melting pot and by Frederick Jackson Turner's frontier hypothesis. Immigrants could scarcely set foot on Plymouth Rock or Staten Island, the story went, before they began to shed their alien ways and emerge as a new breed, the unique American. There was, moreover, the illusion that in colonial America the people whom some now call 'ethnics' were rare. The histories of the two most visible groups of 'ethnics' – blacks and Indians – were treated as subjects separate from that of colonial history. And, even after allowing for the various German and Dutch settlements and a scattering of Scandinavians, French, and Spanish, the overwhelming majority of whites in British America were known to have originated in the British archipelago and were treated accordingly as one group.

Nonetheless, I believe it can be shown that the cultural attributes immigrants brought with them differed, that they persisted with only gradual and relatively minor modifications, and that they go a long way toward explaining the regional differences that emerged within the colonies. Here, I shall employ concepts adapted from cultural geography and anthropology in an attempt to sketch out the way the development of the society of one set of colonies – those in the South – was influenced, and in considerable measure shaped, by the previously existing cultural traits of the people who settled them.

---

[3] For a definition of diffusion, see A. L. Kroeber, 'Diffusionism', in *Encyclopedia of the Social Sciences*, eds. Edwin R. A. Seligman and Alvin Johnson (6 vols, Macmillan, New York, 1930–5). The works mentioned are Sumner Chilton Powell, *Puritan Village: The Formation of a New England Town* (Wesleyan University Press, Middletown, Connecticut, 1963); David Grayson Allen, *In English Ways: The Movement of Societies and the Transferral of English Local Law and Custom to Massachusetts Bay in the Seventeenth Century* (University of North Carolina Press, Chapel Hill, 1981). See also T. H. Breen, 'Persistent Localism: English Social Change and the Shaping of New England Institutions', *William and Mary Quarterly* 32 (1975), pp. 3–28. James G. Leyburn, *The Scotch-Irish: A Social History* (University of North Carolina, Chapel Hill, 1962), is a pioneering study in the direction indicated; it contains much useful information, but it suffers from filiopietism and is often erroneous.

Three principles, I believe, were involved in the interaction between frontier and pioneer. The first has to do with the insular quality of life on the frontier. A long succession of commentators, from Crèvecoeur to Frederick Jackson Turner and his disciples, insisted that the American wilderness functioned as a great environmental grindstone, pulverizing the cultural attributes that Europeans brought over and transforming the immigrants into a new and homogenized species. Misguided nationalism and faddish evolutionism conditioned the formulation and acceptance of that notion, but it is difficult to imagine how a view so contrary to common sense and regard for history could have perdured. A moment's reflection should be sufficient to indicate what, above all else, the essentially uninhabited American frontier provided that Europe could not: places where people could, by choice, live among like-minded people and in isolation from others. In such surroundings, they were at liberty to retain their accustomed norms, whereas those who remained in the British Isles were subjected, during the seventeenth and eighteenth centuries, to a combination of pressures, events, and circumstances which made resistance to change far more difficult.

The second principle is that of cultural conservatism or inertia. Change, we are wont to believe, is the stuff of history; but the stuff of society, if cultural anthropologists are to be credited, is resistance to change, or at least resistance to the changing of fundamental patterns in life's rhythms, rituals, and belief-structures. To be more precise, cultural conservatism is the tendency to continue to think and behave in customary, socially conditioned, and familiar ways unless wars, conquest, technology, interaction with alien groups, or other forces necessitate change; and it is the tendency to retain or revert to those norms in modified form despite the forces of change.[4]

This principle is most readily apparent when one observes relatively primitive societies, but it can be equally operative among the more

[4] Specialists appear to be in general agreement as to the force of cultural conservatism, though they disagree about the dynamics of cultural change. See, for example, George C. Homans, *The Human Group* (Harcourt, Brace, New York, 1950); George Peter Murdock, 'How Culture Changes', in *Man, Culture, and Society*, ed. Harry L. Shapiro (Oxford University Press, New York, 1956), pp. 247–60; Raymond Firth, *Elements of Social Organization* (Watts, London, 1951); Michael Hechter, 'The Political Economy of Ethnic Change', *American Journal of Sociology*, 79 (1974), pp. 1151–78; Ralf Dahrendorf, *Essays in the Theory of Society* (Stanford University Press, Stanford, 1968). My reading on the subject has been extensive but unsystematic and untutored.

advanced. In eastern Europe, successions of regimes have been trying for a thousand years and more to impose a viable political hegemony on the scores of ethnic and national groups in the area, invariably in vain. Present Communist regimes, for all their ruthlessness and their modern technology, have been no more able to homogenize even such small, multi-ethnic countries as Czechoslovakia and Yugoslavia, than were Hapsburgs, Jagiellonians, Ottomans, and Romanovs before them. As for the West, Eugen Weber has demonstrated that in France, that epitome of nineteenth-century nationalism, nearly half the population, six decades after the Revolution, still not only read no French but did not even speak it. In Spain, the Civil War of the 1930s now seems to have been less a contest between classes and ideologies than one between ethnic groups – Basques, Catalonians, Murcians, Andalucians, Castilians – which had retained their identities even though the kingdom had been politically unified for nearly four and a half centuries.[5]

If cultural conservatism could be so potent in a Europe that experienced absolutism, the scientific revolution, the Enlightenment, the French Revolution, and the industrial revolution, it seems likely that it would have been even stronger in colonial America. As Thomas Jefferson wrote in the Declaration of Independence, 'All experience hath shown, that mankind are more disposed to suffer, while evils are sufferable, than to right themselves by abolishing the forms to which they are accustomed.' Alexander Hamilton in his *Report on Manufactures* (1791) described his countrymen in just these terms. 'Experience teaches', Hamilton wrote, 'that men are often so much governed by what they are accustomed to see and practice, that the simplest and most obvious improvements, in the most ordinary occupations, are adopted with hesitation, reluctance, and by slow gradations.' Men would resist changes, he believed, so long as even 'a bare support could be ensured by an adherence to ancient courses', and perhaps even longer.

The third principle, associated with the geographers Milton Newton and Fred Kniffen, is that of cultural preadaptation or preselection.[6]

---

[5] Richard V. Burks, *East European History: An Ethnic Approach*, American Historical Association Pamphlets, 425 (American Historical Association, Washington, DC, 1961, 1973); Eugen Joseph Weber, *Peasants into Frenchmen: The Modernization of Rural France, 1870–1914* (Stanford University Press, Stanford, 1976). See also Michael Hechter, *Internal Colonialism: The Celtic Fringe in British National Development, 1536–1966* (University of California Press, Berkeley, Calif., 1975).

[6] Milton Newton, 'Cultural Preadaptation and the Upland South', *Geoscience and Man*, 5 (1974), pp. 143–54; Fred Kniffen, 'Folk Housing: Key to Diffusion', *Annals of the Association of American Geographers*, 55 (1965), pp. 549–77.

Like most other sound scientific principles, that of cultural preadaptation is obvious once someone else has thought it up. It is this: over the course of time, a society will develop combinations of traits and habits of behaviour which have survival value in a particular human or physical environment, along with other traits that may be irrelevant or even detrimental to survival. Placed in a different environment, members of the society will fare well or ill, depending less upon their adaptability to new surroundings than upon the compatibility between their previously evolved ways and those new surroundings.

Let us now turn to the peopling of the colonies. In so doing, it will be useful to bear in mind an obvious but easily overlooked fact about the British Isles, namely that they were economically and historically far from monolithic. Topographically, Britain is divided along a southwest-to-northeast line that runs roughly from Bournemouth to York, uplands to the north and west, lowlands to the south and east. And the line was a cultural and agricultural watershed as well. When American settlement began the most visible difference between the material cultures of the uplands and lowlands of England lay, in the words of Joan Thirsk, in 'two contrasted kinds of farming. In the grass-growing uplands, where the principal asset was stock, men either specialized in rearing sheep and cattle, or . . . pig-keeping, or horse-breeding or did a little of each.' And tillage there was minimal. In the lowlands, 'mixed farming' with extensive tillage was the norm, and commercial intercourse was far more frequent. The Scottish Lowlands, during the eighteenth-century Age of Improvement, began to adopt a pattern similar to that in the English lowlands. Elsewhere, not only in the west and north of England but throughout the Celtic fringe – Cornwall, Wales, the Scottish Highlands, the Hebrides, and Ireland – the upland herding pattern prevailed, and warfare rather than commerce was the common non-agricultural pursuit.[7]

[7] Joan Thirsk, ed., *The Agrarian History of England and Wales, 1500–1640*, (Cambridge University Press, Cambridge, 1967) vol. IV, pp. 2–6. A. Fenton, 'The Traditional Pastoral Economy', in *The Making of the Scottish Countryside*, eds. M. L. Parry and T. R. Slater (Croom Helm, London and Montreal, 1980), pp. 93–110; E. Estyn Evans, *Irish Heritage: The Landscape, The People and Their Work* (W. Tempest, Dundalganfres, Dundalk, 1977). For detailed documentation of pastoral culture of the uplands and the Celtic fringe, see Grady McWhiney and Forrest McDonald, 'Celtic Origins of Southern Herding Practices', *Journal of Southern History*, 51 (1985), pp. 165–82. For a critique

Migrants from both sides of the upland–lowland line settled in all parts of British America, but it is significant that New England and New England alone was populated overwhelmingly by people from the English lowlands. The settlers moved from particular places in England to particular places in New England, and sometimes so small a change in the environment as moving from one kind of soil to another made adjustment difficult for them. As David Grayson Allen has shown in his meticulous study of five Massachusetts towns, however, 'New England settlers were able to perpetuate old English practice and usually did so.' In those towns the process of 'Americanization', which took about sixty years, consisted not in shedding 'English ways', but in gradually abandoning the subtle local characteristics that had at first distinguished one from another, and thus in becoming a homogenized English whole.[8]

Settlement of the colonial South was a longer and more complex affair. Whereas settlers migrated to New England on an appreciable scale only during the Great Migration of 1629–42 and in a secondary wave during the 1660s, emigrants continued to pour into the South throughout the colonial period. Although there were several distinct patterns to the movement over the course of time, most of the settlers in the South originated in the English uplands or the Celtic fringe.

The first round of southern settlement was in the Chesapeake region. More than 5000 immigrants went there during the first two decades after 1607, but the mortality rate was so high that scarcely a quarter of them survived. By 1640 the population of Virginia had grown to about 8000 and that of Maryland to about 1500, mostly by additional migrations: presumably the new settlers had come from all over England and Wales. The decisive emigration to the Chesapeake colonies began when that to New England ended, around 1642, with the outbreak of the Civil War. Royalist strength was concentrated in the English uplands and

---

of Thirsk's work from the perspective of cultural conservatism or pre-adaptation, see George C. Homans, 'The Explanation of English Regional Differences', *Past and Present*, 42 (1969), pp. 18–34.

[8] Allen, *In English Ways*, pp. 8–18, 205–24, 245–89. At pp. 8–9, n. 6, Allen surveys the bibliography of sources and studies of English migration to New England. It is to be noted that extreme northern New England was settled by different stock, west-country Englishmen primarily.

Wales, and when the Puritan-Parliamentarian 'Roundheads' triumphed, a sizable exodus from 'Cavalier' country to the Chesapeake area ensued. This is not to suggest that more than a handful of the approximately 15,000 who emigrated were Cavaliers in the sense of nobility or landed gentry, or even that most went for political or religious reasons. Indeed, 70 to 90 per cent apparently went as indentured servants, and most seem to have gone mainly to escape severe economic hardship at home. Nonetheless, in striking contrast to New England, Virginia and Maryland were peopled mainly from the upland, pastoral, Anglican north and west of England, from Wales, and – another element in the equation – from Ireland.[9]

The Irish had long been in the habit of migrating from their homeland. After each of the rebellions during the sixteenth century, thousands of Irishmen followed their chieftains to the Continent – where, in the service of European crowns, they could continue to ply their ancient trade as warriors. During the seventeenth century, even before the great rebellion of 1641, many young men and women went from Ireland to the Chesapeake area, some kidnapped or transported but most voluntarily as indentured servants. During the 1640s and 1650s thousands more fled or were deported as felons or rebels. Considerable numbers of these went to the Chesapeake, but most went to the West Indies. By the time of the Restoration, Irish people constituted a large majority of the perhaps 80,000 white inhabitants of the English Caribbean islands of Barbados, St Christopher, Nevis, and Jamaica. Barbados had, at that time, about 30,000 black slaves and about 20,000 indentured white, overwhelmingly Irish, felons and rebels. St Christopher was said to contain 20,000 Irish.[10]

---

[9] Edmund S. Morgan, *American Slavery, American Freedom: The Ordeal of Colonial Virginia* (W. W. Norton, New York, 1975), pp. 136, 180, 395–410; Bureau of the Census, *Historical Statistics of the United States: Colonial Times to 1957* (US Government Printing Office, Washington, DC, 1960), p. 756; James Horn, 'Servant Emigration to the Chesapeake in the Seventeenth Century', *in The Chesapeake in the Seventeenth Century: Essays on Anglo-American Society*, eds. Thaddeus W. Tate and David L. Ammerman (University of North Carolina Press, Chapel Hill, 1979), pp. 51–95, esp. the maps on pp. 67 and 71; John Eacott Manahan, 'The Cavalier Remounted: A Study of the Origins of Virginia's Population, 1607–1700' (unpublished PhD dissertation, University of Virginia, 1947).

[10] G. A. Hayes-McCoy, 'The Tudor Conquest (1534–1603)', and Aidan Clarke, 'The Colonisation of Ulster and the Rebellion of 1641 (1603–60)', in *The Course of Irish History*, eds. T. W. Moody and F. X. Martin (Mercier Press, Cork, 1967), pp. 174–88, 189–203; Edward MacLysaght, *Irish Life in the Seventeenth Century* (Oxford

Remigration to the mainland began in 1669. During the next three decades the Irish labor force in the English West Indies was substantially replaced by blacks imported from Africa, and most of the Irish moved to the new Carolina colonies. There their numbers were augmented by immigrants arriving directly from Ireland. English people and Huguenots went to the Carolinas as well, but in the words of Robert Mills, an early South Carolina historian, 'No country furnished the province with as many inhabitants as Ireland.' Mills, writing in 1826, added, 'Scarcely a ship sailed from any of [Ireland's] ports, for Charleston, that was not crowded with men, women, and children.' In addition, 25,000 to 30,000 were transported as convicts between the 1720s and the 1760s, mainly to Maryland and Virginia, and perhaps as many more emigrated as indentured servants during that period, again mainly to Maryland and Virginia.[11]

The last and greatest wave of immigration to the South, that of the Scotch-Irish, is the most difficult to describe, but only because the Scotch-Irish themselves are difficult to define. It is generally recognized that not many Scots emigrated directly from Scotland to America: a few hundred a year went from the Lowlands, mainly to the Chesapeake region, and about 20,000 went from the Highlands during the decade before the Revolution, mainly to the Carolinas. By contrast, the number of putative 'Scots' who migrated from northern Ireland during the six decades before the Revolution has been estimated variously from 130,000 to 500,000. It is well known that about a third of these landed in southern ports and that all but a handful of the rest landed in Philadelphia, from which they moved inland and thence down the interior uplands from

---

University Press, New York, 1969, reprint of 1950 edn); Carl and Roberta Bridenbaugh, *No Peace Beyond the Line: The English in the Caribbean, 1624–1690* (Oxford University Press, New York, 1972), pp. 12–21, 225–8; Richard S. Dunn, *Sugar and Slaves: The Rise of the Planter Class in the English West Indies, 1624–1713* (University of North Carolina Press, Chapel Hill, 1972), pp. 56–7, 69.

[11] Richard S. Dunn, 'The English Sugar Islands and the Founding of South Carolina', *South Carolina Historical Magazine*, 72 (1971), pp. 82–3; Edward McGrady, *The History of South Carolina Under the Proprietary Government, 1670–1719* (Macmillan, New York, 1897), pp. 73–128, 143ff; Robert Mills, *Statistics of South Carolina . . .* (Hurlbut and Lloyd, Charleston, 1826), p. 175; Abbot Emerson Smith, *Colonists in Bondage: White Servitude and Convict Labor in America, 1607–1776* (University of North Carolina Press, Chapel Hill, 1947), pp. 48–9, 52, 134; Carl Bridenbaugh, *Myths and Realities: Societies of the Colonial South* (Atheneum, New York, 1963), p. 7.

Maryland to Georgia. Historians have been confused, however, as to just who the Scotch-Irish were.[12]

The prevailing understanding – or, rather, misunderstanding – is that the Scotch-Irish were descendants of Scots who settled on the Ulster plantations created by James I in 1610 and rarely intermingled with the 'mere' or pure Irish. There are several things wrong with that view. One is that Ulstermen, Hebrideans, and western Highlanders were all but indistinguishable, having for centuries been a part of a single herding, seafaring, and warrior culture that as a practical matter had been politically autonomous under the Lordship of the Isles until the end of the fifteenth century. No less important, the seventeenth-century migrations from Scotland to Ireland cannot be squared with the myth that the eighteenth-century Scotch-Irish were descended from settlers on the Ulster plantations. From the time of the death of James VI and I, about 14,000 new Scots had been settled in Ulster, perhaps half Lowlanders, the rest from the Hebrides and western Highlands. The number approximately doubled during the 1630s, but the newcomers came mainly from the northeastern Highlands, between Aberdeenshire and Inverness, and they went not to the plantation areas but to counties Antrim and Down. Many of the newly arrived Scots in Ulster fled or were killed during the turbulent 1640s, and by 1652 the total number had declined to about 20,000. Another large migration took place during the next two decades, and Sir William Petty estimated that in 1672 there were 100,000 Scots in northern Ireland. Few Scots went to Ireland during the next generation, but in 1695 a devastating famine swept the Highlands and Islands, and a mass exodus ensued. The Bishop of Baphoe estimated that no fewer than 50,000 Scots families – overwhelmingly Western Highlanders and Hebrideans – moved

---

[12] Bridenbaugh, *Myths and Realities*, pp. 124–33; Ian C. C. Graham, *Colonists from Scotland: Emigration to North America, 1707–1783* (Cornell University Press, Ithaca, New York, 1956), pp. 25, 38–42; R. J. Dickson, *Ulster Emigration to Colonial America, 1718–1775* (Routledge & Kegan Paul, Belfast, 1966), *passim*. Dickson takes considerable pains to disprove the claim of Michael J. O'Brien (in *A Hidden Phase of American History: Ireland's Part in America's Struggle for Liberty* [Dodd Mead and Co., New York, 1919] and in 'Shipping Statistics of the Philadelphia Customs House, 1773 to 1774, Refute the Scotch-Irish Theory', *American-Irish Historical Society Journal* [1923], pp. 132–41) that 150,000 emigrants left Ireland for America in the early 1770s and that two-thirds of these were Catholic Irish. Dickson's argument is sometimes inconsistent and not altogether convincing, yet O'Brien's claims clearly seem extravagant.

to northern Ireland during the late seventeenth and early eighteenth centuries.[13]

The point is this: the great masses of Scotch-Irish who migrated to America and came to dominate the interior uplands of the American South during the eighteenth century were not Lowland Scots of the stereotype – dour, orderly, industrious, rigidly moralistic Presbyterians. Rather, they were, for the most part, almost a mirror opposite of that stereotype, and were the least Anglicized of all the traditionally Celtic peoples.

Bringing these immigration data together, it is possible to arrive at a general picture of the ethnic makeup of the white southern population at the time of the Revolution. A tabulation based upon analysis of family names as recorded in the extant records of the first United States census, that of 1790, is revealing. People of Celtic origins – Welsh, Scots, Irish, and Scotch-Irish – constituted 41.7 per cent of the white population of Virginia in 1790, as compared with 49.6 per cent English; in North Carolina, people of Celtic origin constituted 52.5 per cent, and those of English origin 40.6 per cent; in South Carolina, people of Celtic origin constituted 53.4 per cent, those of English 36.7 per cent. In the backcountry the ratios were higher: Celts constituted 60 to 80 per cent

---

[13] Regarding the Ulster–Hebrides–Highland culture in general, see Jennifer M. Brown, ed., *Scottish Society in the Fifteenth Century* (St Martin's Press, New York, 1977); and Jenny Wormald, *Court, Kirk, and Community: Scotland, 1470–1625* (University of Toronto, Toronto, 1981); Ramsay Colles, *The History of Ulster, from the Earliest Times to the Present Day* (4 vols, Gresham Publishing Co., London, 1919–20); G. A. Hayes-McCoy, *Scots Mercenary Forces in Ireland, 1565–1603* (Burns, Oates, and Washbourne Ltd, Dublin and London, 1937); Donald Gregory, *The History of the Western Highlands and Isles of Scotland* (Edinburgh, 1881); and Michael Sheane, *Ulster and the Lords of the North* (Highfield Press, Stockport, Cheshire, 1980), esp. pp. 112–22. For migrations from Scotland to Ulster, see M. Perceval-Maxwell, *The Scottish Migration to Ulster in the Reign of James I* (Routledge & Kegan Paul, London, and Humanities Press, New York, 1973); Colles, *History of Ulster*, vol. 3, pp. 180, 183–4; Charles Henry Hull, ed., *The Economic Writings of Sir William Petty* (2 vols, A. M. Kelley, New York, 1963–4), vol. 1, p. 149; L. M. Cullen and T. C. Smout, eds., *Comparative Aspects of Scottish and Irish Economic and Social History, 1600–1900* (Donald, Edinburgh, n.d. [*c.*1977]), pp. 4, 24; T. C. Smout, *A History of the Scottish People, 1560–1830* (Collins, London, 1969), pp. 144–5; Audrey Lockhart, *Some Aspects of Emigration from Ireland to the North American Colonies between 1660 and 1775* (Arno Press, New York, 1976), p. 19.

of the population.[14] And, if it can be assumed that seventeenth-century English emigration patterns continued in the eighteenth century, the vast majority of English origin in the South would have come from the northern and western uplands. Or, even if it be assumed that the seventeenth-century patterns were reversed in the eighteenth, it would still follow that about half of the English in the South had roots in the uplands.

Overall, then, it seems conservative to estimate that approximately three-quarters of the white population of the South had originated in the uplands of the British archipelago. This was precisely the opposite of the situation in New England.

In the larger study of which the present essay is a part, my colleague Grady McWhiney and I shall attempt to describe the process by which Southerners reconciled the many particular differences in their backgrounds, adapted to the American environment, accommodated negro slavery and the plantation system, and emerged as a more or less homogeneous society. For now I shall offer a modest effort to survey briefly some of the cultural baggage of the Celtic and upland English immigrants that survived the Atlantic crossing and the early phases of the frontier experience. Three broad sources will be drawn upon: the contributions of cultural geographers, the findings of historical sociologists, and the observations of contemporary travelers.

The most obvious carry-over was that the immigrants had been herders in the Old World and continued to be herders in the New. Despite the expansion of tobacco culture, herding remained the principal occupation of Virginians and Marylanders throughout the seventeenth century and during much of the eighteenth. It was in the Carolinas, however, that herding flourished most: untended swine and cattle multiplied there faster than their owners could eat or market them. True, rice planting began on a sizable scale in the South Carolina low country during the 1720s, and by the time of the Revolution most of the suitable coastal lands had been put under rice. In the 1770s and 1780s tobacco culture spread over portions of both Carolinas, as did cotton in the 1790s. Nonetheless, livestock raising continued to be important in the seaboard states

[14] Forrest McDonald and Ellen Shapiro McDonald, 'The Ethnic Origins of the American People, 1790', *William and Mary Quarterly*, 37 (1980), pp. 179–99; and subsequent articles by Thomas L. Purvis and Donald H. Akenson, and commentary by Purvis, Akenson, and McDonald and McDonald in 'The Population of the United States, 1790: A Symposium', *William and Mary Quarterly*, 41 (1984), pp. 85–135.

throughout the antebellum period, and as late as the eve of the war between the states, the value of hogs and cattle in the South exceeded that of all its agricultural staples combined. In other words, the vast majority of white Southerners continued to be animal raisers first and tillage farmers only second if at all, even as their Irish, Scotch-Irish, Welsh, and upland English ancestors had been.[15]

The foremost student of southern animal-raising practices, Terry G. Jordan, has isolated a unique complex of seventeen traits that characterized Carolina herding in the late seventeenth century, and which persisted essentially without change as southerners moved westward over the course of the next two hundred years. These were: (1) use of the open range; (2) accumulation by individual owners of large herds, amounting to hundreds and even thousands of animals; (3) neglect of the livestock; (4) branding of cattle (hogs were marked by clipping their ears); (5) collection of herds at established cowpens at regular intervals; (6) use of hired, indentured, or enslaved cowhands and swineherds; (7) absentee ownership in some instances; (8) heavy reliance on dogs; (9) use of salt in herd control; (10) use of whips to manage stock; (11) occasional use of horses in cattle tending; (12) overland drives to feeder areas or markets along regular trails, performed by professional drovers; (13) transhumance, or seasonal movement of stock; (14) periodic burning of the range; (15) the combination of cattle and hogs on the same range; (16) a predominance of cattle breeds of British origin, typically rather small animals; and (17) the raising of some field and garden crops but a heavy emphasis on livestock production.[16] Jordan himself found no European or African antecedents for this complex; but McWhiney and I have demonstrated that it had long existed in the Celtic fringe and English uplands and not among any other peoples known to have come to America.

Since immigrants to the South did not change their primary mode of obtaining a livelihood, which in the hospitable southern environment

---

[15] The data in this and the following paragraph are developed and documented at length in McWhiney and McDonald, 'Celtic Origins of Southern Herding Practices'. See also Forrest McDonald and Grady McWhiney, 'The Antebellum Southern Herdsman: A Reinterpretation', *Journal of Southern History*, 41 (1975), pp. 147–66, and the same authors' 'The South from Self-Sufficiency to Peonage: An Interpretation', *American Historical Review*, 85 (1980), pp. 1095–118.

[16] Terry G. Jordan, *Trails to Texas: Southern Roots of Western Cattle Ranching* (University of Nebraska Press, Lincoln, Nebraska, 1981), pp. 25–6 and *passim*.

yielded a far more bountiful existence than it normally had in the British Isles, it is unsurprising that they retained many other characteristics of their traditional material culture as well. The housing of the Scotch-Irish frontiersmen affords a good example. The Scotch-Irish had been inexperienced in building with wood, the most readily available material in America; they learned the techniques, especially of corner timbering for log structures, from the Germans in Pennsylvania. But otherwise their dwellings were duplicates of what they had been accustomed to in Ulster and Scotland. The interior dimensions of their houses in America were sixteen by twenty-two feet, as compared to fifteen by twenty-one in their Ulster houses; the external dimensions were the same as in Ulster. The dimensions had originally been set by the limits on roof sizes imposed by the scarcity of wood in Scotland and Ireland; they were retained in America out of habit despite the abundance of wood. The dog-trot house that became common in the South later was simply two of the traditional houses spaced a few feet apart and enclosed under a single roof. By contrast, English Americans who moved into the interior South from the tidewater typically built log houses about sixteen feet square – the dimensions of the English single-bay cottage.[17]

As for barns, the southern frontiersmen did not build them. The first barns in Maryland were built in the 1690s, after a severe winter killed many thousands of the cattle. Further south they remained almost unknown in the interior: animals either shared the house with the settlers or were left to brave the elements without shelter, both of which were common practices in Scotland and Ireland. Fencing, too, was rare. Whereas the building of fences was the norm in lowland England and New England, it was uncommon in Scotland, Ireland, and Wales; and in the southern backcountry the only people who regularly fenced their land were the Germans. Indeed, the law in every southern jurisdiction prevented the fencing of any land except that which was actually under cultivation, and permitted animal owners to graze their beasts on all

[17] E. Estyn Evans, 'The Scotch-Irish: Their Cultural Adaptation and Heritage in the American Old West', in *Essays in Scotch-Irish History*, ed. E. R. R. Green (Routledge & Kegan Paul, London, 1969), pp. 78–80; Fred B. Kniffen and Henry H. Glassie, 'Building in Wood in the Eastern United States: A Time–Place Perspective', *Geographical Review*, 56 (1966), pp. 40–66; Wayland F. Dunaway, *The Scotch-Irish of Colonial Pennsylvania* (University of North Carolina Press, Chapel Hill, 1944), p. 185.

other land, no matter who 'owned' it. Such legal arrangements persisted into the twentieth century.[18]

In farming practices and the preparation of foods too cultural geographers have identified carry-overs and adaptations. Obviously, southerners of Celtic and English upland origins adapted, as did New England Yankees, by raising plants learned about from Indians – tobacco, 'Irish' potatoes, and 'Indian' corn, among others. But there were striking differences in the ways Yankees and southerners did so. The Indians planted corn in small, easily prepared mounds and then neglected it until harvest, for its rapid growth outstripped that of the surrounding weeds. The transplanted lowland Englishmen in New England, traditionally 'compulsive ploughers', were unable to bring themselves to employ such a primitive method and instead cultivated and tended the plant with as much laborious attention as they devoted to wheat or rye. The Scotch-Irish took readily to the easier Indian way; indeed, since corn required even less labor than potatoes grown in Irish 'lazy beds' and could be distilled into a liquor that more nearly resembled their traditional drink, they increasingly favored corn over the potato. To prepare the land for planting – or for grazing – they employed a traditional technique of the Celtic areas, which the Indians also used, that of setting fire to the countryside. To prepare their maize for eating once it was ripe, they used implements and methods that the Irish had used for processing oats and barley, which were perfectly workable with maize. The knocking-stone became the hominy block, and hominy was made into porridge. Corn breads of many kinds were baked on the hearth or in the pot-oven, and the open hearth retained its place at the center of the home. Beside the hearth was a bundle of feathers, a native replacement for the traditional Irish goose-wing 'tidy'.[19]

[18] Lewis Cecil Gray, *History of Agriculture in the Southern United States to 1860* (2 vols, Peter Smith, Gloucester, Mass., 1958), vol. 1, pp. 142–7, 151, 200, vol. 2, p. 843; Raymond D. Crotty, *Irish Agricultural Production: Its Volume and Structure* (Cork University Press, Cork, 1966), pp. 2–6; MacLysaght, *Irish Life in the Seventeenth Century*, pp. 88, 171–2, 243–4; Leonard T. Davies and Averyl Edwards, *Welsh Life in the Eighteenth Century* (Country Life, London, 1939), pp. 2–3; J. Crawford King, Jr, 'The Closing of the Southern Range: An Exploratory Study', *Journal of Southern History*, 48 (1982), pp. 53–70.

[19] Gray, *Southern Agriculture*, vol. 1, pp. 27, 161–2, 173–4; Percy Wells Bidwell and John I. Falconer, *History of Agriculture in the Northern United States, 1620–1860* (P. Smith, New York, 1941), pp. 10–12; John Fraser Hart, 'Land Rotation in Appalachia', *Geographical Review*, 67 (1977), pp. 148–51; J. S. Otto and N. E. Anderson, 'Slash-and-Burn Cultivation in the Highlands South: A Problem in Comparative Agricultural History', *Comparative Studies in Society and History*, 24 (1982), pp. 131–47; Evans, 'The Scotch-Irish', pp. 82–4.

Many other attributes of Scots and Irish material culture were carried out of habit and continued irrespective of their suitability in the new environment. As indicated, a preference for open-range pastoralism was the most obvious and important of these, and the Scotch-Irish could thrive in America by following the complex of practices that had yielded their ancestors only a marginal livelihood. With regard to tillage two features of the agricultural landscape in Scotland and Ulster were especially conspicuous. One was the infield-outfield system, whereby a central area was cultivated and the surrounding countryside reserved for grazing. This was pretty much duplicated in America, except that in the heavy oak forests swine were kept more often than cattle. The other was the runrig system, whereby individuals plowed, tended, and harvested several separated strips or furrows. The practice was a function of the shortage of good arable land in Scotland and Ireland, and it occurred to no one to replicate it on the sparsely settled, land-rich southern frontier. But one curious aspect of it, which had a practical value in Britain and Ireland, was continued in America even though it was extremely impractical there, namely, plowing in straight vertical lines up and down hills. Given the heavy rainfall, the poor drainage, and the ubiquitous peat bogs in Ireland and western Scotland, such a method was useful in helping dry the land; given the climate and soils of North America, it led rapidly to depletion of the earth by erosion. (During the 1780s Thomas Jefferson 'discovered' contour plowing in France and sought excitedly to persuade his countrymen to adopt it as an erosion preventative. His efforts proved fruitless; New England had no need for the innovation since there, as in England, contour plowing had long been practiced. Southerners, seeing no reason to change their ways, went on washing away their soil.)[20]

It did not trouble southerners that they were destroying the land, partly because there seemed to be an infinite quantity of it but partly also because of another cultural trait that they had brought with them. The Celts had traditionally been somewhat nomadic, as primitive pastoralists are wont to be, migration to uplands for summer grazing having been the norm in Wales, Scotland, and Ireland. Centuries of violence – rival

---

[20] Evans, 'The Scotch-Irish', pp. 80, 84; R. A. Dodgshon, 'The Origins of Traditional Field Systems', in Parry and Slater, *The Making of the Scottish Countryside*, pp. 69–92; Gray, *Southern Agriculture*, vol. 2, p. 796. See also plates 1, 3, and 4 in Parry and Slater for illustrations of Scottish vertical plowing.

clans pushing one another about and English invaders harassing, overrunning and pursuing – had reinforced the tendency. Thus, unlike the German immigrants who preferred to stay in a place and develop it intensively once they had found a suitable location, or the New Englanders who generally migrated only in communities or congregations of saints, the Celtic Americans seem 'to have had a psychological repugnance to making permanent homes until they had moved several times'.[21]

Related to this restlessness was a characteristic that is less in the province of the geographer than of the sociologist or sociologically oriented historian. One ready measure of the differences among social groups is residential patterns. Outside of the few genuine cities in colonial America, three distinct types of residential patterns appeared among the English-speaking inhabitants, each of which represented a transplantation of patterns in the British archipelago. In most of England the nucleated settlement – clusters of houses into villages, no matter what the system of landholding or land utilization – was the norm, and so was it in New England. In the northern and western uplands and in Wales and much of Ireland, dispersed settlement was the norm; that is, each family had its dwelling-place more or less in the middle of the land it owned or leased, in isolation from all others. The same pattern prevailed in the southern tidewater. But in Scotland and Ulster the common folk lived in partly nucleated, partly dispersed clusters of six to ten dwellings called ferm-touns – or bailes in the Highlands – each cluster isolated from the others, each family within it being prone to pack up its roof timbers and move elsewhere to another cluster. That curious pattern was characteristic among Scots and Scotch-Irish settlers wherever they were to be found in colonial America.[22]

Several other characteristics, noted almost uniformly by travelers in Scotland, Ireland, Wales, and the southern colonies, further indicate the remarkable extent to which habits and customary ways survived the

---

[21] John Rhys, ed., *Tour in Wales, by Thomas Pennant* (3 vols, H. Humphreys, Caernarvon, 1883), vol. 2, p. 325; Alexander Fenton, *Scottish Country Life* (John Donald, Edinburgh, 1976), pp. 124–6; E. Estyn Evans, *Irish Folk Ways* (Routledge & Kegan Paul, London, 1957), pp. 34–7; Bridenbaugh, *Myths and Realities*, p. 132; Leyburn, *Scotch-Irish*, pp. 199–200, 214, 222–3.

[22] Hechter, *Internal Colonialism*; Dodgshon, 'Origins of Traditional Field Systems', pp. 68–89; Smout, *History of the Scottish People*, pp. 111–18. The pattern of living in such isolated clusters persists in much of the rural South to this day.

Atlantic crossing. One such attribute was an aversion to work: laziness and/or love of leisure. The Scots, as one traveler put it, were 'brought up from their infancy in tending sheep and cattle, and seeing no other object to rouse their attention, they grow callous and indifferent and . . . delight to drone on doing nothing'. Arthur Young, after remarking upon the wholesomeness of the diet of the Irish, confessed to being puzzled by their indolence: 'I will candidly allow that I have seen such an excess in the laziness of great numbers, even when working for themselves, and such an apparent weakness in their exertions when encouraged to work, that I have had my doubts of the heartiness of their food.' Young added that 'when they are encouraged, or animate themselves to work hard, it is all by whisky.' Whether their reluctance to work arose from diet, whiskey, or 'habitual laziness', Young was at a loss to say. Writing about the same time of the Scotch-Irish frontiersmen in America, Andrew Burnaby attributed the same quality to the environment. 'The climate and external appearance of the country', Burnaby wrote, 'conspire to make them indolent, easy, and good-natured. They seldom show any spirit of enterprise, or expose themselves willingly to fatigue.' The Reverend Charles Woodmason, on the other hand, saw a defect of character. Describing the backcountrymen of South Carolina, Woodmason averred that 'they are very Poor – owing to their extreme Indolence for they possess the finest Country in America, and could raise but ev'ry thing. They delight in their present low, lazy, sluttish, heathenish, hellish Life, and seem not desirous of changing it.' Others regarded the 'constitutional indolence' of southerners as deriving from slavery: 'Man will not labour where he can substitute slaves.'[23]

[23] The quotations are from Wallace Notestein, *The Scot in History* (Greenwood Press, Westport, Connecticut, 1970), p. 197; Arthur Wollaston Hutton, ed., *Arthur Young's Tour in Ireland, 1776–1779* (2 vols, G. Bell and Sons, London, 1892), vol. 2, p. 44; Andrew Burnaby, *Travels Through the Middle Settlements in North-America, in the Years 1759 and 1760* (Cornell University Press, Ithaca, New York, 1968), pp. 22, 27; Richard J. Hooker, ed., *The Carolina Backcountry on the Eve of the Revolution: The Journal and Other Writings of Charles Woodmason, Anglican Itinerant* (University of North Carolina Press, Chapel Hill, 1953), p. 52; and Warren S. Tryon, ed., *A Mirror for Americans: Life and Manners in the United States, 1790–1870, As Recorded by American Travelers* (University of Chicago Press, Chicago, 1952), vol. 1, p. 20. I have studied scores of accounts of travelers and other observers of the Celtic areas and English uplands and of the antebellum South; Grady McWhiney has done exhaustive research in hundreds of such sources in virtually all the major repositories in England, Scotland, Ireland, and Wales as well as in the United States. These materials constitute a major portion of the primary research – as opposed to what we have learned from geographers, anthropologists, and social and economic historians – of our larger study.

One of the few commentators who perceived Celtic indolence as a social norm rather than as an aberration was a Celt himself, the Welsh traveler Thomas Pennant. Pennant – who, Samuel Johnson said, 'observes more things than anyone else does' – put the matter in perspective in describing the Highlanders. They were, he wrote, 'indolent to a high degree', but they could be extremely energetic when 'roused to war' or, for that matter, 'to any animating amusement'. They were also industrious in lending 'assistance to the distressed traveller, either in directing him on his way, or affording their aid in passing the dangerous torrents of the Highlands', for they were 'hospitable to the highest degree', though they were 'impatient of affronts, and revengeful of injuries'. Pennant added several other comments that are to be found, in one form or another, in journals of travelers in Wales, Ireland, and the American South. The Highlanders, he said, were, despite their 'natural politeness', no respecters of the privacy of others; rather, they were 'excessively inquisitive after your business, your name, and other particulars of little consequence to them'. They were 'inclined to superstition; yet attentive to the duties of religion, and are capable of giving a most distinct account of the principals of their faith'.[24]

Arthur Young's description of the manners and customs of the common Irish is remarkably similar. Most striking, he wrote, 'were vivacity and a great and eloquent volubility of speech; one would think they could take snuff and talk without tiring till doomsday. They are infinitely more chearful and lively than anything we commonly see in England. . . . Lazy to an extent at work, but so spiritedly active at play, that . . . they show the greatest feats of agility. Their love of society is as remarkable as their curiosity is insatiable; and their hospitality to all comers, be their own poverty ever so pinching, has too much merit to be forgotten. . . . Warm friends and revengeful enemies . . . hard drinkers and quarrelsome.'[25]

[24] Thomas Pennant, *A Tour in Scotland* (5th edn, B. White, London, 1790), p. 214.

[25] Hutton, *Young's Tour in Ireland*, vol. 2, pp. 146–7. The violence and vengefulness of southerners is treated in many places; among others, see Edward L. Ayers, *Vengeance and Justice: Crime and Punishment in the 19th-Century American South* (Oxford University Press, New York, 1984); Dickson D. Bruce, Jr., *Violence and Culture in the Antebellum South* (University of Texas Press, Austin, 1979); Bertram Wyatt-Brown, *Southern Honor: Ethics and Behavior in the Old South* (Oxford University Press, New York, 1982). Students of the subject, however, rarely connect the patterns of violence in the South with those in the Celtic fringe.

Additional features of the immigrants' cultural baggage, as described by travelers in the Old World and New, may be summarized briefly. In attitude and behavior, they tended toward extremes either of apathy or enthusiasm; they were alien to compromise and had no love for the golden mean. They were oral and aural people who distrusted the printed word, except in the Bible, and who treasured indiscriminately boasting, arguing, sermonizing, speechifying, singing, and fiddling. They respected learning, especially when it was displayed in an emotional sermon, but most were contemptuous of making the effort to obtain learning for themselves. They were inconstant, long on dreaming grand projects but short on bringing them to completion, and improvident, content to live from day to day without a thought of the morrow.

Finally, they had special attitudes toward the family. The clan system did not survive the crossing – efforts to transplant it were half-hearted and few, confined mainly to a handful of Highlanders in North Carolina – but the habit of intense loyalty to the extended, and partly fictitious, kin group persisted among them, along with loyalty to the squire as a kind of clan-chieftain surrogate. Indeed, the extended family continued to be the principal unit of government to them, and their traditional disdain for formal institutions of government went unabated on the frontier. For all their sense of family, however, they placed no premium on sexual fidelity, despite the frenzied efforts of Presbyterian ministers to instil chastity among them. Many started families without bothering to be formally married, and when they did marry it was common for the bride to be pregnant. The Reverend Woodmason said that ninety-four of every hundred South Carolina girls whose weddings he conducted were with child at the time – a norm that persisted in Scotland not only through the eighteenth century but through most of the nineteenth as well.[26]

None of this is intended to suggest that Celtic and upland English society was transplanted *in toto* to the American South. Indeed, the region was sufficiently diverse as late as 1789 that no one said of it, as the geographer Jedidiah Morse said of New England, that the people of the

[26] Smout, *History of the Scottish People*, p. 75; T. C. Smout, 'Aspects of Sexual Behavior in Nineteenth Century Scotland', in *Social Class in Scotland: Past and Present*, ed. A. Allan MacLaren (John Donald, Edinburgh, 1976), pp. 55–85; Ian Carter, 'Illegitimate Births and Illegitimate Inferences', *The Scottish Journal of Sociology*, I (1977), 125–35; Woodmason, *Journal*, pp. 15, 99–100.

region had in common 'their religion, manners, customs, and character; their climate, soil, productions, natural history, &c.'[27] Southerners still lacked the social adhesives – a shared fund of experience as southerners, common religious and ideological rituals, generally accepted myths – that are prerequisite to the formation of integrated social structures in which everyone has the security of knowing his or her place. The process of integration had begun in Virginia; it was more than a generation away in South Carolina.

What is suggested is that the South was fashioned mainly from traditional Celtic and upland English materials. Slavery influenced the shape of the final product, to be sure, and so did the climate and soil. But, though those influences are beyond the scope of the present essay, I shall venture an assertion about them: rather than necessitating fundamental changes in social forms and norms, they facilitated the perdurance of the culture that immigrants to the South brought with them. In a manner of speaking, the entire history of the peoples of the uplands of the British archipelago prepared them to be southerners.

[27] Jedidiah Morse, *The American Geography; or, A View of the Present Situation of the United States of America* (Shepard Kollock, Elizabethtown, New Jersey, 1789), pp. 68, 140.

12

Social Classes and Class Struggles in Geographic Perspective

ELIZABETH FOX-GENOVESE
and EUGENE D. GENOVESE

Since human experience remains inescapably bound by space and time, it would seem natural to study it simultaneously in geographic and historical perspective. Yet most historians, including Marxists, have steadfastly slighted the significance of geography and have even been known to ignore its undeniable constraints on the societies they study.

History in Geographic Perspective restores geography to its proper status as a vital dimension of human thought and action. Edward Fox dismisses the more philistine claims of geography as a predictive science: topography does not determine human experience, which depends at least in part on human will, and, therefore, geography as science cannot be taken as a body of rules to explain that experience. And he recalls Hegel's observation that where geography had once produced Greeks, he now saw only Turks. Drawing on the work of geographers, Fox further argues that it is naive to speak of geography as the constant, unchanging scene of human experience. Humans alter the topography that surrounds them by the ways in which they live in it. The environment, as the modern protestors of its abuse are forcefully reminding us, takes shape under human use and abuse. Or, as Loren Eiseley has cogently argued, human beings mature to an environment made by other human beings, not by nature.

Indeed, the beginnings of history may be located fruitfully in the beginnings of humans' use or organization of the environment to promote their own survival as a group. Even if impossible to date, this 'disembedding' of men and women from nature – to paraphrase

Karl Polanyi – offers an arresting and heuristic myth of the interdependence of human self-consciousness and technical expertise. In those
beginnings lay the seeds of the systematic subjugation of nature to men and
women and the systematic subjugation of men and women to each other.
For the production of the surplus to which Fox attributes the fragile possibilities of civilization, before the rise and triumph of capitalism, depended
as much upon the organization of the human community as upon the
exploitation of nature. In both, the changes over time modified and sometimes revolutionized the space in which they unfolded, just as the space
itself imposed limits upon their unfolding. The exploitation of nature
and the (potentially) oppressive organization of human communities
transformed space, or geography, into what Fox calls the environment –
by which he seems to mean the physical context or dimension of human
experience as forged by successive generations of humans from the raw
material of geography. Fox, early in his book, virtually equates environment
with geography and uses the term to mean precisely geography as modified
by purposeful and self-conscious – what might be called 'goal-oriented' –
human occupation. His recognition of the environment as inseparable from
human experience leads him to formulate a series of 'propositions' with
which to raise the understanding of its impact from empirical observation
to general theory. All of the propositions rest upon his fundamental insight
that societies tend to divide into two kinds as a result of their occupation
of two kinds of environments. The first environment derives from the
presence of navigable seas, oceans, or rivers; the second from the absence of
opportunities for navigation. Societies that benefit from the proximity
of substantial waterways engage in 'transport'; those which do not engage
in 'travel'. Transport encompasses the ability to move bulky goods, initially
grains, subseqently timber and coal, over long distances. This ability
permits societies or settlements to grow beyond their natural environmental
constraints – to grow, that is, beyond the size that could be supported by
the resources available to a population that commanded only human and
animal energy. Thus 'travel' designates the kinds of exchange in which non-
trading societies engage, notably the exchange of money, women, and
messages. In other words, societies based on travel exchange signs rather
than goods. The differentiation between transport and travel may, Fox
contends, constitute 'the historian's most important, as well as most
neglected, tool of geographical analysis' (p. 25).

Fox does not discuss in detail the early development of the two kinds
of societies, which, presumably, can vary considerably. After a glance

at the Ancient World, in which he finds his models confirmed by the contrast between the Greeks and the Persians, he picks them up in early medieval Europe, in which he again finds confirmation in the contrast between the great Frankish hinterland and the Mediterranean littoral. That Frankish hinterland, in his view, exemplifies the uneasy dominance of a feudal elite over parochial, agricultural units. The relations between these two 'systems' remain essentially tangential and do not constitute a state in anything that resembles the modern sense. Nor does he agree that villagers and overlords should be understood as 'classes'. If the overlords constitute an elite, they remain essentially extrinsic to the dynamics of the village community over which they preside, although both groups will eventually constitute the core members of an administrative state based on trade. By contrast, the societies of the Mediterranean littoral are assuming the commercial identities that derive from their ability to transport. Negotiation lies at the very marrow of commercial societies' relations both among their own members and among other similar societies.

Where the mature administrative society associates its own prosperity with the control of territory, the mature commercial society associates its prosperity with the control of resources that can be moved elsewhere. Both types of society achieved their most nearly perfect form during that 'long' eighteenth century between the revolutions of the seventeenth century and the great French Revolution. And social theorists of the time, notably Montesquieu and the Physiocrats, readily identified them. For Fox's commercial and administrative societies can readily be recognized as Montesquieu's monarchy and republic, or as the Physiocrats' landed monarchy and mercantile republic. Quesnay always dismissed the denizens of the latter as unreliable precisely because they could always gather their assets and move elsewhere. The rise of capitalism, especially industrial capitalism, eventually eroded the limitations under which the landed societies suffered. But, in France, the primary subject of the book, they may not have materialized until the Fifth Republic finally drew the peasantry into the national market. And even as the material foundations of the two Frances began to crumble, their legacy left its imprint upon the political preferences of their members.

Fox's specific discussion of the development of the French state from the crisis of the Hundred Years War to the great Revolution and on to the Gaullist 'jacobin' republic offers innumerable insights that provide the essential elements of a coherent narrative. He politely but firmly rejects such previous attempts to make sense of the apparent chaos of French political development as the distinction between urban and rural or between northeastern and southwestern. Having begun with the electoral patterns of the Fourth and Fifth Republics, he found that those standard analyses did not mesh with the patterns he was observing. Nor, in his opinion, did a Marxist class analysis or the class-oriented, interest-group analysis of Beau de Lomenie.

The quest for intelligible pattern led him, in the first instance, to posit an underlying coherence to French political life – an 'unwritten constitution' as capable of insuring the appropriate combination of stability and change as its famed, and more widely acknowledged, English prototype. The French should not, as horrified English and American observers have been wont to claim, be dismissed as rowdies incapable of creating a viable political order. At least from the time of the Great Revolution, France has followed a discernible political path: periods of constitutional, normally republican, government alternated with periods of administrative government. The French instinctively trusted authoritarian administrators, whether Jacobin or Bonapartist, to preside over their business as usual. When administration could no longer encompass and resolve differences of opinion over the path of future development, the French resorted to revolutions and revolutionary legislatures, normally a single 'constitutive' assembly that enjoyed full power to change the rules of the game. Those assemblies inevitably carried through basic changes and then ran into their own irreconcilable conflicts with their executive agents. There ensued a coup and the installation of a new administrative government. This analysis restored coherence and purpose to French political life, but did not adequately explain the resolute refusal of the French to employ the kind of institutionalized negotiation that characterized English political life. Certainly, the specific forms and intensity of French class conflict could hardly account for the difference. The quest for an explanation – specifically an explanation that could transcend the narrow perspective of class analysis – led him back to the Great Revolution and beyond.

The patterns that would characterize French politics during the nineteenth and twentieth centuries assumed their modern guise precisely during the Revolution that effectively gave birth to them. In Fox's judgement, that politics and its attendant struggles again defied the neat compartments of a Marxist class analysis. Rather, they gradually revealed a deeper contest between two different societies. The political patterns of the period cloaked an intense struggle between two very different Frances for control of French destiny. In effect, he sees two minds warring for control of a single body – and vice versa: the territory that had, since the fourteenth century, taken shape as the nation, France. Those societies have consisted respectively in a landed agrarian kingdom and in the series of maritime republics located in the great port cities and commercial centers that ringed it. France, the nation, contained within itself representatives of the two principal types of societies known to human history, the agricultural and the commercial. The incompatibility of their social systems, principles, goals, and forms of discourse have accounted for the superficial upheavals that have punctuated French history. Their frequent ability to coexist under a single set of institutions accounted for the long periods of administrative government.

The force of the rich analysis summarized, if too schematically, here surely derives from the insistence upon understanding the history and significance of political struggles in their specific context – derives, to be blunt, from the author's intransigent materialism. In truth, Fox's opposition to Marxism notwithstanding, he can fairly be charged with a highly original and thought-provoking historical materialism. For, in the end, if he has developed his propositions in order to understand the specific case of France, by the end of the book he makes it clear that France has come to stand as a specific case of the general analysis. The geographic perspective emerges as essential to the unraveling of the mysteries of history, although he wisely avoids claims of predictive or deterministic power. In this respect, this slim volume challenges all other general theories of history. Notwithstanding Fox's anti-Marxism, his introduction of a geographic perspective constitutes a potential advance from, although hardly an alternative to, a Marxist interpretation of history. For Marxists, the struggle between classes constitutes the motive force of history. To place classes in geographic perspective means to locate them within specific societies and therefore should mean the deepening of class analysis. Conversely, we believe that the introduction of a class analysis can only deepen and strengthen the geographic analysis.

Fox's assumptions emerge from his discussions of the origins and development of village society and of the origins and development of the feudal elite and the monarchy in relation to village society. And they remain closely tied to his open rejection of determinism and his more veiled rejection of exploitation and oppression as a central feature of social organization. Although Fox never describes the social relations that produced village society, he does identify its origins with human beings' original *prise de conscience* of their condition – with the fundamental distinction between self and other. Indisputably, he views that human self-consciousness as the necessary and sufficient escape from the trap of determinism. If, as he acknowledges, the environment that shapes human possibilities 'exists only in terms of man's needs, desires, and capacities for satisfying them from materials at hand', it also necessarily 'depends on his conscious awareness of his situation' (pp. 21–2). Or, as Marx put it, men make their own history but only within the limits of definite material conditions. People and their environment exist in a complex state of interdependence in which neither determines the other. This formulation, with which no serious defender of the humanities or of human agency in history would be likely to disagree, but which probably does not meet philosophic standards of explanation, satisfies Fox that the critics of Arnold Toynbee's formulation of 'challenge and response' have missed the point. At the very least, he implicitly identifies his own effort with Toynbee's project to write the history of civilizations. More, he identifies himself with Toynbee's commitment to the possibility of a general history that will simultaneously embrace the principles of human motivation and the manifestations of human activity. He insists – and Marxists should agree – that man (and woman) is a historical animal.

Sharing with Toynbee the view of societies (Toynbee's civilizations) as, in fundamental respects, organic units, Fox's materialism parts company with Marx's in slighting exploitation and oppression in their origins. In effect, he displaces the entire problem of class struggle to the relations between villages and their overlords. And having displaced it, he repudiates its validity. Villagers and their dominant elites belonged to different systems and shared common interests. Thus, the elites cannot really have exploited the villagers from whom they merely extracted a small surplus that permitted their own specialization in warfare and in the cultivation of glimmers of civilization. The uses to which the elite put the surplus benefited the villagers, who, accordingly, were not prone to challenge the elite's dominance. The discussion could, with no trouble, be recast as a problem of hegemony. But to recast it in that way would be to call attention to the possible differences of opinion and even struggles that informed the general acceptance. A class analysis would in fact strengthen and enrich Fox's analysis, but its introduction would expose possible conflicts and inequalities within the organic village community and between the villagers and their rulers.

Fox does not introduce the concept of inequality here, or indeed elsewhere. And he might, fairly enough, contend that inequality or, for that matter, equality have little to do with his tight argument. He never falls into the utopian trap of suggesting that equality prevailed in early societies or even that equality ranks as a special historical desideratum. He fully understands the ubiquity of inequality in human societies. Nor does he ever suggest that all members of all societies entirely enjoyed their position within that society. We suspect, however, that, if pressed, he would argue that identification with the society transcended the dissatisfactions that might arise from particular positions or statuses.

The great strength of his vision lies in the ability to grasp the totality and to recast social and political relations in quasi-spatial terms. Thus in one sense he hits the mark in pointing to the tangential relation between the feudal elite and the village communities. The Catholic Church, struggling on the same terrain, certainly understood the depth of pagan self-containment that characterized village culture and modified its own doctrine in order to capture the pagan imagination. Well into the seventeenth century, and long after the emergence of the administrative monarchy, the nobles continued to view the peasants as so alien as more closely to resemble animals than humans. But the distance between social groups, including significant differences in their cultures, did not vitiate either the class relations that bound them together nor, and perhaps more important, the internal class (and gender) relations that constituted the different groups as communities.

For the concept of class to make sense as more than an arbitrary scheme of classification, it must be understood as the social relations of production. In this perspective, a Marxist class analysis would hold that classes assume their identity only in relation to other classes – that the social relations of production are, precisely, social relations. The economy does not, as in the bourgeois caricature of Marxism, determine class identification as narrow economic self-interest. Rather, the ways in which men and women produce and reproduce constitute a set of social relations that shapes politics, society, and the economy itself. In this perspective, Marxists might say of the economy what Fox says of the environment: it shapes, even as it is shaped by, human beings in a complex web of interdependence. Determinism is no more inherent to Marxism than it is to geography.

From Marx and Engels on, Marxist scholars have looked to human beings' first self-conscious differentiation of themselves from nature for the origins of inequality, exploitation, and oppression. In other words, they have assumed that any specialization among members of the human community has meant some kind of division of labor and has rapidly resulted in the domination of some by others. Differences persist about the precise moment of the emergence of domination and subordination and about the nature of the earliest forms of exploitation. But no form of specialization, even in the religious-magical-medical realm, much less the production of a surplus, should be treated as an event innocent of domination and hierarchy. In all likelihood, the original domination was that of men over women, although the specific causes of that domination remain in dispute. Engels sought to link the emergence of gender hierarchy and exploitation to the emergence of private property – to a specific form of class relations – while others have preferred to attribute it to nature. And there are many viewpoints in between. Fox invokes the exchange of women as one feature of a society based on travel, but to be exchanged, women had to be in some measure dominated or controlled. Their exchange indicates some form of division of labor, and many societies that exchanged women moved on to exchange slaves. Even societies that did not exchange slaves did exchange various kinds of signs that reflected their own internal division of labor, presumably first by gender, but not long after by class as well.

Somewhere between that original moment of human consciousness, when men and women constructed their surroundings as the environment, and the meeting between the villagers of Gaul and their new Germanic overlords, human beings began to dominate and exploit each other in innumerable forms. The domination and exploitation may have seemed tolerable when superiors and inferiors shared ethnicity, lineage, gender, generation, and culture. Probably, the earliest forms of domination followed either the natural lines of gender and generation or the alien lines of ethnic and cultural difference. Most early societies, much like their more complex successors, found it easier to enslave strangers – Aristotle's barbarians – than their own kind. Most early societies also tended to favor assimilating indigenous forms of domination and exploitation to the familial norms of gender and generation. No matter how they cast the legitimation of dominance, they not merely engaged in it, they also profited from it.

Rousseau began his *Confessions* with the announcement that he was neither better nor worse than others, only different, but the habit of mind that led human beings to distinguish between self and other inescapably led them to cast that difference as better and worse, as higher and lower, as man and woman, as master and slave. No known pre-capitalist people endowed work with the high value with which it would be endowed by the Euro-American bourgeoisie. Feudal lords early learned to associate their own excellence not merely with their specialization in warfare and civilization but with their freedom from demeaning toil, yet there is scant evidence that the unfree laborers whose toil permitted them that specialization valued work any higher than they – viewed it as anything more than an unhappy condition of a largely unhappy life. The villagers who produced the surplus off which the feudal knights fed had their own ideas about the appropriate division of labor by gender and generation, and they defended the essential core of those ideas against the pressures of their feudal 'protectors'. But the pressure resulted in their producing more than their own subsistence, and in so doing they forced changes in internal social relations.

The protection provided by the feudal lords came at a high price for the villagers of Gaul, as it did subsequently for their Anglo-Saxon counterparts. Many villagers bought protection by slipping from free to unfree status, although few slipped into slavery. The Frankish conquerors, unlike the Romans they supplanted, did not stand to benefit from a costly enslavement of their laborers. They had no interest in organizing *latifundia* to feed distant cities. They had every interest in being able to count on a steady supply of dues or tribute in kind or in labor, and they organized their relations with the villagers so as to ensure themselves both. At the very least, a village that found itself newly obliged to contribute, say, ten days' worth of labor of an able-bodied man per week had to compensate for the loss of that labor on village fields or accept a decline in standard of living. To the extent that the overlords held the villages as units accountable for the tribute, the villages had to modify their internal organization to ensure collective responsibility for collective obligations. The nature of these relations, as well as their breakdown, appeared in the pitiable fate of the village tax collector at the end of the *ancien régime*: if he could not gather sufficient taxes from his fellow villagers, he had to make up the deficit himself.

From Fox's point of view the difference between the tribute in labor or kind and the taxes of the late *ancien régime* amounts to that between apples and oranges – that is, the shift from feudal lordship and monarchy to the administrative state constitutes a watershed. From a Marxist point of view, the distinction is less stark. For the patterns of social relations among villagers and between villagers and lords retain important continuities from the beginnings of European serfdom to the collapse of the *ancien régime*.

Fox properly insists that both the monarchy that collapsed in 1789 and the feudal nobility 'rested on . . . the agricultural base of rural France' (p. 32) and that monarchy and nobility constituted radically different institutions that competed for control of the agricultural surplus. But he concludes that the monarchy was not the logical outgrowth of feudalism. And perhaps not, although Montesquieu, who warned Louis XV 'no nobility, no monarchy', would have demurred. But then feudalism itself requires a closer look. For Fox appears to identify feudalism as a political system with the seigneurialism on which both it and the monarchy rested.

The history of fifth- to eleventh-century France remains difficult to unravel, despite the scholarship generated by the Carolingian interlude. The hesitant attempts to piece together a new agricultural and a new political order proceeded unevenly and experimentally, with serious retreats in both. The excessively ambitious Carolingian state collapsed from ill-advised extension and inadequate local foundations. Only after the death of Charlemagne, towards the middle of the ninth century, did the process of feudalization emerge as irreversible. Even thereafter, it never attained the symmetry and neat relation to seigneurialism that William the Conqueror would impose on England. The growth of seigneurialism followed its own rhythm. Knights and lords sought to assure themselves control of the surplus that could be produced by the combination of land and labor even when their political entitlement remained uncertain. By the time that Charles the Bald was coerced into promising his vassals – or, more accurately, warlords – that their sons would be permitted to inherit their fiefs should they die in battle, the issue that divided king and lords had more to do with title than with substance. The king could no longer seriously challenge his vassals' control of their fiefs, but their demand demonstrates that, even in that chaotic age, they attached considerable importance to the title.

As Georges Duby has shown, those dark, dark ages of the late ninth and early tenth centuries also produced the codification of nobility as a legal status. The nobles insisted out of fear that they or their progeny might lose their privileged class position were it left open to the fluctuations of economic fortune. No Marxist, Duby intended only to refine Marc Bloch's classic periodization of the feudal ages, but he called attention to the relations among class formation, political development, and economic organization. The consolidation of the nobility as a class and an estate – a privileged and legally guaranteed order – depended both upon politics and economics, that is, upon social relations as the link between politics and economics.

The feudal/seigneurial noble took shape as two persons in one body. As feudal lord and vassal, he constituted the basic common denominator in a political system based on personal relations, notably the personal provision of military service and political deference. As seigneur, he presided over one or more manors that owed him tribute in labor and kind in return for his primarily military protection. The two systems interlocked in the person of the knight or lord but remained inexorably separate. Serfs, or for that matter villagers, who lacked *gentillesse* or *race* or *noblesse* did homage to no one. They constituted, from the perspective of the feudal order, so many economic building blocks or objects. They were 'the other' with a vengeance, but even such objectified others commanded recognition. If both villagers and lords had their own customs and laws, if, in some essential respects they belonged, as Fox demonstrates, to different systems, they also shared those customs and laws that bound them together in the emerging seigneurial system. The exactions of the lords could not long have survived had they been purely arbitrary. The exchange of tribute for protection gradually became systematized and itself acquired the status of custom or of law. When the lords infringed upon recognized rights, the villagers rejected their 'illegitimate' demands. Conversely, the lords exercised their own retribution against villagers who refused to comply with 'legitimate' demands.

The growth of towns, the increased circulation of money, and the emergence of the administrative monarchy did dramatically undermine the role and character of feudalism, but had far less impact on seigneurialism. Serfdom had begun its steady decline at least with the appearance of vigorous towns in the twelfth century, and by the fifteenth century most of the erstwhile serfs had become peasants. But if their persons had been unshackled, their lands had not. A wide variety of what would soon be viewed as infamous dues and services continued to adhere to the occupation of land. The seigneurial lords retained the power to collect tribute in kind, and even to demand various labor services. They could force their peasants to grind their grain at the lords' mills and to pay the attendant charge. A variety of customary rights impeded the free sale of land and even its free inheritance. These 'feudal' dues and services accounted for the principal part of the income of many nobles who, not without reason, hired lawyers to secure old titles and invent new ones. The Physiocrats and other reformers loudly protested these many infractions on economic freedom, but before the Revolution swept the residue away, they did not succeed in dismantling the system, much less the class relations it embodied.

The administrative monarchy may have revolutionized the character of its feudal predecessor, but it inherited its social base. In effect, the administrative monarchy stripped its nobility of their last serious claims to participate effectively as a group in the exercise of political power. The Parlements, which began to proliferate following the Hundred Years' War and which acquired new life with the inheritability of office in the early seventeenth century, constituted a pale, although by no means impotent, remnant of feudal prerogative. Yet the nobility's loss of its feudal political pretensions did little to undermine its social and economic – in a word, its class – power. To the contrary, it could be argued that, by opening the nobilty of blood to infiltration by an aspiring nobility of office and fortune, the new monarchy gave its old nobility a new lease on life. But new life or old, the nobility's class position depended both upon its legal sanction by the monarchy and its economic base in the seigneurial system. And down to the Revolution, no significant segment of the French nobility showed serious interest in stripping itself of either. Nor did the crown mount a systematic attack on noble privileges. Even the frequently underrated Maupeou revolution attacked its proto-political arm, the Parlements, not its fundamental legal or economic foundations.

The French monarchy, even in its new administrative guise, sank its roots into the same seigneurial system as its nobility: the monarchy derived its legitimacy from its relation to the specific system of class relations that it guaranteed and that was itself grounded in seigneurialism. Nothing, perhaps, better illustrates this seigneurial grounding than the history of those maritime republics – that 'other France' – which flourished in the port cities of the Atlantic littoral. However much a city like Bordeaux might belong to a commercial and, by the eighteenth century, an Atlantic society, after the end of the Hundred Years' War it also developed in symbiosis with agricultural France and under the aegis of the French administrative monarchy.

The feudal monarchy had, in fact, allowed Bordeaux and its hinterland considerable autonomy. The vicissitudes of feudal inheritance laws, which eventually contributed to the outbreak of the Hundred Years' War, even took Bordeaux into the web of the Anglo-Norman monarchy. But the same events that launched the French monarchy on its administrative course reunited Bordeaux's course to that of the French kingdom.

Fox's concept of a commercial society makes sense of Bordelais history, which previous interpretations had failed to make. Once the history of the city during the early modern period is considered from that perspective, no other will do. Bordeaux developed as a classic maritime republic, albeit more cautiously from the fifteenth to the late seventeenth century than it would thereafter. The possibilities of Atlantic commerce, notably in sugar, roused the Bordelais from their rather lethargic interest in overseas trade: they had previously engaged in it, but had let others provide the ships. Even before their commitment to the Atlantic trade, the Bordelais had displayed a vigorous regionalism that included a series of rejections of the crown's attempts to impose its authority. That tradition culminated in 1675, when Louis XIV took yet another Bordelais rejection of yet another royal tax as a personal provocation. His displeasure took the form of occupying troops and of the razing of the city's fortress, the Chateau Trompette. From then until the end of the *ancien régime*, the Bordelais directed their attention outward, leaving their Parlement and Chamber of Commerce to defend their interests vis-a-vis the crown. They had been brought into line as much as anything by Colbert's threats to deprive them of their privileges should they fail to comply with his wishes, in this instance by investing in one of his innumerable trading companies.

By the late seventeenth century, Colbert had to threaten the Bordelais to make them commit themselves to the monarchy's attempts to promote commerce. The Bordelais distinctly preferred to launch their own ventures. This preference again confirms the sagacity of Fox's analysis. Bordeaux in the eighteenth century enjoyed the spectacular growth rate of 4 per cent a year on the basis of its trade with the French islands. It had no interest in monarchical interference, red tape, and bureaucracy. Bordelais merchants understood the Atlantic trades better than any royal official, whom they frequently advised on these and related matters. And the crown, wisely, came to recognize the danger of smothering geese that lay golden eggs. It sought other ways to share in Bordeaux's prosperity, notably through tapping its wealthiest merchants for loans.

Fox underscores the importance of the port merchants' contributions to the royal debt and minimizes the other factors that bound them to the agricultural kingdom of administrative France. Some port merchants, notably those of Nantes, did lend the monarchy staggering sums, but those of Bordeaux, on the whole, did not. They nonetheless retained a deep interest in the fate of the monarchy. That interest arose, as much as anything, from their having to depend on the monarchy to secure local privilege in general, and class relations in particular. The Bordelais merchants forged a deep and abiding alliance with the members of their own Parlement, whose noble status they frequently sought to share. The culmination of a successful career as a merchant in Bordeaux lay in the purchase of a patent of nobility, if not an office that conferred nobility. The Parlement, for its part, valiantly defended all local interests from a preference for free trade in grain to opposition to any form of taxation on the nobility or any restriction of the privileges that granted nobles and bourgeois an effective monopoly of the sale of the famous Bordelais wines.

The pressure of the monarchy on Bordeaux's independent life may fruitfully be compared to the pressure of the feudal lords on the village communities during the early Middle Ages. In the case of Bordeaux, not all of the pressure was even perceived as such, for the Bordelais did not develop a precocious revolutionary culture, much less a precocious opposition to the system of estates and privileges – the class relations – that the monarchy guaranteed. The internal cohesion of Bordeaux society resulted from class relations formally similar to those of agricultural France. Bordeaux, like the rest of France, was divided into three estates. Even the great merchants whose prosperity embodied the commanding role of merchant capital – Fox's commercial society – in urban life did not fully break free of the legal or ideological constraints of French society as a whole. Their wealth and lavish entertaining earned them the astonished comments of visitors from abroad and from the rest of France, but did not clearly mark them as of a different order from, say, the great financiers. Nor did that wealth ever free them from the temptations of noble status. The role of the famous Bordeaux wine trade in establishing merchant and *parlementaire* fortunes depended as much on royal privilege – in particular a monopolistic control of wine sales during the most profitable months – as it did on the free play of the market.

The monarchy also imposed constraints on Bordeaux's economic fortunes by never diverting adequate resources to the protection of French merchants' commerce in the Atlantic. With every war with Britain during the eighteenth century, Bordelais trade came close to a standstill, and the monarchy's financial needs diverted funds from overseas trade. Bordeaux's commerce was financed locally, through the archaic patterns of individuals' buying shares of a ship for a specific voyage. French law did not permit the development of joint stock companies, and no adequate system of maritime insurance emerged. The greatest of the merchants presided over family enterprises clearly envisaged as high-risk attempts to provide a solid, landed foundation for family fortunes. They never, like their counterparts in Nantes, expanded into nascent textile production or any other significant manufacturing ventures. The measure of their economic conservatism can be seen in Bordeaux's collapse into economic underdevelopment after the Revolution in France and that in Saint-Domingue, which stripped France of its great sugar colony.

Bordeaux developed the commercial potential inherent in its location on the Atlantic littoral under special conditions. The opportunity for transport did not alone produce the commercial republic; the opportunity for a special kind of highly lucrative transport did. And even the emergence of that Atlantic commerce did not entirely alter the character of the city and did not divorce it from the class relations and legal system of the monarchy on which it depended.

Bordeaux's great Atlantic adventure during the eighteenth century yielded changes that differentiated the city from its counterparts in the interior. The potentially most significant change resulted from the combination of the cultivation of and trade in wines. Much like the wine-growing region of Portugal, the wine-growing region around Bordeaux witnessed a mini-agricultural revolution that began in the seventeenth century. That revolution led to the widespread expropriation of peasant holdings and to a concentration of vineyards in the hands of the members of the Parlementary nobility. The 'liberated' peasants constituted a pool of potential laborers for the city's commerce, and during the eighteenth century, Bordeaux developed a precociously active market in 'free labor' that ranged from dockworkers to governesses. Notwithstanding the advertisements for employment, sought and offered, in the principal newspaper, these new departures remained hostage to the fate of Bordeaux's Atlantic commerce, which itself remained hostage to the Bordelais's abiding commitment to the class structure and privileges guaranteed by the monarchy.

Bordeaux's great eighteenth century also included a cultural flowering that manifested the mixed character of the city. Bordeaux, with its long-standing commercial contacts, developed an even more severe case of Anglomania than the rest of France. Yet the fascination with things British primarily focused on such harmless concerns as gardens and sentimental fiction. The Bordelais had a time-honoured habit of religious tolerance and usually refused to interfere with the lives of their large Protestant and Jewish communities, but they developed no special ideological justification of their own practice. Nor did they manifest any sustained tradition of political opposition. Montesquieu's great defense of the separation of powers – if that is what he really meant – concerned a defense of the prerogatives of the Parlements, from whose ranks he came, not a defense of representative government in the modern, that is, English, sense.

When the Revolution threatened and then broke, many Bordelais did, in fact, rapidly discover their own predisposition for what we would today call liberalism. They viewed the defense of private property and the individual right that emanated from property holding as the cornerstone of any sane political order. Even the 'left wing' of the Bordelais political spectrum supported the defense of slavery as a form of property and as the basis of their community's prosperity. By 1791, Bordeaux had, in fact, spawned a distinctive political discourse that its representatives and their allies – the Girondins – carried to the center of national debates. Historians have frequently doubted the coherence of the Girondins as a party or even as the spokesmen for a particular point of view. Fox, in developing his geographic perspective, demolishes the basis for those doubts. The Girondins make sense only as the Atlantic or commercial faction of the Jacobins. Compared to other revolutionary groups like the Feuillants, they, like the Robespierristes with whom they warred, rank on the left of the revolutionary spectrum. Yet from the perspective of Paris they represented an idiosyncratic left. For the Girondins did defend negotiation against administration, did defend property as an innate rather than a social right, did defend slavery as property against radical egalitarianism. Above all, they did, to the best of their (limited) abilities defend the views of another France. Their defeat at the hands of Robespierre and his allies represented the defeat of that France's aspirations to frame France's political future.

The course of the Revolution did not merely reveal the defeat of the Gironde in the national arena, but also in Bordeaux. Prosperity had permitted the political representatives of the mercantile bourgeois to consolidate their hegemony over their fellow Bordelais. The revolutionary wars that undermined that prosperity also undermined the hegemony. By 1793, Bordeaux itself witnessed the emergence of a hard radical core of sans-culottes, primarily urban artisans, and a hard counter-revolutionary opposition. The hegemony of the Atlantic bourgeoisie had contained the opposition of those representatives of administrative France by offering them a combination of prosperity and non-interference. The strains of war revealed the fragility of the compromise and the vigorous persistence of the class system of the administrative monarchy. After Bordeaux had failed in its attempt to resist the centralizing pressures of administrative France, the classes that composed Bordeaux struggled against each other in alliance with national groups.

Fox demonstrates that Bordeaux and its sister port cities did not emerge as simple, unmediated products of their specific environment. He clearly states that the environment posed a challenge to which human beings responded, but here as elsewhere he denies the centrality of social classes and class struggles. Yet the classes that composed Bordeaux took shape as a result of struggles among themselves and within the interlocking contexts of the Atlantic littoral and the administrative, seigneurial monarchy. Those class relations distinguished Bordeaux from cities like Bristol, Liverpool, Boston, and Charleston, which it in many other respects resembled. The class relations informed every aspect of the city's development from its economic performance to its political culture. The monarchy intruded itself into the interstices of urban life even more through the class system than through its specific regulations and prohibitions. The class system made the actions of the monarchy, as well as the opportunities of commerce, a living presence in the lives of individuals.

Cities like Bordeaux especially prospered as a result of concentrations of merchant capital. Those restless funds which dominated so much of European and American history from the fourteenth century to the early nineteenth latched on to commercial opportunities of every kind. Merchant capitalists especially flourished from their investment in commerce or transport in the eras before the triumph of industrial capitalism. They did not necessarily transform social relations or promote economic development, which they may even have retarded. They fastened onto existing societies or enclaves in existing societies.

To the extent that merchant capitalists imprinted a distinctive character on the regions they touched, they tended to organize them as social formations – as social units that might range in size from a household to a colony and might vary widely in social composition – from which they extracted a surplus. Whether the extraction took the form of collecting the cloths prepared by peasant women or of bringing slaves from Africa to Virginia, the manipulators of merchant capital left their mark on everything they touched. But to the extent that they affected the social relations within any particular social formation, they did so by exerting pressure at the periphery. In this respect, they, like Fox's feudal lords, could give the appearance of only taking a surplus. They did not control, nor intend to control, the relations among genders or classes that resulted in the production of the surplus. They remained indifferent to consequences, which varied widely. The migration of Bordelais families and capital before, during and after the Revolution confirms Quesnay's acid comments about merchants who had no need to be loyal to the government that facilitated their enterprises or the country off which they fed. The merchants who helped to create and who crested with Bordeaux's extraordinary eighteenth-century commercial venture worked within a context established by the class relations and seigneurial base of the French monarchy.

The mercantile Girondist bourgeoisie defended modern bourgeois private property, which was theoretically grounded in the principle of 'each man's property in himself', and simultaneously defended colonial slavery, which was theoretically grounded in a contrary principle. Its contradictory, not to say hypocritical, attitude exposed the specific class nature of the merchant bourgeoisie of the France of the Atlantic ports, in contradistinction to the petty bourgeoisie and incipient agrarian and industrial bourgeoisies of the France of the interior. Recognition of the different class nature of the principal bourgeoisies of the two Frances dramatically confirms Fox's thesis of two societies, which we do not contest. Rather we would suggest that the dynamics of those two societies and the conflict between them cannot be fully understood without a discrete analysis of the classes that were contending within and between them.

The heuristic power as well as the limits of Fox's thesis appears with special force when we consider the effects of the penetration of merchant capital in the colonies. And we know of no better illustration than the American South, in which slavery arose as a social formation intrinsic to the developing Atlantic commercial society.

The settlers of the southern colonies of North America came from a society in the throes of bourgeois revolution and emerging capitalism. With temporary and marginal exceptions, even the most aspiring aristocrats among them arrived without the trappings of a residual seigneurialism. Bourgeois notions of absolute property informed their institutions from the start. But the exigencies of staple crop production for a world market, combined with apparently endless supplies of land and severe shortages of labor, led them to adopt slavery by the end of the seventeenth century. By the end of the eighteenth century, they had consolidated a society based on slavery as a social system. The great southern planters, for all their nostalgic cultivation of traditional aristocratic style, belonged as surely as the Bordeaux merchant bourgeoisie to Fox's commercial society. The very existence of their plantation world depended on the world market. And, also like the Bordeaux merchants, they intermarried and traded with members of its other outposts, especially in the northern North American colonies. But, again like the Bordeaux merchants, they remained inextricably bound to social classes that inhabited largely self-sufficient agricultural hinterlands and that viewed the pretensions and way of life of the southern slaveholders with deep suspicion.

At least from the time of the American Revolution, the southern slaveholders had to contend with struggles on two flanks. In their own hinterland, they confronted a staunchly independent yeomanry that depended primarily on largely self-sufficient household farms and that deeply mistrusted interference from its commercially-oriented cousins of the coastal plantation belt. In the northern and emerging western states, they confronted increasingly antagonistic farmers, mechanics, and businessmen who, by the second quarter of the nineteenth century, increasingly favored tariff protection for nascent manufactures, internal improvements, and free land. Northerners, like southerners, remained as divided by class and specific interests, but by the end of the antebellum period each region coalesced around its attitude towards slavery – or towards the freedom of labor, that is, the class question.

American historians have long resisted the application of a class analysis to the United States on the grounds that it cannot accurately apprehend American experience. Fox's geographic perspective helps resolve one set of difficulties by calling attention to different social systems along the coasts and in the interiors. But the American case also suggests the limits of that perspective. For, during the early nineteenth century, commerce or transport expanded apace in the northern part of the country, and each new frontier succumbed more rapidly than its predecessors to the incursions of canals and rails. Transport became dominant as more and more lands were pressed into the service of feeding coastal cities which themselves were becoming manufacturing centers. The expansion of industrial capitalism significantly eroded the distinction between agricultural and commercial areas. Northern and western farmers may have born a superficial resemblance to the yeomen of the upcountry South, but beneath the surface, they constituted a very different class – embedded in a different society.

The outstanding difference between North and South, conditioned by geography or environment, lay in class relations. The slavery upon which the plantation South depended deeply affected the nature of the yeomanry as a class. In fact, the importance of slavery as a social system powerfully assisted the yeomen in maintaining the kind of life they cherished. For slavery held to a minimum free white wage-labor, restricted the growth of manufacturing, and prevented a general commercialization of social relations. Slavery permitted the yeomen to protect the independence of their households and even, paradoxically, their political significance as independent freeholders who might even own or aspire to own a couple of slaves. The yeomen's relations to the slaveholders helped to define them as a class and to differentiate them from their northern prototypes.

The slaveholders and yeomen worked out an understanding according to which heads of households did not interfere in the affairs of other heads of households. For the yeomen the understanding meant above all that the slaveholders granted them assistance in times of need in return for political support on the slavery question and did not presume to burden them with heavy demands for taxes or other services. The understanding effectively glossed over the dramatic class differences between free white men – although the slaveholders and especially the slaveholding women were not above considerable social snobbery – by stressing the 'free' and 'white' and by respecting every man's vote. It worked so well that the yeomen initially accepted secession in about the same proportions as the slaveholders. Only after the Confederacy found itself obliged to make unacceptable demands upon the yeomen for money and men did the understanding collapse. And when it did, it also exposed the depths of the coastal/hinterland split, much as Fox's thesis would have led us to expect.

Fox's thesis might not have led us to expect the contradictory nature of the 'commercial' southern society. For at the very moment that it became commercial with a vengeance, creating itself, as it were, within the broader commercial Atlantic world – inseparable from and unimaginable without the world market – it was also creating itself as a system of households. Each household, dominated by a male slaveholder, included not merely wife and children but slaves: it comprised a 'family, black and white'. It aspired to, but rarely achieved, self-sufficiency, and to constituting a world apart and independent of the very commercial relations in which it was embedded, for its internal social relations were the antithesis of the commercial. The southern plantation world represents an anomaly both for Fox's thesis and for classical Marxist analysis. Its existence and the power it manifested for so long nonetheless invite a deepening, not a rejection, of the geographic perspective and of Marxism. But, like the case of France, that deepening can only proceed with due attention to the centrality and extraordinary complexity of social class relations.

13

The Segmentary State and
La Grande Nation

TRAIAN STOIANOVICH

Concern for the ties between a people's history and its geographic and territorial setting compels attention to some little studied questions, among which are: the lateness of cantonal development in Serbia and the neighboring territories of the Ottoman, Habsburg, and Napoleonic empires; the consequent struggle between the great and little county or potential canton; the prospects for an embryonic national economy under the impact of the dislocated and thwarted circulation of elites, and of economic reterritorialization, ideology, and continental war.[1]

By 1800, the world's settled human societies had been organized into at least six main types of territorial units. Four of these territorial categories were old: a customary space of matrimonial exchange, the county or *pays*, the province, and the world economy – a territorial unit that functioned in the plural, often as a political entity organized sometimes as an 'empire'. The other two were new: the canton, and the nation constituted or at the point of being constituted as a national market.[2] In a few parts of the world – western Europe and the lowlands of China, perhaps also Japan – the cantonal structure was almost complete

[1] On the relationship between revolution and the thwarted circulation of elites, see Suzanne Donner Vromen, 'Pareto on the Inevitability of Revolutions', *American Behavioral Scientist*, 20 (March/April 1977), pp. 521–8.

[2] I myself have made the distinction between the older and newer types of territorial organization. For the identification of the six main types of territorial units, see Fernand Braudel, *Civilisation Matérielle, Économie et Capitalisme, XVe–XVIIIe Siècle* (3 vols, Armand Colin, Paris, 1979), vol. III: *Le Temps du Monde*, pp. 11–33, 238–49.

by the end of the eighteenth century. Elsewhere, as in the adjacent territories of the Ottoman, Habsburg, and Napoleonic empires, the development of the canton was in an early stage or had not yet begun.

Considerably smaller than a county, a canton may affirm its utility as an economic or administrative entity only as it attains a certain population density. As that density nears fifteen persons per square kilometer, some residents usually perceive the need to form a territorial unit in which little-county interests are recognized and little-county elites – rural notables who aspire to form flourishing little market towns – are allowed to function as part of a larger territorial system. The older elites may perceive cantonal growth as a further means of promoting county, provincial, and national interests, or they may regard it as an obstacle to such interests. Under the technological conditions prevalent before 1850, however, the absence of little-county organization imposed limits on demographic and economic growth. It prevented the rise of an integrated economy.

In some of the territories of the middle and lower Danube during the eighteenth century, little-county interests – from which may evolve cantonal interests – began to approach the minimum demographic requirement for cantonal formation. The great-county elites immediately took countermeasures to frustrate the ambitions of their little-county rivals. The sovereign states, Habsburg and Ottoman, of which the great and little counties were component territories, were forced thereupon to side with the great counties or to support the idea of a little-county organization, either as a substitute for or as a complement to the great counties. To explain their ambivalent behavior we are obliged to undertake a brief inquiry into the dilemmas of state sovereignty.

A political state must strive to organize itself as an ultimate, legitimate, and – in some spheres of action – comprehensive authority.[3] In point of fact, the authority of no state is so complete or legitimate that some of its subjects may not seek to abolish it. One of the primary needs of states, therefore, is to limit the duration, scale, and intensity of internal violence. This must be done not only by acquiring a quasi-monopoly over the utility known as protection and, with it, over the instruments of

---

[3] Gabriel A. Almond, 'Comparative Political Systems', *Journal of Politics*, 18 (August 1956), pp. 391–409.

violence,[4] but by establishing a territorial base compatible with the exercise of that monopoly.

The direst threat to the integrity of small states has been the cupidity of larger and more powerful ones. To be bigger often does mean to be better. As Richard Bean has stressed, size may offer the advantages of a variety of resources, of a wider zone for the circulation of goods, and of lower per capita costs for defense. But as he has also noted, the optimum size of states varies with changes in technology and administration.[5] A one-time optimum, according to Fernand Braudel, was achieved whenever the distance between a state's peripheries and its chief post of command and main points of supply neither much exceeded nor much fell below forty days of travel by the slowest customary means of transport.[6] Presumably, such a representative optimum obtained during the era in which the ideology of the balance of power did not govern relations between states, and in which utilizable sources of energy were both available from and restricted to human, plant, animal, water, and aeolian power. The proper functioning of that highly precarious optimum depended upon the simultaneous existence of workable autonomy at the lower levels of territorial organization and of administrative effectiveness at the higher levels of territoriality – incidentally, the two means by which internal violence could be kept manageable.

As Malte-Brun, the geographer, observed more than a century and a half ago, the civilization to which agriculture gave birth was local. Each local culture was separated from the others by law and custom, if not by impregnable physical walls. The invention of navigation, he contended, then shook the pillars of such supposed 'Chinese felicity'.[7]

---

[4] Frederic C. Lane, 'The economic Meaning of War and Protection', *Journal of Social Philosophy and Jurisprudence*, 7 (1942), pp. 254–70; Charles Tilly and James Rule, *Measuring Political Upheaval*, Research Monograph No. 19 (Center of International Studies, Woodrow Wilson School of Public and International Affairs, Princeton University, Princeton, 1965), p. 4; John R. Gillis, 'Political Decay and the European Revolutions, 1789–1848', *World Politics*, 22 (April 1970), pp. 344–70.

[5] Richard Bean, 'War and the Birth of the Nation State', *Journal of Economic History*, 33 (March 1973), pp. 203–21.

[6] Fernand Braudel, *La Méditerranée et le Monde Méditerranéen à l'Époque de Philippe II*, 2nd edn (2 vols, Armand Colin, Paris, 1966), vol. I, pp. 339–40.

[7] Conrad Malte-Brun [Malthe-Bruun], *Précis de la Géographie Universelle, ou Description de Toutes les Parties du Monde, sur un Plan Nouveau d'après les Grandes Divisions Naturelles du Globe* (8 vols, François Buisson, Volland, and Aimé-André, Paris, 1810–29), vol. II: *Théorie Générale de la Géographie* (1810), pp. 614–15.

Until the nineteenth century only ripples of that disturbance had spread beyond the world's maritime fringes. In effect, most states continued to be organized around a principle of center–periphery relations that required state control of the routes between cities, if not always of the cities themselves. That organization demanded a large degree of household and village autonomy and some (but a highly variable) degree of provincial and great-county autonomy, especially for distant lands, so long as the inhabitants paid their taxes and did not rebel against the legitimate political authority.

That, too, was the mechanism of Ottoman rule. In the Ottoman system, in fact, certain rural collectivities were put in charge of security between places of difficult access. In areas in which less than 20 per cent of the population was Moslem, as in peninsular Greece, Christian settlements endowed with local autonomy were organized as *armatoliks* or captaincies (a special form of great county) and were freed of part of the tax burden. In frontier areas in which more than a third of the population was Moslem, as in Hercegovina and Bosnia, local Moslem families managed the captaincies. Along the imperial route between Edirne and Sofia, Christian *voynuk* (paramilitary) villages performed analogous tasks and enjoyed similar privileges.[8]

LITTLE COUNTY AGAINST GREAT COUNTY

Being closer to the Habsburg system of states, Serbia had more opportunities for rebellion against Ottoman authority. As a result, its *voynuk* villages were deprived of their former functions. Principal responsibility for security along the imperial route between Niš and Belgrade had, by the middle of the seventeenth century, fallen to a

---

[8] Branislav Djurdjev, 'O Vojnucima', *Glasnik Zemaljskog Muzeja*, 2 (Sarajevo, 1947), pp. 75–137; Spyros J. Asdrachas, 'Quelques Aspects du Banditisme Social en Grèce au XVIIIe Siècle', *Études Balkaniques*, 8 (Sofia, 1972), pp. 97–112; Dennis N. Skiotis, 'Mountain Warriors and the Greek Revolution', in *War, Technology, and Society in the Middle East*, ed. V. J. Parry and M. E. Yapp (Oxford University Press, London, 1975), pp. 308–29; Hamdija Kreševljaković, 'Kapetanije i Kapetani u Bosni i Hercegovini', *Godišnjak Istoriskog Društva Bosne i Hercegovine*, 2 (Sarajevo, 1950), pp. 89–141; Traian Stoianovich, *Mediterranean and Balkan Dimensions* (2 vols, Charles Schlacks, Jr, Irvine, Calif., forthcoming), vol. II: *Material Culture and 'Mentalités', Power and Ideology, Land and Sea*, esp. the last few pages of the final chapter, 'Prospective: Third and Fourth Levels of History'.

network of palisades or palanques manned by soldiers of the central government at a day's march from each other. Three-fifths of the palanque population was Moslem, while the surrounding rural population was overwhelmingly Christian.[9]

Under circumstances still obscure, a *knežina* territorial organization arose in that part of Serbia that formed the sanjak/pashalik of Smederevo/Belgrade. Originally, the knežina may have been a lineal unit defined as a group of families that acknowledged a common real or fictive ancestor, as among the Vlachs of the Danubian principalities. Probably as a result of frequent in- and out-migration, the lineal bonds weakened. In any event, during the economic and demographic recovery of the second half of the eighteenth century, without wholly losing their lineal basis, the knežinas of the Belgrade pashalik acquired a territorial foundation.[10] Often known as *kmet* – from *comes*, count – at the village level, the *knez* – etymologically, king – was the unofficial mediator through whom the government collected taxes in a village or cluster of villages. In 1793 and succeeding years, in order to obtain the aid of the knezes against the rebel governor of Vidin, the Porte issued a number of firmans that assented to the role of the knezes, thereby conferring semi-official recognition upon a customary institution.

The urban notables of the pashalik of Belgrade – propertied persons of the fortress towns of the Danube, Sava, and Drina rivers and of the great-county or *nahiye* (*nahija*) towns, the only towns apart from Belgrade with a population of 2,000 or more – sensed immediately their community of interest with the governor and great-county and provincial notables of Vidin. Themselves an elite of recent origin, they viewed with alarm the formation of an elite with rural, little-county, and communal foundations, which might obstruct their own circulation as an elite with an urban, great-county, and provincial basis.

[9] Dušan Pantelić, 'Vojno-etnografski opisi Srbije pred Kočinu Krajinu od 1783 i 1784 god.', *Spomenik*, 19, drugi razred, knj. 54 (Srpska Kraljevska Akademija, Belgrade, 1929), pp. 20–1, 83–91; Olga Ziroević, 'Palanka', *Studia Balcanica*, 3: *La Ville Balkanique, XVe–XIXe Siècles* (Sofia, 1970), pp. 173–80; Ilhan Tekeli, 'On Institutionalized External Relations of Cities in the Ottoman Empire–A Settlement Models Approach', *Études Balkaniques*, 8/2 (Sofia, 1972), pp. 49–72, esp. 54–6.

[10] Ružica Guzina, '*Knežina* i Postanak srpske Buržoaske, Države' (Kultura, Belgrade, 1955), *passim*; Branislav Djurdjev, 'O Knezovima pod Turskom Upravom', *Istoriski Časopis*, Nos 1–2 (Belgrade, 1948), pp. 132–66; Michael Boro Petrovich, *A History of Modern Serbia, 1804–1918* (2 vols, Harcourt Brace Jovanovich, New York, 1976), vol. I, pp. 18–19.

Designated in Ragusan documents as *primati* and *superiuri et principali del paese*, the urban and provincial notables known to the Turks as *ayan* had received official recognition of their status only in 1768 at the start of war with Russia. Ayan status then became venal, but by paying for the charge the buyer obtained the right to participate in decisions about the allocation of fiscal and military resources in a particular *kaza* (township or military-judicial district), nahiye, or province. In 1785, in an effort to reaffirm its control, the government attempted to abolish the privileges it had only recently granted. It nonetheless had to restore them, tacitly upon the outbreak of war with Russia and Austria in 1787 and 1788, and officially in 1790.[11] Between 1793 and 1807, striving to model its military, fiscal, and administrative institutions on those of Austria, the government again disputed the authority of the ayans.[12] In that dispute the Serbian knezes sided with the central government.

Comprising about 39,000 square kilometers, the pashalik of Belgrade represented barely one-fifteenth of the Ottoman territories in Europe and less than 2 per cent of its tricontinental territories. In 1800, it embraced a population of 40,000 Moslems, who resided almost

---

[11] Avdo Sućeska, 'Vilajetski Ajani', *Godišnjak Društva Istoričara Bosne i Hercegovine*, 13 (Sarajevo, 1962), pp. 167–98; A. Sućeska, 'Bedeutung und Entwicklung des Begriffes, A'yân im Osmanischen Reich', *Südost-Forschungen*, 25 (1966), pp. 3–26; Deena Sadat, 'Urban Notables in the Ottoman Empire: The Ayan', (Unpublished PhD dissertation, Rutgers University, New Brunswick, New Jersey, 1969); Deena R. Sadat, 'Rumeli Ayanlari: The Eighteenth Century', *Journal of Modern History*, 44 (September, 1972), pp. 346–63; Halil Inalcik, 'Centralization and Decentralization in Ottoman Administration', in *Studies in Eighteenth Century Islamic History*, ed. Thomas Naff and Roger Owen, published under the auspices of the Near Eastern History Group, Oxford, and the Middle East Center, University of Pennsylvania (Southern Illinois University Press, Carbondale and Edwardsville, Ill., 1977), pp. 27–52; Stanford J. Shaw, *Between Old and New: The Ottoman Empire under Sultan Selim III, 1789–1807* (Harvard University Press, Cambridge, Mass., 1971), pp. 167–79, 211–46, 283–327; Kemal H. Karpat, 'The Land Regime, Social Structure, and Modernization in the Ottoman Empire', in *Beginnings of Modernization in the Middle East: The Nineteenth Century*, ed. William R. Polk and Richard L. Chambers (University of Chicago Press, Chicago and London, 1968), pp. 76–83; Kemal H. Karpat, 'The Transformation of the Ottoman State, 1789–1908', *International Journal of Middle East Studies*, 3 (1972), pp. 251–3; E. Ziya Karal, 'The Ottoman Empire and the Serbian Uprising, 1807–1812', in *The First Serbian Uprising, 1804–1813*, ed. Wayne S. Vucinich (Social Science Monographs, Boulder–Brooklyn College Press, distributed by Columbia Univesity Press, New York, 1982), pp. 207–26, esp. p. 208.

[12] E. Ziya Karal, 'La Transformation de la Turquie d'un Empire Oriental en un État Moderne et National', *Cahiers d'Historie Mondiale; Journal of World History; Cuadernos de Historia Mundial*, 4 (1958), pp. 426–45.

exclusively in the towns, fortresses, and palanques, a small number of Jews and Gypsies, a handful of Armenians, and 200,000 Orthodox Christians, largely Serbs but including a small number of Vlachs, Greeks, and Bulgars. At least 180,000 of the Christians resided in 1,800 villages, most of which presumably were members of one of approximately forty-five knežinas. An average knežina thus included forty villages and a rural population of 4,000 Christians spread over an approximate area of 800 square kilometers. Since there were thirteen nahiyes in the pashalik, we may assume that the great county was three to four times as large as the little county. Even when a town lay within its nominal territory, the little county lacked an urban foundation.[13]

Ayan strength lay in the towns. But the urban economy was blocked. Intended primarily for local urban needs and secondarily for other towns, urban craft production had virtually no outlet in the countryside, whose consumption was restricted almost wholly to the production of its own household economy. In such an uninviting environment, the ayans logically concluded that they could enrich themselves more easily by creating their own redistributive system than by serving simply as the stewards of redistribution. They seized a share in the production of the peasantry, levied illegal tolls on the passage of livestock, and retained a portion of the fees collected at the customs stations of the Sava and Danube entrepôts, especially Belgrade, through which passed the cotton exports of Serres and Salonika destined for Vienna and Germany. In particular, they asserted their right to the *deveto*, ostensibly an illegal tribute of one-ninth of a peasant's harvest after the collection by the timariot (in return for cavalry service to the state) of the *deseto* or tenth. By this action and other acts of violence against person or property, the

[13] Milenko S. Filipović, 'Selo u Srbiji Krajem 18 i Početkom 19 Veka (Le Village de Serbie vers la Fin du XVIIIe Siècle)', in *Geografski Lik Srbije u Doba Prvog Ustanka (L'aspect Géographique de la Serbie à l'Époque du Premier Soulèvement, 1804–1813)*, Srpsko Geografsko Društvo, fasc. 32 (Belgrade, 1954), pp. 76–7; Borivoje M. Drobnjaković, 'Stanovništvo u Srbiji za Vreme Prvog Ustanka (La Population de la Serbie au Temps du Premier Soulèvement)', ibid., pp. 136–52; Vuk Vinaver, 'Tursko Stanovništvo u Srbiji za Vreme Prvog Srpskog Ustanka (Die Türkische Bevölkerung Serbiens im Zeitalter der Serbischen Revolution)', *Istoriski Glasnik*, No. 2 (Belgrade, 1955), pp. 41–80; Stojan Novaković, *Ustanak na Dahije 1804: Ocena Izvora, Karakter Ustanka, Vojevanje 1804, s Kartom Beogradskog Pašaluka* (Zadužbina Ilije M. Kolarca, Belgrade, 1904), pp. 196–201; Vladimir Stojančević, 'Karadjordje and Serbia in His Time', in *The First Serbian Uprising*, ed. Vucinich, pp. 23–39.

dues in kind exacted from many Serbian peasants were suddenly doubled, sometimes tripled.[14]

Like their fellow notables in Vidin, Janina, Bosnia, and Anatolia and Syria, the ayans of the pashalik of Belgrade sought to build a provincial redistributive economy. As in earlier centuries, writes Ilkay Sunar, market exchange in the Ottoman Empire continued to function primarily as 'a transactional form' rather than as 'a social organizational mode'[15]. Sunar evidently means that the productive and commercial economies had to play a subordinate role to the redistributive economy. In fact, the growth of ayan power entailed the subjection of the commercial and productive economies to two rival redistributive economies, each with its own territorial base: a central redistributive and a provincial redistributive economy.

The blockage of the urban economy facilitated the recruitment of an ayan fighting arm. In 1794, for example, an unskilled worker in the Morea earned about thirty paras a day or twenty piasters for a full month's employment. A master mason or master locksmith earned twice as much.[16] Wages in Belgrade were at a similar level. But a craftsman inscribed on the Belgrade janissary rolls obtained in addition ten piasters equivalent at the current rate of exchange to 2.5 francs per month for his militia duties. In 1792, however, as part of its reform projects, the government discharged the janissaries, reducing them to the status of artisans and workers or casting them into the ranks of the unemployed.[17] Their debasement came in the wake of a continuing rise in the price of bread. Between 1800 and 1819, bread prices in Ottoman towns doubled, whereas the earnings of journeymen rose by only 25 per cent.[18] The one-time janissaries were therefore eager to enter the service of the ayans.

[14] Vuk Stefanović Karadžić, *Danica: Zabavnik za Godinu 1827* (Printing Press of the Armenian Monastery, Vienna, 1827), pp. 80–1.

[15] Ilkay Sunar, 'Anthropologie Politique et Économique: l'Empire Ottoman et sa Transformation', *Annales: Économies, Sociétés, Civilisations*, 35 (May–August 1980), pp. 551–79, esp. pp. 551–60.

[16] Saverio Scrofani, *Voyage en Grèce de Xavier Scrofani, Sicilien, Fait en 1794 et 1795*, tr. J. F. C. Blanvillain (3 vols, Treuttel et Würtz, Strasbourg, an. IX/1801), vol. III, p. 93.

[17] Barthélemy-Sylvestre Cunibert, *Essai Historique sur les Révolutions et l'Indépendance de la Serbie depuis 1804 jusqu'à 1850* (2 vols, F. A. Brockhaus, Leipzig, 1855), vol. I, pp. 11, 15, 20.

[18] François-Charles-Hugues-Laurent Pouqueville, *Voyages dans la Grèce* (5 vols, Firmin Didot, Paris, 1820–1), vol. III, pp. 443–44; Louis-Auguste Félix de Beaujour, *Tableau du Commerce de la Grèce, Formé d'après une Année Moyenne depuis 1787 jusqu'en 1792* (2 vols, Imprimerie de Crapelet, Paris, an. VIII), vol. II, p. 168.

They were all the more zealous to do so since their own dismissal as a protection-production enterprise had been followed by official Ottoman recognition of a Christian enterprise of protection producers. In 1794, in effect, the governor of Belgrade had acceded to the scheme of little-county chiefs to allow the Serbians, several thousands of whom only recently (1788–91) had made war against Turkey in the service of Austria, to keep and use their arms against the rebel governor of Vidin. The knezes had argued that the Serbs could not bear the burden of heavier taxes but that they could reduce protection costs to the central government by becoming their own protectors.[19]

Serbian troops fought successfully against the dissident ayans, dislodging them from Belgrade. Napoleon's landing in Egypt in 1798, however, gave rise to a wave of Turkish reaction against all innovation, including Sultan Selim's 'new order'. For the Moslems of Bosnia, France became the *vampir* or bloodsucker empire of irreligion, revolution, and error.[20] In Belgrade and four other Serbian fortress towns, the janissaries were reinstated on the rolls, and ayan authority was restored.

Dividing the pashalik into four regions, each under the authority of a grand notable or *dey*, the ayans sent out agents to establish inns of office (*hans*, *konaks*) at regular intervals across the Serbian countryside. The function of these agents was to police their circumscription, collect the deveto and other tributes, and assume the authority of the knezes. In February 1804, after completing the territorial reorganization, the ayans summarily executed seventy-two knezes and other rural primates, perhaps even twice as many. The presumed object of their action was the removal of a rival elite and abolition of the knežina as an autonomous territorial organization.[21]

But the Serbians already possessed a military leadership, constituted between 1788 and 1791, acknowledged by the Ottoman government itself in 1794, and confirmed by their actions during the next ten years. As the

---

[19] Emile Haumant, 'Les Origines de la Liberté Serbe d'après les Mémoires du Protopope Matia Nénadovitch', *Revue Historique*, 118 (1915), pp. 54–69; Guzina, *Knežina*, p. 48.

[20] Midhat Šamić, 'Un Consul Français en Bosnie et la *Chronique de Travnik* de M. Ivo Andrić', *Annales de l'Institut Français de Zagreb*, 2nd series, No. 1 (1952), pp. 69–80.

[21] Cunibert, *Essai Historique*, vol. I, pp. 23–4, 28; Barbara Jelavich, *History of the Balkans: Eighteenth and Nineteenth Centuries* (2 vols, Cambridge University Press, Cambridge, 1983), vol. I, pp. 193–200; Wayne S. Vucinich, 'Introductory Remarks: Genesis and Essence of the First Serbian Uprising', in *The First Serbian Uprising*, pp. 1–21.

government kept its distance after 1798 and especially after 1801 and during 1804, and as the rural and little-county notables were intimidated, the Serbian military leaders were able to assert and extend their own authority.

The ayans found supporters among Moslem craftsmen and janissaries, among the urban poor, among cattle rustlers, and among Moslem loggers and raftsmen. According to Dušan Popović, the Serbian commanders found recruits among haiduks, bachelors (*bećari*) – many of them from other Balkan provinces and without roots in the pashalik – men without house or family (*beskućnici*), and the naked and barefoot (*goli i bosi*).[22] Numerous rootless and poor swelled both camps. Ayan partisans were largely Moslems; the Serbian fighting arm was made up almost wholly of orthodox Christians. But what chiefly distinguished the two adversaries was the urban and non-peasant character of the former and the rural character of the latter.

The ensuing struggle, generally known as the First Serbian Insurrection, did not begin as a movement of national independence. From the start, it was a struggle between exponents of two – and more than two – different conceptions of territorial and resource (property) management. Upon seizing arms against the great-county interests (1794–1804) and then (in 1805) against the Ottoman Empire itself, Serbian leaders did not clearly envisage their own affirmation as an ultimate, comprehensive, and legitimate political authority. Ružica Guzina is right: there were certain incomplete features in the Serbian state as it evolved between 1804 and 1813.[23] An embryonic and segmentary state, it remained incomplete because it lacked a legitimate basis – although a claim was made to continuity with Serbia's medieval political heritage – and because its leaders were never wholly convinced that it should become an ultimate authority.[24]

On January 14, 1805, the *Journal des Débats* carried a report from Semlin (Zemun) with a 25 December dateline about the tumultuous national assembly of that same month in Smederevo, the last capital of medieval

[22] Dušan J. Popović, *O Hajducima* (2 vols, Narodna Štamparija, Belgrade, 1930–1), vol. II, p. 139. See also Karadžić, *Danica*, pp. 91–6.

[23] Guzina, *Knežina*, pp. 100, 255. A review by Adam Nikolić, in *Istoriski Glasnik*, No. 1 (Belgrade, 1956), pp. 125–32, disputes the view that the Serbian political formation lacked the full features of a state.

[24] R. W. Seton-Watson, 'Some Aspects of Dynastic Policy in the Balkans', *Transactions of the Royal Historical Society*, 4th series, 32 (1950), pp. 1–14.

Serbia and first capital of the rebel state. Observing that the rebellion was backed at last by a 'general plan', the Semlin correspondent believed that its implementation would be sure to bring about 'great changes' in eastern Europe. The plan included the Serbs' decision to concentrate their military effort on the capture of Belgrade, the one substantial city in the pashalik and the provincial base of the great-county ideology of property relations.[25]

PRODUCT SPECIALIZATION AND THE SAVA-KUPA AXIS

The Serbs ultimately took Belgrade. In addition to the incitement of their own military achievements, external factors contributed to the persistence of the rebellion. Present as opportunities, symbols, and interests, the external factors were derived from the opposite shores of the Sava and Danube, namely, from the Habsburg territories of the Military Frontier and from Habsburg Styria, Carniola, Carinthia, Croatia, and southern Hungary.

As in the Ottoman Empire, a conflict of territorial jurisdictions raged in Hungary during the eighteenth century. The central government sought to establish its own royal officials in the counties – territories with an average area of more than 4,000 square kilometers, thus great counties by definition. Under the inspiration of noble or agrarian interests, the county (*comitatus*, *vármegye*, *županija*) governments sought to preserve and extend their authority and influence.[26] With minor modifications, therefore, one may apply Theda Skocpol's structural analysis to the Ottoman and Habsburg empires alike:

[25] *Journal des Débats*, lundi 24 nivôse an 13 (January 14, 1805), dateline Semlin, December 25, 1804, reproduced in Dragoslav Janković, *Francuska Štampa o Prvom Srpskom Ustanku*, Srpska Akademija Nauka, 'Gradja', knj. XIII, Istoriski Institut, knj. 10 (Naučno Delo, Belgrade, 1959), p. 85 (Doc. No. 102).

[26] Malte-Brun, *Précis de la Géographie universelle*, vol. VI: *Description de l'Europe Orientale* (1826), pp. 372–3; Slavko Gavrilović, 'Obnova Slavonskih Županija i Njihovo Razgraničavanje sa Vojnom Granicom (1745–1749)', *Matica Srpska: Zbornik za Društvene Nauke*, No. 25 (Novi Sad, 1960), pp. 49–92; Slavko Gavrilović, 'Urbarijalno Pitanje u Sremskoj Županiji Sredinom XVIII Stoleća', ibid., No. 27 (Novi Sad, 1960), pp. 5–32; Ivo Banac, 'The Role of Vojvodina in Karadjordje's Revolution', *Südost-Forschungen*, 11 (1981), pp. 31–61, esp. p. 36; Jelavich, *History of the Balkans*, vol. I, pp. 142–3.

Inherent in all agrarian bureaucratic regimes were tensions between, on the one hand, state elites interested in preserving, using, and extending the powers of armies and administrative organizations and, on the other hand, landed upper classes interested in defending locally and regionally based social networks [at the great-county level], influence over peasants, and powers and privileges associated with control of land and agrarian surpluses.[27]

Tensions between nobility and officialdom were softened somewhat in Hungary by the successful expansion of cereal production and subsequent development of a cereal export economy. By 1800, according to my conversions of J. A. Demian's data, the grain production of Hungary proper – without Transylvania, Croatia, and Slavonia – included in good years more than 168,000 tonnes (1,845,000 hectoliters) of barley, 224,000 tonnes (2,460,000 hectoliters) of wheat, and large quantities of maize, millet, buckwheat, and oats: perhaps a total grain production of 1.12 million tonnes (12,300,000 hectoliters).[28] In addition, my conversions of Malte-Brun's data give a grain production to Croatia and Slavonia, in good years just before 1826, of 431,200 tonnes (4,735,500 hectoliters).[29]

Geographic and topographic factors encouraged the formation of zones of product specialization (Figure 13.1). South of a line from the vicinity of Györ eastward to Máramaros county lay a zone of stock raising and wheat, maize, millet, tobacco, and fruit production. Máramaros county was the chief source of rock salt for Hungary, part of Slavonia, and the eastern or Sava portions of the Military Frontier. North of the Györ–Máramaros line lay a zone of barley, rye, and

[27] Theda Skocpol, 'France, Russia, China: A Structural Analysis of Social Revolutions', *Comparative Studies in Society and History*, 18 (April 1976), pp. 175–210, esp. p. 184.

[28] Johann A. Demian, *Tableau Géographique et Politique des Royaumes de Hongrie, d'Esclavonie, de Croatie et de la Grande Principauté de Transilvanie*, tr. (2 vols, S. C. L'Huillier, Paris, 1809), vol. I, pp. 89–91. According to Milan Vlajinac, *Rečnik Naših Starih Mera u Toku Vekova* (4 vols, Srpska Akademija Nauka i Umetnosti, Belgrade, 1961–74), vol. I, p. 56; vol. III, pp. 596–98, the Vienna or Pressburg *Metzen* of grain weighed about 56 kilograms. I have further calculated the Vienna or Pressburg *Metzen* of grain as a measure of capacity at about 61.5 liters.

[29] Malte-Brun, *Précis de la Géographie Universelle*, vol. VI, pp. 343–4. Malte-Brun shows an annual grain production of 3.7 million *Metzen* in Croatia and 4 million *Metzen* in Slavonia.

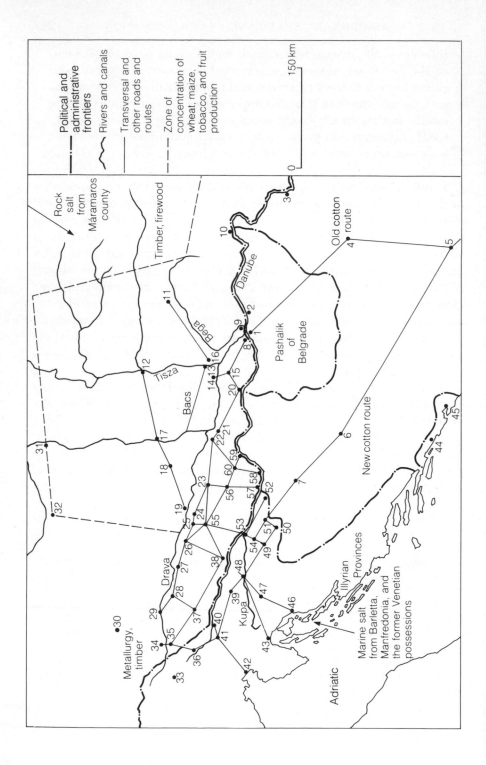

Political and
administrative
frontiers

Rivers and canals

Transversal and
other roads and
routes

Zone of
concentration of
wheat, maize,
tobacco, and fruit
production

0   150 km

Rock
salt
from
Máramaros
county

Timber, firewood

Danube

Old cotton
route

Bega

Pashalik
of
Belgrade

Tisza

Bacs

New cotton
route

Drava

Kupa

Metallurgy,
timber

Illyrian
Provinces

Adriatic

Marine salt
from Barletta,
Manfredonia, and
the former Venetian
possessions

1 Belgrade (Beograd)
2 Smederevo (Semendria)
3 Vidin
4 Niš
5 Üsküb
6 Sarajevo
7 Banja Luka (Banjaluka)
8 Zemun (Semlin)
9 Pánčevo (Pancsova)
10 Orsova
11 Temesvár (Timişoara)
12 Szeged (Szegedin)
13 Novi Sad (Neusatz, Ujvidék)
14 Petrovaradin (Peterwardein)
15 Sremski Karlovci (Carlowitz, Karlowtz)
16 Nagy Becskerek (Veliki Bečkerek, Gross-Becskerek)
17 Baja
18 Pécs (Fünfkirchen)
19 Légrád
20 Mitrovica (Sremska Mitrovica, Mitrowitz)

21 Vukovár (Bukovar)
22 Osijek (Eszek, Esseg, Essegg)
23 Virovitica (Verőcze, Verovditz, Virovititz)
24 Drnje
25 Križevci (Kreutz)
26 Koprivnica (Kopreinitz)
27 Varaždin (Warasdin, Varasd)
28 Ptuj (Pettau)
29 Maribor (Marburg)
30 Graz
31 Buda
32 Györ
33 Villach
34 Klagenfurt
35 Ferlach
36 Kranj (Krainburg)
37 Celje (Cilli)
38 Zagreb (Agram)
39 Novo Mesto
40 Salloch (Szalok)

41 Ljubljana (Laibach)
42 Trieste
43 Fiume (Rijeka)
44 Dubrovnik (Ragusa)
45 Kotor (Cattaro)
46 Senj (Zengg, Segna)
47 Ogulin
48 Karlovac (Carlstadt, Karlstadt, Gornji Karlovci)
49 Glina
50 Novi
51 Kostajnica
52 Dubica
53 Sisak (Sissek)
54 Petrinja
55 Bjelovar (Belovár)
56 Daruvar (Daruvár)
57 Jasenovac
58 Gradiška
59 Brod
60 Požega (Slavonska Požega)

FIGURE 13.1   Production and exchange economy, 1780–1810

oats production, and of cereal deficiency. East (Transylvania) and west (Croatia and Slavonia) of the zone of maize and wheat production was a zone of timber and firewood resources, scarce in the southern Hungarian counties. Slavonia was a mixed zone with products of all kinds, while the Croatian Military Frontier was a zone of salt and grain deficiency.

The growing cereal surpluses, virtually nonexistent until the mid-eighteenth century, circulated in three directions. More than 5 per cent and sometimes as much as 7.5 per cent of Hungary's cereal production – limited, however, to wheat, barley, and oats – reached Vienna by way of the Danube. Probably more than 2 per cent and sometimes as much as 5 per cent went by way of the Danube, Sava, and Kupa to the grain-deficient areas of the southwest and to Adriatic ports. A further amount reached the cereal-deficient regions of the north. Partly by way of the Drava, a portion of the Slavonian grains went to Venice and other parts of Italy.[30]

The noble estates produced most of the cereal surpluses, but the merchants, many of them Hungarian Serbs, moved them. By 1800, hardly a village in Hungary lacked one or more Rahz (Serb, Rascian) or Jewish peddlers,[31] and Serb wholesale merchants were numerous in the towns. Demian and Malte-Brun attest that in Hungary proper, in the Military Frontier, and in Civil Slavonia, there were more than 6,000 villages, 278 towns, and 21 cities.[32] Serb merchants were probably active in at least half these villages, in more than a hundred towns, and in most of the cities. At a presumed average of sixty Serb wholesale merchants to a city, and twenty to a town, one may estimate the number of Serb merchants at 3,000, in addition to thousands of peddlers.[33]

Indeed, according to Demian and Martin von Schwartner, a whole new system of structures increasingly evident between 1750 and 1800 favored mercantile activity: population growth, agricultural expansion,

---

[30] Demian, *Tableau Géographique*, vol. I, pp. 15–18, 58, 73, 82–3, 87–91, 231–40; vol. II, pp. 1–3, 22–3, 33, 49, 94–5.

[31] Ibid., vol. I, pp. 232–4.

[32] Ibid., vol. II, p. 20; Malte-Brun, *Précis de la Géographie Universelle*, vol. VI, pp. 390–2.

[33] I have estimated the average number of wholesale merchants in towns and cities on the basis of the suggestive data in Demian, *Tableau Géographique*, vol. II, part 2, pp. 55–8, 207–10.

navigable rivers, appropriate entrepôts, two new canals (Bega and Bacs) and a third under construction, new main roads, and improved transversal roads made lively by the growth of fairs, complements of the river entrepôts. By 1800, there were 1,640 fairs in Hungary proper and probably several hundred more in Slavonia. Of the major Slavonian fairs, six were held in Požega and four each at the fortress towns of Eszek (Osijek) and Peterwardein (Petrovaradin) and at Djakovo (Diakovár, Deakovár), Virovitica (Veröcze, Veroviditz), Vukovar (Bukovar), Mitrovica, Orahowitz (Orahovica), and Sid (Šid).[34]

The Drava became navigable at Légrád, the Sava at Salloch (Szalok) several kilometers from Laibach (Ljubljana), and the Kupa at Carlstadt (Karlovac, Gornji Karlovci). A French report maintains that the towpaths between Semlin and Sissek (Sisak) were especially well kept up. At Sissek on the Sava at the confluence with the Kupa, the larger boats and rafts – a few of them with a carrying capacity of 200–250 tonnes (4,000–5,000 hundredweights) or more – unloaded their grains, tobacco, and other goods, for the Kupa and the Sava between Sissek and Salloch were unsuitable for carriers of more than 3,000 or 4,000 hundredweights.[35] With the major exception of rock salt, the commercial traffic within the entire quadrilateral of river and canal – Sava, Drava, Danube, Tisza, Bacs, and Bega – and transversal road systems bounded by Pančevo, Nagy Becskerek (Veliki Bečkerek), Szegedin, Drnje, and Sissek was largely in the hands of Orthodox Serb merchants. Around this quadrilateral lay a secondary zone of Orthodox Serb mercantile penetration that extended westward to Karlovac and Salloch and eastward to Temesvár and Orsova. In the western sector of this secondary zone, at the western fringes of the primary zone, and at the Slavonian fairs in general, the Orthodox Serb merchants made contact with German (Austrian) artisans whose own craft production required the existence of a further area of product specialization – Carniola, Carinthia, and Styria – or with traders from these provinces, notably, from such places

[34] Ibid., vol. I, pp. 232–4, 241–3, 265–71; Martin von Schwartner, *Statistik des Königreichs Ungern*, 2nd edn (2 vols in 3 parts, n. p., Ofen, 1809–11), vol. I, part 1, pp. 425–34.

[35] Service Historique de l'Armée (Vincennes), Mémoires et Reconnaissances 1598: 'Reconnaissance sur l'Unna, l'Isle et le Château de Costanicza', Laybach, September 5, 1810, the report of Isnard, Chief of the Battalion of Engineers; 'Rapport sur la Navigation de la Save', General Lauriston to the Emperor, Trieste, December 26, 1810. The previous footnote confirms and complements the French reports.

as Laibach, Pettau (Ptuj), Ferlach, and Graz, perhaps also from Klagenfurt and Krainburg (Kranj): a supply base of iron ware. The general route of hardware supply seems to have been Graz, Marburg (Maribor), Pettau, and Varaždin, whence the goods attained the Sava or one of the Slavonian fairs, especially those at Eszek.

During the Serbian insurrection part of the hardware so obtained consisted of munitions, small arms, and cannon, often bought from German gunsmiths in Slavonia, delivered to Novi Sad and Petrovaradin, and then sent on to the rebels in Serbia. While some munitions for rebel use were produced in the eastern Civil Slavonian county of Srem and in the Banat of Temesvár (east of Srem county), a good portion came from the western territories.[36] The ability of the Serbian rebels to obtain imports of grains, salt, and limited supplies of arms and munitions – for which they often paid in livestock – depended, let us stress, upon the earlier, albeit recent, commercial assertion of Habsburg Serb merchants on the Sava and at the fairs between the Sava and Drava.[37]

Interest probably bound several score of the three thousand Habsburg Serb merchants – cereal merchants and gunrunners in particular – to the Serbian cause. The territories north of the Sava and middle Danube contained at the same time a large Serb Orthodox population, among a portion of whom, namely the manipulators of symbols and ideas, patriotism often complemented self-interest.

A case in point is the secularized Orthodox monk Dositej Obradović, son of a Csakova (Čakovo) pelt monger. Envisioning an early end to 'the time of weeping and lamentation, hunger and wailing . . . of the lenten fast', to the rule of haricots, peas, lentils, and cabbage, Obradović looked forward to a 'golden age' of reason and 'evangelical freedom'. He was probably the first person to introduce into the written Serbian language, in 1788 and 1789, the terms (borrowed from French and other

[36] Slavko Benović, 'Sremski Trgovci i Prvi Srpski Ustanak do 1809 Godine', *Zbornik Matice Srpske*, serija društvenih nauka, No. 5 (Novi Sad, 1953), pp. 5–25, esp. pp. 10–13; Slavko Gavrilović, *Vojvodina i Srbija u Vreme Prvog Srpskog Ustanka* (Institut za Izučavanje Istorije Vojvodine, Novi Sad, 1974), pp. 58–60; Banac, 'The Role of Vojvodina', pp. 37–9.

[37] On Serbian imports from the Habsburg territories, see Gavrilović, *Vojvodina i Srbija*, pp. 40–52; Mijo Mirković, *Ekonomska Historija Jugoslavije* (Ekonomski Pregled, Zagreb, 1958), p. 165; Danica Milić, 'Austro-srpska Trgovina 1813–1815 Godine i Pokušaj Osnivanja Austriskog Konzulata u Srbiji', *Istoriski Časopis*, Nos 9–10 (Belgrade, 1959, publication date 1960), pp. 333–44, esp. pp. 340–1.

Romance languages by way of German) *kapital* for accumulated wealth, and *nacia* for nation.[38] Obradović was ultimately called to peasant Serbia to take charge of the newly created department of education.

By that time the word nacia (or *naciia*) was part of the vocabulary of other educated Habsburg Serbs,[39] some of whom similarly emigrated to insurgent Serbia to serve as secretaries, administrators, wordspinners, and advisers. The new political state offered as a mode of communication a written language in which they had no superiors and in which competition favored their success. It afforded them advantages that they lacked in Hungary, where they had to face the competition of more privileged or better educated ethnic groups.

Habsburg Serb merchants and wordspinners alike had broadly regional or national spatial conceptions, whereas Serb and Croat peasants had communal and small-county conceptions. The peasant stirrings of 1806, 1807, and 1808 in Slavonia and the Banat, like those in Turkey's southern Balkan territories during the same years, may have found some inspiration in the resumption of war between Russia and Turkey in 1806 and in the acquisition by Napoleonic France of Istria, Dalmatia, and Ragusa, and of the right to move troops between Venetia and Dalmatia across the territory of the Carlstadt regiment of the Croatian Military Frontier. But while they were sympathetic to Serbia, the Slavonian and other peasants aspired to aid neither the Serbian nor any other state. Like the peasants of Serbia itself, they sought rather to obtain a fairer share of the agricultural product and assert or augment their local autonomies. These segmented short-lived jacqueries did not turn

---

[38] Dositej Obradović, *Dela*, with a biography by Jovan Skerlić, 5th edn (Državna Štamparija, Belgrade, 1911), p. 3; *The Life and Adventures of Dimitrije Obradović, Who as a Monk Was Given the Name Dositej, Written and Published by Himself*, tr. and ed. with an introduction by George Rapall Noyes (University of California Press, Berkeley and Los Angeles, 1953), p. 131. In the subsequently devised modern and secularized orthography, *nacia* (or *naciia*) was written with a 'j' as *nacija*.

[39] Kosta Milutinović, 'Iz Istorije Novog Sada u Doba Kočine Krajine i Prvog Srpskog Ustanka', *Zbornik Matice Srpske*, serija društvenih nauka, No. 7 (Novi Sad, 1954), pp. 49–85, esp. pp. 68–9. For an examination of the ideology of nationhood among Serbs and other South Slavs, see Banac, 'The Role of Vojvodina', pp. 31–61; Dimitrije Djordjević, *Révolutions Nationales des Peuples Balkaniques, 1804–1914* (Institut d'Histoire, Belgrade, 1965), pp. 11–38; Roger Viers Paxton, 'Nationalism and Revolution: A Re-examination of the Origins of the First Serbian Insurrection, 1804–1807', *East European Quarterly*, 6 (September 1972), pp. 337–62.

into a general uprising; they retained their local focus and were suppressed.[40]

More important to a new conceptualization of territory was the contribution of officers and soldiers of the Military Frontier, several thousands of whom joined the rebellion in Serbia, became bandits, or defected to the French.[41] Since 1740 at least, according to Ivo Banac, Serb and Croat historians had embraced the imaginary goal of an Illyrian state (Serb, Croat, Serb and Croat, or Serb and Bulgar) conceived in pseudo-medieval terms, stretching sometimes from the Adriatic to the Black Sea.[42] Merchants and officers of the Sava and Kupa basin did not reject this baroque conception, but some began to emphasize the need to give that state, or group of associated states, the commercial foundations of the Sava and Kupa, which until 1750 had been virtually nonexistent and were not well developed until 1780.

LA GRANDE NATION

By the treaty of Schönbrunn, 14 October 1809, Austria concluded a six-month war with Napoleon, ceding to France the territories of the Carlstadt and Banal (Viceregal) regiments – the latter situated along the right bank of the Sava – as well as Dalmatia, Istria, Carinthia, and part of Carniola. The French reconstituted these territories as the Illyrian Provinces.

Among the officers brought to Serbia by the disaffection in the Military Frontier was a certain Rade (Rado, Rada) Vučinić (Vučenić). Born apparently in Carlstadt, Rade Vučinić was the scion of a family that had achieved distinction in the mid-eighteenth century for its opposition to efforts to bring the Orthodox Serbs into union with Rome. Acknowledging the existence of Orthodox and Roman Catholic Serbs alike, he did not regard religion as the main criterion of nationality. In a letter to Champagny, French Minister of Foreign Affairs, he swore

[40] Banac, 'The Role of Vojvodina', pp. 53–60; Slavko Gavrilović, 'Seljački Pokret u Sremu u Doba Prvog Srpskog Ustanka', *Zbornik Matice Srpske*, serija društvenih nauka, No. 7 (Novi Sad, 1954), pp. 7–48.

[41] Gunther E. Rothenberg, *The Military Border in Croatia, 1740–1881: A Study of an Imperial Institution* (University of Chicago Press, Chicago, 1966), pp. 102–21.

[42] Banac, 'The Role of Vojvodina', pp. 46–52.

that he would put country and nationality above 'all the riches of the Universe' and all 'particular interests'.[43]

'Patriot' Captain Rade Vučinić was thus the choice of commander-in-chief Karageorge (Karadjordje Petrović) and of the Serbian Executive Council as emissary to Napoleon during the six-month war between France and Austria: bearer of a resolution dated August 16/28 that proclaimed the Serbian people's decision 'to confide its destiny to the puissant protection of the Great Napoleon'. They would thus welcome the garrisoning of all Serbian fortresses by soldiers of the *Veliki Narod* or *Velika Nacia* (*Grande Nation*), and their compatriots in Bosnia, Hercegovina, Hungary, and Bulgaria would join them in battle. Serbs and Bulgars would advance toward the frontiers of Dalmatia and Ragusa. The 'Magyar colossus', support of Austria, would collapse as Serbian and French troops moved into Slavonia, Srem, and the Banat, where the Serbs detested their Magyar lords. To carry out the project, Serbia required financial and technical aid: cannoneers, engineers, sappers, and mineralogists. In return for such aid, France would obtain access to Serbia's livestock, timber, and mineral resources.[44]

Carrying the mesage, for reasons of security, by a roundabout route to Bucharest and Lwów, Vučinić arrived in Vienna too late. He did not meet Napoleon, who by the peace of Schönbrunn had achieved his objective of closing Trieste to British commerce. France thereby deprived Austria of a direct outlet to the sea and thus of opportunity for physical contact with Britain. At the same time, it gained entry to a land route for Franco-Levantine commerce.[45] Napoleon thereupon sought to resolve other urgent problems: the continuing insurgence of the Iberian peninsula, the threat of an English invasion of the Low Countries. Champagny did not neglect, however, to issue the following cautionary instructions to Ledoulx, France's vice-consul in Bucharest:

---

[43] Mihailo Gavrilović, *Ispisi iz Pariskih Arhiva (Gradja za Istoriju Prvoga Srpskoga Ustanka)* (Srpska Kraljevska Akademija, Belgrade, 1904), pp. 565–6.

[44] Ibid., pp. 465–7, for the Serbian text; Auguste Boppe, *Documents Inédits sur les Relations de la Serbie avec Napoléon I (1809–1814)* (Imprimerie d'État, Paris, 1888), pp. 6–8, for the French translation.

[45] Gellio Cassi, 'Le Populazioni Giulio-Illiriche Durante il Dominio Napoleonico (1806–1814)', *Rassegna Storica del Risorgimento*, 17 (1930), pp. 1–70, esp. p. 2; Melitta Pivec-Stelè, *La Vie Économique des Provinces Illyriennes (1809–1813)* (Éditions Bossard, Paris, 1930), pp. 12, 146, 176.

Being and desiring to remain at peace with the Porte, the Emperor surely will not accord open protection to those whom the former regards as rebels. His Majesty cannot remain totally indifferent, however, to the fate of a people that has shown such constancy and courage. Welcome its overtures, look with favor on its effort to establish communications with France. Let it take hope in the concern of the Emperor. But act without arousing the suspicion either of the Porte or of Russia.

Above all, Ledoulx was not to compromise himself or France by any written document.[46]

After returning to Belgrade, Vučinić was sent on a second mission to request French arbitration and protection. On 20 February 1810, he arrived in Trieste by way of Carlstadt with Serbia's message. Serbia would agree to peace or to an armistice in return for Ottoman recognition of the approximate frontiers of the pashalik of Belgrade as Serbia's frontiers and acknowledgment of Karageorge and his legitimate male descendants as Serbia's hereditary chiefs. Peace would allow it to provide the Illyrian Provinces with cheap supplies of cattle, sheep, goats, pigs, tallow, honey, and beeswax. Of equal importance, it would ensure the restoration of the cheaper Belgrade cotton route, diverted by war to Vidin and Odessa – and to Sarajevo. If Turkey persisted in war, Vučinić was to try to persuade France to provide Serbia with geometers, miners, and sappers, several units of properly armed infantry, and 2,000 quintals of gunpowder, 4,000 quintals of lead, 10,000 muskets with bayonets, and 20 pieces of field artillery with gun carriages. Payment was to be made in raw materials. Significantly, the solicited munitions and arms were supposed to be entrused to reliable merchants in Carlstadt who would deliver them to Belgrade by way of the Kupa and Sava.

To complete his charge Vučinić journeyed from Trieste to Vienna and then to Paris in an effort to seek as well a loan of 1,500,000 francs and authorization to import sulfur, lead, and arms from the Kingdom of Italy. He did not receive satisfaction. But Champagny did not fail to inform Napoleon of Vučinić's comment that Serbia must seek the protection of one great power or another. Serbia, observed the French

---

[46] Gavrilović, *Ispisi iz Pariskih Arhiva*, pp. 488–90; Boppe, *Documents Inédits*, pp. 11–13.

Minister, might therefore turn, as in earlier years, to Russia. In that event, Russian influence would spread south of the Danube to the proximity of the Adriatic and to Russia's ally, Montenegro. As a Russian vassal, Serbia might extend its authority northward into Hungary, weakening Austria's function as a counterweight to Russia.[47]

Immediately thereafter, Napoleon assured Metternich of his unalterable opposition to Russian occupation of strongholds on the right bank of the Danube, which was higher than the left – an occupation tantamount in his eyes to the conquest of Constantinople and ruin of the Ottoman Empire.[48]

Serbian goals did not suit Napoleon's scheme of things, and their affirmation came at a time of lagging French interest in Serbian affairs (see Figure 13.2). Nor did they correspond to the basic features of French foreign policy, conditioned by history, position, and size, and by the French leaders' need to pursue policies in conformity with their country's role as a world power locked in a struggle with other European powers.

From time to time, Napoleon may have been tempted by the Comte de Volney's territorial solution: the partitioning of backward states and empires among the chief states of the superior European technological and scientific civilization.[49] But the great powers were unable to agree on their respective shares. For a basic statement of French foreign policy, therefore, it may be preferable to turn to a book by Jean-Louis Favier, *Politique de Tous les Cabinets de l'Europe* (1793), and to a second (1801) and third (1802) edition of the book with the critique of Louis-Philippe de Ségur.

Favier contended that Russia's wars of the eighteenth century had been 'national' wars of 'real interests'. For the commerce of the Black Sea was 'as precious for Russia as that of America was for France, Spain,

---

[47] Ibid., pp. 30–1, 61; Gavrilović, *Ispisi iz Pariskih Arhiva*, pp. 526–8, 534–47, 557–9.

[48] Clemens Lothar Wenzel, Fürst von Metternich-Winneburg, *Aus Metternich's Nachgelassenen Papieren*, ed. Alfons von Klinkowström (8 vols in 3 parts, Wilhelm Braumüller, Wien, 1880–4), vol. II, book 3, pp. 156–64, 377–85.

[49] Constantin-François de Chasseboeuf, Comte de Volney, *Considérations sur la Guerre Actuelle des Turcs* (n. p., London, 1788), pp. 61, 71. The indicated place of publication may be fictive, designed to elude censorship.

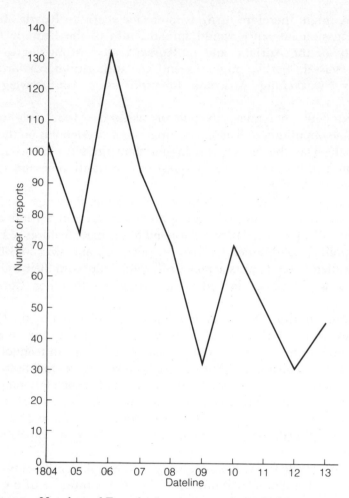

FIGURE 13.2   Number of French news reports about Serbia, 1804–13 (based
on data in Janković, 1959)

or England, with the difference that [for Russia it was] a natural
commerce, lying at its door'. No wonder, then, that Russia should strive
to crush or dominate the Ottoman Empire. For France, however,
Turkey's destruction would be a 'most baleful' blow.[50]

[50] Jean-Louis Favier, *Politique de Tous les Cabinets de L'Europe pendant les Règnes de Louis
XV et de Louis XVI, Contenant des Pièces Authentiques sur la Correspondance Secrète du Comte
de Broglie* (2 vols, François Buisson, Paris, 1793), vol. I, pp. 289, 307, 357–63.

Hostile to the 'spirit of system', Ségur argued that in relations between states there were no 'natural' friends or enemies. Whereas Favier had favored alliance with Prussia, Ségur would look with disfavor on no alliance if it worked to France's advantage. Insisting that security depended much more on consensus and effective internal administration than upon alliances, he regretted Favier's emphasis of geographic 'position', which had led to a belief in 'the possibility of a permanent alliance system'. Despite his different argument, Ségur came to the same conclusion in regard to the Ottoman Empire. As the victim of internal violence, Turkey was great only in area. It would therefore be a transgression of French interest to allow its destruction or domination by another great power, specifically, Russia.[51]

French and Serbian conceptions of territorial organization could not be reconciled. But the French Revolutionary and Napoleonic reality and ideology of a *grande nation*, or nation of nations, served as a catalyst to the idea of using the Sava–Kupa commercial system as a link between the Adriatic and Serbia and of founding a large Serbian state or system of Serbian or Illyrian states.

The attempt was an act of will and consciousness applied to geography – a temporal product of two dialectics. It began as a struggle of newly prospering but threatened little-county and peasant interests against the blocked economy and aggressive redistributive ideology of urban and great-county notables. To fight effectively, the leaders of the peasant rebels had to have recourse to another ideology and to other forms of social and political organization. Serb merchants, officers, and wordspinners from southern Hungary, Slavonia, and the Sava-Kupa basin filled that need, providing peasant Serbia with an embryonic ideology of a nation state that would function as a national market in an essentially commercial rather than redistributive world economy.

In the context of a history of larger scope, the attempt was part of an unco-ordinated general revision of spatial relationships, of which the most striking examples, in the order of their occurrence, were the internal customs unions of the United States, France, and Germany, and the

---

[51] Jean-Louis Favier, *Politique de Tous les Cabinets de l'Europe pendant les Règnes de Louis XV et de Louis XVI, Contenant des Pièces Authentiques sur la Correspondance Secrète du Comte de Broglie, avec des Notes et Commentaires, un Mémoire sur le Pacte de Famille et l'Examen du Système Fédératif Qui Peut le Mieux Convenir à la France*, ed. Louis-Philippe de Ségur, 3rd ed. (3 vols, François Buisson, Paris, an. XI/1802), vol. I, pp. 12–13, 16–19; vol. III, pp. 367–79.

new nation states of nineteenth-century Europe. An important difference exists, however, between the western European and Serbian solutions. In western Europe, a centuries-old cantonal and political organization preceded and facilitated the formation of nation states as national markets. In Serbia, as in much of eastern Europe, cantonal development or the linking of market towns to the countryside had to follow the formation of a political state.

The suppression of the First Serbian Insurrection in 1813 delayed that political development. When a new Serbian state was formed between 1817 and 1878, the opportunities of the Napoleonic wars were no longer present. Serbian leaders and thinkers therefore turned to other territorial solutions. Upon the establishment of a state of the Serbs, Croats, and Slovenes at the end of World War I, the Sava, Kupa, lower Drava, and middle Danube basins became part of that state, later renamed Jugoslavia (or Yugoslavia). Despite, and as a consequence of, the pursuit of several different political and ideological solutions since then, the creation of a viable political and economic entity continues to be a challenging unfinished task.

14

Commodity Production, Subsistence, and the State in Colonial Africa: Peasant Cotton Agriculture in the Lower Tchiri (Shire) Valley of Malawi, 1907–51[1]

ELIAS MANDALA

. . . we must begin by stating the first presupposition of all human existence, and therefore of all history, namely, that men must be in a position to live in order to 'make history.' But life involves before everything else eating and drinking, a habitation, clothing and many other things. The first historical act is, therefore, the production of material life itself. This is indeed a historical act, a fundamental condition of all history. . . . In any conception of history, therefore, the first requirement is to observe this basic fact in all its significance and all its implications and to give it its proper importance.

Karl Marx[2]

[1] Field research for this paper was conducted in the Lower Tchiri Valley as well as in the Malawi National Archives, the Public Record Office and the National Library of Scotland between 1976 and 1980. I would like to express my gratitude to the men and women of the Tchiri valley for sharing with me their experiences and the memoirs of their ancestors. No archives can replace them. The essay benefited from comments by Eugene Genovese, Joel Gregory, and Jane Guyer. The Social Science Research Council and the American Council of Learned Societies provided valuable financial support for the project. I would also like to thank the Secretarial Services of the History Department (University of Rochester) under Jean DeGroat and Helen Hull.

[2] T. B. Bottomore, *Karl Marx* (Mc-Graw-Hill, New York, 1956), p. 60.

Older people who remember the days when there were big European estates in the Lower Shire and Chikwawa districts will also remember that the cotton crop on these estates often failed and that nearly always gardens then planted by the Africans gave good cotton. This was because the Africans' gardens were all planted after they had hoed their food crops and their cotton grew and flowered after the bad time for the pests which destroyed so much of the European cotton.

H. C. Ducker[3]

The claim that commodity, or cash-crop, production has exacerbated the present food crisis in Africa[4] does not, as yet, rest on a firm empirical or theoretical basis. Research in African studies is virtually silent on the historical relation between commodity production and African systems of food cultivation and supply. Most analyses of cash-crop agriculture are grounded in one or another version of neoclassical economic theory, which makes export agriculture a painless development that amounted to nothing more than the deployment of the supposedly underutilized land and labor resources in precolonial African economies. It equates peasant initiative in the reorganization of village economies in this century with responsiveness to market incentives.[5] Under-development theory, which many hailed as an alternative to the neoclassical, has also skirted the issue of subsistence in the rise of export production and posited the dynamics of commodity agriculture in the structural conflict between peasants and capitalists in a political setting dominated by capitalist interests. Theorists of underdevelopment have, for example, argued that colonial authorities kept rural momentum in cash crop production either by underwriting peasant subsistence in the form of food distribution or through political coercion.[6] The more

[3] H. C. Ducker, 'A Talk on Cotton Growing in the Lower Shire and Chikwawa Districts,' *Nyasaland Agricultural Quarterly Journal (NAQJ)*, I, 1 (January 1941), pp. 14–15.

[4] For a critical review of the subject, see Sara S. Berry, 'The Food Crisis and Agrarian Change in Africa: A Review Essay,' *African Studies Review*, XXVII, 2 (June 1984), pp. 59–112.

[5] For a general critique of this position, see John Tosh, 'The Cash-Crop Revolution in Tropical Africa: An Agricultural Reappraisal,' *African Affairs*, 79, 314 (1980), pp. 79–94.

[6] Deborah Fahy Bryceson, 'Changes in Peasant Food Production and Food Supply in Relation to the Historical Development of Commodity Production in Pre-Colonial and Colonial Tanganyika,' *Journal of Peasant Studies*, VII, 3 (April 1980), pp. 281–311; Allen Isaacman, *et al.* '"Cotton is the Mother of Poverty": Peasant Resistance to Forced

widespread variation of the same theme holds that colonial rulers constrained peasant initiative in cash-crop production in order to make land, labor, and market opportunities available to local, European capitalist farmers.[7] Some scholars who recognize that colonial states were not simply the handmaids of mercantile interests,[8] have altered the terms but not the nature of the debate. Their new argument concerns the relative autonomy of state structures – the capacity to promote simultaneously capitalist production, social order, and peasant agriculture. They have not advanced a theory about the social and technical factors that have affected peasant decisions to resist or participate in commodity production. The proponents of the modes-of-production paradigm, who might have shed new light on this critical problem, have not fulfilled their promise. They have reduced the often violent penetration of capital to abstract and neat formulations about the 'subordination' of 'precapitalist' to the 'logic' of capitalist production.[9] The unquestioned assumption about the primacy of 'social' over 'technical' relations has further deflected the theorists from the issue of

Cotton Production in Mozambique, 1936–1961,' *International Journal of African Historical Studies*, XIII, 4 (1980), pp. 581–615; Bogumil Jewsiewicki, 'African Peasants in the Totalitarian Colonial Society of the Belgian Congo,' Martin A. Klein, ed. *Peasants in Africa: Historical and Contemporary Perspectives* (Sage, Beverly Hills, Ca., 1980), pp. 45–75.

[7] Robin Palmer and Neil Parsons, eds, *The Roots of Rural Poverty in Central and Southern Africa* (Heinemann Educational, London, 1977) and most of the essays in Robert I. Rotberg, ed., *Imperialism, Colonialism, and Hunger: East and Central Africa* (Lexington Books, Lexington, Mass., 1983). For critical appraisals of this and other versions of dependency, see Frederick Cooper, 'Peasants, Capitalists and Historians: A Review Article,' *Journal of Southern African Studies*, VII, 2 (1981), pp. 284–314; 'Africa and the World Economy,' *African Studies Review*, XXIV, 2 and 3 (June/Sept. 1981), pp. 1–86; Gavin Kitching, 'Capitalism and Colonialism in Mozambique: Review Article,' *Journal of Southern African Studies*, IX, 2 (April 1983), pp. 258–63; Jack Lewis, 'The Rise and Fall of the South African Peasantry: A Critique and Reassessment,' *Journal of Southern African Studies*, XI, 1 (Oct. 1984), pp. 1–24; Elias Mandala, 'Gold Seekers, *Prazo*-Holders and Capitalists in Mozambique: A Review,' *Canadian Journal of African Studies*, XVII, 3 (1983), pp. 545–7; Terence O. Ranger, 'Growing from the Roots: Reflections on Peasant Research in Central and Southern Africa,' *Journal of Southern African Studies*, V, 1 (1978), pp. 99–133

[8] John Lonsdale and Bruce Berman, 'Coping with the Contradictions: The Development of the Colonial State in Kenya, 1895–1914,' *Journal of African History*, XX, 4 (1979), pp. 487–505.

[9] See, for instance, Henry Bernstein, 'African Peasantries: A Theoretical Framework,' *Journal of Peasant Studies*, VI, 4 (1979), pp. 421–44; and Sara Berry's critique, 'The Food Crisis.'

production. The premise has only reinforced the anthropological presupposition that, unlike wage labor, labor for subsistence production is too immersed in the 'social' schedules of peasants to be subjected to historical investigation.[10] Thus, while wage labor has been the subject of much historical discussion in African studies, agricultural labor has been treated either as a 'backdrop' and the exclusive province of agricultural economics and geography, or as a variable that changed automatically in response to shifts in the market and politics.

Despite its many links with the political, social and ecological systems, food production in the Tchiri Valley can be analysed as an autonomous subject of historical inquiry, with its own dynamics and contradictions. The contradiction between the social and technical requirements of food production had reached a new stage by the end of the nineteenth century. Peasants resisted tenant and wage labor, and adopted cotton cultivation on their own, rather than on the terms dictated by the colonial state. The subsequent interaction between cotton and food cultivation also reveals an important dimension of commodity production which had been ignored by Africanist scholars: through their quiet and laborious work in the fields, peasants could significantly alter colonial beliefs and agricultural policy.

CHANGE AND CONTINUITY IN LOCAL FARMING PRACTICES IN THE LATE NINETEENTH CENTURY

The farming practices of the Mang'anja people of the Tchiri Valley during the second half of the nineteenth century contradict the static and vent-for-surplus models of agricultural production in precolonial Africa.[11] Land was abundant only in absolute terms. Erratic and low rainfalls, which averaged 32 inches in a normal wet season from November to March, combined with frequent droughts (one every five to seven years), to reduce the agricultural significance of the extensive *mphala*-land.[12] *Mphala* is the raid-dependent dryland of light, sandy soils

---

[10] Keith Hart, *The Political Economy of West African Agriculture* (Cambridge Univ. Press, Cambridge, 1982), p. 10.

[11] John Tosh, 'The Cash Crop Revolution.'

[12] Elias C. Mandala, 'Capitalism, Ecology and Society: the Lower Tchiri (Shire) Valley of Malawi, 1860–1960,' (Unpublished PhD dissertation, University of Minnesota, 1983), pp. 1–8.

found at a distance of two to ten miles away from the Tchiri river, extending towards the mountains that run parallel to the river on the east and west. The *mphala* accounts for over 85 per cent of the arable land in the region. Only the remaining 15 per cent (400 square miles) of the land is immune to drought. This was the *dambo* floodland that bordered the Tchiri river. In most places the *dambo* did not extend two miles beyond the river banks. The two notable exceptions are the large Dabanyi (also known as 'Elephant' since the 1850s) and Dinde marshes in the central and southern portions of the Valley. The demand for this fertile land always far exceeded supply.[13]

Most peasant households tried to insulate themselves from the vagaries of the weather, especially drought, by maintaining a plot on the *dambo* in addition to the regular *munda* (plural: *minda*) field on the *mphala*. The combination of the two agricultural systems made cultivation an all-year round activity. The view of the idle, precolonial peasant reduces to arrogant ideology, for, in addition to the labor demands of the two agricultural systems, the people of the Tchiri Valley also supported a complex nonagricultural sector before the 1890s.[14] To meet the existing subsistence levels, peasants allocated their labor among many economic activities.

Under the rain-dependent or *munda* system, the Mang'anja grew staple crops: millet (of the *gonkho* variety) and sorghum (*m[a]chewere*). Other crops raised on the *munda* included the small-grained but heat resistant maize, locally known as *kanjere-mkwera* and more significantly, cotton (*thonje*), which was made into cloth for local use and for sale in the Tchiri

[13] This is the basis of the *nchoche* system under which growers from the local hills and the Tchiri Highlands leased gardens on the *dambo* from headmen in the valley plain on a fee – usually part of the harvest. See 'Tchiri Valley Economy and Society' TVES (a collection of oral testimonies recorded by the author in the valley in 1980): 3/2; Waller Diaries (Rhodes House, Oxford University, Gen. 1803–9): August 6, 1862; A. W. R. Duly, 'The Lower Shire District: Notes on Land Tenure and Individual Rights,' *Nyasaland Journal*, I, 2 (July 1948), p. 44. 'Ownership' of the highly prized *dambo* rather than that of the extensive *mphala* signified a social relation.

[14] For a more detailed discussion of nonagricultural production and exchange during the late nineteenth century, see Elias Mandala, 'Capitalism, Ecology and Society,' pp. 24–31, 83–107. The use of the term *dimba* for the floodlands – as I have done in my previous writings – is not correct. The floodlands in their natural state are known as *dambo*. The term *dimba* refers only to the gardens and the agricultural system as a whole. Similarly, the term *mphala* refers to the land only. The gardens based on the cultivation of the *mphala* are known as *munda* (plural: *minda*).

Highlands and the Lower Zembezi. The preparatory work started in
September. The amount of labor required at this stage varied according
to the age of the *munda*. The arduous work of opening fresh gardens
(*kuswa mphanje*) was done by men. It included the cutting of grass and
the pruning of branches of large trees, like the *mtondo*, the trunks of which
were left to wither before being set on fire. The short-handled iron hoe
and axe were the only instruments of labor.[15]

A free Mang'anja male would be required to open a fresh *munda* only
when he moved to a new village either as an immigrant or as a prospective
son-in-law (*mkamwini*). Under the Mang'anja *chikamwini* or brideservice
arrangement, a young man had to open a fresh *munda* for his parents-
in-law and for himself as proof of his ability to maintain a household.
Well established married males maintained their old *minda* for an
indefinite number of years. Shifting cultivation was a rare practice in
the Valley during the nineteenth century,[16] partly because of the labor
requirements of the second cultivation system to be described below.

Preparatory work on the perennial *minda* was a relatively lighter
exercise, and women generally joined their husbands. The work was
limited to the felling of new grass and the stalks of old crops, which were
later burned for ashes to be used as fertilizer. All crops were planted
on the flat ground. Mound cultivation (*mathutu*) was applied only for
the growing of *kanjera-mkwera* on the sloping *mphala*. In other localities
even the *kanjera-mkwera* was planted on the flat ground, intercropped with
millet and sorghum.[17]

Labor on all *minda* gardens became intensive during the rainy season,
from late December to March. The fields were continually weeded, and
in the event of a drought, peasants replanted where the initial November
plantings had failed. Sorghum and maize were harvested in April, while
the slower maturing *gonkho* millet remained on the fields until the
commencement of the second or *dimba* agricultural system on the *dambo*
floodlands.

Until the 1890s *dimba* farming did not conflict with the *munda* system.
The *dambo* became available for farming from June to December after

[15] Mandala, 'Capitalism, Ecology and Society,' pp. 22–4.

[16] Mandala, 'Capitalism, Ecology and Society,' pp. 21–4; see also Megan Vaughan,
'Social and Economic Change in Southern Malawi: A Study of Rural Communities
in the Shire Highlands and Upper Shire from the Mid-Nineteenth Century to 1915'
(PhD. Dissertation, University of London, 1981), pp. 37–60.

[17] Mandala, 'Capitalism, Ecology and Society,' pp. 20–4.

the floods had receded for a period of less than six months. The onerous task of opening *dimba* gardens was performed exclusively by men. Each flood season brought to the marshes a thick floating bush of grass, reeds and the common *bande*.[18] The *bande* formed a sinuous structure after the floods, making the opening of even old *dimba* gardens a muscle-breaking, if worthwhile, exercise. The highly fertile *dambo* supported a wider range of crops than the *mphala*: the dry season maize (*chimanga chamgwera* or *murope*), sweet potatoes (*mbatata* or *bambaya*), sugar cane (*mzimbe* or *misale*), and many vegetables (*masamba*) – all intercropped in the same field. In the Dinde marsh peasants also raised wetland rice (*mpunga*), planted before the floods in December after the other crops had just been harvested. The rice was reaped in May, and a substantial amount was exported to the Lower Zembezi before and after the escalation of the slave trade in the 1860s.[19]

The *dimba* and *munda* agricultural cycles began to overlap in the 1880s as a result of the lowering of the Tchiri levels, which exposed more *dambo* for cultivation and for a longer period of time than previously. Instead of June, *dimba* work now started in February and lasted until December. This permitted the cultivation of several, consecutive food crops on the *dambo*. It also created the problem of labor distribution between *dimba* and *munda* farming, particularly during the latter part of the wet season from December to March. Many peasants found their work schedules devoted almost entirely to agriculture, which after the 1880s contributed to the rapid decline of many important branches of the nonagricultural sector when the Mang'anja also grew sesame for market.[20]

No structural change in the patterns of labor mobilization accompanied the new pressures on labor. The early nineteenth-century division of labor persisted well into the twentieth both as material reality and as

[18] The botanical name for *bande* is *Echinochloa haploclada*. See G. Jackson and P. O. Wieche, *An Annotated Check List of Nyasaland Grasses* (Government Press, Zomba, Nyasaland, 1958), p. 37, where it is described as: 'Perennial, up to 2 m. tall, forming loose straggling tufts; stems often floating when growing adjacent to open water; inflorescence very regular with conspicuous awns; spikelets green or reddish-purple.'

[19] Mandala, 'Capitalism, Ecology and Society,' pp. 24, 30, 83–107; Norman Robert Bennett and Marguerite Ylvisaker, eds., *The Central African Journal of Lovell J. Procter, 1860–64* (Boston Univ. Press, Boston, 1971), p. 322; Reginald Foskett, ed., *The Zambesi Journal and Letters of Dr. John Kirk 1858–63* (Oliver and Boyd, Edinburgh, 1965): I, pp. 209–210; John Peter Richard Wallis, ed., *The Zambezi Expedition of David Livingstone, 1858–1863* (Chatto and Windus, London, 1956), I, p. 105.

[20] Mandala, 'Capitalism, Ecology and Society,' pp. 83–107.

ideology. This regime assigned the matrilineage (*mbumba*) – a community of matrilineally related households (*banja*) – as the primary unit of nonagricultural production and exchange. Agricultural production was considered a 'private' activity, carried out by the wife, her husband, and her dependent children as members of the *banja* household.[21] Only chiefs and heads of important households enjoyed institutional access to the labor of non-*banja* members in agriculture. The idea that one does not exploit extra-household or kinship ties for agricultural production continued to inform the practice of ordinary peasants even after the decline of the nonagricultural sector and the increase in agricultural activities. So firm was the separation of agricultural labor from the communally based nonagricultural production in the Mang'anja economy and thought that during the twentieth century all new channels of labor recruitment developed outside kinship ties.[22] This discrepancy between the patterns of labor recruitment and those of labor usage would have important repercussions for the rise of the colonial economy and for cotton agriculture.

COTTON CULTIVATION, THE FOOD ECONOMY AND THE STATE, 1907–40

Nyasaland's colonial rulers discriminated against African farming systems in favor of capitalist production. Despite their knowledge of the Valley as an important cotton growing area before the 1880s,[23] they introduced cotton in 1902 as a settler crop to be grown exclusively by Europeans on the Highlands. Africans were to participate only as tenant and wage laborers. But the Highlands proved unsuitable for cotton cultivation. The administration then encouraged European farmers to move to the lowlands, including the Tchiri Valley. An estate economy struggled for survival in the valley from 1905 to the 1920s, when it collapsed in competition with a vigorous peasant cotton regime.[24] A major

[21] Mandala, 'Capitalism, Ecology and Society,' pp. 24–31.

[22] See p. 16–17 below.

[23] Public Record Office (PRO), FO2/66: Harry Johnston, 'Report on the First Three Years' Administration of British Central Africa,' March 31, 1894.

[24] Joseph Elias Chakanza, 'The Rise and Decline of a Plantation Economy in Nsanje District, 1895–1945' (Unpublished Student Seminar Paper, History Department, University of Malawi, 1976–77); Mandala, 'Capitalism, Ecology and Society,' pp. 118–36.

implication of the noted divergence in the development of labor usage and recruitment patterns was a sharpened awareness of the value of household labor in meeting the current standards of subsistence. Any new system of production that diverted labor from the food economy became a potential focus of rural resistance.

Peasants perceived estate agriculture as the most formidable threat to subsistence production. The notorious *thangata* regime, first developed by European tea and tobacco farmers on the Highlands, required tenants to pay rent in labor.[25] The head of every tenant household had to work for the landlord at least two months during the wet season from December to March, when cultivators weeded their *munda* fields, replanted where crops failed, and after 1890, also the time that cultivation on the *dambo* started. In the Valley, *thangata* came to be known as *uzungu*, or slavery under the white man, and tenants tried everything to withold their labor. Some demanded that rent be paid in cash rather than labor; some refused to pay any rent at all; the majority, either as individuals or in groups, simply deserted their landlords. From its inception, estate agriculture in the Valley depended on migrant and particularly Lomwe labor from Mozambique. The only time that local labor satisfied the demands of the estate sector was in 1918–1923, when a combination of drought, floods, and small-pox and influenza epidemics severely disrupted peasant production and undermined resistance. The end of these calamities dried up the local labor supply, and European farmers began to compete with African growers for foreign, Lomwe labor. Labor shortages after the Mwamthota famine of 1920–23 aggravated other problems of the estate sector and speeded its collapse.[26]

Before the calamities of 1918–23, 'free' peasants on unclaimed or Crown land had adopted several cash-earning strategies to avoid employment on the European estates. These included beer brewing, the sale of surplus foodstuffs, head-porterage and, after 1908, railway construction work, none of which required the long-term withdrawal of labor from food cultivation, as did work on the estates. Railway construction attracted mostly unmarried and the recently married males who had little or no access to *dimba* farming. They sold their labor-power during the sluggish *munda* cultivation period and returned to their fields

[25] John A. Kamchitete Kandawire, *Thangata: Forced Labour or Reciprocal Asistance?* (Research and Publication Committee of the University of Malawi, Zomba, 1978).

[26] Mandala, 'Capitalism, Ecology and Society,' pp. 118–36.

soon afterwards. Colonial attempts to bind the local labor force more or less permanently and the unfavorable work conditions made employment on the railways as unpopular as work on the estates. Young Mang'anja men who had to pay taxes, and their Sena counterparts who had to pay both bridewealth and the taxes, left the valley to work in South Africa and Southern Rhodesia (Zimbabwe).[27] The emigration, which Mang'anja elders came to accept only as an alternative to the more exploitative and inhumane wage-labor regime, tapered off once peasant cotton agriculture became securely established after the Mwamthota famine of 1921-23. Smallholder cotton production became the most effective form of resistance to tenancy and wage labor for it embraced all sectors of the rural population: women and men, the young and the old.

The development of peasant cotton agriculture in the Valley highlights two main issues in the debate over the relation of the state to production in colonial Africa. The first concerns the nature of colonial agricultural policy. Study of Nyasaland's policy indicates that colonial planners were more responsive to changes in material conditions than scholars in the underdevelopment tradition have recognized. Colonial policy proved as inconsistent as the many and contradictory objectives it was supposed to serve. The goals of Nyasaland's planners ranged from the preservation of rural social relations to the promotion of capitalist production and from the regulation of the conflict between peasants and European traders and farmers to the monitoring of the relations of metropolitan and local capitalists. To preserve the integrity of the state and its primary mission of serving metropolitan, British, capitalist interests, colonial officials shifted their alliances from one to another class or fraction.

The conflict between settler and peasant production in colonial planning surfaced early. It did not begin with a theoretical discussion about the merits of the government's commitment to settler production, for most colonial officials believed in the intrinsic superiority of capitalist over peasant production. Rather, the performance of the estate sector provoked it. Mr. S. Simpson, the officially designated cotton 'expert' who arrived in 1905, was so appalled by European cotton farming on the Highlands that he began to question the administration's belief that only capitalist enterprise could 'develop' the country. He subsequently translated into action his verbal attacks on the 'inefficient' European

---

[27] Mandala, 'Capitalism, Ecology and Society,' pp. 114-25.

farms by asking district administrators to distribute cotton seeds to peasants in the Lakeshore area, Mulanje and the Tchiri Valley.[28] And while the experiment did not prove a spectacular success, it compared favorably enough to estate production to weaken the state's alliance with European farmers. It enabled Mr. Simpson to gain some converts to his vision of a peasant cotton economy that straddled the officially sponsored settler agriculture. High on the list of converts was Mr. J. McCall, who arrived in 1909 as the first Director of the newly established Department of Agriculture.

In a major policy shift, Mr. McCall called upon the state to take a more positive role in peasant cotton agriculture. He successfully lobbied for the passage of the first peasant cotton legislation in the country. Amidst strong opposition from the settler community, the state extended to peasant cotton growers the tax rebate (originally designed to cover only wage laborers). A peasant could fulfil his or her 'hut' tax obligation (3 shillings per year) by selling to the government or any European 36 lbs of cotton in the Valley and 42 lbs elsewhere.[29]

In the Valley the rebate strengthened rural opposition to wage employment on the estate and the railways, and it transformed the nature of struggle for tenants. The tenants demanded the right to grow cotton in their estate plots, so that they could pay their rent in cash.[30] When landlords refused permission or offered lower prices than those which prevailed in the state-controlled markets, tenants deserted the estates to join 'free' peasants on the land still unoccupied by Europeans – the Crownland.

The passage of the tax bill also represented the triumph of metropolitan over local capitalist interests. Unlike the settlers, metropolitan capitalists, like the empire-wide British Cotton Growing Association (BCGA), were more interested in cotton as a finished product than in the specific system of labor control under which it was raised. They sided with any group that made cotton available on the market. The BCGA, through its operations in countries like Nigeria or Uganda, knew that the peasants could grow cotton – and more cheaply than European settlers could.

[28] Malawi National Archives (MNA), NSB1/1/1: Simpson to District Resident, Blantyre, June 17, 1908; PRO, CO525/13: Simpson to Colonial Office, July 11, 1906.

[29] MNA, A2/1/3: 'Cotton Growing by Natives, 1909.'

[30] MNA, A/1/4: Ruo District Commissioner to Director of Agriculture (hereinafter as DA) Feb. 10, 1913; TVES1/10; TVES2/3, 7–9; TVES5/1–3.

Thus, while granting soft loans to European farmers, the BCGA also supported the movement toward smallholder production, if not as an alternative, then as a supplement to the fragile estate economy. Mr. J. Percival, who arrived in 1910 as the first representative of the BCGA,[31] became a close ally of Mr. McCall, although he too entertained the idea that the estate sector would become the mainstay of the country's cotton production. The hope began to fade as the estate sector continued to perform poorly and many farmers defaulted on their loans. The Tchiri Valley was officially removed from the list of areas to be 'developed' through capitalism in 1923, when many planters could not cultivate their land because of a labor shortage. The Director of Agriculture then declared that no more land was to be sold or leased to European settlers.[32] Metropolitan, capitalist interests could be served effectively at no political cost through an alliance with the productive peasantry. Colonial agricultural policy was more dynamic than is suggested by such simplistic formulas as 'promotion-or-strangulation,' which have dominated the literature on agrarian change in Central and Southern Africa.

The second issue concerns the state's ability to enforce its own programs, for scholars have exaggerated state power in colonial Africa. The Director of Agriculture's circular letter of 1909 went further than merely announcing the tax rebate. It contained a list of instructions that together sought to establish the primacy of cotton over food cultivation. According to the blueprint for estate farming, peasants were required to plant cotton seeds during 'the first month of the rains . . . in November,' when peasants also sowed their seeds of sorghum, millet and maize on the *munda*. The regulations required peasants to grow cotton on fields separate from food crops and on 'long ridges' of about four feet apart.[33] Cotton was to be treated differently than food crops, which peasants continued to raise on the flat ground.

The colonial regime had only limited success in enforcing its first agricultural program, for colonial power was derivative. The effectiveness of colonial rule depended on the degree of its 'consumption' of the powers

[31] MNA, A2/1/6: Acting DA, 'Report on the Operations of the BCGA in Nyasaland During the Year 1911'; J. McCall, 'Special Report on the Operations of the BCGA, 1910–12,' August 2, 1912; MNA, A1/1/4: BCGA (Manchester) to DA, March 31, 1913.

[32] MNA, A3/2/68 (same as S1/2004/23): DA, 'Report on a Visit to the Lower Shire District,' June 1923.

[33] MNA, A2/1/3: 'Cotton Growing by Natives, 1909'; 'Report for June, 1909.'

of the indigenous rulers who, [34] notwithstanding their presentation in the literature as a homogeneous category, were a composite of fractions. Village headmen (leaders of village communities) and 'chiefs' (territorial leaders) had differing relations with the colonial state and the peasantry in different localities over time.[35] It was comparatively easier for the state to enforce elements of its program in much of the Chikwawa area, where the foreign Kololo chiefs had effectively undermined the position of the indigenous Mang'anja headmen since the mid-nineteenth century.[36] They only had to convert the handful of powerful members of the Kololo aristocracy into faithful administrators. The task proved much more complicated in much of Nsanje district, where headmen continued to contest the power of their peers, who had suddenly been raised to the position of chiefs by the colonial state. Mang'anja and Sena headmen pursued their personal and heightened sense of group interest by insulating their communities from outside intervention by chiefs and the British administration.[37] They proved to be the least reliable allies of the colonial state, particularly in matters of labor recruitment and cotton production.

These political rivalries, in demographic and ecological context, strengthened rural opposition to the cotton blueprint, which entirely ignored the labor and land requirements of the food economy. Only a small percentage of growers adopted elements of the blueprint. These were predominantly Mang'anja peasants living in western Chikwawa and in the Tengani chiefdom of Nsanje district. Both areas were ruled by strong and autocratic chiefs, the Kololo in Chikwawa and the Tengani in Nsanje – sparsely populated areas with little or no *dimba* agriculture. The peasants continued to reject the provision that cotton be grown on ridges (*mitumbira*), but for the most part planted cotton in November in fields separate from food crops. Both fields were sometimes located on the *mphala*. In areas bordering the Dabanyi marsh the

[34] For an illuminating examination of this issue, see Karen E. Fields, *Revival and Rebellion in Colonial Central Africa* (Princeton Univ. Press, Princeton, 1985).

[35] The distinction between chiefs and headmen became problematic after the collapse of the Lundu state in the eighteenth century and continued to be so in the southern part of the valley until the imposition of British colonialism. (Mandala, 'Capitalism, Ecology and Society,' pp. 222–30).

[36] Elias C. Mandala, 'The Kololo Interlude in Southern Malawi, 1861–1895' (MA Thesis, University of Malawi, 1977), pp. 96–120.

[37] Mandala, 'Capitalism, Ecology and Society,' pp. 123, 222–30.

general practice was to grow food on the *dambo* and cotton on the *mphala*.[38]

The majority of growers in the Valley rejected the entire set of cotton rules. High population densities in southern Nsanje and eastern Chikwawa made the goal of pure cotton fields unrealizable for most peasants. The combination of *dimba* and *munda* farming left little or no room in the agricultural work schedules of the cultivators, who had to treat cotton as a supplementary (catch) crop, subject to the requirements of food cultivation. Village headmen received the seeds for distribution but ignored the instructions of district administrators and agricultural officers. The primacy of cotton was equated with tenant and wage labor.

Ironically, cotton agriculture never 'took off' where state ('chiefly') power was strongest, as in western Chikwawa and the Tegani chiefdom. Smallholder production was strongest in precisely those areas in which state power was weakest and rural protest most effective.

With the support of their headmen, growers in the south and the northeast continued to apply the techniques used since 1907, before the state became interested in their enterprise. Some of these techniques originated in the precolonial era, when cotton production constituted an integral part of the local and regional economy. Chief among the revived methods was a variation of crop rotation on the *munda*, according to which peasants planted cotton not in November, as the Agricultural Department stipulated, but in March-April after sorghum and maize had been harvested. Cotton grew together with the slow-maturing *gonkho* millet on the same field until the latter was reaped in May-June. The cotton was harvested in August-September.[39] Peasants in these areas had neither the land nor the labor to treat cotton separately.

Colonial authorities were either too contented with peasant performance or too busy devising ways to improve the estate sector to take notice of the rotation technique. The report by the Director of Agriculture in 1915 – the earliest known reference to the technique – summarized his observations on cotton growing in the southern section of Nsanje (Port Herald) District:

[38] TVES2/3; TVES4/1, 6, 9; TVES6/2, 4.
[39] TVES2/3, TVES4/1, 6, 9; TVES 6/2, 4; MNA, A3/1/3: DA to BCGA (Manchester), Dec. 23, 1915.

The Lower Shire District is very heavily populated south of Port Herald and a large number of villagers are situated on light soil along the foot hills and the cotton in this area is largely planted on the *same* soil as the food crops *after* they have been harvested.[40]

The suggestion that this deviation from the Department's original blueprint resulted from experimental work done at the government farm at Nyachiperi, must be considered a face-saving mechanism. No experimental work worthy of the name had been done at the farm by this time.

Elsewhere, peasants tried a completely new technique of growing cotton. They breached the Department of Agriculture's ruling 'never to mix cotton with food crops' by growing it together with maize, beans, sweet potatoes on a land (the *dambo*) that no colonial expert had thought suitable for cotton. Planted immediately after the floods had receded in February and March, the cotton was harvested in September and October. The bulk of the cotton, which the African Lakes Corporation bought on behalf of the BCGA in 1907–1909 and which the Director of Agriculture used in support of his argument for a peasant alternative, had been raised under this method in the Dinde marsh.[41] The technique became widely used in the Dabanyi marsh during World War I. Observers were then able to contrast the relative merits of *dimba* and *munda* farming, as the following report implies:

> On walking across the (Dinde) marsh I saw that the quality of the cotton was very good. Probably here is grown the most satisfactory native cotton in the Lower Shire. . . . On the other side of Port Herald (i.e. Tengani area) a different state of affairs exists . . . the crop in this district will not be very good. . . . The size of the plants gets smaller as one goes further out (on the *mphala*).[42]

The undeclared war against state intervention in the production process had been won for the time being. The victory made the Crownlands

---

[40] MNA, A3/13: DA to BCGA (Manchester), Dec. 23, 1915. Emphasis added.

[41] MNA, A2/1/3: 'Cotton Growing by Natives, 1910.' See also TVES1/12; TVES3/9; TVES5/2, 4–5, 9; TVES6/6–7. The system was described in greater detail by agricultural officers after 1930: MNA, A3/2/53,54,65,200–203: Annual and Monthly Reports, 1930–38.

[42] MNA, A3/1/3: District Agricultural Officer (H. Munro) to DA, Aug. 16, 1915.

on which 'free' peasants lived more attractive to tenants who were struggling against the tyranny of rent-labor. The Tchiri Valley came out of World War I with two distinct cotton cultures: the first in several variations, based on the *mphala*, and the second on the *dambo*.

Intercropping and rotation reduced the level of conflict over good agricultural land, which in some areas had already become a scarce resource before the outbreak of the war. The two techniques also minimized the problem of labor distribution between food and commodity production. Rotation merely extended the period of cultivation on the *mphala*, and intercropping only intensified *dimba* agriculture. The two methods also ensured the popularity of cotton farming in the Valley. Single women, as well as wives of polygamous husbands who had no other sources of labor besides their dependent children, were able to participate fully in the cotton economy. They raised cotton at the same time and in the same fields as food crops. Over 97 per cent of all households in Nsanje district were registered cotton growers in 1925.[43] The Valley emerged as the center of peasant cotton agriculture in colonial Malawi, producing between 50–98 per cent of all the cotton exported from 1909 to 1940.[44]

Much of this cotton was grown in Nsanje (Port Herald) district, and one BCGA representative admitted that peasants in this district were more exploited than those in other parts of the country, including the Chikwawa district: 'The Port Herald District has been the mainstay of the Protectorate for many years, and the natives have done more for the country than all the others put together . . . they had the least done for them.'[45] The larger Chikwawa district contributed less than fifty per cent of all the cotton exported from the Valley during 1909–40, partly because of its smaller population. But the main reason appears to lie in the cultivation techniques. Whether practised on the *dimba* or on the *mphala*, the pure cotton field method placed a heavier burden on household labor than did rotation or intercropping. Only 76 per cent of the households in the district grew cotton in 1925.[46]

While the *mbumba* extended family continued to exercise influence on matters relative to land distribution, actual production rested on

[43] MNA, A3/2/233: 'Production Per Head of Export Crops, 1925.' The comparative figure for Chikwawa was 76.6.

[44] Mandala, 'Capitalism, Ecology and Society,' Table IV, p. 148a.

[45] MNA, A3/2/233: 'Production Per Head of Export Crops.

[46] *Ibid.*

household labor. Kinship retained its precolonial 'invisibility' in agricultural work. The lack of institutional access to the labor of one's kinspeople may have contributed to the popularity of the labor-saving techniques of rotation and intercropping and the weakness of the cotton economy in those areas in which for political, ecological and demographic reasons, peasants did not sufficiently subordinate cotton to food production. The cultivation techniques employed in western Chikwawa and the Tengani chiefdom might have been effective under a different system of division of labor. In many parts of colonial Africa commodity production developed in the context of a labor division that consigned female and male labor to food and cash crop production, respectively. Such a transformation, which often gave men more control over the cash economy, was staunchly resisted by the traditionally independent Mang'anja women.[47]

The two popular channels of labor control that developed in the aftermath of the cotton economy had no roots in precolonial Mang'anja society and arose outside the domain of kinship ties. The first was wage labor, which, as in colonial Ghana, employed migrants, particularly the Lomwe from Mozambique.[48] The other major source of extra-household labor was the *nomi* – inter-village, youth labor associations brought to the Valley by Sena immigrants from the Lower Zembezi. *Nomi* members rendered agricultural and other services against payment in cash or kind. Rich peasants (or *zunde*-holders) and European estate farmers benefited from both types of labor. *Nomi* services became accessible to the predominantly Sena peasantry in the south and northeast between the two world wars.[49] Before, Sena and Mang'anja growers depended almost entirely on household labor, just as their counterparts in the northwest did throughout the colonial era.

Cotton agriculture, despite a negligible impact on the precolonial division of labor, did shape the course of food production and supply. The impact was largely negative, although the degree of disruption varied

[47] Elias Mandala, 'Capitalism, Kinship and Gender in the Lower Tchiri (Shire) Valley of Malawi, 1860–1960: An Alternative Theoretical Framework,' *African Economic History*, 13 (1984), pp. 137–69.

[48] TVES5/2,3; TVES6/2; MNA, A3/2/201: Monthly Reports for June and July 1933; MNA, S1/79A/36 (NSP2/1/5) and S1/79B/36: Annual Reports for respectively Port Herald and Chikwawa Districts, 1935.

[49] Matthew Schoffeleers, 'From Socialization to Personal Enterprise: A History of the *nomi* Labor Societies in the Nsanje District of Malawi, c.1891–1972,' *Rural Africana*, 20 (Spring 1973), pp. 11–25; Mandala, 'Capitalism, Ecology and Society,' pp. 126–7, 170–4.

between techniques over time. The adoption of the Department of Agriculture's requirement that cotton be grown in separate fields created a labor distribution problem that adversely affected food production. In order to raise first-grade cotton,[50] labor-deficient households spent more time in looking after cotton than food crops. The amount of cash realized from cotton sales was directly related to the degree of attention given to the cotton field during the weeding season. Often, in areas like the Tengani chiefdom, where peasants adopted the pure cotton garden method because of political pressure, well-cultivated cotton fields flourished alongside untidy gardens of food crops. As one perceptive administrator commented upon returning to the Valley after several years of absence:

> Much has been done to improve cotton growing but practically nothing with regard to the far more important food crops. When I came back to the District after four years of absence I was very much struck with the lack of progress in the production of food crops. *In some respects thing have changed for the worse.*[51]

Other reports lamented the peasants' neglect of such essential tasks as the scaring of birds from sorghum and millet fields.[52] Food crops raised alongside cotton on the *mphala* were particularly vulnerable to the labor diversion effect of commodity agriculture. The two *munda* fields fell within the same agricultural cycle.

That the food economy also suffered under crop rotation and intercropping cautions against romanticizing peasant initiative and technical knowledge. Rotation may have accelerated the depletion of the fragile *mphala* soils, as some colonial observers have remarked. More significantly, the technique led to the disappearance of *gonkho* millet in many parts of the Valley since the 1920s. Villagers discovered that cotton mixed with *gonkho* after the harvesting of maize and sorghum yielded

---

[50] Cotton was classified into three categories. The prices for grades 1, 2 and 3 at Karonga market in 1922 were 1.75, 1.25 and 0.75 pennies per lb. (MNA, A3/2/75: Karonga District Commissioner to DA, Sept. 19, 1922). During the depression buyers refused to buy grades 2 and 3.

[51] MNA, NSP2/1/3: Port Herald (Nsanje) District Annual Report, 1930. Emphasis added.

[52] MNA, A3/2/200: Monthly Reports, Feb. 1931; Jan. 1932. The reason actually cited was, of course, that peasants were lazy.

poor results. The tall *gonkho* shaded the shorter cotton plants at the time of flowering. The resulting elimination of the *gonkho* and the increasing reliance on maize were recognized as significantly contributing to the recurrence of food shortages during the 1920s and 1930s. *Gonkho* was the most heat resilient cereal in the area, and its disappearance exposed the food economy to the dangers of drought.[53]

Less conspicuous but no less distorting for production was the popular method of intercropping cotton with food crops on the *dambo*. Cotton on the *dambo* permitted only one maize crop, planted at the beginning of the *dimba* cycle. No other maize crop was grown after the harvesting of the first since the slower maturing cotton was still on the ground. In contrast, growers, like those in northwestern Chikwawa, who reserved the *dambo* exclusively for food production, were able to raise several, consecutive maize cultures, as their precolonial ancestors had done when cotton was restricted to the *mphala*.[54]

The periodic food shortages aggravated by cotton agriculture did not lead to general famines during 1922 to 1940 – generally considered a period of 'prosperity' in the Valley. The rise of an intricate system of food distribution moderated the largely negative effects of cotton farming. The new system, largely the creation of the cotton economy, superimposed itself on the older patterns of supply that had linked the *mphala* and *dambo* ecological zones and Valley with the Highlands. While peasants kept the state at arms-length with regard to production, they had little choice but to accept the paternalistic intervention of the state in the sale of cotton. The state established an elaborate and tightly controlled marketing system, which it used to raise revenue, to regulate the antagonistic relations of peasants with cotton buyers, and to guarantee the supremacy of metropolitan over local traders.[55]

New centers of food distribution arose as extensions to the cotton markets. Some of the new food markets later came under the control of Native Authorities, as chiefs were called after 1932. But most were in the hands of Indian traders. Indians operated many shops, especially after 1923 when the state expelled them from cotton markets and granted

[53] TVES5/6; MNA, NSP2/1/1: Port Herald District Annual Report, 1925/6; MNA, A3/2/200: Monthly Reports, Feb. 1932; Feb. and Nov. 1934.

[54] Foskett, Reginald, ed., *The Zambesi Journal of Dr. John Kirk*, I, p. 164; TVES1/2,14.

[55] Mandala, 'Capitalism, Ecology and Society,' p. 151–9.

the BCGA a monopoly over all peasant-grown cotton in the Valley.[56] Indians then concentrated their efforts in those trades in which they faced no competition from Europeans: cloth, hoes, and food. They purchased the peasants' surplus food at the time of harvest and imported other cereals from the Highlands,[57] which they later sold to peasants at inflated prices.

Indian traders made this food available even to poor peasants by giving credit to anyone who grew cotton. Peasants pledged against the cotton in the field. Thus, Indians, although legally barred from cotton growing and purchasing, succeeded in controlling the cotton economy by indirectly employing peasants to grow cotton for them. The link between cotton and the food economy became apparent during the depression. Indians took legal action against villagers who defaulted on their loans. Such traders were often forced to accept cotton in lieu of cash.[58] The end of the depression re-established the increasingly false sense of prosperity among the peasants and their British rulers.

FROM ACCOMMODATION TO INTERVENTION:
CHANGES IN STATE POLICY, 1909–51

Nyasaland's colonial rulers, contented with the performance of the peasant sector, neither attempted to introduce new cotton techniques nor to revive the Agricultural Department's blueprint of 1909. Instead, a growing number of experts began to accept the rationality of peasant farming systems. Two factors, together with the relative weakness of state power, undermined the position of the interventionists in the production of cotton. First, the government extended its participation in the lucrative marketing system, and the organization of markets absorbed all of the country's meager resources. All local administrators

[56] MNA, A3/2/67: 'Agreement with the BCGA,' 1922; MNA, A3/2/68: 'Development of the Native Cotton Industry,' May 9, 1923. The initial contract was for a five year period and was to be renewed every three years thereafter.

[57] MNA, A3/2/200: Agricultural Monthly Reports: Dec. 1931; April, 1934; MNA, NSP2/1/4: Port Herald District Annual report, 1933; MNA, S1/88B/35: Chikwawa District Annual Report, 1934.

[58] MNA, S1/225/20: Memorandum by the DA; MNA, S1/60F/32, NSP2/1/4: Port Herald District Annual Reports, 1931, 1933, respectively; MNA, Lower Shire District Book IV (1928–32); MNA, NSC2/1/3: Chikwawa District Annual Report, 1934.

and the personnel of the Department of Agriculture were engaged in the marketing of cotton.[59] Second, the estate sector collapsed. Intervention in peasant cotton cultivation had grown out of the government's concern with estate production, the demise of which removed the Tchiri Valley from a colonial obsession with soil conservation.

The state signaled its retreat from the sphere of production in 1922, when it closed the Nyachiperi farm near Nsanje township, which had been established in the early 1910s to conduct experiments for the benefit of European farming. In 1923 the state turned down the request of the Director of Agriculture for the reopening of the farm under an officer who would be paid an annual salary of £150, to come from the £7,259,000 received by the state from the BCGA. Under the terms granted the monopoly, the BCGA had to share its profits with the state.[60] The station was only partially re-opened in 1925, when it was taken over by the Empire Cotton Growing Corporation (ECGC), a research consortium under Mr. H. D. Ducker. Mr. Ducker lived in Zomba, and no experiments were done until 1930 when the ECGC employed Mr. E. Lawrence as the first agricultural officer posted since 1922.

The ability of peasants to feed themselves while increasing their cotton output transformed official detachment from production into the policy of accommodation or inactivity. The accommodation with African farming systems had started during World War I, when startled by the effectiveness of the techniques of rotation and intercropping, some officials tried to 'appropriate' them by falsely claiming that the methods had been developed at the Nyachiperi farm.[61] This claim, designed to re-establish shaken confidence in the rationality of colonial technical knowledge, did not stand against time. Officials who came later and with no knowledge of the Department of Agriculture's original plan accepted and praised peasant initiative in cotton cultivation and even defended the techniques against the imposition of new ones. Mr. Lawrence expressed the view of many other experts in 1930: 'Until more is known about the optimum spacings, etc. for millet in the district, the Native Agricultural Instructors are told not to advise anything very drastic in the way of change'.[62]

[59] MNA, A3/2/54: H. C. Ducker to DA, Dec. 15, 1936; Mandala, 'Capitalism, Ecology and Society,' pp. 151–9.

[60] MNA, A3/2/180: Agricultural Report for 1924; MNA, S1/481/21: Report on the African Cotton Industry, 1923.

[61] MNA, A3/1/3: DA to BCGA (Manchester), Dec. 23, 1915.

[62] MNA, A3/2/200: Agricultural Monthly Report, Dec. 1930.

Mr. Ducker went so far as to suggest that European agriculture failed in the area because of the white farmers' unwillingness to learn from African growers. He later introduced the local *dimba* cultivation techniques to the Karonga district on the northern shores of Lake Malawi.[63] The Director of Agriculture reiterated the policy of accommodation in the annual report for 1933:

> A close study of native methods on the Lower River has shown that the native practice of growing millets, cotton and legumes in the same garden is a sound one when the time at his disposal for agricultural work, his way of living and his fear of hunger are taken into account.[64]

Colonial rulers did not relentlessly and uniformly pursue their cherished beliefs, as most recent studies suggest. Colonial policy did not operate in a social or political vacuum. British rulers may have come to understand that under certain conditions the absence of any policy could also serve the cause of imperialism.

The Director of Agriculture had to take a stand on the farming practices of the Valley because of the resurgence of interventionist sentiment among some of the country's rulers during the 1930s. A few, 'enlightened,' mostly young administrators, familiar with developments in the more 'advanced' colonies like South Africa and Southern Rhodesia (Zimbabwe), wanted to see the state assume a more positive role in peasant production in order to forestall what they perceived as an impending environmental disaster. But it was not until after the war that some of these ideas became part of official policy. The delay resulted not so much from the controversial nature of the 'scientific' arguments that were being advanced by the proponents of intervention, as from lack of political resources, and, more significant, from the continued ability of the condemned methods to deliver cotton and generate much needed foreign exchange. The victory of the interventionists after the war was to a large measure determined by the diminishing capacity of the peasantry in Nsanje district to increase cotton output and to finance their own oppression.

---

[63] Ducker, 'A Talk on Cotton Growing,' *NAQJ*, I, 1 (Jan. 1941), pp. 14–15; 'The Nyasaland Cotton Crop.' *NAQJ*, X, 4 (Dec. 1951), p. 129.

[64] *Annual Report of the Department of Agriculture for the Year 1933* (Zomba), p. 27.

Prominent among the new critics of the cotton-growing practices of the Valley was Mr. F. Barker, who succeeded Mr. Lawrence as the agricultural officer of the Valley in 1933, when the Nyachiperi farm was handed over to the state.[65] He was well informed about the conservationist debate in Central and Southern Africa. What he observed in the Valley jostled against what conservationists defined as 'sound' farming methods. Instead of large fields, planted to a single crop on neatly constructed ridges, he saw small and irregularly shaped plots, each planted to a host of crops on the flat ground. He concluded that these systems could only lead to all sorts of environmental problems, particularly soil erosion and the spread of the red bollworm (diparopsis castanea).

The red bollworm, which destroyed cotton bolls before they reached full flower, was first identified in 1911,[66] but nothing was done to understand its etiology or methods of control until the ECGC took over the Nyachiperi farm in 1930. The ECGC and the Department of Agriculture advanced several theories to explain its incidence. These included: the disappearance of the indigenous kidney cotton, thought to have hosted the pest in the precolonial past; the end of largescale bush fires; the rise in the moisture content of some soils because of the rise in the levels of the Tchiri River and, more significant, the lack of a universal dead or close season that separated one cotton crop from another.[67]

The lack of a universal dead season resulted from the multiplicity of cotton cultures, each with its own planting and harvesting times. The pure-stand or 'summer' cotton raised alone on the *munda*, was planted in November and picked up in May and June. The cotton rotated with maize and sorghum on *munda* gardens was sown in March and April and harvested only in September. Finally, the *dimba* (or 'winter') cotton intercropped with food crops was planted in March and April and remained in the ground until October and November, when the pure-stand cotton cultivation on the *mphala* was about to begin. There was no time during the year when there was no cotton growing somewhere

[65] MNA, A3/2/201: Agricultural Monthly Report, Nov. 1933.

[66] MNA, A2/12/5: Temporary Agricultural Assistant's (E. B. Gamlen) Report on a Visit to the Ruo District, May 8–20, 1911.

[67] MNA, A3/2/54: BCGA Local Manager to DA, Aug. 4, 1937; MNA, A3/2/65: Ducker to DA, Oct. 6, 1936; MNA, S1/189/38: B. L. Mitchell, 'Survey on the Work in Progress in Nyasaland on the Red Bollworm, Diparopsis Castanea,' Aug., 1939.

in the Valley. The experts argued that the red bollworm of one cotton culture was easily passed over to the next culture.

No further investigation was carried out once the local farming methods were assumed to be the cause. The focus changed from questions about etiology to measures to be taken to combat the pest. This was the 'optimum planting time' debate which, predictably, divided colonial experts into two warring factions. The first, the chief architect of which was Mr. Ducker of the ECGC, proposed late planting. He argued for a planting period that would extend from mid-January to the end of March and for a dead season from mid-November to mid-January. According to his plan, which was also supported by the country's entomologist, Mr. Smee, all cotton stalks were to be uprooted and burned by November 15, and no planting was to take place until January 15.[68] The second faction, the most articulate spokesman of which was Mr. Barker of the Agricultural Department, argued for early planting. In his schedule, the optimum planting period should lie between December and February, preceded by a dead season of five weeks from October to November.[69]

The debate remained unresolved throughout the 1930s and 1940s. The stalemate resulted partly from the appeal of both parties, especially the proponents of early planting, to science as their arbitrator under circumstances in which the controversy had little to do with experimental knowledge. Principally, it concerned differing opinions about African cultivation systems and their relation with commodity production. Embedded in the early planting proposal was the belief that commodity production should take precedence over food cultivation from the perspectives of both land and labor. Cotton was to be treated as an autonomous culture rather than as a catch-crop. But no one who had observed with admiration the success of the locally derived cultivation techniques was ready to accept the scientific garb under which the interventionist argument was cloaked.

The proponents of late planting and of the methods of rotation and intercropping, pointed to several inconsistencies in the 'scientific' argument. They noted that very little research had been done at the

---

[68] MNA, A3/2/54: Entomologist (Smee) to DA, July 23, 1937; Lawrence to DA, 1937; MNA A3/2/65: Ducker to DA, 1933; Oct. 1936.

[69] MNA, A3/2/65: Barker to DA, Feb. 1, 1934; Nov. 8, 1934; DA, 'Cotton Returns, 1923–1936.' MNA, A3/2/71: Barker to DA, 1935.

Nyachiperi farm and that the little that had been done since 1930 had yielded no conclusive evidence to link the red bollworm with the prevailing techniques. They reminded their adversaries that the pest was first identified in 1911 – long before intercropping, rotation, or any form of cotton cultivation had become established in the area. They also recalled how in 1936 the pest did more damage in the northern parts of the country, where peasants neither intercropped nor rotated their cotton with food crops.[70] Mr. Ducker also contended in 1937 that any experiment done at Nyachiperi since 1930 could not be relied upon for prediction in the whole Valley. The soils at the farm carried more moisture than those found elsewhere in the Valley because of the farm's proximity to the Tchiri river. He concluded that much of the failure of cotton output in Nsanje district in 1936 directly resulted from Mr. Barker's unofficial attempts to implement the early planting proposal.[71]

The arguments divided high ranking officials, and nothing was done to resolve the conflict until 1950.[72] No amount of experimental work was sufficient to convert the proponents of late planting. For most elderly statesmen in Zomba the controversy looked esoteric. The cultivation techniques that were being attacked continued to yield more cotton than any other method. Only changes in the specific political and economic situation would decide the issue, as the debate about soil erosion demonstrated.

Soil erosion, was from the beginning, a national rather than local issue. It arose from the colonial government's concern with both cash crop and food production, and by the 1930s there were few disagreements about its causes. Colonial officials at all levels blamed population pressure and African cultivation methods:

> Put very briefly, this position is caused by too many people multiplying too fast and attempting by traditional and inefficient methods to derive an ever-increasing standard of living from a limited amount of land.[73]

[70] MNA, A3/2/54: BCGA Local Manager to Assistant DA, Aug. 4, 1937.

[71] MNA, A3/2/65: Ducker to DA, Oct. 6, 1936; Ducker to Assistant DA, Dec. 5, 1937.

[72] A conference convened in 1937 failed to reach a consensus on the debate. See MNA, A3/2/54: 'Record of a Meeting Held at Zomba on the 26th November, 1937, of the Special Committee Appointed to Consider the Question of the Planting Date for Cotton in Nyasaland.' Also: E. O. Pearson and B. L. Mitchell, *A Report on the Status and Control of Insect Pests of Cotton in the Lower River Districts of Nyasaland* (Zomba, 1945).

[73] Nyasaland Government, *An Outline of Agrarian Problems and Policy in Nyasaland* (Zomba, 1955), p. 2.

And once a region or locality was identified as having the problem, disagreements arose only over the extent of the damage, the measures to be taken, and, sometimes, their effects on soil structures and yields.

As in colonial Southern Rhodesia and South Africa, the problem of erosion in the Valley was first raised in the context of settler rather than peasant farming. In 1915 the Director of Agriculture singled out erosion as one of the two causes – the others being poor procedures of seed selection – for the reduction in the length of cotton staples that originated on European estates. Soil erosion, he wrote to the East Africa Committee of the BCGA in Manchester, resulted from lack of rotation. He estimated that 'at least half of the crop [cotton] produced during the past three years' came from 'land which has grown cotton continuously for periods of 5 to 7 years.' He ended with a note of despair: 'I have preached continuously against this system but with European estates, one cannot control their operations.'[74] The issue died together with the collapse of the estate sector, to re-emerge in the 1930s as a peasant problem in both cotton and noncotton-growing areas.

Two areas in the Valley were singled out as the worst affected by erosion: northeastern Chikwawa, which bordered the Thyolo escarpment, and the whole Nsanje district to the south of Chiromo. The two areas had all the properties that according to the prevailing theory, everywhere precipitated erosion. A census report of 1929 placed southern Nsanje as the most densely populated region in the country, with an average of 300 persons per square mile.[75] Much of the population in the northeast and south was immigrant, consisting of Lomwe and Sena peasants who had fled Portuguese rule in Mozambique. The majority of the Lomwe had initially come from the east as laborers on European estates and their settlements were concentrated along the Thyolo escarpment. The Sena who migrated from the Lower Zembezi before the outbreak of World War I occupied the Dinde and the eastern portion of the Dabanyi marshes. They took an active part in the rise of the peasant cotton economy.[76]

Sena and Lomwe immigrants who came during and after the war found much of the fertile *dambo* already occupied. They settled on the

[74] MNA, A3/1/3: DA to BCGA (Manchester), Dec. 23, 1915: 'Alleged Depreciation of Nyasaland Cotton.'

[75] F. Dixey, 'The Distribution of the Population of Nyasaland,' *Geographical Review*, XVIII, 2 (1928), pp. 274–90.

[76] Mandala, 'Capitalism, Ecology and Society,' pp. 119–22.

mphala, cultivating the light sandy soils, including the foothills that the Mang'anja indigenes had rarely used before. Reports since the late 1910s that the foothills were being denuded of their original vegetation[77] raised the specter of gully in addition to sheet erosion.

The extent of the actual damage remains debatable. Writing while still an employee of the ECGC under Mr. Ducker, Mr. Lawrence denied claims of extensive damage:

> Soil erosion does not present such a great problem on the Lower River plain as in other places. The plain is very flat and the little erosion that would take place during heavy rains is held in check by the native methods of farming – when there is no crop on the ground there are weeds and grass.[78]

Mr. Lawrence changed his position, which was shared by many other noninterventionists, a few years later after being transferred to the Department of Agriculture. He became one of the most outspoken proponents of the Department's anti-erosion campaign in the Valley and elsewhere.

In the period from 1931 to 1937 officials of the Department proposed four different remedies against erosion in the Valley. Only limited action was taken on two of the schemes. The remaining died in the books, including the proposals to plant bands of trees at intervals of about a mile, to run parallel to the mountains and the railway line from Bangula to Nsanje, and to resettle peasants from the congested south to the sparsely populated west bank, between the Thangadzi and the Mkombedz-wa-fodya rivers. Peasants resisted resettlement, whereas some experts objected to the tree planting program. They argued that any plan that reduced the amount of land for cultivation would exaggerate

---

[77] MNA, S1/430/19: Lower Shire District Annual Report, 1918–19 (July 1919 entry).

[78] MNA, A3/2/109: Lawrence to DA, Jan. 21, 1931; see also MNA, A3/2/53: Lawrence to DA, Feb. 17, 1934 in which Mr. Lawrence cites the 'clean weeding fetish' as being responsible for soil erosion against the African system of scatter planting. But see also MNA, A3/2/200: E. Lawrence, 'Soil Erosion on the Lower Shire,' April 3, 1931; Conservator of Forests, 'Memorandum on Soil Erosion,' April 9, 1931; District Agricultural Officer, 'Memorandum on Soil Erosion,' April 17, 1931; DA to District Agricultural Officer, 'Memorandum on Soil Erosion' May 2, 1931.

the problem of erosion and defeat its own purpose. Behind this argument was the fact that the plan was expensive.[79]

The two schemes on which limited action was taken before the war were those which cost nothing to the colonial state: These called upon peasants to box or contour ridge (*mitumbira*) their *munda* gardens and to plant 'village forest areas.'[80] Despite initial success in certain parts of the Valley, the village reforestation program lost its momentum in the late 1930s. The Department of Agriculture became narrowly committed to the *mitumbira* scheme, but until the 1950s the *mitumbira* scheme was limited to northeastern Chikwawa, where it had been introduced in 1937.[81] Peasant opposition was too strong and colonial opinion too polarized for any conservationist agenda, including the 'cheap' ones, to succeed, particularly when the cotton economy was still thriving.

Wartime and postwar ideological, political and economic contingencies, rather than the coherence of any scientific argument, decided the outcome of the debates over erosion and the red bollworm. The movement for political union, which in 1953 resulted in the ill-fated federation of the Rhodesias and Nyasaland, provided the context for greater cooperation between Nyasaland's Agricultural Department and its counterpart in Southern Rhodesia, where extensive research on various agricultural problems was under way.[82] The exchanges strengthened the position of the local conversationists, who scored their first major victory in 1946 with the passage of the Natural Resources Ordinance. The Ordinance was revised in 1948 against the backdrop of increased world demand for African commodities and obvious strains in the peasant sector.

More significant for the history of conservationism in Nyasaland was the countrywide famine of 1949. The famine raised food production to the same pre-eminence as cash crop agriculture in colonial planning. It helped to convert the remaining skeptics to the need for a more thorough land reform than that stipulated by the 1948 Natural Resources Ordinance:

[79] MNA, Lower Shire District Book, IV (1928–32); MNA, NSP2/1/7: Port Herald District Annual Report, 1935.

[80] By 1934 there were 19 village forest areas, covering some 16,513 acres in Nsanje district alone (MNA, S1/88A/34: Port Herald District Annual Report, 1934).

[81] MNA, NSC2/1/5: Chikwawa District Annual Reports, 1938, 1939.

[82] For a more detailed discussion of the connection, see William Beinart, 'Soil Erosion, Conservationism and Ideas about Development: a Southern African Exploration, 1900–1960,' *Journal of Southern African Studies*, XI, 1 (Oct. 1984), pp. 52–83.

It is becoming increasingly obvious that this country must make a complete change in its agricultural policy within the very near future unless it is to meet disaster. The population continues to increase and there is as yet no sign that the African cultivator is willing or able to change his ways. A few of the more intelligent are willing, and a few of them are able, to carry out better methods of farming and to adopt simple soil conservation methods, but they are quickly submerged and lost in a sea of inertia and suspicion. The need is urgent and cannot afford to wait. A method of mass attack must be found and put into operation quickly.[83]

Many officials, after passing the threshold of their own inertia, took conservation as an end in itself in the 1950s.

The Tchiri Valley had no chance of escaping the conservationist movement of the late 1940s and 1950s. Several changes since the late 1930s had, from an agricultural viewpoint, brought the area in line with the rest of the country. The most significant related to the permanent inundation of the *dambo*. The waters of Lake Malawi had been rising steadily until 1935, when they overflowed the sandbar that had separated the Tchiri river from Lake Malawi since the 1880s. The levels of the Tchiri began to rise as a consequence. The Bomani floods of 1939 left large tracts of the Dabanyi and Dinde marshes permanently submerged.[84]

The ramifications of this change proved dramatic and far-reaching. *Dimba* cotton agriculture died almost instantaneously:

The rise of the Lake, and consequent perennial flooding by the Shire, eliminated the flood lands and forced all cotton growing on the higher and drier areas. This changed the situation completely and it now became a matter of mixing semi-summer (i.e. rotation) and summer crops.[85]

For the first time the Valley had to depend almost entirely on *munda* cotton. *Dimba* cultivation became restricted to a few fast maturing potatoes and legumes raised on a limited number of spots of high

---

[83] *Annual Report of the Department of Agriculture* (ARDA), 1949 (Zomba), Part I, p. 8.

[84] An estimated 120,000 acres of the *dambo* were lost in that year alone (*ARDA*, 1939, Pt. I, p. 5).

[85] Ducker, 'The Nyasaland Cotton Crop.' *NAQJ*, X, 4 (Dec. 1951), p. 128.

elevation. The change exacerbated the problem of overpopulation on the *mphala* in the south and northeast as some of the former occupants of the *dambo* moved to higher grounds. The change also exposed the area to the frequent dangers of drought, especially in the south where over 66 per cent of all cotton cultivation had been based on the *dambo*. The countrywide famine of 1949 had been preceded by a more severe local famine in 1941.[86]

The end of *dimba* agriculture undermined the position of the noninterventionists and the proponents of late planting, who had defended such *dimba* techniques as intercropping. The conservationists no longer needed the authority of science to justify their beliefs in early planting or new conservation measures. Food crises and cotton failures plagued the 1940s: 'the effects of insect pests were enhanced and the gamble on the late rains intensified. If the June-July rains failed to arrive cotton late sown on really dry sites was apt to fail completely as a crop.'[87]

The timing of the government's decision to impose by force the *mitumbira* (ridging) and early planting schemes dramatized the importance of local political struggles. Before the 1930s, the state could not rely on village headmen to administer its program, but during the 1940s it could count upon the support of some indigenous leaders throughout the Valley. These were Native Authorities, as chiefs came to be known under the Native Authorities Ordinance of 1933, which introduced Indirect Rule in the country.[88] One outcome of the Ordinance was the emergence of a small group of 'progressive' chiefs. The village headmen had often defended their interests by insulating their communities from interference by the state and the 'conservative' chiefs had tried to use the Ordinance for such traditional goals as the preservation of the Mang'anja 'purity.'[89] But the 'progressive' Native Authorities sought to further their personal and class interests by proving their loyalty to the state in all measures, including soil conservation.

---

[86] *ARDA*, 1941, Part I, p. 9. For the percentage of the *dambo* under cotton cultivation in the South, see MNA, A3/2/201: Agricultural Monthly Report, June, 1933.

[87] Ducker, 'The Nyasaland Cotton Crop,' p. 128.

[88] Mandala, 'Capitalism, Ecology and Society,' pp. 230–48.

[89] Top among the demands of the 'conservative' chiefs under Indirect rule were the reinstatement of the Lundu Paramountcy and the restoration of *salima* mediums at the Khulubvi Mbona shrine. Mandala, 'Capitalism, Ecology and Society,' pp. 227–32.

The man who best exemplified the new breed of 'progressive' chiefs was Mollen Tengani,[90] who came to power in 1936 and was one of the few chiefs who lent unqualified support to the attempt of the local agricultural officer, Mr. Carral-Wilcocks, to introduce the early planting proposal on an experimental basis in 1938. Tengani then asked Mr. Carral-Wilcocks to force the people of his area to ridge their sweet potato gardens.[91] Tengani's subsequent cooperation with colonial authorities in such measures as latrine construction made him a natural ally of all district administrators who were looking for a traditional ruler capable of breaking rural resistance to the soil conservation program. One such administrator, Mr. P. M. Lewis, had been posted to Nsanje district in 1947. Nicknamed Thengo-ya-m'madzi ('Thorn-in-the-water') for his ambiguous relations with the Africans as a man and as an administrator, Mr. Lewis established cordial working relations with Tengani and promised him more territory for his cooperation in the conservation scheme.[92]

Assured of the support of Tengani and other 'progressive' chiefs like Liva Mlolo, Mr. Lewis brushed aside the opposition of 'conservative' chiefs and uncooperative headmen, and introduced the *mitumbira* scheme throughout the district in 1948.[93] A British visitor to the Valley in late 1949 declared the project a complete success in Tengani's chiefdom: 'Much of it (land) was box-ridged, that is to say one set of ridges was crossed by another so that the general effect was that of a waffle-iron, each little "box" ready to hold the rain when it fell and to keep it from running along croding the parallel trenches.'[94] Tengani had accomplished this pictorial beauty, which so well satisfied the British vision of order, by jailing and fining those peasants who failed to abide by the new regulations. And while 'conservative' chiefs and traditional religious leaders interpreted the subsequent drought and famine of

---

[90] Mandala, 'The Tengani Chieftaincy and Its Relations with Other Chieftaincies in Nsanje District, c.1850 to 1951,' (Unpublished Student Seminar Paper, History Department, University of Malawi, 1973/74).

[91] MNA, A3/2/202: Agricultural Monthly Report, March 1938.

[92] Mandala, 'The Tengani Chieftaincy.'

[93] *ARDA*, 1948: Part I, p. 12: 'the inhabitants of the Chiromo-Port Herald area, who had previously resisted attempts to introduce ridge cropping, were subjected to a special drive and substantial progress followed vigorous action by the Administration.'

[94] Frank Debenham, *Nyasaland: the Land of the Lake* (H. M. Stationery Office, London, 1955), p. 199.

1949–50 as a sign of displeasure by the region's guardian spirit (M'bona) with the new rules,[95] Tengani and Lewis read the same events as a mandate for a more draconian agricultural reform.

As soon as the famine ended, the state inaugurated the long-debated early planting proposal in 1951. This completed the conservation package considered necessary for the long-term economic viability of the Valley. The other components of the package were, in addition to *mitumbira*, the stillborn 'Shire Valley' and peasant resettlement projects. The new rules went beyond what people like Mr. Barker had called for during the 1930s. No cotton was to be planted after January; the practice of rotating cotton with maize and sorghum on the *munda* was legally abolished. The uprooting of cotton stalks was to be completed by July 31 to allow a four-month dead or close season considered a necessary step towards the elimination of the red bollworm. And to make certain that peasants did not revive the practice of intercropping in the event the *dambo* became available for cotton cultivation, cotton was to occupy a separate field 'in order to obviate the retarding effect of maize on cotton. . . .' Finally, like food crops, cotton was to be grown on 'ridges 8–9 inches high at 3 feet intervals.'[96]

The new regulations, while bringing the Valley in line with other cotton-growing areas of the country, constituted an all-out onslaught on regional practices, particularly in the Nsane district. Like the original blueprint of 1909, they sought to draw a clear line between the production of food and that of cotton, which would be raised from its subordinate status as a catch-crop – a status that colonial officials learned to live with only as a necessary evil. The most eloquent voice of the new regime turned out to be none other than Mr. Ducker of the ECGC, who had previously seen no reason for reforming the techniques of the Valley. In 1951 he defended the government's position in a language no different than that of his adversaries of the 1930s:

An extensive, low efficient, system of agriculture is to be replaced by a more efficient system, which will have its repercussions not only for cotton growing but also on the production of food and other

[95] Matthew Schoffeleers, 'The History and Political Role of the M'bona cult of the Mang'anja.' Terence O. Ranger and I. N. Kimambo, eds., *The Historical Study of African Religion* (Univ. of California Press, Berkeley, 1976), p. 88.

[96] H. C. Ducker, 'Cotton in Nyasaland,' *NAQJ*, X, 3 (Sept. 1951), p. 87; *ARDA*, 1952, Part I, p. 6.

cash crops. Without such a development the economic future of the Lower River would be far from bright.[97]

The need to preserve a system of control based upon the ability of the colonized to finance their own oppression had united the various fractions of the ruling class. Conventional wisdom rather than science had revealed the bankruptcy of liberalism in colonial planning.

PREVIEW

Peasant reactions to the new regulations followed predictable lines. Opposition was weakest in Chikwawa district outside the east bank. Growers on the west bank had, for political, demographic, and ecological reasons, raised cotton according to the original proposal of the Department of Agriculture, except for the provision that cotton be planted on ridges (*mitumbira*). Political coercion after 1951 undercut this element of resistance, particularly in the area of chief Ngabu, where serious cotton cultivation started only after the collapse of *dimba* agriculture in the late 1930s. The heavier *makande* soils in the chiefdom did not only prove capable of producing cotton. They also withstood ridging better than the more common *mphala* soils. Ridges constructed on the *makande* did not collapse as easily as those on the lighter sandy soils. The Ngabu chiefdom, which received a large proportion of the peasants evicted from the *dambo*, emerged as the new center of cotton agriculture in the Valley. In the early 1960s it was made the headquarters of the 'Shire Valley Agricultural Project,' which was the post-colonial successor of the aborted 'Shire Valley' project of the late colonial era.

In the southern or Nsanje district the story was completely different. Instead of reviving cotton, the new rules actually facilitated its demise. Ridging (*mitumbira*) and early planting schemes precipitated a wide protest movement known as *nkhondo ya mitumbira* ('the war of the ridges'), during which peasants, particularly women, stopped growing cotton altogether. The movement received the support of traditional religious leaders, 'conservative' chiefs, as well as the educated elites who merged the local protests with the national movement for political independence.[98]

[97] H. C. Ducker, 'Cotton in Nyasaland,' p. 93.

[98] A sequel to this study will explore in detail the nature of the protests and their relation to the changing patterns of food production, division of labor, and social differentiation.

SUMMARY

Since peasants grew part or all their food, their response to commodity production, as well as wage and tenant labor, was in the first instance informed by the requirements of the food economy. Meeting subsistence needs was for the inhabitants of the Valley a real struggle that included maximum utilization of the available land and labor resources. Because of its links with the locally specific political, social, and ecological systems, this struggle changed over time. The colonial cotton economy of the Valley arose out of the uneven developments between the technical and social arrangements of food cultivation during the latter part of the nineteenth century. This type of change cannot be accounted for in either neoclassical or the modes-of-production theory, the former because of the belief in the unlimitedness of production resources in precolonial peasant economies, and the latter because of the assumption about the universal priority of social over technical relations.

An understanding of the food economy in its sociopolitical context has permitted a re-interpretation of the role of the colonial state in commodity production. The history of the Valley demonstrates how, on the one hand, the combination of local political struggles with the dynamics of food production severely limited the abilty of the state to implement its programs and, how on the other hand, official agricultural policy shifted constantly in response to the actions of both capitalists and peasants. The peasants, through their quiet work in the fields, affected colonial planning in a manner that has not been sufficiently recognized by Africanist scholars. I do not, however, mean to suggest that colonial policy was 'ungrounded,' as some analyses seem to imply.[99] The Nyasaland state was autonomous only with respect to the means of achieving its goals, not with respect to the nature of the mission itself. Decision-makers struck an alliance with the peasantry only because of the failure of European settlers to satisfy the demands of metropolitan British capital. Even the most accommodating of the British colonizers did not hesitate to take unpopular measures during the 1940s and 1950s when it became apparent that peasants might finally refuse to subsidize their own oppression and the development of metropolitan capital.

---

[99] See Lonsdale and Berman, 'Coping with the Contradictions.'

15

The Commercial Society and International Relations

RICHARD ROSECRANCE

Edward Whiting Fox has explained how it is possible for there to be two societies within one 'country'.[1] France, in the period Fox examines, contained within it the administrative order of the great kings as well as the commercial society of the oceanic ports. Their rivalry and alternating influence in French history is the subject of his magnum opus, *History in Geographic Perspective*. But the key to this shifting preponderance is transport: the relative efficiency of river/ocean v. land transport in carrying goods and messages from one place to another. Unlike England, a country covered by navigable waterways and canals, France did not have the means of getting grain to distant markets until fairly recently. Railways were the necessary first step, but it was not until the vast network of highways and the advent of motor trucks fomented a transport revolution after World War II that larger scale agriculture, some of it directed toward export, became possible.

Thus from the seventeenth to the nineteenth centuries France could not be represented as a trading nation. Its concerns were territorial and administrative, to some degree reflecting a partial self-sufficiency in agricultural and manufactured goods. In the twentieth century, the EEC's Common Agricultural Policy move to export high-cost French agricultural products was a measure of the degree to which subsidies and price incentives were necessary to bring France into a trading relationship with other countries. The delay in France's transport

---

[1] Edward Whiting Fox, *History in Geographic Perspective: The Other France* (W. W. Norton, New York, 1971), pp. 19–53.

revolution was one reason for its hesitancy in moving toward a general trading strategy in world politics. France's past success with an administrative, territorial, and military organization was another. In the second half of the seventeenth century Louis XIV could think that the conquest of territory on the Rhine and in North Italy could substitute for English and Dutch pre-eminence in overseas trade. New peasants and increased grain supplies would add to the revenue and power of the French monarch.

Other countries had similar orientations. The great Russian monarchy sprawled over an area that extended from the Neva to the Pacific. Russian tsars, from Peter I on, had hesitated to rely upon trade with the more developed West, fearing that they would thereby subject themselves to control by more advanced commercial and naval countries. Walther Kirchner writes:

> In relation to maritime access, Russia is the most disadvantageously situated of all large powers. The grand duchy of Muscovy, which was to give rise eventually to modern Russia, had no access whatever to the sea. In the nineteenth century, Russia, after having expanded for six hundred years, had a seacoast extending thousands of miles in the Arctic which was almost useless for transport purposes. She also secured ports on the Baltic and Black Seas which were suitable for peaceful trade but which lacked free exit. The straits connecting the Baltic with the open sea were dominated by Denmark, those of the Black Sea by Turkey; and Europe saw to it that neither of these two countries would fall under Russian rule. Thus, strategically, the ports formed a liability rather than an 'asset'.[2]

In the twentieth century, Russian victories after the Revolution stimulated an even more paranoid reliance upon territorial and military resources to advance Russian and Soviet positions in world politics. Russia's control of Eastern Europe was facilitated by the Soviet military dispositions there. The separation of its territories from those in central and western Europe was designed to put a barrier between the Russian–East European Communist apparatus and the social infection of western

---

[2] Walther Kirchner, *History of Russia* (Barnes and Noble Books, New York, 1976), p. 5.

and trading ideas. In sum, Russia's relative success with the military control of territory, and its inexperience and ineptitude with trading strategies, fostered a continued reliance on the former. Even after transport methods, still backward in the USSR, made possible a wider and more outward looking orientation, the Soviet Union clung to traditional attitudes and autarkic policies.

The United States also evinced primarily territorial and continental concerns in the development of a market large enough to sustain US industry, without major recourse to trade with the outside world. This was not true in the nineteenth century when North America had to repay British loans and offer recompense for the investment of British capital in the railways and other industrial infrastructure. Agricultural exports (both cotton and grain), the early means of repayment, were supplemented by manufacturing exports in the late nineteenth century after the infant industry period was over. In World War I the United States became a great exporter of arms and industrial equipment, winning markets in third countries where Britain and Germany had been preponderant before the war. Yet in the 1920s the United States returned to a hemispheric policy in trade, though its capital exports financed German reparations to allied powers.[3] With the Depression, the Smoot-Hawley tariff of 1930, and Roosevelt's devaluation of the dollar, the inward looking, self-sufficient orientation of American economic policy became a kind of national obsession. The United States made it very difficult for others to sell in its home market and at least temporarily accepted the risk that continental tariffs and British Commonwealth preference arrangements would represent formidable barriers to its exports abroad.

The shortages and European inflation that followed World War II gave US goods a competitive edge in world markets, but this advantage did not last for long. In the 1970s the dollar was pressed into formal devaluation, and after that it was forced to float lower still. The cheaper dollar sustained the US trade balance for a time, but in the 1980s high US interest rates generated by a large and persistent government deficit initially raised the dollar to levels almost unprecedented in recent history. That in turn brought on a massive balance of trade deficit of more than $100 billion. The United States turned from a creditor nation into one whose

[3] Stephen Schucker, 'American Reparations to Germany, 1919–1933' (Unpublished paper, Department of History, Brandeis University).

liabilities exceeded its assets. It was no longer clear whether US industrial and manufacturing productivity would increase sufficiently to allow the United States to become an effective competitor of large Japanese, East Asian and European firms on a worldwide basis.[4] The uncertainty in the long-term economic position of the United States was compounded by its territorial rivalry with the Soviet Union.

In the flush of US victory and Soviet weakness after World War II, US strategists had adopted the policy of 'containment', in the belief that the United States was so strong economically and industrially that it could stand long term competition with the USSR, and that it could afford to intervene, as it did in Korea and Vietnam, in areas where the outcome was uncertain. Even in the Third World the United States could send its forces or proxies against insurgents and expect to be successful. The struggle with the Soviet Union was viewed essentially in territorial terms: if one area or region of the world adopted a pro-Russian or Marxist stance, this was equivalent to extending the territorial glacis of Soviet power, and sooner or later Americans would find themselves fighting on the beaches in California. In the Kennedy Administration the forward thrust of US foreign policy was most explicit: citizens would be asked to 'bear any burden' or 'pay any price' in defense of liberty and the American way. United States' military preparations in strategic and conventional terms were designed not only to deter the USSR in Europe and the Third World but also to convince them that the United States was superior: militarily, economically, technologically and politically. The confidence verging on hubris of the mid-1960s was not likely to yield to a more detached or dispassionate view of US security interests: these continued to be interpreted in territorial terms that would have been familiar to Louis XIV.

The basic distinction that Edward Fox made between commercial and areal societies had much to do with the structure of political organization. For the areal, political organization was territorial and compact, a distinct and formed land mass with boundaries on other states. The commercial organization of society, however, was not compact or areal; it was linear. Cities were nodes on these linear communication links, and it is not surprising that Fox lists Bordeaux, Venice, the city states of the Aegean, Amsterdam, and London as cities in the commercial society. In different

[4] Lester C. Thurow, *The Zero Sum Solution: Building A World Class American Economy* (Simon & Schuster, New York, 1985).

time periods the networks between them produced a distinct way of life that was as marked as that within territorial states. The networks were not always peaceful; in certain periods they were racist and survived on the slave trade; they frequently depended upon a monopoly of products from particular regions of the world. Venice and Lisbon alternately captured the market for Far Eastern spices, textiles, wood, and dyes. Amsterdam was the purveyor of Baltic produce; London was the center of a profitable re-export trade in North American and Caribbean goods. The conflict between London and Amsterdam was a major factor of the 1660s and 1670s; Genoa and Venice warred throughout the thirteenth and fourteenth centuries. London emerged victorious in all areas except the Baltic in the mid-eighteenth century, but even British fleets were unable to capture control of the production of sugar in the Caribbean. The eighteenth century was not to see a forerunner of the OPEC cartel in sweets and sweeteners.

With all the conflict among trading cities, however, their competition was not quite like that of territorial states. In imperial relations their objective was trade, not settlement; control of production, not conquest. One of the reasons for the relative fragility of both Dutch and Portuguese empires was the slender base of metropolitan population on which they rested. England was different, and here commercial, territorial, and religious objectives fused and refracted upon one another. North America had few initial products to offer to Europe; it was not a sugar island; but in time timber, indigo, cotton, tobacco and grain emerged as useful exports. The growth and continuing migration of population to North America, however, transformed it into a territorial province (and also a liability) not merely a trading enclave. Nonetheless, the conflict and competition of trading cities, especially when these were not buttressed with the resources of the territorial state, were limited. Instead of each trying to monopolize the key Eastern or Caribbean wares, when they began to specialize, the co-operation among them grew. The consensus among the cities of the Hanseatic League was more typical of the role of trading cities than the monopolist and mercantilist conflict of the Mediterranean and the Caribbean. Finally, when mercantilist restrictions were dismantled in the nineteenth century, cities could compete with one another, but on the basis of free and open trade. London then had ties with Hamburg, Bordeaux, the Dutch cities, and Lisbon, to say nothing of Charleston, Mobile, and New Orleans. Monopolies no longer existed, but there was sufficient differentiation of function in the exports from each for a co-operative trading network to emerge among them.

One other advantage of the experience of London was that the territorial enterprise succeeded only briefly. During the great conflict in Europe, India, and the Caribbean in the mid-eighteenth century, William Pitt had announced that 'commerce had been made to prosper through 'war.' '[5] The cutting down of the French edge in sugar plantations, and the capture of India and Canada, seemed to be a commercial victory as much as a military one. Soon after, however, the American colonies, freed from the French threat, revolted against the mother country. The British Navy was no longer superior to a combination of other fleets, and even if it had been, the British faced crucial difficulties fighting with determined continentals thousands of miles from Europe. The victory of Washington over Cornwallis, abetted by the victories of De Grasse at sea, made the British rethink their entire strategic position. If colonies would demand independence when they reached a mature stage of political and economic development, there no longer seemed warrant to conquer them.

Afterwards, the leaders of the British Colonial Office began to ready their charges for autonomy and responsible self-government, and annexationist sentiment abruptly declined, not to be revived until the 1870s. Britain's liberal empire of the 1840s to 1870s allowed colonies and dominions to set their separate tariffs. The British did not demand preference since the colonial markets belonged territorially to the empire. At the same time they also encouraged Europeans to move toward free trade, arguing that all would benefit thereby. Some have claimed in response that Britain's policy at mid-nineteenth century was a kind of 'imperialism of free trade' in that, as the first industrial nation, Britain would be the greatest beneficiary of the abolition of 'tariffs'.[6] This may be true, but England did not switch to protection when she was no longer the premier industrial country. In the 1860s she was not seeking new colonies and indeed disdained them in notable cases. She could do nothing about the higher American tariffs after the Civil War, and was not able even to get the continentals to move all the way to free trade. It was

[5] Quoted in Walter L. Dorn, *Competition for Empire, 1740–1763* (Harper and Row, Inc, New York, 1963), p. 370.

[6] William Roger Louis (ed.), *Imperialism: The Robinson–Gallagher Controversy* (New View Points, New York, 1965).

after the German adoption of higher tariffs in 1879 that England began to recognize that France and Germany would extend their protectionist barriers to any new territory they might acquire. After the British occupation of Egypt in 1882, the French came back into the colonial game with a vengeance, backed by Berlin. Britain began to see the African subcontinent parcelled out into separate tariff zones that corresponded to political ones. Unless it re-entered the quest Britain faced the problem of exclusion from markets of the colonial territories of other states. And the scramble for Africa, parts of the Far East, and Oceania began.

By the 1880s Fox's commercial society saw its links attenuated or severed by a new rash of customs increases and political acquisitions. Until World War I, with the exception of the 1900–13 interlude, trade and investment expanded at a reduced rate. Tariffs joined hands with imperialism and the world was increasingly subdivided into French, British, German and US markets, each commanded by a national capital. Funds continued to flow freely in and out of national and imperial jurisdictions, however, and foreign investment had a brief rebirth before 1914. Lloyds of London had ensured the German merchant marine and planned to pay compensation for any ships that British vessels sunk, should there be a 'war'.[7] All such arrangements, however, were destroyed by World War I. Nor were the commercial links, broken by tariffs, economic nationalism, and war, fully re-established after 1918. With the Dawes Plan of 1924 loans, reparations payments, and capital flows began to move relatively freely from one national jurisdiction to another. But trade was hemmed in by restrictions, and the US market was largely denied to other states. Britain and France tried to maintain relatively open trade, but the under-valued franc and the over-valued pound sterling combined to draw reserves to Paris. When London could not stand the strain in 1931 the British jettisoned their traditional policy and erected Commonwealth preference and a tariff wall against outsiders. The burgeoning commercial links between countries were broken once again.

Yet transport, the key variable in the Fox synthesis, operated to make possible a wider trading system than ever before. The completion in the late nineteenth century of railway feeder lines and the advent of the

[7] Paul M. Kennedy, *The Rise and Fall of British Naval Mastery* (Allen Lane, London, 1976), pp. 152–5.

tramp steamer had reduced transport costs greatly. The first effect of national and international transport that linked the world with the village was, however, always a flow of goods inward. France, the United States, Germany, and other countries reacted at the end of the nineteenth century and in the 1920s to limit highly competitive foreign imports: textiles, grain, machinery, and the like. It was not until after World War II that the new possibilities of transport fashioned a trading and exporting response to the outside world, facilitated by the development of superhighway networks in Europe and the United States that could carry bulk commodities rapidly from one point to another. More important still, governments changed their policies and came to endorse a trading strategy in international politics. They had failed to conquer a vast internal market for their own industries and were partly disabused of war as a prime means of policy. Accordingly, they had to export to live – to gain the wherewithal to import food and energy.

The commercial strategy was connected with a reversal in the trend toward ever larger continental states. From the end of the fifteenth century to the beginning of the twentieth century, states were growing larger in size and fewer in number. The Spanish and Portuguese empires forwarded this development outside of Europe; inside, gunpowder and the development of territorial monarchies extinguished the independence of small principalities and city states in one period of warfare after another. The Thirty Years War, the wars of Louis XIV, and finally the Revolutionary and Napoleonic Wars brought a wholesale consolidation. The German states, particularly, were molded into larger units to resist the invader. Brandenburg-Prussia was first strengthened as a French ally in the struggle with the Habsburgs; later England, Russia and Austria added to its territory and power to provide a bulwark against France. The final unification of Germany and Italy after the mid-nineteenth century carried the process further still. Overseas the European imperialism of the period 1880–1914 divided up the rest of the world in the drive for colonies. By 1914 a few Great Powers controlled the earth.

This initial period of political and territorial amalgamation, however, gave way to a new trend that is still with us: the breakup of empires and the establishment of new and smaller nationalist states. The process began as early as the first part of the nineteenth century with the independence of Latin American states; it continued with freedom for Turkish territories in the Balkans; and it was speeded greatly in

World War I with the collapse of the Austrian and Russian empires. After World War II, the British, French, Portuguese, Dutch and Belgian empires followed suit, and it is still not clear where the process of national subdivision will end. If ethnic nationalist movements have their way, there will be more new states in Europe, Oceania and South Asia.

Endemic political cleavage has renewed national candidacy for the commercial society. Small states were not axiomatic protagonists of oceanic trade, but many of them were located on international waterways and still more had no means of support short of commerce with other nations. The nearly one hundred nations that have joined the international system since the end of World War II have had to export to live. Dependent in many cases on imports of energy, raw materials or food, they have had to fashion a trading strategy to meet essential needs. In many cases in Africa, South Asia, or the Middle East, such strategies have not been entirely successful, and in some they have not been successful at all. African nations of the Sahel have been mired in poverty and drought and have existed on a precarious subsistence level. One-crop or one-mineral economies have been persistently vulnerable to a sudden drop in the market price and have suffered periodically, as Chile, Ghana, and Senegal have demonstrated. Those countries which have shifted to cash-crops for export have sometimes neglected their own food supplies, and the remedy has frequently been worse than the disease. The heavy indebtedness of many Third World nations has made the problem worse, for exports to the North and West in world politics have been the vital means of repaying loans or financing investments. While commercial obligations have created some of the problem that such nations face, however, it is difficult to think of a long-term solution – and multilateral aid offers no such remedy – that does not involve exports and finding a niche in the structure of international comparative advantage. At most, assistance from outside can tide such countries over the shoals of start-up and debt costs, but it cannot substitute for productive efficiencies at home.

The renewal of the commercial society on a worldwide basis depends upon a series of facilitating causes. First and foremost, as Edward Fox saw, transport must be cheap and efficient. Even rural hinterlands must be accessible to the sea. Tariffs must be low enough to permit a circulation of goods, and capital must be freely mobile. Such conditions were not met in the latter part of the nineteenth century or in the 1930s, and if there were a new economic collapse in the 1990s protectionism and economic nationalism would arise again. In addition a renaissance of the commercial society depends on restraints on military conquest. So long as the areal order of French kings could be expanded at will, there was little temptation to follow the linear trading path of the port cities in a national and foreign policy strategy. On the Rhine, in Italy, and overseas, new territories could still be taken. The success of European imperialism in the late nineteenth century was a tribute to the still territorial organization of international politics. When small states began to emerge from the grasp of the large powers at the beginning of the twentieth century, the balance shifted. Now it was harder to govern new territories.

In World War II, Nazi Germany briefly controlled an empire the size of Caesar's, conquering and then subduing populations from Brittany to Kiev. For a time, German victories and popular quiescence sustained an anti-Bolshevist political order in Europe. But resistance gradually developed in Yugoslavia, France, Norway, and the Low Countries. The German *blitzkrieg* failed in Russia and Hitler's hold on North Africa was shattered. After the war, the atomic bomb and new delivery capabilities raised great quandaries for any aggressor nation. Territory could be attacked, but at the risk of rendering it a radioactive wasteland. Conventional war was possible in areas of low strategic importance, but no great shift in the balance in world politics could be produced by campaigns in Korea, South Asia, Vietnam, or Afghanistan. China and Russia could have an occasional engagement over the Ussury River and Vietnam, and China could engage in artillery duels, but no decisive advantage would be gained one way or the other. In Europe, or Japan, however, political, military and economic issues of the greatest magnitude were involved in the territorial balance. No power could assume that nuclear weapons would not be used in a military conflict in those regions. It did not, therefore, take place.

But even where conventional and irregular warfare occurred – in the Middle East, Africa or South Asia – the results were seldom decisive. One Arab-Israeli war followed another, but the balance did not change very much. Superpower involvement there as well as in South Asia dampened the results and rearmed the parties afterward. In Africa, Somalia and Ethiopia switched sides, and Egypt withdrew from the Soviet embrace in 1972. Marxist victories in Angola are exceedingly fragile and in Mozambique a self-proclaimed Marxist government seeks to improve its ties with the capitalists. The Soviet 'victory' in China has turned to ashes. Political fluidity in fact dominates allegiences in the Third World, and territorial victories sometimes are reversed. The temptation to stake all the chips on the ideological or military conversion of an opponent has greatly declined.

This outcome is not only a result of military standoff in world politics, it is also a reflection of the growing cost of foreign intervention. Politically mobilized populations now await any invader; they will not follow tribal or traditional leaders who agree to 'indirect rule' by the imperialist. In most conflicts today both sides are heavily armed, so heavily that complete victory for one side is virtually out of the question. In Lebanon all factions possess modern weapons; none can be eliminated; each has outside suppliers; and none can be forced to compromise. A temporary victory for an intervening power does not last, as both the Soviet Union and Israel have increasingly found. Strictly, the political or military position may be maintained, but the cost grows so high that no benefit is thereby derived. The United States was not defeated in Vietnam, but chose to withdraw given the costs, military, economic, and political. The rise in the costs of military victory, the inability to govern the society once it has theoretically been 'pacified', and the continuance of military resistance all call for an alternative strategy in world politics. And it is precisely the failure of territorial expansion in the manner of the French kings that brings the commercial society to the fore once again. Small trading states with commercial cities embedded within them can once again enjoy an independent existence, since the drive for military domination seldom succeeds. Such states typically make their way in the world by trading for the necessaries of a national existence. Warfare is an ultimate distraction from this task.

This does not mean that war does not occur, and particularly, it does not mean that war does not occur in the Third World. The very recentness of autonomy and independence, the lack of well-formed internal institutions, the uncertainty of political support, and the presence of ethnic divisions within society have sometimes led to war with other jurisdictions. It is perhaps no accident that when the European state system was being formed in the seventeenth century, there was continual 'war'.[8] Latin American states fought among themselves in the aftermath of independence from Spain. Turkish subjects in the Balkans

[8] This is the thesis of Darryl Roberts, *Origins of War in the Periphery* (Doctoral dissertation, Cornell University, Ithaca, New York, 1984).

progressively sought and gained independence, in the last part of the nineteenth century, but the process involved war between successor states as well as with the weakening imperial power. After 1945 new nations like India and Pakistan, Israel and Egypt, Indonesia and Malaysia, Somalia and Ethiopia, China and Vietnam, Morocco and Algeria, Iraq and Iran engaged in military confrontations with one another. Some of these quarrels were abetted or stimulated by superpower rivalries. Most, however, reflected nascent and local hostility. The aggressive nationalism of such newly formed states might theoretically come to characterize much of Third World international relations and doom new commercial orientations.

Yet what is astounding about the period since World War II is not the rivalries and occasional military conflicts of new nations; it is their relative absence. Nearly a hundred new states have joined the international system since 1945, and they have generally abided in peace with their neighbors. Few have tried to conquer new territory, and most disputes have had to do with ethnic rivalries and *irredenta* – conflicts that stemmed from domestic instabilities. And even where tribal religions or ethnic boundaries differed from national loyalties, conflict within and between states was often moderated. India, Pakistan, Kenya, Nigeria, Zimbabwe, Malaysia, Burma, and many other countries were able to maintain themselves despite internal divisions that might once have fomented internecine strife and continual conflict. Certainly, the acquisition of territory for territory's sake (the typical objective of Louis XIV and other traditional monarchs) had little attraction to the overwhelming majority of new nations.

Nationalism in the Third World, therefore, is of a particular type. Unlike the European nineteenth-century variety which frequently merged with imperialism, nationalism in the southern and eastern hemisphere has been largely confined to the maintenance of existing frontiers. Vietnamese expansion (a kind of European sport) has not produced a general mutation in world politics. It is surprising how many states have defined their identity, not in ethnic terms, but rather in terms of the territory previously ruled by the imperialist. As a result historic and idiosyncratic frontiers have been endowed with the legitimacy they did not enjoy in the nineteenth century. This delimitation of national identity provides an even more effective pattern of deterrence and defense. With the exception of still traditional and unmobilized polities, the new nation states will fight vigorously to protect their independence, and even the superpowers have had to reduce their expectations of social and political transformation induced through military means. Nationalism, in short, has served to integrate new political communities and protect them from attack; it has only occasionally engendered new chauvinism and territorial expansion.

The commercial society will take shape only under favorable conditions: the costs of territorial expansion must be palpable if a commercial strategy is even to occur to states that have the theoretical means to implement it. Transport and communications must permit the efficient carrying of bulk commodities great distances from their points of origin. But such negative conditions will still not produce a commercial society unless the benefits of trade with far-flung suppliers and markets are large and continuing. This in turn means low tariffs, the provision of insurance and financing, enforcement of contract in local courts, and the absence of cultural and other impediments to trade. It is not enough that the actual interdependencies among nations increase; nations, or, in this case, trading groups within nations must believe that they should be extended and expanded. One of the causes of warfare in recent western history was the rejection of the interdependence that began to develop among nations following the industrial revolution. Foreign policy leaders sometimes sought to cut the ties of dependence on the outside world and strove to bring all needed resources and markets within a single national 'compass'.[9] Only if such ambitions are believed certain to fail will countries consider commercial interdependence as an acceptable alternative.

It is of course not enough that a given nation abjures the use of force and thinks in terms of commercial co-operation with other countries. The entire international system must be largely peaceful to permit trade to prevail over military force. In the Iran–Iraq War, for example, Iraq's attacks on the tankers bound to or from Iran did not totally disrupt trade because new subsidized insurance, supplementing Lloyds of London, made it possible for shipowners to bear the associated risks. Commercial activities require long term conditions of peace, for the benefits of trade are not reaped in one or two years.

Some have argued that a military hegemony is necessary to hold the ring in international relations, thus allowing others to pursue commercial

[9] Alan S. Milward, *The German Economy at War* (University of London, Athlone Press, London, 1965).

vocations. Britain, so it is said, performed such a function in the nineteenth century, as did the United States after 1945. But if this were true, the so-called balance of power system could not have operated before 1914. Instead, nations should have deferred to British preponderance. After 1945, the United States should have gone from strength to strength, imposing its will in Vietnam as well as upon Cuba. Short of such well-nigh complete victories, the international economic system, so some claim, could not function. But, of course, in neither case was there a military hegemony. Britain did not rule the continent in the nineteenth century, nor did the United States control the outside world (or all of Europe) in the period after 1945. A balance existed in both cases: primarily multipolar in the one case, and bipolar in the other. Great Britain and the German Empire got along as well as they did between 1871 and 1890 because of a division of tasks and responsibilities: Bismarck saw to the balance in Europe, Disraeli and later Salisbury to the stability of the outside world. After 1945 the American position in Europe provided deterrence and 'reassurance',[10] but it did not prevent the rise of new powers in other regions: Japan, China, India, Brazil and Mexico. The Soviet Union did not contribute to commercial development, even though it occasionally benefited from western capital and goods in eastern European markets. Rather, the commercial system eddied around the Russian rock, flowing outward. The failure of the United States to dominate the world militarily had little effect upon commercial, assumptions and prospects so long as other balancing forces were in place. Generally speaking, the Soviet Union sought ideological and paramilitary conversion of opponents, not full-scale war. It did not seek to extend its borders in Europe and could hardly think of taking a populous Chinese province. In the Third World it gave arms and support to Cuba, but this did not guarantee a fixed political outcome. The Soviet Union's efforts were slender enough to permit commerce (as, for example, in Angola) to function and even to determine major economic orientations. Perhaps strangely, the capitalists of western Europe have not been hostile to the Soviet system in the east; they seek to trade and extract needed raw materials from it. They operate on the assumption that the Soviet bloc trade can ultimately be reoriented along western lines.

[10] Michael Howard, 'Reassurance and Deterrence: Western Defense in the 1980s', *Foreign Affairs*, 61 (Winter, 1982–3), pp. 309–24.

All these peaceful assumptions could change if a major war loomed in the 1990s. But few, certainly not capitalists, think it is likely. And if small or insurgent wars occur, they can be isolated within compartments and will not restrict overall commercial exchanges. In fact, one of the most interesting tendencies of the international commercial society since 1945 has been its relative immunity to crisis: Hungarian, Czech or Afghan. In the aftermath of each, business continued as usual and even the stock markets did not get out of hand. For some, this almost amounts to the view that commercial links will survive upward or downward blips in East–West relations. The presence of Japan as a new trading nation has if anything strengthened such views, because Japanese calculations have always been of longer range than those of the western industrial nations.

For reasons similar, no economic hegemony has been needed to keep international markets in order and to serve as market or lender of last resort. As US economic leverage declined, others came to the fore to help hold tariffs down, and keep restraint agreements within limits. The results in the international monetary system today are perverse if one requires hegemony to produce stability. The dollar was a much less strong currency when the United States was at its relative economic peak than it was in 1985 when the US's position declined. The collapse of the dollar in 1971–3 did not cause trading nations to embrace other currencies or to set up exclusive commercial blocs. The renaissance of the dollar has served the interest of European, Japanese, and Third World investors as well as or even better than it has served those of the United States. In any event the relative weakness of the US economy has not led to a flight of capital elsewhere as happened in the 1920s and 1930s, when Britain's economic and commercial decline made it impossible to maintain a high fixed value of sterling.

Can the commercial society continue and prosper? This question cannot yet be answered. Wars could still occur. An economic crisis or collapse could lead to a reimposition of tariff and exchange controls, like those of the 1930s. Commercial interests do not necessarily have the same influence in each nation. Large territorial states still think in terms of self-sufficiency. The choices of the United States and the Soviet Union will ultimately be decisive. The Soviet Union seems likely to continue aiming at autarky for as long as its bountiful natural resources last. The United States is past this stage, but there are some who believe that a new technological innovation in biotechnology, fusion power, or resource recovery will ultimately emancipate the US from the restraints and limits of the world economy. What is not fully realized in either of these states is that it is not simply a matter of resources and markets. Information and technology require links to the outside world, which cannot be provided solely by indigenous research and development. Market research may be one of the most important bases of commercial knowledge in the next generation or so, and there is no area in which the Soviet Union more grievously lags behind. Awareness of what the outside world is doing is necessary to fashion an effective commercial strategy and to find a niche in international trade. Here the Japanese excel, and the Americans, for all of their computer wizardry, sometimes lag seriously behind.

It may even be that commercial interests will have to begin thinking of states as a congeries of trading and research regions. What New York is doing may be quite different from Silicon Valley. Biotechnology firms on the West Coast may have a distinct interest and economic orientation different from that of software producers in the north east. Certain decisions concerning commercial and manufacturing strategies rest on a continuance of low oil prices and low inflation. Agricultural and exploration industries, however, frequently base their assumptions on inflation and a rise in the cost of energy. They cannot all be right and, as farmers have recently found, the combination of high interest rates, a high US dollar, and low agricultural prices spells ruin to many. In this degree, the existence of different commercial interests with partly conflicting claims can even induce paralysis in social and governmental policy. In such circumstances commercial alliances may be formed with colleagues in other countries that partly cut across or contradict the so-called 'national' interests of a single state. But this was the fundamental point that Edward Whiting Fox was raising, and that has recently been reinforced by Jane Jacobs: there is more than one society in a 'country.'[11] There is certainly a commercial society and a territorial order, but there may also be different trading societies as countries become more disparate internally. The size of national units has been declining since the end of the nineteenth century. But for political and economic reasons, it may have to become smaller still.

[11] Jane Jacobs, *Cities and the Wealth of Nations* (Random House, New York, 1984), pp. 204–20.

16

The Argument: Some Reinforcements and Projections

EDWARD WHITING FOX

Originally *History in Geographic Perspective* was the product of my efforts
to explain a widely noted but never adequately-explicated split in the
French body politic. When it finally came to me that I was in fact
contending with two separate and distinct 'societies', I realized that I
needed a definition of this term. What I found in a standard anthropology
text was that 'societies' consisted of individuals and groups who
communicated with one another through the exchange of 'goods, wives
and messages'. While these particular categories of exchange were
identified in the anthropologist's primitive societies, I found that both
the 'goods' and the 'messages' proved to be critical in my historical units
as well, for it was the exchange of goods that created the economic base
of a community, and the promulgation of messages, or orders, that
established its governmental and military organization.

When I tried to project these exchanges onto the topography of pre-
industrial France, I then ran into what turned out to be the critical double
distinction between travel and transport over land and over water. That
is, while it would be relatively easy for individuals or groups to travel
overland along an unobstructed path if supplies were available on the
way, it would be difficult to move objects of any weight or bulk – such
as staple foods or fuel – across the landscape. Over water, however, the
situation would be roughly reversed: once a ship and crew were organized,
heavy goods could be transported easily, while travel would be much
more cumbersome than by land. In the one case, over land, economic
co-operation would be restricted while governmental or military activity
would not; in the other case, over water, easy transport would facilitate

and extend the range of economic exchange, but less flexible travel would tend to hamper military or administrative efforts.

Thus the two different societies began to emerge in my mind's eye as I pictured France, and ultimately the rest of Europe as well, in the millennium before the coming of modern forms of transport and communication. Under the *ancien régime* in France, for example, royal agents circulated freely in the hinterlands on the king's business, supported by the endless subsistence units that blanketed the countryside, while along the coasts the merchants of the port cities grew rich by trading overseas with other merchants from widely scattered ports. For practical purposes the two communication systems operated quite independently of one another.

Although this analysis is foreign to most historians today, I found that it was taken for granted by any number of major commentators in the eighteenth century. Perhaps the most useful for our purposes is François Quesnay, who wrote about the 'agricultural kingdom', which he viewed as the source of all true wealth, and a contrasting waterborne 'republic of commerce', which he viewed as morally flawed by its traffic in the empty currency of money.

One of the most important – and most contested – conclusions of this analysis is that, given the difficulty of overland transport, the agricultural units of the hinterland must have been strictly limited in size and function to the exchange of staples within the radius of a day or two's travel around a market town. Usually critics object that local inhabitants appear to have participated in the exchange of a variety of goods brought from both near and far, and thus that they could not have been as effectively isolated as I claimed. In my book I tried to deal with this objection by examining the specific items exchanged in the markets of the interior, dividing them into two categories according to whether they had been transported over long or short distances. I thereby tried to demonstrate that long-distance transactions (which I termed 'commerce' as opposed to 'trade') played a relatively minor role in the economic life of the agricultural community. It would have clarified my point, I now realize, if I had drawn my distinction not between the distance goods had traveled but between those goods that added to the society's basic resources and those that drew upon such resources to serve some other purpose. It was this distinction that Quesnay used to formulate his theory of the 'net product', his term for the agricultural surplus that remained to a society after the producers and their families had been provided with the bare necessities for the coming year. This residual supply was his measure of the society's wealth, which by implication divided all members of the society into those who contributed to, and those who were supported by, this surplus.

From our present perspective we can see that Quesnay was really dealing with the society's store of surplus energy, largely in the form of food and fuel, and that there were therefore basically two types of trade: that which contributed to this store of energy, and that which consumed it in the pursuit of other aims. The purpose of belaboring this point is to eliminate luxuries and trinkets from our calculations in estimating the size and character of basic economic units. The pound of pepper brought from the Indies to some Rhineland prince might have made a handsome profit for the merchant, but it added nothing to the 'net product' of the Rhineland. Rather, its transport consumed energy all along the route. In more general historical terms this means that the growing luxury trade of the Mediterranean did not actually enrich Europe or enlarge the economic units of which Europe was composed; rather, it was attracted by Europe's growing agricultural surpluses, which it tapped without adding to the real wealth of the agricultural community.

The case for the concept of isolated, self-contained subsistence units of peasant agriculture is perhaps best put by J. von Thünen in his book *The Isolated State*. A scientific farmer and economic theorist who lived in northwest Germany in the early nineteenth century, von Thünen is still far less known than he deserves to be; I did not discover him until after I had completed by own book. In the course of demonstrating the limits of overland transport on an inland agricultural community, von Thünen recounts his experiment to see how far two drivers could take a wagonload of grain, drawn by four horses along a straight, flat road, if they fed themselves and their team exclusively from their load and saved half of it for the return trip. The distance, he reports, was fifty miles, but he adds that in everyday life the working radius was likely to be closer to twenty or thirty miles. In any event, the existence of a fixed point beyond which the transport of grain is counterproductive establishes the inevitability of an impassable 'transport barrier' – the logical conclusion of which is that the agricultural hinterland will be divided by such barriers into small, self-sufficient units.

For von Thünen, escape from this isolation would normally be provided only by navigable waterways, particularly rivers and canals. Contrary to what he may have seen in the Rhineland, however, I found in France that most rivers played only a limited role in either transportation or communication, and certainly none served to merge the land- and water-based societies. At the same time I realized that some rivers, or segments of rivers, must have figured in the organization of the two societies, and I have tried to establish some general categories of rivers and their functions that would be useful in any geographic analysis. What I learned was that rivers should first be divided according to whether or not they had practical two-way access to the sea; those that did were usually assimilated into the oceanic community, while those that did not would be integrated into the society of the hinterland, often contributing to the development of inland towns and cities by bringing them staple supplies from their adjacent banks. Such inland cities, it must be added, tended to become military and administrative centers, large or small – right up to a royal capital like Paris, which in spite of its size never became a full commercial center like London.

To account for or explain the two radically dissimilar societies created by these two different economic organizations, it may be useful to see them as fostering opposite social responses. In the 'agricultural kingdom' human effort was dispersed over as wide an area as possible, in order to bring the maximum amount of territory under cultivation and taxation, whereas the 'republic of commerce' concentrated both people and goods in points connected to one another by linear patterns of transportation. The chief expression of the 'areal' response was military and administrative, and operated over land with limited access to water transport; by contrast, the 'linear' reaction was commercial and depended on waterborne circulation of goods and people.

Although the two systems derived from quite different situations, they frequently overlapped and fell into unequal conflict, in which the areal form of organization would have gross advantages in a military confrontation, and the linear would enjoy even greater superiority in an economic or monetary confrontation. To understand this relation it is useful to look at some examples.

The classic model of a waterborne society was the ancient Aegean, with its many ports and trading cities. Although these communities seem to have grown out of a base of subsistence agriculture, their citizens early took to the sea to fish, and to exchange odds and ends with one another, until eventually they began to procure grain from the great plantations of the Black Sea and the Nile to supplement their own limited harvests. Because the food they obtained from these new sources was so abundant and cheap, it significantly increased their 'net product', which they used to develop their own special exports, often such other staples as wine or oil. In consequence their production costs fell, and the surplus wealth (that is, energy) available to them to use for purposes beyond subsistence increased. Obviously this economic development involved a geographical division of labor that was beyond the reach of land-bound subsistence farming units, and that turned this inland sea into a powerful economic engine capable of generating unprecedented wealth. In time this trading society permeated the entire Mediterranean and dominated much of the history of ancient world.

In the later Middle Ages, lesser but similar commercial communities developed in the western Mediterranean and the Baltic. Gradually these communities established patterns of exchange with each other, first across the Alps and down the rivers, and later by water around Europe's Atlantic coast. It was this Atlantic coastal circulation which led eventually to the establishment of the oceanic trading society of the seventeenth and eighteenth centuries, and thus to the world economic community in which we live today.

Normally the wealth of a commercial community would be concentrated in its port cities, thus making them tempting prey for the adjacent land powers. Unless they enjoyed particularly favorable terrain, as did Athens or Venice, the trading cities were generally vulnerable to military attack from the land, and were eventually swallowed by neighboring territorial states. Often the conquerors, in their zeal to extract the maximum profit from their conquests, defeated their own interests by disrupting the commercial relations of their ports with other members of the trading community – a tendency that could still be discerned in eighteenth-century mercantilism. Only once, it might be added, has the entire littoral of a sea been brought under the control of a single land-based power, and that was when Rome turned the Mediterranean into *mare nostrum* following the Second Punic War. With this total control of the sea the Roman Empire became not only the most powerful, but also the richest, of the ancient world.

All of this is to say that geography must play an essential role in the division of labor. Limited in size by the overland transport barrier, Europe's characteristic subsistence units were too small to foster economies of scale, whether in agriculture or manufacture, as can be demonstrated by considering Adam Smith's famous example of the pin factory. To accommodate its prodigious production there must be a society large and complex enough to have ten workers available to do nothing but carry out the various functions he assigns to them in the pin manufacturing process, as well as a sufficient population to purchase 48,000 pins a day, day after day – certainly not any average market town. In other words, a necessary precondition for the division of labor and resulting economies of scale is the assemblage of sufficient numbers of both producers and consumers, as well as sufficient quantities of raw materials and food to sustain the workers. The capacity for all this concentration would depend upon a favorable geographic situation, particularly one that provides fertile land to feed an increased population or access to navigable waterways that extend the transport range of supplies. Throughout the continental hinterland, however, even the most favorably located towns tended to remain market towns writ large, extending their limits slowly, and serving primarily to reinforce the organization of Quesnay's 'agricultural kingdom'. Lacking the capacity to transport their staple products any distance, such towns could not expand their economic base individually. As they grew, however, they could and did mobilize men in the service of the ruling lord or monarch; they thereby formed an important link in a society that was unified by the imposition of a centralized administration and a fiscal economy. This economy was based on the purchase of local supplies by royal agents with the cash that they had collected as taxes, and that they would then tax back repeatedly.

This pattern, which was repeated with endless variations across the map of Europe, was territorial in origin and operation. It drew its sustenance from subsistence agriculture, and produced ample reserves of manpower for the royal armies, with the consequence that territory itself represented both wealth and power for a ruler – a form of wealth and power that could only be defended, and extended, by military force. The monarchies that took shape through this process reached relatively stable form by the seventeenth-century, and finally became the nation states of today. The history of modern Europe has of course reflected the obsessive preoccupation with boundaries that follows from the territorial organization of these societies.

The contrasting pattern of organization can be seen in Europe as early as the tenth-century revival of the 'republic of commerce' in the western Mediterranean. Even earlier, Venice had begun importing the plentiful cheap grain from around the Black Sea that was the basic source of her wealth, since it fed the workers who manufactured the city's famous wares. Venice also had easy access to timber and other shipbuilding supplies, which contributed to her all-important transport capacity. In the meantime, the other Italian communes followed more or less the same pattern of concentrating population and materials, and producing the finished goods that they circulated among one another and to the scattered markets of the 'agricultural kingdom' to the north.

With time, similar centers of concentration and production also developed in the north – primarily in the lower Rhineland and the Baltic, where cheap grain was readily available up the Vistula and naval supplies abounded around the ocean littoral. Not surprisingly, this northern commercial center early developed waterborne communication with that of the Mediterranean along Europe's Atlantic shore, and, although this traffic made little contact with the French, Spanish or Portuguese coasts until the opening of the North Atlantic trade, it did transform London and the Netherlands ports into major centers of the new commercial system.

London's location could hardly have been more favorable to become the eventual capital of the growing 'republic of commerce'. At the head of the Thames estuary, it was a splendid ocean port, but it also drew on the unrivaled fertility of the Thames Valley for plentiful supplies of grain, and it could depend on an all-water route to Newcastle to supply its enormous need for coal.

One of the hazards of advancing the hypothesis of an oceanic commercial community is the difficulty of thinking in terms of an interacting system of port cities rather than of national merchant marines, and of a 'republic' that was governed without the sort of formal institutions developed by the land-based states. Characteristically, trading communities did not form states like their land-based counterparts; the most they usually attempted was an exchange of ambassadors or the organization of leagues, like the Delian of the ancient Aegean and the Hanseatic of the medieval Baltic. One of the main reasons for this difference between oceanic and territorial communities is that, whereas laws and orders can be imposed on territory by military force, it is difficult to do the same at sea; there, the rules that govern the society generally arise out of negotiation and compromise among its members. The ultimate political consequences of this geographic principle are profound, for right to our own times the land-based societies have tended to have administrative government by king or despot, while their water-based counterparts are likely to favor some consultative or parliamentary form of government. Typically political values within the two types of societies also reflect their separate realities. For the territorial state, political virtue often finds its ultimate form in the 'perfect plan perfectly implemented', while for the oceanic community it is likely to be defined as the freely accepted compromise. This is not to claim that one form or ideal of government is inherently superior to the other, since the administrator of a territorial state could be a philosopher-king or even a sovereign people who use the government to implement a democratic policy, while the governing council of a 'republic of commerce' could be corrupt and self-serving.

Although the wealth of the commercial community was regularly taxed by the inland regimes, economic relations between the two systems were normally prevented by the transport factor, which rapidly raised the cost of commercial grain or coal as it was moved inland from the water's edge. Individual members of the two societies often entered into financial transactions, however, as landowners borrowed from merchants the cash that their estates had no means of generating. Since they also had no means of liquidating such debts in cash, the landowners frequently found themselves transferring land to the merchants instead. The result of many such loans was a relatively steady erosion of noble property by default, beginning with the Crusades and continuing to the French Revolution.

A different version of this relationship between the two societies is provided by the long history of royal borrowing. An early example is seen with Charles VII, who in the mid-fifteenth century created Europe's first standing army with cash provided by his friend and banker Jaques Coeur. The sources of Coeur's fortune were German silver mines and some Mediterranean slave trading, both of which generated money profits that Charles used to pay his troops, and, through them, the peasants who provided the troops with their surplus grain. This example raises interesting questions about the transfer of commercial wealth into the royal fiscal economy. Jaques Coeur's coins from the Mediterranean started as a commodity (gold), but, transferred to France and distributed by the king, became in effect a royal requisition of supplies for provisioning the troops and royal agents. While this transaction stimulated an exchange of goods, the exchange was limited to the subsistence unit of the land-based system, generating an agricultural surplus for local consumption but producing no commercial return on Coeur's original advance, and thus no way for the king to repay his loan.

The early and effective response of the monarchy to such indebtedness was confiscation and repudiation, or at best more borrowing to meet interest payments on the earlier loans. Thus we are left with the question of how and why the monarchy was usually able to secure loan after loan from a commercial society that had no rational prospect of being repaid. Since the king usually obtained these funds without the use or threat of military force, it would seem that the merchants' action reveals their participation in the value system of the agricultural society, in which only ownership of land conferred nobility, and the king, as the greatest landlord of all, had overwhelming prestige.

While the fiscal exploitation of the 'agricultural kingdoms' of the hinterland was being pushed to its logical conclusions, the Atlantic 'republic of commerce' was undergoing a parallel development. Thanks to a growing accumulation of improvements in ship design and construction, as well as important advances in navigational skill and knowledge, waterborne commerce in the seventeenth century crossed a threshold that made possible the generation of unprecedented wealth, in a spiraling process that led to ever further expansion and greater riches.

Obviously, such a spectacular phenomenon did not go unnoticed, but because of its linear, as opposed to areal, organization, the commercial community of the Atlantic was not widely recognized as a coherent social system. Instead, shipping was generally viewed as an extension of the state that controlled the home port of a given ship – a view that still shapes our own tendency in looking at the commerce of the Atlantic. England was by far the most important unit in that commerce, followed by the Netherlands and then all the others with ocean ports. But particularly in the case of England one should question whether the port 'belonged' to the 'state' or the 'state' to the port – especially after the English Civil War, which was fought in large measure to protect London from absorption into an administrative monarchy backed by a standing army. Indeed, the Glorious Revolution and the elevation of William of Orange to the English throne as William III can be seen as a triumph of the Atlantic system, which would last for at least two centuries.

This brings us to the modern period and the critical question of the impact on our two societies of the industrial revolution – particularly of the railroads, which removed a major obstacle to overland transport and might therefore have been expected to lead to a merging of the hinterland with the oceanic community. In fact, such merging as did take place was both slow and incomplete – which requires some explanation.

Europe's 'agricultural monarchies' reached their apogee almost simultaneously with the late eighteenth-century industrial revolution and the Napoleonic wars of the early nineteenth century. Because of the wars, England's new industry was slow in crossing the Channel, and no coherent rail lines were in place in continental Europe before the middle of the nineteenth century. Instead, the century began with Europe's agricultural monarchies making a major effort, at the Congress of Vienna, to balance their military forces in order to prevent another general war. And to this end their chief means was to adjust territorial holdings. In the long-established tradition of these monarchies, land was generally accepted as the base and practical equivalent of military power. It was into this situation that the new railroads would begin to be introduced.

Given the size and nature of the undertaking, almost all rails in Europe were built, and often operated, by the state, which inevitably placed administrative and military considerations among its top priorities. Extending the reach of oceanic commerce into the hinterland was not a major goal of the central government; instead, the early rails were intended to mechanize the administrative and military lines of communication, with the result of transforming Europe's traditional agrigultural kingdoms into the modern nation states that dominated Europe on the eve of World War I. While these 'Great Powers', as they called themselves, were more or less industrialized, they retained their economic base of peasant agriculture, which continued to make them nearly self-sufficient and essentially independent of the developing oceanic commerce until World War I. Although that conflict began as a battle for continental Europe, it ended as a struggle for control of the Atlantic. Both Germany and France, no less than Britain, depended upon oceanic communications for critical supplies and reinforcements, and it was the entry into the war of the United States and its ships that proved decisive in the outcome.

When the fighting ceased, Britain and the United States failed to recognize their continuing interest in the military balance of power in continental Europe until it was too late to block Germany's second attempt at dominance without another major war. World War II was, even more clearly than World War I, a double conflict in the two arenas of land and sea. The territorial struggle began in central Europe with the non-agression pact between Germany and Russia, which united the two major land powers on the Eurasian continent in an arrangement that Hitler intended to transform into conquest. In the meantime, however, he seized western Europe to protect his rear against the Atlantic intervention that had proved so disastrous to Germany in the last war. For similar reasons, the Japanese opened hostilities with the United States because it had threatened to interfere with their plan of creating a territorial nation state through conquest on China's mainland.

The outcome of the war revealed most clearly the continued operation of the two very different kinds of social and economic organization we have examined. For in many ways the two superpowers that emerged from the war can be seen as paradigms of the land-based administrative state and the oceanic trading community. Both the United States and the Soviet Union projected their power over land and sea, but the very different structures and outlooks of the two victors are obvious in their disposition of the vanquished. Surrendering directly to the United States, Japan was forced to abandon its dreams of territorial conquest and accept metamorphosis into an oceanic trading state. Defeated Germany, however, ended by being split between the eastern and western conquerors; the eastern territory and conquests were swallowed by the Soviet Union, while the westward-oriented territory was incorporated under American hegemony into the North Atlantic economic and military system.

The nation-state 'Great Powers' of World War I were now replaced by the two superpowers and their circles of satellite allies. The territorial orientation of the Soviet Union was emphasized by its administrative government and heavily fortified boundaries, backed by its massive army. Further, its economy manifested strong autarkic tendencies as well as tight domestic control of both production and distribution. And while it is necessary to resist the temptation to see this closed society as the inevitable product of Russia's continental character, it is also obvious that this sort of social organization would be difficult to impose over sea. Over-land, however, the system was readily installed in each of the Warsaw Pact allies, and reinforced whenever necessary by military intervention.

By contrast, the postwar orientation of the United States was oceanic. During the war the US economy had poured out the flood of arms and materials that had made victory possible in both the Atlantic and Pacific theaters of combat. With peace, the flow was redirected to supply and restore friend and foe alike, creating in the process a new global economy. The result was a widespread and unprecedented new prosperity, which

Americans feared might tempt the military might of their continental rivals. To meet this potential threat the United States and its partners along Europe's Atlantic and Mediterranean coasts formed a classic league, under the title of the North Atlantic Treaty Organization. And while nothing comparable was developed in the Pacific, special arrangements were established with various trading partners around that ocean's rim.

In addition to this model confrontation between land-based and waterborne superpowers, there exist similar divisions within the body politic of any number of territorial states – most notably the United States – which enjoy full access to oceanic trade. This persistence into the present of these two separate and different social organizations, long after industrial and technological developments have eliminated the geographic restraints within which they first developed, calls for some explanation or speculation. For example, if the industrial revolution dismantled the transport barrier, it also created new and acute social problems that only the state seemed capable of alleviating. Thus it would seem to be from its own inherent resources that the state derived its unequaled strength as both an engine for war and a mechanism for social control. At the same time the commercial community also expanded its range, thanks to technological advances, but it was generally unable to escape all interference by the various coastal states on whose territory it operated, or to take over such state functions as defense or social legislation.

Now, near the end of the twentieth century, we find the patterns of communication and exchange in human societies in bewildering flux. The technological development of weapons – air power, missiles and nuclear explosives – has altered the 'ground rules' of human organization beyond our present capacity for grasping the consequences or extrapolating even tentative projections of future consequences. One constant would seem to remain: human dependence on a geographical base for existence. But it is changing conditions that determine, in the veiled future as in the more accessible past, how territory will be exploited and allocated, contested and defined.

Index

Index compiled by Meg Davies